D1570100

Choosing the Right Pond

"I changed my mind. I'd rather be a big enchanted prince in a small pond than a small enchanted prince in a big pond."

Choosing the Right Pond

HUMAN BEHAVIOR AND THE QUEST FOR STATUS

Robert H. Frank

New York   Oxford
OXFORD UNIVERSITY PRESS
1 9 8 5

Oxford University Press

Oxford   London   New York   Toronto
Delhi   Bombay   Calcutta   Madras   Karachi
Kuala Lumpur   Singapore   Hong Kong   Tokyo
Nairobi   Dar es Salaam   Cape Town
Melbourne   Auckland

and associated companies in
Beirut   Berlin   Ibadan   Mexico City   Nicosia

Published by Oxford University Press, Inc.,
200 Madison Avenue, New York, New York 10016

Library of Congress Cataloging in Publication Data
Frank, Robert H.
Choosing the right pond.
Includes bibliographical references.
1. Economics.   2. Welfare economics.   3. Wages.   4. Social status.
I. Title.
HB71.F6955   1984   330   84-19099
ISBN 0-19-503520-8

Parts of the following copyrighted material were reproduced by permission:

James Abegglen, *Management and Worker*, Tokyo: Sophia University, 1973.
Roald Dahl, *The Best of Roald Dahl: Stories from Over to You, Someone Like You, Kiss Kiss, and Switch Bitch*, New York: Vintage Press, Inc., 1978, and London: Michael Joseph, Ltd, and Penguin Books Ltd.
Robert H. Frank, "Are Workers Paid Their Marginal Products," *American Economic Review, 74,* September 1984.
Robert H. Frank, "The Demand for Unobservable and Other Nonpositional Goods," *American Economic Review, 75,* March, 1985.
Milton Friedman, *Capitalism and Freedom*, Chicago: University of Chicago Press, 1962.
John Stuart Mill, *On Liberty,* edited by Alburey Castell, Arlington Heights, Ill.: Harlan Davison, Inc., copyright © 1947.
Robert Nozick, *Anarchy, State, and Utopia*, New York: Basic Books, Inc., copyright © 1974.

Printing (last digit):   9 8 7 6 5 4 3 2 1

Printed in the United States of America

Preface

This book is about the consequences of people's concerns about where they stand on the economic totem pole. Its primary theme is that these concerns shape people's behavior in systematic, observable, and often unexpected ways.

Some of the consequences of concerns about status are of only trifling importance—having to do, for example, with the labels we assign to things. When a Mercedes is sold for the second time, it is described as a previously owned, not a used, car.

But other consequences of people's concerns about economic status are more serious. These concerns, I will argue, play dominant roles in many of our most important private transactions and underlie much of the regulatory apparatus we observe in modern Western societies.

In arguing these claims, my approach will be to assume that people and firms take their economic environments as given, and then try to do the best they can for themselves and their families. This approach does not deny the existence of altruistic and other community-minded behavior. But it does stress the rich predictive power of the view that people generally behave in self-interested ways. It is the same approach as the one taken by Milton Friedman in his classic, *Capitalism and Freedom*. But the conclusions that emerge from my use of it here are often strikingly different from Friedman's.

In reaching these conclusions, I will deal with issues that go far beyond what most people would think of as the normal domain of economics. And because many of these issues are also important in other fields, I have tried to keep all of the arguments accessible to people with no formal training in economics.

Much of what I discuss here touches directly on some of the strongest concerns we feel as we struggle to define our roles and to affirm our importance in the world around us. The very intensity with which we feel and express these concerns makes them subjects of fascination in their own right. The inherent allure of this book's subject matter, together with the accessibility of its arguments, lead me to hope that reading it will help persuade noneconomists that economics is a much less narrow and dismal science than it often appears.

My deepest hope for this book, however, is that it will help persuade my fellow economists, at least some of them, that we have too often neglected fundamental elements of human nature in our study of the ways people behave. The penalty for this neglect has been that we have failed to ask many important questions; and, moreover, that we have offered wrong, or at least misleading, answers to many of the most important questions we do ask.

Our failure as economists to acknowledge basic elements of human nature has also served to isolate us from the broader community. Our isolation shows up, for example, in the way we are regarded by scholars in other fields. As a member of the nominations committee at the university where I teach, I must ask faculty members, both in economics and in other fields, to stand for election to various university committees. My own economics colleagues almost always consent because they know that most people in other departments always vote for the candidates from other fields. (I myself ended up on the nominations committee only because the psychologist who defeated me in the election for that post subsequently went away on leave.)

Our isolation is also clearly captured by the report of two economists who reviewed several evaluations of federal job-training programs. The two were particularly critical of one study that counted as a benefit of the programs the fact that trainees committed fewer robberies and burglaries after becoming trainees. Since the victim's loss in any theft is counterbalanced by the thief's gain, these economists pointed out, theft is not properly reckoned as a net loss at all. Instead, it is merely a transfer of existing resources from the victim to the thief, and its prevention therefore cannot be recorded as a social gain. But outside the world studied by economists, everyone knows that people are much more concerned about how the economic pie is distributed than about how large it actually is. And those economists who say that the prevention of theft is a neutral act because it doesn't affect the size of the pie are properly dismissed by outsiders as having failed to grasp the essence of the problem.

Most economists are of course well aware of such distributional concerns, but we have generally taken pains to steer clear of them, apparently in the belief that economics has little useful to say about them. I will attempt to show, however, that people's concerns about distributional matters have a very natural expression within the same analytical framework we have used to such advantage in our study of efficiency; and that once these concerns are properly incorporated into this framework, the conclusions that emerge from standard economic models often fall effortlessly into harmony with those that have always struck most noneconomists as self-evident.

As noted, the subjects I confront in this book have forced me to stray into fields other than economics. Such forays have never been much favored among economists, and for good reason: It is difficult enough just to keep ideas straight within the confines of our own field. The only justification for studies of this sort can be the belief that the problems at hand are so broad that the errors we expect to make by venturing outside our field are less serious than the errors we will inevitably make by remaining strictly within it. Such is my belief about the problems I confront here.

In drawing from the works of biologists, psychologists, and sociologists in assembling a description of human motivation, I hope I have not interpreted important ideas from those disciplines in naive or misleading ways. I hope also that philosophers will react patiently to my attempts to sort through the various ethical questions that arise throughout the book. Perhaps they will be amused by an outsider's attempt to deal with such questions (in the same paternalistic way that my colleagues and I are often amused when we overhear heated discussions about professional football taking place among our newly arrived foreign graduate students). My hope is that, having failed to express myself in the proper idiom, I will at least have avoided violating basic tenets of common sense in my attempts to discuss issues outside my own field.

These are lofty hopes for any book. I suspect many readers will have difficulty accepting all of the explanations I offer for the various puzzles and anomalies they will encounter in these pages. To be sure, many of these explanations are speculative. Yet I feel sure that many readers will find these problems deeply engaging, as I have, and be stimulated by the alternative perspective offered here to ponder them afresh.

Ithaca, New York   R. H. F.
January 1985

Acknowledgments

The interval between writing something and experiencing others' reactions to it is for me often unbearably long. Foremost among the many debts I have accumulated in writing this book is the gratitude I owe to Philip Cook and Larry Seidman for the almost instantaneous feedback they provided as I worked through several earlier drafts. Their unremitting support and encouragement, not to mention their many helpful comments and suggestions, have meant more to me than I can ever hope to tell them.

I am also grateful for the encouragement I received from Professor Robert Clower, editor of the *American Economic Review*, where two of the three technical papers on which the book is based appear. I began work on this manuscript in May of 1983, by which time each of these papers had experienced considerable difficulty finding space in the leading professional economics journals. Professor Clower's expression of support for my research came at a time when I sorely needed it, and freed me from having to burden the readers of this book with many of the technical details of the supporting arguments.

I am also especially in debt to my Cornell colleagues, John Bennett, George Hay, and Dick Thaler, whose detailed suggestions on earlier drafts led to many improvements. John Bennett's lengthy comments on Chapters 6, 10, and 11 were particularly valuable and have spared me much embarassment (by which I do not mean to suggest that John would agree with all of what I chose to retain in those chapters).

Numerous other friends, relatives and colleagues read various parts of the manuscript and provided helpful suggestions. I especially thank Dana Ansuini, David Easley, Ronald Ehrenberg, Micky Falkson, Dick Freeman, Paul Geroski, Ned Gramlich, Alfred Kahn, Harriet and Dick King, Bill Lambert, the late Steve Marston, Lars Muus, Mary Beth Norton, Jeremy Rabkin, Bob Reynolds, and Amartya Sen, and apologize to those many others whom I have failed to mention here.

I have also benefitted from other valuable support at many stages of the project. My thanks to Steve Bunson, Joe Kennedy, Randy Lutter, Danny Sastrowardoyo, and Janet Young for their extremely able research assistance; to Verma McClary for her boundless patience in typing draft after draft; to Gini Curl for her similar patience in producing so well the drawings I described to her so vaguely; to Joan Bossert and Janice Lemmo for helping reshape my often tedious and elliptical academic prose; and to George Boyer, Anne Farley, Julia Grant, George Kosicki, and Naufel Vilcassim for their able and generous assistance in proofreading the final manuscript.

My special thanks go to Herb Addison, my editor at Oxford, for his early enthusiasm for the manuscript and for his unflagging faith that others besides economists will want to read it.

And I would like, finally, to thank my wife, both for her forebearance during my periods of most intense involvement with the project, and for contributing so much to the environment in which I live and work.

Contents

1. Contests, Leagues, and Rules   3

2. Local Status   17

3. Choosing the Right Pond   39

4. How Much Is Local Status Worth?   64

5. Further Indications of the Value of Local Status   87

6. Why Redistributive Taxation   108

7. The Positional Treadmill   132

8. Collective Protection of Inconspicuous Consumption   154

9. The Left's Critique of Capitalism   174

10. Why Do Ethical Systems Try to Limit the Role of Money?   192

11. Freedom of Association, Economies of Scale, and the
Limits of Government Paternalism   214

12. The Libertarian Welfare State   244

Notes   271

Bibliography   281

Index   295

Choosing the Right Pond

One

Contests, Leagues, and Rules

In Ithaca, New York, where I live, the cable TV system carries most New York Yankee baseball games. One August night, sportscasters Phil Rizzuto and Bobby Murcer were calling a slow game between the Yankees and the Milwaukee Brewers. Between pitches, Rizzuto was looking over his record sheets and remarked that the Brewers had done much better in day games than in games played at night. Murcer checked his own records and found that the Yankees, too, had a much higher winning percentage during the day. With characteristic enthusiasm, Rizzuto then conjectured that *all* teams have better records for day games. In a brisk exchange of the sort that makes summer evenings in Ithaca seem to fly by, the two then spent the rest of the inning discussing the poor lighting conditions in American League parks and various other difficulties that might help account for why teams do so poorly at night.

But the "fact" that Rizzuto and Murcer were trying to explain was of course not a fact at all. Without consulting any baseball records, we know that it is mathematically impossible for all teams to have better records during the day than at night. For every team that loses a night game, some other team must win one. Lighting conditions at night may indeed be poor, but they are poor for both sides. Taken as a whole, teams play .500 ball at night, the same as they do during the day.*

---

*Rizzuto and Murcer are in distinguished company in having overlooked the inherent reciprocity between winning and losing. As we will see in Chapter 3, leading economic thinkers of the past two centuries have overlooked a similar reciprocity that exists in the labor market.

The exchange between Rizzuto and Murcer calls our attention to two simple but important properties of contests in general: (*1*) *For any contest to have a winner, it must also have a loser;* and (*2*) *measures that provide equal advantages* (*or disadvantages*) *to all contestants do not affect the expected outcome of a contest.* To these two properties, we can add a third—(*3*) *participation in many important contests takes place on a voluntary basis.* In this book, I argue that these three simple properties have profound consequences for the contests that determine who gets the most important prizes in life— that is, for the contests whose winners get the best education, the most desirable jobs, the most sought-after mates, the highest quality health care, and so on.

Various combinations of these three properties suggest new interpretations of many of our most important economic, legal, and ethical structures. In particular, they help us gain useful insights into the following seemingly disparate questions:

- Why are wage rates among co-workers so much more egalitarian than predicted by standard economic theories of the labor market?
- Why do most countries have redistributive tax programs?
- Can these programs be altered in a way that would make them both more fair *and* more efficient?
- Would trade unions, occupational safety and health regulations, minimum wage laws, and overtime laws play useful roles even in perfectly competitive labor markets?
- Would forced savings programs be beneficial even if people had perfect foresight and ample self-discipline?
- Why do many societies impose ethical sanctions against the sale of transplantable organs, babies, and sex?
- Why, similarly, are there ethical objections to using cost-benefit analysis for health, safety, and environmental issues?
- Why is there widespread aversion to relying primarily on private markets for the provision of educational services?

These three simple properties of contests also suggest possible avenues along which to reconcile many of the classical disputes that have simmered through the years, both between the socialist and the free marketeer, and between the libertarian and the paternalistic regulator. In the eyes of its staunchest defenders, the market system can do little wrong. Guided by Adam Smith's invisible hand, people pursue their own goals in the marketplace in ways that happen also to promote what is best for all. Yet critics of the market system insist that it poisons everything it touches. Far from serving society's desires, they argue, it serves up limitless arrays of frivolous products, disbursing incomes that bear little relationship to the social value of the work people do. Throughout this book, I oppose the conventional view that the marketplace stands on some convenient middle ground between these two extremes. The market system I portray here is very much the energized, responsive mechanism its defenders claim it to be; but it nonetheless produces a litany of social ills very much like those described by critics on the left. It does so, however, for reasons that differ sharply from the ones offered by these critics. And these reasons, in turn, suggest alternative ways of thinking about the state's proper role in regulating economic activity—ways of approaching economic and social problems that are very different from the ones suggested by left-wing critics.

Keeping Up with the Joneses

H. L. Mencken once defined wealth as any income that is at least one hundred dollars more a year than the income of one's wife's sister's husband. And abundant evidence suggests that people do in fact care much more about how their incomes compare with those of their peers than about how large their incomes are in any absolute sense. Most poor citizens of the United States enjoy an absolute consumption standard that would be the envy of all but the richest citizens of, say, India. Yet the poor here are often said to be much less content with their lot than are the upper-middle class citizens of many poorer nations.

Our concerns about where we stand on the economic totem pole have numerous consequences, not all of them bad. Still, the moral teachings of

Drawing by Leo Cullum. Copyright © 1983 The New Yorker Magazine, Inc.

"I was at my sister's today. They have two pots."

most cultures, including our own, exhort people to try to suppress these concerns. These teachings obviously serve a useful purpose under many circumstances. But they also cause us to view our concerns about relative standing with an overriding sense of disdain, even contempt. This attitude, in turn, has kept us from clearly seeing the ways in which these concerns serve people, and has obscured the various consequences they produce in social settings. Had it not done so, I suspect that our common knowledge would have long since encompassed my claim that these concerns lie at the very heart of many of our most important economic, legal, and ethical structures.

My arguments in support of this claim are neither complex nor arcane. But they will be much more easily digested if you can suspend for the moment whatever negative attitudes you may have toward people's concerns about "keeping up with the Joneses." Think of these concerns instead as being just another aspect of human nature—to be understood, appreciated when useful, and controlled effectively when their consequences are harmful.

If you, or someone you know, have two small children for whom you feel an abiding affection, perhaps an account of the following experiment will encourage a neutral mindset toward people's concerns about relative economic standing. The experiment is carried out at breakfast time. For the first two days, pour the young siblings their usual glass of orange juice, taking special care that their glasses are the same size and that each is filled to capacity. We use orange juice here because, unlike ice cream, it is not something that children always value highly in its own right. ("Do I *have* to drink all my juice?") On the third day of the experiment, fill each glass exactly half full. Finally, on the fourth day, fill one child's glass to the top, the other's only three-quarters of the way. Record what happens each day.

What almost always happens in this experiment is that neither child complains when the glasses are reduced from full to only half full. But when one is given a full glass and the other a glass that is only three-quarters full, there is trouble. The child with less looks first at his brother's glass, then at his own, then back at his brother's. Tension obviously building within him, a moment passes, after which any number of actions may follow. At minimum, he will address a bitter complaint to the pourer of the juice. ("He *always* gets more than me!") Or perhaps the child with less will attempt to switch glasses with his brother, who, though completely innocent in the matter, is by this time seen as a hostile force.

Before things get too far out of hand, the experimenter probably will yield to his own impulse to explain to the two that it really doesn't matter who has how much orange juice; that there is more in the pitcher if they want it; and finally, that it is bad form to carry on about such a petty matter. After all, if half a glass was sufficient the previous day, why is three-quarters of a glass suddenly too little?

Yet with whom may we really find fault here (other than the experimenter, who has probably broken some law by using human subjects in an experiment without first having had them sign a consent form)? With the complaining child? Surely it is hard to view him as particularly blameworthy. The parent who knows and loves him realizes that in those first few seconds, while he was sizing the situation up, he was really doing his best *not* to complain. Perhaps his parents should have taken greater care all along about instructing him in the proper ways to behave. Yet most parents miss no opportunity to chide their children for just such behavior, whenever and wherever it occurs.

Sooner or later, of course, most children do learn to stifle their complaints in such situations. But learning in this case means only that the impulse to complain goes underground. Years hence, the complaining child having reached adulthood, the same impulse will be present when, seated at a dinner party, his host pours a full glass of wine for the person sitting next to him and only three-quarters of a glass for him. But he will keep quiet about it then. In the full maturity of his cognitive forces, he will realize that the stakes are not really high enough to matter and that, if he were to complain, he would succeed only in making a fool of himself. Indeed, he may even laugh at himself for having such an impulse here.

But given that such impulses can be kept under control for the most part, would parents really want their children to be stripped of them entirely? Given the kind of world we live in, would they feel completely at ease knowing that their children, unlike others, were not motivated to do as well as they could in relation to their classmates? Would they want their children to marry people who didn't care where they stood in relation to their peers? For all of the difficulties concerns with status create, few parents would feel comfortable seeing their children go off to confront the world without them.

Our focus here will in any event be not on the acceptability of these concerns, but on their specific consequences. Does the behavior of people who are deeply concerned about relative economic standing differ systematically in important, observable ways from the behavior of others who are less concerned about position? Where important differences do exist, are there circumstances under which we can agree that their consequences are undesirable? And are there specific measures we might use to counter such consequences?

Contests for Position

Many of the prizes in life are what Fred Hirsch has called "positional goods"[1] —goods that are sought after less because of any absolute property they possess than because they compare favorably with others in their own class. A "good" school, for example, is sought after less for its absolute quality than for its high rank among schools in general. If the quality of instruction at all universities were suddenly cut by half tomorrow, students admitted to Harvard would still have the same obvious reasons for celebrating their good fortune as before.

The diamond ring I wear, which was once my father's, is similarly a positional good. It is an exceptionally clear, deep canary-yellow stone, valuable less for the inherently pleasing way it refracts the light than for the fact that stones of its particular type and quality are so rare. (Stones that have only a slight yellow hue are much more common and are thus actually worth less

than white ones.) The ring was beyond my father's means, one of the few
luxuries he allowed himself. And on more than a few occasions, he was forced
to borrow against it. Yet he always managed somehow to get it back, and
wore it with obvious pride, a statement to the world about himself. The ring is
as incongruous with my own financial station in life as it was with his, and it
was a long time after his death before I began to feel comfortable wearing it.
But I too wear it with pride now, and not only for the fond memories it kindles
of him. (I take it off, though, when visiting New York City or when dickering
with the seller of an oriental rug.) So it is with understandable displeasure that
I read of an inexpensive new process claimed to make synthetic diamonds that
are indistinguishable from real ones. Positional goods are, by their very
nature, things in fixed supply. If flawless diamonds can someday be synthe-
sized at little cost, there will no longer be anything special about having one.

But some things will always remain positional goods. The most sought-after
jobs, for example, are defined not by the particular characteristics they
possess, but by how those characteristics compare with those of other jobs. If
everyone wants jobs on the top 10 percent of the job ladder, no new process
can ever alter the fact that only 10 percent of the job-seekers will be able to
occupy those jobs, no matter how hard everyone tries. The top jobs will always
be the prizes in a contest, and those who get them will always be the contest
winners.

In the next chapter I look at evidence suggesting that we come into the
world equipped with a nervous system that worries about rank. Something
inherent in our biological makeup motivates us to try to improve, or at least
maintain, our standing against those with whom we compete for important
positional resources. A critical feature of this motivating mechanism, often
too little emphasized, is that it is much more responsive to local than to global
comparisons. Negative feelings are much more strongly evoked by adverse

*"I admit it does look very impressive. But you see, nowadays
everyone graduates in the top ten per cent of his class."*

comparisons with our immediate associates than by those with people who are distant in place or time. We are little troubled when we hear that one of the Rockefellers, somewhere, has acquired a stately mansion. But we often become very agitated indeed when we learn that one of our co-workers got a slightly higher pay raise than we did. This local nature of our concerns about where we stand among our peers is important because it makes one aspect of our participation in contests for position genuinely voluntary.

The voluntary aspect stems from the fact that our "needs" depend very strongly on the identities of those with whom we *choose* to associate closely. When we associate with people of modest means, the things we feel we need are more modest than when we associate with people of greater means. As Richard Layard aptly put it, "in a poor society a man proves to his wife that he loves her by giving her a rose but in a rich society he must give a dozen roses."[2] Someone whose close associates all earn $50,000 a year is likely to feel actively dissatisfied with his material standard of living if his own salary is only $40,000. He can afford a comfortable home in a safe neighborhood, but what he really wants is a home with a view. Yet that same person would likely be content if his closest associates earned not $50,000 but $30,000 a year. His same house would then be no longer an object of disdain but a symbol of the type of house others aspired to own someday.

Because we have considerable latitude in our choice of friends, neighbors, co-workers, and other close associates, we are in a position to choose the level at which we conduct our contests for position. Someone who is tired of feeling bad about the kind of house she lives in can start to feel good about that same house by simply switching to a less wealthy circle of friends. She can play in a different league.

Why We Sort Ourselves into Leagues

It is thus easy to see why a frog might choose to live in a pond populated by frogs smaller than himself. What is less apparent, though, is why frogs already in that pond would permit the larger frog to enter their circle. After all, status in any peer group is a two-way street: The larger frog gains in status from the favorable comparison with the smaller frogs, but the smaller frogs suffer a loss in status from that very same comparison.

Our properties of contests thus impose an immediate obstacle in the way of forming a heterogeneous peer group. A favorable comparison cannot take place in the absence of its reciprocal invidious comparison—if there is a winner, there must also be a loser (property 1). And if people are free to choose their own associates (property 3), why would anyone then agree to participate in a group in which he was a low-ranking member? Presumably, he would prefer to form a separate peer group composed of others whose status is roughly the same as his own. Caring about "local status" and having the freedom to choose our own associates thus create strong pressures to stratify us into homogeneous groups. And leagues of various sorts do seem to form among people, much as they do in competitive sports.

Yet these leagues are not completely homogeneous. In baseball, for example, we find many consistently strong teams in the National League, but we also find the San Francisco Giants. Similarly, within each private firm, we find substantial differences in productivity among workers.

The ranges of ability within firms are not only broad but also overlapping: The average worker in one firm will be more productive than most workers in a second firm, but less productive than all but a few workers in a third. In the first half of this book, I take up the question of what makes such diverse collections of people hang together. What keeps a low-ranked worker in one firm from moving to some other firm in which her rank would be much higher?

The answer—an answer—to this question is that people often *can* improve their rankings by switching to another group, but they will always incur a cost in the process. If high-ranked positions are valuable things that almost everyone would like to have, then we should not expect these positions to be had for free. On the contrary, a well-developed implicit market exists for them and their prices are often very steep. The sellers in this market are of course the occupants of the low-ranked positions without whose presence the corresponding high-ranked positions would simply not exist.

In these observations, we have the rudiments of a theory in which status within groups emerges as a good like any other that is traded in the marketplace. Traditional economic theory insists that workers are paid the value of what they produce by the firms they work for. By contrast, both the theory and evidence I will uncover here say that wages are as much or more influenced by people's concerns about the wages earned by their co-workers. The most productive workers in a firm get paid substantially less than the value of what they produce, while the least productive workers are paid substantially more.

"Fairness" and "equity," which are concepts usually discussed in abstract, philosophical terms, are very closely linked to the concept of local status. Local status, in turn, is like various more concrete things, in that it has a price and can be traded for material things that have value. These connections will reveal that the redistributive tax systems most societies have need not be viewed as burdens nobly tolerated by the rich in the name of fairness, as the rich are often wont to say. We may view such tax systems instead as an embodiment of the same phenomenon that reduces wage inequality among co-workers in competitive firms. If people were free at the outset to form societies with others of their own choosing, and if there were no redistributive taxation, the rich would then be foreclosed from the favored positions they now occupy in the social hierarchy.

Making the League Rules

Our concerns about position influence not only our incomes but also how we spend them. No matter what group we choose to define as our peers, there will remain contests for the most sought-after resources. And the proportion of winners and losers in these contests remains fixed by the laws of simple arithmetic (our first property of contests again). But if the proportion of winners is necessarily fixed at the outset, the identities of those winners are not. By expending additional effort in a contest, we can affect the outcome of that contest, provided our added efforts do not call forth similar extra efforts by others. If other contestants alter their own efforts in parallel ways, however, the original balance between contestants will be restored (our second property of contests). In the end, the additional effort will have been expended largely for naught. In the familiar metaphor, all spectators in a sports arena leap to their feet to get a better view of an exciting play, but in the end everyone's view is no better than if all had remained seated.

In the second half of this book, I argue that our first two properties of contests cause us to place various restrictions on our contests for position. That we often seek to keep other sorts of contests from getting out of hand is evident from a host of familiar experiences. The poker game my colleagues and I hold every other Thursday night, for example, has several rules to keep our betting within reasonable limits. We have a 50-cent ceiling on each bet and we limit the number of raises to two per person per betting round. Our one exception to these limits is that each person is permitted to make one $2 bet during the course of the evening. Even with these rules, there is much excitement in our games (calling a $2 bet is probably the biggest risk any of us ever takes), and ample good cheer. Some nights, when the cards fall right, it seems we *all* walk away from the table with extra cash in our pockets.

Winning and losing is what matters for us in these games, much as it would be in a game with much higher stakes; yet the constraints we impose keep our game affordable even on an academic salary. The particular stakes we set, of course, would not be right for every group. Several of my friends, who as economic consultants in New York City earn salaries that are four times as high as ours, would no doubt find our limits too confining. But even they will set at least *some* limits on the stakes they play for.

"And I think I've got the winning hand, but in case Ed Crawford beats it, would you be willing to go and stay with him for a weekend?"

By now most countries have laws that prohibit dueling. But before the existence of these laws, people often faced situations in which the only acceptable way to respond to a blatant insult to their honor was to challenge the offending party to a face-off with pistols at 100 paces. (Even here, note the limits: Why not 10 paces?) With dueling forbidden by common consent, however, we are free to defend our honor in a variety of less costly ways. Occasional outbursts by Norman Mailer and Billy Martin notwithstanding, dueling and assault laws have enabled most of us to keep our pride well enough intact without risking even so much as a black eye.

In the Ivy League, teams play a game that bears only a remote resemblance to what at many other universities is known as college football. Ivy League rules require, among other things, that spring practice be limited to one day; that athletic scholarships not be given; and that athletes be admitted according to the same academic standards applied to other students. Such restrictions have obvious consequences for the level at which our games are played.

New arrivals accustomed to watching Big Eight teams are often amused at first by the spectacle of an Ivy League football contest. But if they remain in this environment for long, they usually come to appreciate these contests for the spirited, hard-fought encounters they really are. In Ivy League games, half of the teams win each autumn Saturday, and half of them lose—the same as in other football conferences. Yet the scale of what is sacrificed in the process is in many ways much lower here than in other conferences.

Where to set the stakes in such contests will obviously be decided differently in different leagues. But all leagues adopt at least some measures that limit the stakes of their contests. Even the National Football League, in many ways the most fiercely competitive arena in this country, has its roughness penalties and 49-man roster limits.

Like the contests just discussed, unconstrained contests for position also have a tendency to get out of hand. Because having a tasteful wardrobe helps us get a job or win the attention of a potential mate, for example, many of us feel strong pressure to spend a lot on clothing. Yet parallel spending by others will offset the intended effects of these efforts. The concept of a tasteful wardrobe, like so many others, is a relative one. What would have qualified as a tasteful wardrobe had others not invested in parallel ways will again be only an ordinary wardrobe once they do. The same jobs and the same mates will end up pairing with the same people as if none had made the additional investments.

As a group, we might have chosen to save much larger fractions of our incomes and spend considerably smaller amounts on clothing. But it would not necessarily have been in the interests of any one of us, acting alone, to do so. After all, as the clothing manufacturers are fond of reminding us, first impressions count for a lot, and we never get a second chance to make a first impression.

With these observations in mind, it will become clear that the forced savings programs most societies have (such as our Social Security System*) might still play an important role even if people had perfect foresight and complete self-control. Indeed, forced savings programs may be most needed not because people fail to perceive their interests as individuals, but because they perceive those interests only too clearly.

Similar reasoning can help us interpret numerous other apparently paternalistic laws and practices. Occupational safety regulations, for example, often explained as a means of protecting workers from exploitation by firms, will make more sense when viewed as a means of mitigating the consequences of mutually destructive contests for position. Overtime laws, minimum wage laws, and a variety of other labor regulations will be more easily understood, not as devices for keeping workers from being ravaged by greedy capitalist firms, but as ways of keeping workers from ravaging one another.

People seek such collective restrictions not to *eliminate* the contests for important positional resources, but to *restructure* the terms on which they are fought. The boxers who today wear padded gloves fight one another just as intensely as those who fought bare-fisted in years past. But in the process of deciding their contests, they inflict much less damage on one another than fighters used to. Various social regulations similarly limit the damage that contestants for position inflict on one another.

The nature of contests for position also sheds light on why ethical and cultural systems go to such great lengths to deemphasize the role of money as a yardstick for assigning value to human activities. Many people recoil in disgust when they hear of economists who say that the cost of safety measures and what people are willing to pay for safety should be balanced against one another in deciding, for example, how safe a commercial airliner should be. It is unethical, many feel, to use monetary values when making decisions about life and safety.

Yet it is clear that these same people do not, and would not want to, completely ignore monetary costs and benefits when making their own decisions about safety. They could, for example, reduce the likelihood of being killed in an automobile accident by having the brakes on their cars replaced once a week. Even so, no one replaces his brakes that often. The reason, presumably, is that the costs would so greatly outweigh the expected benefits. The desirability of neutralizing contests for position will make clear that accepting additional risk exposure in exchange for extra money is not objectionable in and of itself; rather, as we will see, the problem is that people

---

*Strictly speaking, the social security system is not a savings program, but a transfer from those who work to those who receive benefits. From the point of view of the individual, however, it is much the same as the pension programs that most private companies have. In both, people give up some of their income during their working years in return for benefit payments during retirement.

struggling for position are often led to sell their safety too cheaply. The nature of contests for position will suggest similar interpretations of ethical sanctions against prostitution, the sale of babies, and a variety of other monetary transactions whose principal effects appear largely confined to direct participants.

The Paternalism Question

It is one thing to be constrained by the rules of a private club or league but a very different matter to be held in check by the laws of the state. Few of us would object if two workers freely signed a contract in which workplace safety standards prevented each from trying to outdo the other by accepting greater safety risks in return for higher wages. But many people do object strenuously when the state uses the force of law to impose such standards on workers and firms who want no part of them.

The dilemma posed by this objection lies in the reciprocal nature of the problem. Many people want a Social Security program because they know that, without one, it will be in their interests to spend more than they really want to on positional goods. Yet Barry Goldwater and others insist, correctly, that such programs deprive them of their liberty to decide for themselves when and how much to save. If people could form separate societies of their own, each group could obviously have its own way on such issues. As long as we are committed to a single society, however, it is clearly no longer possible for each group to get all of what it wants. To affirm one group's position means necessarily to deny the other's. We need some criterion for deciding which position is the more important to uphold.

We may feel tempted to say that we cannot properly force people to save just because others might envy their standard of living. But this response leaves out something important. Although the desire to escape feelings of envy may be part of what makes people want forced savings programs, there are also more concrete issues at stake here. In our contests for position, how the amounts we spend compare with what others spend often plays a decisive role. Saving a "prudent" amount will sometimes mean not being selected for a job. And it is the very real outcomes of such contests, not just our feelings, that we have to live with.

Yet it is by no means clear that people's feelings will never constitute legitimate grounds for imposing restrictive government rules. Our intuitive belief that one person's freedom should not be restricted because what he does might make others feel bad rests implicitly on the notion that, by minding our own business, we can avoid bad feelings caused by what others do. This principle obviously provides useful guidance much of the time. But it does not imply that bad feelings alone are *always* insufficient to warrant constraining the actions of others.

Consider, for example, a recent episode involving a member of the immigrant community of Tongans living in Salt Lake City, Utah.[3] The Tongan went one afternoon to purchase a pony for his son's birthday. After agreeing with the pony rancher on a price for a particular pony, the Tongan backed his pickup truck up to the barn and emerged with a stout section of lumber. With it, he then delivered a powerful blow to the pony's head, killing the animal instantly. The horrified rancher quickly summoned the police, who tracked the Tongan to his home, where they found him roasting the pony on a barbeque spit. Their interrogation revealed that it is common practice in Tonga to honor a loved one by killing and roasting a pony. (The investigating officer called the incident a "cross-cultural misunderstanding.")

In the United States, we do not permit people to kill and roast ponies.* Here, we encourage children to develop strong emotional attachments to ponies, and the very knowledge that one has been disposed of in this fashion therefore causes many of us great anguish. By denying the Tongan's right to kill the pony, we affirm the right of children to persist in their views about ponies. The children's gain, by our reckoning, exceeds the loss to those who are prevented from killing ponies.

On their own territory, Tongans have of course demonstrated that it is possible to resolve the matter differently. By not encouraging the development of strong emotional attachments to ponies, they are able to kill them for food, just as we kill beef cattle for food here.

But it is difficult to imagine a closely intermingled population that consists partly of pony lovers and partly of pony eaters. Having committed our emotional energies to the love of ponies, we cannot simply tune out the fact that others close by are killing and eating them. Our feelings about what others do are what govern our decisions about rules here. And where the scope for altering how we feel about what others do is inherently limited, it is difficult to argue that such an influence is always wrong as a matter of general principle.

Our concerns about position, like our concerns about our pets, sometimes cause us trouble. Yet we would no more willingly abandon one than the other. We can and do try to make our own accommodations to the negative feelings evoked by disparities in income, but there are clear limits to our ability to ignore these feelings. Sometimes, we reluctantly call on the state to intervene. Where we do regulate contests for position, however, we almost always offer spurious explanations for our actions. And, having failed to perceive clearly why we regulate in the ways we do, we often adopt policies ill-suited to the tasks at hand. From a clearer understanding of the real purposes behind our

---

*Pony killing, being a rare and recent phenomenon in Salt Lake City, has not yet been formally banned by municipal ordinance. But similar ordinances against the killing and cooking of household pets are commonplace throughout the country. If informal pressures did not dissuade outsiders from roasting ponies, we may be sure that a formal ordinance would soon reinforce those pressures.

regulations, alternative policies will unfold that can enlarge our freedom while at the same time promoting greater efficiency and equity.

To explore the reasons behind these claims, let us begin by looking closely at people's concerns about position, the very wellspring of our attempts to regulate social interaction.

"Of this mountain, that's what I'm king of."

Two
_____

Local Status

Imitative Behavior

The herd instinct is as powerful in humans as in many animal species. Imitative behavior begins early in life and appears to spring from within.

In the psychology laboratory of the University of Edinburgh, a young mother and her six-day-old baby are seated before a camera. On cue, the mother sticks out her tongue, wiggles it briefly and then waits. Ten seconds later, the baby opens its mouth and performs a similar movement. Next, the mother flutters her eyelids, stops and opens her mouth, this time without extending her tongue. A few moments later, the baby's eyelashes flutter, its mouth opens briefly and then closes.[1]

Similar behavior has been observed in infants only a few hours old, suggesting that the urge to imitate cannot be entirely a learned behavior. In part, at least, it seems a consequence of the inherited structures of our nervous systems.

The influence of peer behavior is especially strong among children and adolescents. But the impulse to follow what others do is not confined to the young and inexperienced. In a 1970 film,[2] veteran student of human nature Allen Funt examined how adults conformed in a variety of unusual settings. In one instance, Funt placed his telephone number in a help-wanted advertisement, then arranged personal interviews with those who responded. We are shown an interviewee as he is directed to a small office in which several other persons are already seated, apparently waiting. To the experimental subject, the others appear to be fellow interviewees, but we know they are really confederates of Mr. Funt. Responding to no apparent signal, the others abruptly rise from their seats and begin taking off their clothing. We are shown a close-up of the experimental subject, his face a mask of apprehension as he surveys what is happening. A few moments pass, then he, too, rises from his chair and proceeds to disrobe. At no point during this process does he ask any of the others why they are removing their clothing. As the scene ends, we see him standing there, naked alongside the others, apparently waiting for some clue as to what happens next.

Imitative behavior often occurs when someone who doesn't know exactly what to do identifies other persons who seem to know and are doing it. The discrepancy between his behavior and theirs creates a sense of tension that is at least partly relieved by imitating the others. In the full wisdom of hindsight, people often recognize that having fallen into line may not have led to the best outcome. Perhaps the experimental subject in Funt's film later wished he had remained seated as the others played out their roles. He knows, after all, that we are taught to admire those whose independence of mind enables them to avoid the obvious pitfalls of being swayed too easily by what others do or think.

Yet if we focus exclusively on the occasional negative consequences of imitative behavior, we risk losing sight of how useful such behavior has been in helping people make their way through a complex and uncertain world. Consider, for example, a member of some primitive society who while hunting in a forest encounters a group of frightened fellow tribesmen running at top speed in the direction of their encampment. Numerous possible responses are open to this person. He may, for example, (1) spend several minutes thinking the situation over carefully; or (2) ask the others what the problem is and try to gather more information; or (3) join the others immediately in their flight, no questions asked. None of these strategies is without possible adverse consequences. The delays inherent in the first two may result in his being caught by a tiger, just out of sight, that is in hot pursuit of the others. On the other hand, there may be no tiger at all. Perhaps the others have simply angered some other tribesman and are fleeing from him. To join the fleeing tribesmen would then waste valuable time and energy that could have been devoted to the hunt. Under these circumstances, however, the odds seem to favor imitative behavior. And in the contest for survival, our hunter would probably have been well-served here by an impulse to mimic his fellow tribesmen.

Choosing the Right Role Models

Even in less extreme circumstances, imitative behavior is likely to be adaptive in a variety of ways. People's experiences differ widely, and no one individual's experience is so extensive as to encompass more than a fraction of the combined experiences of others. When people see others doing something unfamiliar, their urge to try it will probably benefit them over the long run, provided they exercise prudent judgment in choosing whom to imitate. For if imitative behavior is to be useful at all, we must choose worthy role models. Surely the time and energy required to explore examples provided by obviously incompetent or reckless persons would be much better spent taking leads from others who show some evidence of knowing what they are doing. Indeed, the most sensible imitative strategy might involve focusing on the behavior of those positioned above ourselves on whatever index of "success" we find most important. After all, if what they are doing seems to work for them, then why not for us?

It seems plausible to think of imitative behavior as reflecting an inner desire to be "like" other people. Yet this description seems to miss something important. Although people want to be like those they consider above them, they show little evidence of wanting to be like those they regard as substantially inferior. It may thus be useful to think of Funt's experimental subject as not so much wanting to be like the others as fearing to be worse than they are in some important respect. When we are thrust into unfamiliar settings, our tendency to behave as others do may spring less from a desire to be similar to them than from a very rational fear that their information is better than ours. From this perspective we can view the desire to imitate as merely a way of trying to avoid being outdone.

In this chapter I describe evidence that suggests people come into the world equipped with an inner voice urging them to rank as high as possible in whatever social hierarchy they belong to. Some of this evidence springs from the emerging consensus among biologists that the structure of human motivation was shaped by the forces of natural selection. The evolutionary biologist's view is that the psychological drive system we have inherited has properties that made our ancestors more likely to survive and leave offspring. Sugar tastes sweet to us, for example, because having a taste for ripened fruit was once helpful to the survival of our primate forebears.

Several reasons suggest that natural selection should have similarly favored those who were driven to seek high rank. Even in a famine, for example, there is still *some* food available, and first claim to whatever food there is will generally go to those with highest rank. If by dint of effort a person can move forward into a position of higher rank, that person's chances of making it through lean times should improve measurably. In general, whatever steps we take to move as far forward as possible in our social hierarchy will improve our access to a variety of other important resources that are in more or less fixed supply. Our chances of ending up with a desirable job, a sought-after mate, and other resources needed to raise large families are all enhanced by having high rank in our social hierarchy.*

Yet these goals might appear no better served by an inner voice saying "Try to rank ahead of as many others as possible" than by one saying simply "Do the best you can." To be sure, Robert Louis Stevenson's observation—"To be what we are, and to become what we are capable of becoming, is the only end of life."—does ring true at an intuitive level. After all, having done the best we can, we gain nothing by driving ourselves to distraction over the fact that others managed to do better. And it is true enough that the two inner voices have the same implications for behavior in many circumstances. Even so, there are at least some important settings where the first inner voice might serve better than the second.

Positive Reinforcement and Effort Monitoring

Consider, for example, the practical difficulties confronting a person who tries to respond to the hopelessly vague charge, "Do the best you can." Few people come into the world equipped with a blueprint that tells them how to "become what they are capable of becoming." Instead, people try many different things along the way and gradually focus their efforts on what seems to work best for them.

The process of determining what works best does not and cannot take place in social isolation. The psychologist's model of learning stresses the role of positive reinforcement throughout this process.[3] And positive reinforcement comes in the form of seeing one's own achievements compare favorably with the achievements of others. Runners don't win races simply by doing the best they can. They must also have discovered the events they are good at. To do so, what more useful motivating force could there be than an inner desire to achieve high rank? Some such desire surely helps explain why Einstein became a physicist instead of a marathon runner and why Martina Navratilova became a tennis player rather than a physicist.

Consider, too, the question of how much effort to expend in pursuit of resources that are important for survival. The expenditure of maximum effort at every moment will surely not be a sensible strategy for everyone. It invites "burnout" and will deplete the reserves of energy required for short-term bursts of effort when environmental conditions are temporarily highly stressful. Yet by spending too little effort, we risk falling into the lower portion of the population distribution, which is vulnerable even when environmental conditions are generally favorable.

The best level of effort to put forward depends on the abilities and efforts of others with whom we are in close competition. The lower we rank on the social scale, the greater is the payoff from efforts to advance. Even today,

---

*In many contemporary societies, family size is of course negatively, not positively, related to economic rank. But the drive system inherited by the members of these societies was forged under conditions in which fertility and economic rank were strongly positively correlated.

impoverished immigrants often work several jobs at once and make numerous other sacrifices in an effort to escape the bottom of the economic ladder. In their eyes, apparently, the risk of burnout is well worth taking in return for a ticket out of their slum neighborhoods. For those further ahead in the social queue, however, there is relatively more breathing room, and the best strategy for them may be to hold something in reserve for lean times.*

Precommitment in Bargaining

Caring about how our incomes compare with the incomes of others may also have had—and may still have—adaptive significance in interpersonal bargaining situations. We constantly confront decisions about the terms on which we engage in transactions with others. And a case can be made for the proposition that we will do better in these bargaining situations if we care more about relative than absolute income.

Support for this proposition comes from Schelling's observation that negotiating parties often do better if they commit themselves in advance to a particular negotiating position.[4] Suppose, for example, that both A and B are needed to perform some task and that the total gain from this task will be $1000. Suppose further that A is a tough bargainer, and threatens to abandon negotiations unless B agrees to perform his share of the task for only $100, leaving the remaining $900 for A. To make his threat credible, A shrewdly instructs his lawyer to draw up a contract that requires A to contribute $900 to some charity in the event that B receives more than $100. (A's threat to abandon negotiations unless B accepts his terms is made credible by his having signed such a contract, because it makes the transaction unprofitable for A unless he gets at least $900 of the $1000 total. Like Ulysses, A has tied himself to the mast; B knows that if he refuses A's offer, A is powerless to renegotiate. B must take it or leave it.)

Although A's offer will raise B's absolute level of income by $100, at the same time, it will worsen his position relative to A. If B cared only about his absolute income, he might accept A's terms rather than forego the transaction altogether. (His only reason for not accepting would be to discourage A from trying the same trick in future negotiations.) But if B cares also about how his position compares with A's, he will be less likely to accept A's proposal. Having a psychological drive mechanism that focuses on relative rather than absolute income is thus itself a precommitment strategy of a sort. If A knew that B would really *prefer* to have no deal at all than to accept the terms offered, A never would have committed himself to those terms in the first place—to do so would have served only to ensure that no agreement be

---

*The observation that many people in the highest-ranked positions tend to be extraordinarily driven personality types is perfectly compatible with the notion that extra effort enhances survival prospects most for those near the bottom of the queue. At any given starting point in the queue, different people will have different drives and capacities to undertake effort, and those with greater capacities will naturally tend to move farthest ahead.

reached at all.* Having strong concerns about position is thus tantamount to signing a contract that prevents participation in one-sided transactions. Indeed, there is ample empirical evidence that notions of equity cause negotiating parties to refuse offers that would enhance their absolute wealth.[5]

Our intuitive understanding of such behavior might be summarized by saying that people are averse to participating in transactions that they regard as "unfair."[6] But this raises the question of just what makes a transaction seem unfair. The preceding discussion suggests that an unfair transaction may simply be one in which one party's position suffers vis-à-vis the other's. If people were sure they had the best possible terms, then an inner voice saying "Do the best you can" would urge them to accept the transaction, no matter how inequitable it seemed. An inner concern about relative standing, by contrast, would move them to reject such transactions. Over the long run, people with an inherent concern about position will be better bargainers.

Arousal and Motivation

The foregoing argument suggests an important distinction between cognitive and noncognitive forces in motivating human behavior. Although the general subject of motivation is one of the least well understood among psychologists, there is wide agreement that at least some human behaviors are caused by inborn drives. The decision to eat, for example, is thought not to be motivated primarily by strictly cognitive considerations. One does not say to oneself, "I consumed 900 calories at 8 A.M. and burn calories at the rate of 300 per hour. Since it is now 12:30 P.M., I have exhausted the calories I consumed in the morning and had better eat something so I won't run out of energy this afternoon." Instead, one simply feels hungry, and goes off in search of something to eat. If cognitive forces get involved at all, it is likely to be to *override* the impulse to eat.

Some investigators have found it useful to think in terms of a model of "arousal," in which many human behaviors are motivated in much the same way as hungry people are motivated to eat.[7] Although the arousal mechanism is described in many different (and sometimes conflicting) ways, I hope the simplified account I offer here will capture at least the flavor of what these psychologists have in mind.[8]

The concept of arousal, broadly speaking, refers to the degree of electrical activity that takes place in the brain. In nontechnical terms, it might be thought of as a measure of mental alertness or agitation. Arousal is lowest during sleep; it rises gradually upon waking, fluctuates about some equilibrium level throughout the day, then declines again as a precondition for sleep.

For each of the various tasks people perform, there is thought to be an optimal level of arousal. Reading a scientific treatise requires a higher level of

---

*One might counter that B is concerned about his rank vis-à-vis other people besides A, and be moved by *that* concern to accept even such one-sided proposals. Although he might accept some such proposals, an obvious distaste for doing so would make him less likely to receive exploitative proposals, and would thus enhance his expected income vis-à-vis those of all other persons.

arousal than does reading a murder novel. Physical activity generally requires a higher level of arousal than does mental activity. Moreover, the arousal level can be elevated merely by engaging in simple physical activity, which may help account for why people yawn, stretch, or get up and walk around when they become fatigued while performing a mental task.

In addition to being elevated by physical activity, arousal can also be elevated by a variety of other factors. The arousal we call hunger, for example, is apparently triggered partly by low levels of sugar in the blood;[9] and, as everyone can attest, it can also be elevated by visual and olfactory stimuli. Mere thoughts can elevate arousal, as when one contemplates being in a dangerous situation.

The arousal mechanism's link to motivation apparently lies in its connection to the limbic system of the brain. The limbic system surrounds the brain stem and is thought to be responsible for the experience and expression of emotion. Pleasure, pain, fear, rage, joy, grief, lust, hunger, thirst, and a variety of other feelings are all believed to be centered there. Both very high and very low levels of arousal evoke feelings of displeasure or tension. These negative feelings, in turn, provide an incentive for the person experiencing them to alter the source of arousal that caused them. Electrical stimulation to specific sites in the limbic system has been shown to produce a variety of specific behaviors even when the environmental conditions that would normally provoke those behaviors are not present. Voracious eating behavior, for example, can be induced even after the subject has just ingested a large meal.[10]

In some important respects, then, it appears that people function more like automatons than like cognitive, willful beings. Just as war is said to be too important to leave to the generals, so perhaps did evolutionary forces feel that getting fed is too important to leave entirely to the organism's cognitive processes. In the same way that going without food for long periods produces uncomfortably high levels of arousal, a variety of evidence suggests that similar feelings are associated with having low relative standing.

Relative Standing and Feelings of Well-Being

BIOLOGICAL EVIDENCE
Sociophysiological experiments have demonstrated, for example, that specific measures of autonomic nervous system arousal are strongly influenced by status in social interactions.[11] In one recent investigation, Long and others found consistently higher heart rate and blood pressure readings among subjects interacting with people who outranked them than among subjects interacting with people of equal rank.[12] (See Figure 2.1.)

There is also evidence from primate studies that experimental manipulation of status orderings can produce fundamental changes in important neurophysiological processes. In a series of provocative studies, McGuire and his colleagues at UCLA have demonstrated that dominant and nondominant vervet monkeys show large differences in their blood concentrations of the neurotransmitter serotonin, one of whose functions is to carry nerve impulses

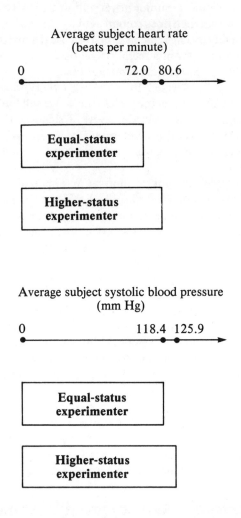

Figure 2.1 Heart Rate and Blood Pressure Are Significantly Elevated by Social
Interactions with Others of Higher Rank
Source: Adapted from Long et al. (1982), Table 1, p. 169.

in the limbic system. (More on the role of serotonin below.) McGuire et al.
first identified the behaviorally dominant member of each of 19 separate
groups of adult vervets and monitored whole blood serotonin concentrations
for both dominant and nondominant animals in all groups. In each group, the
dominant animal had the highest serotonin level, and the differences in
concentration levels between nondominant and dominant animals were consistently large. As shown in Figure 2.2, serotonin concentrations (in nanograms

per milliliter) for dominant animals were almost 50 percent higher than the corresponding average for nondominant animals.[13]

In a sequence of careful steps, the McGuire group then demonstrated that these biochemical differences are likely the result, rather than the cause, of the animals' dominance relationships. They began by removing the dominant animals from eight of the groups, placing each in an isolation cage. With the initially dominant animal gone, one of the remaining animals within each group then became behaviorally dominant, usually within 24 to 48 hours. Whole blood serotonin concentrations were monitored for all animals at intervals throughout the experiments. In these monitorings, serotonin concentrations in the newly dominant animals rose steadily to the levels of the formerly dominant animals. At the same time, the corresponding concentrations in the formerly dominant animals fell to the levels associated with subordinate status.

These changes in serotonin concentrations do not begin to take place until some 72 hours *after* the rearrangement of group membership. This suggests that the serotonin differences play no direct causal role in determining dominance rankings within groups. That these differences are instead the result of status differences is further supported by the observation that, once the formerly dominant animals are returned to their groups, they quickly reestablish their dominant positions. And having reestablished dominance, they show serotonin concentrations equal to their initially high levels. At the same time, the concentrations of the interim-dominant animals fall once again to their initially low levels. The respective time paths of serotonin concentration levels in initially dominant and interim-dominant vervets are represented in Figures 2.3 and 2.4.

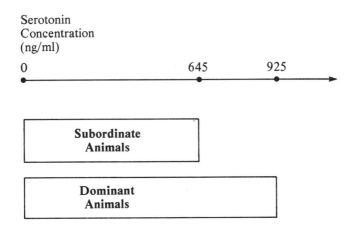

Figure 2.2 Mean Whole Blood Serotonin Concentrations for Dominant and Subordinate Vervet Monkeys

Similar experiments involving humans would present obvious difficulties. And because of the many hierarchies most people are involved in, it is difficult to identify natural experiments that can be used to assess the effect of status on biochemical processes in humans. The McGuire group has been able to determine, however, that serotonin concentrations are approximately 20 percent higher for the officers of college fraternities than they are for the other members of the same groups. Similar differences were identified between leaders and non-leaders of college athletic teams. In an effort to identify the effects of carefully controlled changes in status in humans, the UCLA researchers are currently studying serotonin concentrations in a small group of men before, during, and after their participation as officers and crew members on an extended sailing voyage.

If the findings from these human studies turn out to be similar to those from the primate studies, what would that tell us about the importance of status relationships between people? The answer to this question depends, of course, on the specific role played by serotonin in the central nervous system. Unfortunately, this area of research is still very much in its infancy. But there can be little doubt that serotonin does play an important role in the way people and animals act and feel. Primates and humans synthesize serotonin from the amino acid tryptophan, and investigators are thus able to elevate serotonin levels experimentally by administering controlled amounts of tryptophan. Vervet monkeys given daily doses of tryptophan for a two-week period show an increase in social behaviors and a corresponding decrease in behaviors associated with fear and anxiety.[14]

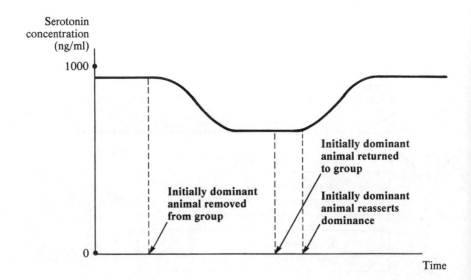

Figure 2.3 Whole Blood Serotonin Concentrations in Initially Dominant Vervets

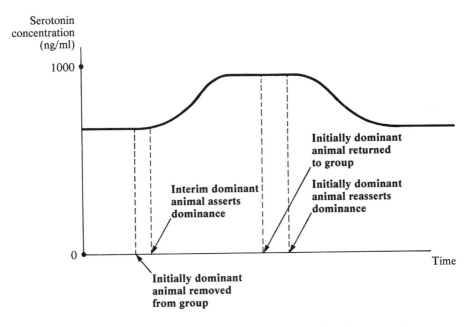

Figure 2.4 Whole Blood Serotonin Concentrations in Interim-Dominant Vervets

In other experiments, researchers have studied the serotonin-behavior relationship by administering drugs that interfere with serotonin biosynthesis.
The compound parachlorophenylalanine, for example, inhibits production of
the enzyme tryptophan hydroxylase, which, in turn, is essential for the biosynthesis of serotonin from tryptophan. Vervet monkeys treated with daily
doses of parachlorophenylalanine for two weeks exhibited irritable, aggressive, and hypermobile behavior.[15] In similar pharmacological experiments
carried out in humans, reduced serotonin levels have been associated with a
variety of affective disorders, including sleep disturbances, irritability, and
heightened aggressiveness.[16] Moreover, serotonin metabolism deficiencies in
humans have been linked to mania and depression.[17]

Status relationships are also thought to be related to blood concentrations
of the sex hormone testosterone in men. Successful efforts to achieve or
maintain status tend to produce elevated plasma testosterone levels, whereas
reductions in status are followed by declines in these levels.[18] (As the father of
two adolescent sons afflicted with testosterone poisoning, I am well aware that
this particular effect of enhanced status is not an unmixed blessing.) The link
between testosterone levels and specific behaviors in humans is very poorly
understood. But there is some evidence from primate studies that heightened
levels facilitate behaviors that achieve dominance, while reduced levels inhibit
such behaviors.[19] Thus, while the status-serotonin linkage apparently operates
in one direction only, the status-testosterone relationship seems to be one of

Drawing by Gini Curl.

Figure 2.5 Dominant vervet monkeys have elevated concentrations of the neurotransmitter serotonin, which affects moods and behavior.

both cause and effect. As tentative as these findings are, they clearly raise the possibility that one's status may have profound effects on the way one feels and functions as a person.

SURVEY EVIDENCE

Shortly after World War II, various public opinion surveys began investigating happiness. Findings from one of these surveys, which asked people to place themselves into one of several happiness categories, are reproduced in Table 2.1. These findings are consistent with the view that relative economic standing exerts a strong influence on reported happiness levels. People in the highest income bracket, for example, are nearly twice as likely as those in the lowest bracket to report that they are "very happy," and less than one-third as likely to say they are "not happy." (One's relative standing in the national income hierarchy, however, cannot be the *only* important factor determining a person's happiness level. After all, nearly 30 percent of those in the lowest income category classified themselves as "very happy.")

The data in Table 2.1 might just as easily be interpreted to mean that happiness increases not with relative but with absolute income levels. The results of nine similar happiness surveys taken between 1946 and 1970, however, rule out this interpretation. (See Table 2.2.) National per capita income, measured in 1970 dollars, rose from $2500 in 1946 to $3890 in 1970, an increase of 56 percent. Even so, there is no clear evidence of a significant change in happiness levels during those years. A similar pattern is reported by Duncan, who found that "[t]here was no change in the distribution of satisfaction with the standard of living among Detroit area wives between 1955 and

Table 2.1 *Percentage Distribution of the Population by Happiness, by Size of Income, in the United States, 1970*

Income (in $000's)	(1) Very Happy	(2) Fairly Happy	(3) Not Happy	(4) No Answer
15+	56	37	4	3
10–15	49	46	3	2
7–10	47	46	5	2
5–7	38	52	7	3
3–5	33	54	7	6
Under 3	29	55	13	3

Source: Data from American Institute of Public Opinion Poll, December 1970, cited in Easterlin (1973), p. 100.

1971, although current-dollar median family income doubled and constant dollar income increased by forty percent."[20]

Survey evidence has its limitations, of course, and we may wonder whether there is really any relationship between how happy people say they are and how happy they actually feel. Woody Allen has made a good living over the

Drawing by George Booth. Reproduced by Special Permission of PLAYBOY Magazine. Copyright © 1974 by PLAYBOY.

"Materially speaking we've been on the decline, but spiritually we're doing much better, thank you."

years telling people how miserable he is. ("Most of the time I don't have much fun. The rest of the time I don't have any fun at all.") Still, one suspects that by now few people take his pronouncements at face value.

Yet a large body of research has shown that self-reported happiness is indeed linked to various objective measures of well-being. For example, people who say they are not happy are much more likely to exhibit physical symptoms of distress, such as rapid heartbeat, frequency of headaches, digestive disorders, and dizziness.[21] Indexes of self-reported happiness are also strongly related to clinical symptoms of depression, irritability, and anxiety,[22] as well as a number of observable behaviors that are commonly taken as symptoms of psychological well-being.[23] People who consider themselves happy are more likely than others, for example, to initiate social contacts with friends. Moreover, measures of self-reported happiness are very stable over time, as measured by the consistency of responses taken for the same sample of people in surveys conducted two years apart.[24] In one pair of surveys taken eight months apart, fewer than 2 percent of the respondents switched between extreme categories (e.g., by reporting "Very Happy" in one survey and "Not Very Happy" in the other.)[25]

Such findings, needless to say, do not force us to accept uncritically what people say about how happy they are. When taken as a whole, however, the evidence we have seen suggests that people's relative economic standing strongly influences the way they feel and act.

Local Versus Global Hierarchies

A person's well-being depends in part on how large his income is relative to the incomes of others. Yet do the incomes of all people matter equally, or are

Table 2.2 *Percentage Distribution of the U.S. Population by Self-Rated Happiness Categories, 1946–70*

Date	Very Happy	Fairly Happy	Not Very Happy	Other
Apr. 1946	39	50	10	1
Dec. 1947	42	47	10	1
Aug. 1948	43	43	11	2
Nov. 1952	47	43	9	1
Sept. 1956	52	42	5	1
Mar. 1957	53	43	3	1
July 1963	47	48	5[a]	1
Oct. 1966	49	46	4[a]	2
Dec. 1970	43	48	6[a]	3

Source: Data from American Institute of Public Opinion Polls 369, 410, 425, 508, 570, 571, 580, 675, 735. Cited in Easterlin (1973), p. 109.

[a]The category in this survey was worded "not happy" rather than "not very happy."

some more important than others? Comparisons of surveys across countries provide little evidence that a person's well-being depends significantly on where he stands relative to people in other nations. Easterlin found, for example, that differences between the reported happiness levels for various countries are generally small, even when per capita gross national products differ between countries by factors of 15 and more.[26] One set of typical findings is reported in Figure 2.6 and shows no clear link between a country's per capita GNP and the average reported happiness levels of its citizens.

Similarly, the findings summarized in Table 2.2 suggest that reported happiness levels are not very sensitive to comparisons across time. Although people know their incomes are larger than those of their parents, this does not seem to count for much.

Other evidence suggests that our "reference groups" are circumscribed even more narrowly than by time and national boundaries. The sociophysiological studies cited above, for example, suggest that face-to-face contact intensifies the status comparisons we make. Even though people know that there are many others who outrank them along various social or economic scales, the very process of direct interaction with such persons often serves to elevate arousal to uncomfortable levels. Nigerians surely know that Germans are much wealthier than they are. Yet because Nigerians don't come in direct contact with Germans often, they don't focus closely on how the incomes of Germans compare with their own—which may help explain why the two countries report the same happiness levels in Figure 2.6. The adage "Out of sight, out of mind" appears to be at work here.

The usefulness of such a rule of thumb seems especially plausible if the forces of natural selection indeed played a central role in molding the structure

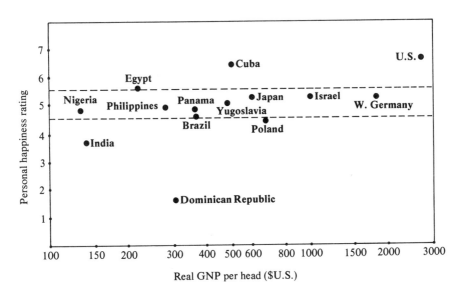

Figure 2.6 Average Personal Happiness Ratings and GNP per Capita
Source: Easterlin (1973), p. 106.

of human psychological drives. After all, Darwinian theory has always stressed the importance of local environments in shaping the evolutionary paths of behavior and physical characteristics. The outcome of the struggle to survive depends much less on one's strength in any absolute or global sense than on how strong one is relative to the others with whom one must compete directly for important resources. The biologically fit organism is the one that carves out a suitable ecological niche for itself—a local environment in which it outranks sufficiently many of its competitors to gain access to the resources it needs to survive. Why should any organism spend scarce resources worrying about how it ranks against others against whom it will never have to compete directly? An arousal mechanism more attuned to relative standing in local than in global environments would surely have conferred at least some advantage under the conditions in which humans evolved.

The psychologist's understanding of the way people perceive and process information lends additional support to the notion that people care more about local than global relative standing. Psychologists stress that our senses are designed to respond less to the absolute measure of any stimulus than to differences between that measure and some norm of reference standard that we adopt from experience.[27] On a 65° day in March, for example, people in

"I don't know how you and I would be rated by the psychiatrists in the Soviet Union, but I'd say we're fairly sane by New York standards."

Miami will be shivering in their sweaters, while residents of Minneapolis go about cheerfully in shirt sleeves.

Kahneman and Tversky have shown that the norms people use in making judgments are strongly governed by the "available" information they have—information that can be accessed easily from memory or constructed readily from imagination.[28] Among the myriad bits of information stored in each human brain, some can be summoned much more easily than others and thus play more important roles in the way we perceive things and make judgments about them. How available a given piece of information is depends on numerous factors. One of the most important is what psychologists call its "vividness"—the extent to which it is "(a) emotionally interesting, (b) concrete and imagery provoking, and (c) proximate in a sensory, temporal, or spatial way."[29]

Using some vivid information of their own, Nisbett and Ross illustrate these ideas as follows:

Consider the difference in the amount of information in the sentence "Jack sustained fatal injuries in an automobile accident" and that in the sentence "Jack was killed by a semi trailer that rolled over on his car and crushed his skull." The amount of codable information in the latter is substantially greater, aside from the additional "information" generated by the involuntary imagery in reading it.

Now contrast the amount of information in the second, concrete sentence with the amount of information that would result from actually viewing a semi trailer rolling over on a car and crushing its occupant. The duration of the event might not exceed the time it takes to read the sentence, yet to describe verbally even a small fraction of the information about the actual event that might be coded could take a very long time. A picture can be worth a thousand words, and real life exposure to the object can be worth many thousands more.[30]

As people grope for a baseline against which to assess their relative standing, they are likely to be influenced disproportionately by the vividness of the information they have about others with whom they come in direct contact. For example, even though economics professors "know" that accounting professors earn 20 percent more than they do, they are much more likely to focus their concerns on their fellow economists who earn 5 percent more than they do.

The fact that people's closest associates may matter most for the purpose of interpersonal income comparisons does not imply, of course, that they are the *only* ones who matter. A large sociological literature has established that close contacts are indeed important, but that more distant comparisons can be important as well.[31] To be sure, people in similar circumstances, even though located far away, can be even more important than people nearby whose circumstances are markedly different. For example, a 35-year-old vice president in a branch bank in San Francisco may take a much greater interest in the salary of her counterpart at the Los Angeles branch than in the salary of the 50-year-old dentist in her own neighborhood. But here, too, a simple, unifying principle governs the membership of people's personal reference groups—people care most about those with whom they compete most directly for important resources.

Self-Perception, Local Status, and Performance

Recently, the passenger sitting next to me on an airplane noticed that I was proofreading an earlier version of this chapter and asked what my work was about. I gave him a brief summary of the chapter, which prompted him to relate the following account of his own circumstances.

The son of a wealthy family, he had always been sent to the best private schools, where he had struggled each year to make passing grades. In his junior year in high school, he was finally dismissed for poor academic performance. Discouraged, and unwilling to invest in further private education, his parents then enrolled him in the local public high school. There, much to his surprise, he emerged as a leading student. He also became much more active socially than he had been before and went on to do very well at a small college. He is now the president of a fast-growing mortgage bank in a small city and, by all external measures, has been very successful in life.

"I would never have gotten off the ground," he explained to me, "if I hadn't flunked out of prep school. I always felt so stupid and depressed all of the time there that I could never really get going on anything. But once I found myself doing well in the public high school, everything started opening up for me."

An intriguing body of psychological research lends support to this man's view that performance can be strongly colored by self-perceptions. In one particularly provocative experiment, Lewinsohn and his colleagues had a sample of clinically depressed persons and a control group assess their own skills and personality traits.[32] An external group of observers also made independent evaluations of the same skills and traits. Not surprisingly, the depressed persons had consistently less favorable self-assessments than did the nondepressed persons. The interesting finding was that, while there was close agreement between the depressed persons' self-assessments and those of the external evaluators, people in the control group consistently rated themselves much more positively than the outsiders did. The depressed subjects, in other words, apparently had a more realistic impression of their own traits and skills than did the ostensibly normal control subjects, who characterized themselves with "a halo or glow that involves an illusory self-enhancement. . . ."[33]

In another experiment, Alloy and Abramson confronted samples of depressed and nondepressed students with an assortment of tasks, the successful completion of which depended to a varying degree on the performance of the person attempting them.[34] Alloy and Abramson found that the depressed students judged the extent to which their success depended on their own performance extremely accurately. By contrast, however, they found that the nondepressed students consistently overestimated the role of their own performance in those tasks in which they achieved desired outcomes and underestimated their own role in those that resulted in undesired outcomes. (The investigators called the depressed students "sadder but wiser.")

Such experiments obviously do not establish that negative self-perceptions cause depression or any other seriously incapacitating psychological condition. But suppose we accept the widely held view that self-confidence enhances a person's performance, and that positive self-perceptions, even if somewhat illusory by objective standards, tend to serve people well in life. It then follows, as it apparently did for the banker, that local environments that discourage positive self-perceptions can adversely affect performance. Viewed from the other side, local environments that help support positive self-assessments can favorably affect performance. Given the importance of vivid information in the process of human inference, having high rank in a local environment will tend to enhance the development of a positive self-image. Self-esteem, after all, derives largely from favorable comparisons with others close at hand. And to the extent that high self-esteem is linked directly to performance, the ability to occupy a high-ranked position relative to others in the same local environment thus becomes an all the more valuable asset to have. Even extremely capable people often have difficulty achieving their full potential in environments that make it difficult to maintain feelings of self-esteem.

Does Absolute Income Matter at All?

The view that to be poor means simply to have less than others have has by now gained broad currency, and the evidence reviewed in this chapter is largely consistent with this view. The public at large seems also to have defined poverty in relativistic terms. In numerous Gallup surveys, for example, people were asked, "What is the smallest amount of money a family of four needs to get along in this community?" Responses, which are summarized in Table 2.3, grew at roughly the same rate as national income.

Many have been led by such evidence to conclude that, beyond some point, absolute income levels do not matter at all as determinants of human happiness. Townsend, for example, writes that "[a]ny rigorous conceptualization of the social determination of need dissolves the idea of absolute need. . . . Lacking an alternate criterion, the best assumption would be to relate sufficiency to the average rise (or fall) of real incomes."[35] By this view, the pursuit of economic growth is thus a futile exercise, one destined to end in frustration and disappointment.

The concept of poverty undeniably does have a strong relative component. Yet the conclusion that absolute income does not matter at all appears just as spurious as the notion that absolute income is the *only* income concept that matters. Granted, the human nervous system tends to focus on the here and now; and people tend to feel dissatisfied in proportion to how far their

*"I was sad because I had no walking stick, Until I saw a
man who had no spats."*

incomes fail to match those of their peers. But that does not mean that people
would be indifferent if everyone's income suddenly became twice what it is
today. After all, people are in competition not only with one another but with
the external environment as well. And the resources available for the struggle
against disease and other external threats will rise more than in proportion to
the rate of increase in absolute material living standards. The family that loses
a child to an illness suffers deeply, no matter what its position on the relative
income scale. The capability to reduce the incidence of such suffering is clearly
enhanced by a rising material standard of living.

Hirsch and others are correct when they say that economic growth often
entails frustration insofar as people's concerns tend to focus on their economic
standing vis-à-vis other people. But that does not mean that economic growth
becomes a matter of social indifference.[36]

Economists and Relative Standing

Although the distinction between local and global relative standing has been
little emphasized in the economics literature, numerous economists have
nonetheless recognized the importance most people seem to place on relative
standing. Duesenberry, for example, wrote in 1949 that "demonstration

effects" cause people to emulate the consumption standard set by those above them in the income hierarchy.[37] Leibenstein wrote in 1950 of "snob goods" and "bandwagon effects" in consumption.[38] Easterlin, cited earlier, produced a thoughtfully documented argument that rising aggregate income levels do not make people happier, a theme also explored recently by Scitovsky and Rainwater.[39] Thurow, too, has focused on the importance of relative standing in many of his writings.[40] Kapteyn and van Praag have made innovative use of survey data in exploring the nature of people's concerns about where they stand in the income hierarchy,[41] and Layard has investigated some of the policy implications of those concerns.[42] Numerous other economists have written about various other aspects of how interpersonal comparisons matter to people.[43]

Still, it is perhaps an understatement to say that the economics profession as a whole has shown little interest in the idea that people are deeply concerned about their relative standing in hierarchies. Duesenberry's theory of consumption behavior, for example, was quickly relegated to historical-footnote status as soon as alternative theories appeared (even though, as I argue in Chapter 8, the alternative theories do not account for the patterns of spending behavior we observe nearly as well as Duesenberry does).

In setting up formal models of economic behavior, economists almost always assume at the outset that a person's sense of well-being, or utility, depends on the absolute quantities of various goods he consumes, not on how those quantities compare with the amounts consumed by others. Sometimes, this assumption works even if it is relative standing that people really care about. Suppose, for example, the identities of the members of a person's reference group are taken as fixed, and their behavior taken as given. Then the

Table 2.3 *"What is the smallest amount of money a family of four needs to get along in this community?"*

Year	Median Response ($/wk)	Median Response as a Percentage of Average Disposable Income for a Family of Four
1952	50	42.7
1957	72	51.8
1961	84	54.9
1966	99	49.3
1967	101	47.6
1968	102	44.9
1970	120	46.0
1971	126	45.3
1972	127	42.8
1973	149	44.9
1974	152	42.3
1975	161	41.2
1976	177	42.0

Source: Gallup (1972 and 1978), and *Economic Report of the President* (1982).

effect of that person's attempt to maximize his absolute income level will be precisely the same as if he attempted to maximize his relative standing in that group. Such similarities between the two approaches (which, we will see, are often more apparent than real) have played at least some role in the economist's implicit decision to leave the study of relative standing to psychologists and sociologists.

Economists are by nature and training much more concerned with what people do than with what they say or feel, and as a group they have never seemed to believe that people's concerns about relative standing have much influence on what they actually do. To be sure, there are good reasons for being skeptical about what people say. The story is told of a famous violinist who was approached after a performance by an admirer who said "I'd give anything to be able to play as beautifully as you do." The violinist responded by asking, "Would you have been willing to practice for 10 hours a day ever since you were four?" Often people do want what they say they want but aren't willing to back up their wants with the necessary sacrifices. Perhaps most economists believe that, when people say that their relative standing is important, what most of them really mean is that it would be nice to have high relative standing, but not at the expense of changing their behavior significantly.

As we will see, however, the effects of people's concerns about relative standing are *not* limited to those invisible attitudes and feelings they carry about privately. Rather, these concerns have profound effects on an array of observable behaviors of just the sort that economists have always taken great efforts to explain—on the wages firms pay their workers, on the tax systems people implement, on the ways in which they spend their incomes, and even on the various legal and ethical structures they adopt. In trying to explain such phenomena without taking people's concerns about relative standing into account, economists have been led to adopt a variety of theories that seem either utterly implausible as descriptions of human behavior or sharply at variance with observed facts. To see why this is so, let us turn now to the economist's traditional theory of competitive labor markets, which suffers from both of these problems.

"I changed my mind. I'd rather be a big enchanted prince in a small pond than a small enchanted prince in a big pond."

Three

Choosing the Right Pond

In the winter of 1978, a leading West Coast university made an attractive job offer to a young economics professor at one of the prestigious institutions overlooking the Charles River in Cambridge, Massachusetts. The eastern institution wanted very much to keep this employee, who is rightfully regarded as one of the most original and productive scholars in the profession. Following an intense period of negotiations, the eastern university was forced to concede defeat. The chairman of its economics department put it to the departing scholar something like this: "You're well worth it to the department, and I'd have no trouble paying you what it would take to keep you here, but we could never afford to handle the fifteen other salary increases your raise would prompt."

Episodes like this one are apparently everyday occurrences in the world of work. Yet when viewed within the framework of the traditional economic theory of competitive labor markets, such a transaction is all but completely unintelligible. According to this theory, if someone is worth what it would take to keep him, then he will be kept on, no ifs, ands, or buts.* To others who then demand higher salaries, only two responses make any sense: (1) If, for some reason, they had been working for less than what they were worth, and in fact are worth what they now ask, then they too will be accommodated; or (2) if they are not worth what they ask, then their requests will be denied and they will be reminded that they may leave if not satisfied.

Traditional economic theory says that a worker will be paid the value of his "marginal product" by the firm that employs him in a competitive labor market. The value of a worker's marginal product is defined, in turn, as the amount by which the value of the firm's production during each time period would decline if he were no longer employed by the firm.

The Marginal Productivity Theory of Wages

The logic of the traditional theory is simple and compelling. The basic argument is that firms are unstable whenever workers are *not* paid the respective values of their marginal products. To see how this argument works, let us consider an example in which firms hire workers to make bricks out of clay. (The details of this example are obvious abstractions from any labor market we might actually observe in practice. But none of the simplifying assumptions changes the main point the example illustrates.) Suppose that clay, a plentiful commodity, is available free of charge and that a firm's only expenses are the wages it pays its workers to mold clay into bricks. If brick-making is like most other activities, we may safely assume that some brick-makers are less productive than others. Suppose that some can mold 10 bricks per hour, others 20, others 30, and still others 40. To complete the picture, suppose that each firm sells its bricks to an exporter who pays 10 cents per brick for whatever quantity of bricks the firm wishes to sell.

In this very simple labor market, the value of a brickmaker's marginal product is 10 cents times the number of bricks he makes per hour.† A worker who makes 30 bricks per hour thus has a marginal product whose value is $3 per hour, for example, whereas one who makes 40 has a marginal product whose value is $4 per hour. The theory of competitive labor markets says that the only outcome that is stable under competition is for the former to be paid $3 per hour, the latter $4 per hour.

If a firm paid more than these amounts, its revenues from the sale of bricks would fail to cover its labor costs, and it would eventually be forced out of business. A firm that paid any less would be unable to retain its workers.

---

*Although normally developed within the context of profit-maximizing firms, the theory of competitive labor markets applies whenever organizations compete with one another for the purchase of labor services. Such competition is in few industries more intense than among leading research institutions.

†To keep the example from becoming needlessly cluttered, I am ignoring entirely here the traditional concept of a declining marginal productivity schedule, along which any given worker's marginal product falls as more workers are employed by the firm. Noneconomists interested in a fuller development of the marginal productivity theory may consult Samuelson (1980), chapter 27, or any other introductory economics text.

Suppose, for example, that a firm paid a 30-brick-per-hour worker a wage of only $2.50. Some other firm, by offering $2.60, could presumably lure him away. By so doing, it would augment its profits by 40 cents per hour (the difference between the $3 worth of bricks he produces per hour and the $2.60 per hour it pays him). But then a third firm could offer this same worker $2.70, thus luring him away from the second firm, and augmenting its own profits by 30 cents per hour. This bidding process will continue until the 30-brick-per-hour worker's wage is driven up to $3 per hour.

Suppose the 30-brick man ends up in a brickmaking firm where the most productive worker until his arrival had been a 20-brick worker who was being paid $2 per hour. With the arrival of the new man, the $2-per-hour worker may feel unhappy at being displaced from his position as top earner in the firm. He may even ask his employer for a raise. But the traditional theory of competitive labor markets holds that it is not in the employer's power to give him one. He is already being paid the value of what he contributes to the firm's revenues, and to pay him more would only push the firm into the loss column.

Now, the labor market in this example is, needless to say, a highly stylized one. More realistically we would have to say something more about what the firm itself contributes to the whole process. Presumably, it would rent land, construct buildings, buy kilns, buy fuel to operate them, and incur a host of other expenses. These expenses too would have to be reflected in the price of bricks. And in a more realistic market workers might not be so freely mobile as in this example. Perhaps workers' inertia would allow a firm to escape for a while paying a 30-brick-per-hour worker only $2.50 per hour. Or perhaps a conspiracy of brick producers might form to depress brickmakers' wages. But despite these possible difficulties, whose consequences I will consider momentarily, the logic of the competitive labor market model is nonetheless airtight. When the conditions of this model are met, its prediction that workers will be paid the respective value of their marginal products is unequivocal.

It is fair to say that economists as a group believe that these conditions are, for the most part, satisfied in practice—not literally so, but perhaps in the way that physicists think of each side of a large block of dry ice as a frictionless surface. There is in fact an easily measurable quantity of friction present when a puck glides across a dry ice surface. But we can nonetheless generate reasonably accurate predictions about what will happen when various forces are applied to the puck if we think of it as traveling along a perfectly frictionless surface. In much the same way, most economists feel comfortable with their view that workers, within close limits,* are paid the values of their marginal products.

---

*Again for the sake of simplicity, I ignore numerous other factors that might affect the relationship between wages and marginal products. Risk aversion (Stiglitz, 1975; Shavell, 1979), specific training expenses (Becker, 1964; Oi, 1962; and Mincer, 1962); measurement problems (Groves, 1973), internal labor market dynamics (Doeringer and Piore, 1971; Thurow, 1975; and Lazear, 1979), for example, have all been shown capable of causing at least momentary divergencies between wages and marginal product values. But I attempt to show in Chapter 4 that these factors cannot satisfactorily account for the patterns of wage payments we observe in actual firms.

Does the Marginal Productivity Theory Work?

Nowhere is the power of a plausible theory to influence the way people interpret what happens in the world more evident than in the way the competitive labor market theory has caused economists to view what happens in the workplace. At a superficial level, at least, the pay schedules we observe in practice seem altogether more egalitarian than would be possible under the marginal productivity theory. Many firms, for example, follow strict pay formulas based on education, experience, and length of tenure, even when there are substantial productivity differences among workers who are paid the same under these formulas. Many prestigious law firms reward their partners according to formulas based exclusively on tenure, even though there are obvious differences in the revenues brought in by partners who are paid the same. Indeed, pure piece-rate pay schemes of the type predicted by economic theory are almost never observed in even the most atomistically competitive labor markets. To business managers, personnel administrators, and almost everyone else in the world who has reflected even briefly on the matter, the economist's claim that workers are paid the values of their marginal products must seem nothing short of absurd.

But if economists have clung too stubbornly to a theory that doesn't fit the facts, their critics have accepted too credulously the various alternative explanations that have been offered. Consider, for example, the following arguments put forward by critics of the competitive theory.

One such argument is that the marginal productivity theory relies too heavily on the assumption that workers will move in response to more favorable wage opportunities.[1] This assumption does indeed appear false for many, if not most, workers. Having located in an area, bought a house, made friends, and started a family, most people are unwilling to pick up stakes in search of a higher wage rate. Yet the fact that most people are reluctant to move is alone insufficient to enable firms to pay workers less than they are worth.

Suppose, for the sake of argument, that firms did feel they could exploit worker inertia by paying people substantially less than the economic value of what they contribute. Why, then, except possibly in a one-company town, would any workers agree at the outset to work for such a firm? Before people make the commitments that make moving so hard, many in fact do move. Marston estimated, for example, that between 1970 and 1978 alone, intercity migration flows exceeded 25 percent of the urban population.[2] Why couldn't a new firm enhance its profits by bidding for the services of these relatively mobile workers? And even where workers cannot or will not move to where job opportunities are, isn't it still possible for firms to bring jobs to them—just as, for example, the availability of unemployed aerospace workers prompted many firms to move to Seattle during the early 1970s?

Some critics of the competitive theory respond that firms offer high starting wages to entice workers to join, and then cut wages once they are hooked. However, employers develop reputations among potential workers, the same way that merchants do among potential buyers, and many workers would not work for such firms. Other things equal, a firm with the reputation of paying fair wages will compete favorably against other firms thought to exploit their workers. By luring workers away from exploitative firms, such a firm would increase its own profits, just as the brickmaking firm did by hiring the underpaid brickmaker.

If the threat of competition thus protects the worker against being exploited here, it is not because of any charitable motives on the part of the entrepreneur. Instead, it is because it is in the selfish interest of any firm to prevent its new employees from being diverted in this fashion. Even if the owner of the firm had decided to retire, to allow such diversion would then cause the price at which the business could be sold to fall by more than the resultant temporary savings in labor costs.

Another common criticism is that the competitive theory of wage determination breaks down because employers conspire to hold down wages. And it is surely true that cartels of various sorts have existed throughout history. But cartels are almost always unstable. Existing members profit greatly when they cheat on their agreements, and there are high payoffs to new firms that organize outside cartel agreements. In the face of such payoffs, cartels seldom hold together for very long.[3]

Perhaps the greatest difficulty for critics of the competitive theory is that the rates of return most firms earn on their investments are too low to support the claim that markets are not highly competitive.[4] Even most critics are willing to concede that when the owner of a firm makes an investment in that firm, she is entitled to expect a reasonable rate of return in exchange. After all, making that investment imposes costs on her, which are the returns she foregoes by not doing something else with those same resources. She could have used those resources to plant trees, for example, in which case her return would have been the extra lumber available for sale at the end of each year. When we adjust for the risks involved and for various other factors that influence the return to an activity, we see that the returns most firms earn are not excessive compared to what the same resources could have earned in such manifestly nonexploitative alternatives as tree growing.

If we assume, to the contrary, that exploitative firms do exist and can hold wage rates down by even as little as 10 percent below competitive levels, we would then expect the rates of return for those firms to be roughly 50 percent higher than competitive rates.* Yet very few firms consistently earn rates of return as high as that. More important, those industries that do have higher than average rates of return almost always turn out to be high-wage rather

---

*Consider the case of a firm that hires labor in competitive markets at a wage W, and that can borrow or lend at the annual rate r. If L denotes its labor force and K its capital stock, and these are its only factors of production, then its total costs, C, are given by $WL + rK = C$. If $r = .10$ and labor costs are 70 percent of total costs, it then follows that $K = 3C$.

Now consider a firm identical to the one above, except that its market power in the labor market enables it to pay its workers only $.9W$. If P denotes the excess profits it receives as a result of its market power, we then have $.9(.7C) + .10(3C) + P = C$, or $P = .07C$. Suppose the firm's equity is one-half of its total capital stock. Its total rate of return on equity will then be the sum of the competitive return ($.10 \times 1.5K = .15C$) and the excess return ($.07C$) divided by total equity ($1.5C$), which is $.22C \div 1.5C = 0.147$.

Volume of
lumber

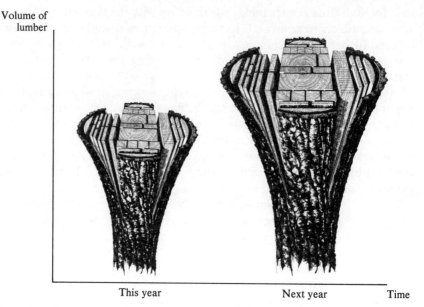

| This year | Next year | Time |

Figure 3.1 A corporation has no reason to remain in business unless it expects to earn at least as much as it could by investing its capital in trees.

than low-wage industries. Empirical studies have repeatedly found that wage rates are positively, not negatively, influenced by profit rates.[5] To be sure, the West Virginia coal miner in a one-mine town does earn a wage that is well below the average wage paid in many other industries. But the mine that employs him probably exists at the margin of economic profitability. And if so, it makes no sense to say that his low wage is the result of exploitation.

These observations are difficult to reconcile with a belief that exploitation in labor markets is substantial and pervasive. As I argue both in this and in later chapters, however, many of the *conclusions* supported by exploitation arguments happen to be largely correct. They are correct, however, for reasons that have little or nothing to do with exploitation. The plausibility of the conclusions attributed to these arguments has lent them credibility all out of proportion to their logical and factual content. This is most unfortunate, because these same exploitation arguments are also used to support a variety of conclusions that are not correct, some of which have had serious adverse consequences for public policy (more on these points in Chapter 12).

If the internal wage structures of firms are far more egalitarian than would be warranted by the marginal productivity theory, and if firms as a whole do not earn abnormally high profits, it follows that the least productive workers in firms are being paid *more* than the value of what they produce; and that firms accomplish this by paying their most productive workers less than the value of what they produce. These observations may cause no tension on ethical grounds (more on this point below). But, to my knowledge, neither critics nor defenders of the market system have yet explained why any profit-seeking firm would ever deliberately and persistently pay some workers more than the value of what they contribute to its revenues. Nor, as noted, has anyone satisfactorily explained why the most productive workers stay in their current firms, if indeed they are being paid less than their true value. Why haven't they instead gone to other firms who offer them what they are worth? The facts as they have been addressed by existing theories just do not add up.

An Alternative Theory of the Internal Wage Structure

By observing that workers care not only about their absolute wage levels but also about how their wages compare with those earned by their co-workers, we can begin to resolve the paradox at hand. Consider the following scenario. A team of economists has somehow seized control of the reins of government in the country where the brickmaking firms in our earlier example operate. Their first act is to decree, in the name of efficiency, that each firm must pay each worker the value of his marginal product, with failure to do so punishable by law. (Presumably, the economists believe their decree is redundant—a mere rhetorical flourish—since competition in the labor market is supposed to accomplish the same result in any event.) If workers care about their rank in the firms they form, one immediate consequence of this decree is that workers of different productivity levels cannot co-exist under the roof of a single firm.

To see why this is so, suppose some firm employed two brickmakers, A and B, whose marginal products are 40 bricks per hour and 30 bricks per hour, respectively; and that, in compliance with the decree, the firm paid A a wage of $4 per hour and B a wage of $3 per hour. Assuming that B cares about his relative standing in the income hierarchy of his firm, why, then, would he remain with this firm? He would clearly prefer to work for a firm that employs only workers like C, who are also paid $3 per hour for the 30 bricks per hour

"Mind if I join you folks? Everyone else here is too smart for me."

they make. For that matter, B would prefer even more to work for a firm that employs only workers like D, who are paid $2 per hour for the 20 bricks per hour they make.

Yet if the latter firm were to hire B, what reason would workers like D have for remaining? They would clearly be happier if they joined some other firm that excluded workers who earned higher salaries. Under the hypothetical decree that workers be paid the respective values of their marginal products, then, the only sustainable outcome is that each firm employs workers whose marginal products are identical. This decree leaves no room for a firm with a heterogeneous workforce.

But status in any hierarchy is a reciprocal phenomenon. B's refusal to experience low status in their two-person hierarchy prevents A from enjoying high status in that same hierarchy. Had he stayed, perhaps B would have lost less than A would have gained. No one is better positioned than A and B themselves to judge. Yet by passing their decree that wages equal the value of marginal products, the ruling economists will have prevented this hierarchy from forming, regardless of how A and B feel.

Now suppose that there had been no such decree, that wages could be set at whatever level each firm chooses, subject only to a law protecting workers from working for a particular firm against their wishes. Then the decision of whether to form a given hierarchy would be left in the hands of its potential members, where it seems to belong. With this in mind, suppose that A and B each would accept up to a 10 percent salary cut in order to be in the top half of the earnings hierarchy in his firm. Suppose further that each would be willing to tolerate being in the bottom half of such a hierarchy in return for a wage of at least 10 percent more than the value of what he produces. (If status brings satisfaction, and one has more than enough food to eat in any event, who is to say that such valuations are unreasonably large?)

Given the way A and B feel, no firm can pay them their marginal products and hope to retain them. (Recall from the earlier discussion that for A and B to be paid their marginal products meant that each would end up in a firm composed only of workers whose marginal products were identical to his own.) With the decree no longer in effect, suppose some new firm then offered to pay B a wage of $3.35 per hour and A a wage of $3.65 per hour. These offers would be attractive to both of them. B, like A, would rather not be in the bottom half of any firm's income hierarchy. But for a boost in his hourly wage of at least 30 cents per hour, he is, by assumption, willing to accept such a position. Similarly, A is willing to give up as much as 40 cents per hour in return for the privilege of being in the top half of an earnings hierarchy. Yet he gets top-half status from this firm by giving up only 35 cents per hour in wages.

A has thus gained a "surplus" of 5 cents per hour by forming this hierarchy with B (the difference between the 40 cents per hour the top-half position is worth to him and the 35 cents per hour he sacrificed to get it). B, too, is 5 cents per hour better off than he would have been had he not joined up with A. By their own reckoning, at least, the exchange in question improves the welfare of both parties.

Recognition of the fact that people's status in local hierarchies is important to them, much more important perhaps than their status in the overall population, thus makes for a significant transformation in the nature of status. When one's rank in the overall population, or "global status," is all that matters, status has something of a predetermined quality, almost like one's caste in the hierarchical societies of the East. When income is the measure of status, one can strive harder to earn more of it, but so too can everyone else. And in the end, each person's rank in the global income hierarchy will be governed to a large extent by his or her talent and upbringing. But when local

Drawing by Wm. Hamilton. Reproduced by Special Permission of PLAYBOY Magazine. Copyright © 1971 by PLAYBOY.

*"Oh, sure, I like to feel loved—but what really gives me
a bang is to feel envied."*

status takes on primary importance, the question of what one's status will be is thrown wide open. Talent and early advantage no longer assure a position of high rank. By the same token, a person's relative lack of talent and early advantage does not mean she is predestined to occupy a position of low status in her local hierarchy. The membership of her local hierarchy, and thus her status in that hierarchy, is to a large extent subject to her own control.

The Market for Local Status

What patterns will emerge in the ways people elect to exercise that control? If status in income hierarchies is like other things that yield satisfaction, people will differ substantially in the sacrifices they are willing to make to attain it. In particular, variations in earning power are likely to cause differences in demands for status. And even among people with the same income, tastes are likely to differ. To some, status will matter a great deal, while to others it will count for very little. As we saw in the earlier example, variations in the monetary valuations people place on status create opportunities for mutual gains through exchange, without which heterogeneous local hierarchies could never coalesce.

When people trade objects they care about in exchange for money, those who place highest value on those objects are the ones who end up with them. At an auction, the highest bidder leaves with the antique clock. This person is not necessarily the one with the highest income. We are not surprised, for example, when someone who wants the clock very badly ends up bidding higher than others who earn much more than he does.

The same holds true with status in local hierarchies. Although people with high earning power are *able* to outbid those with lower earning power, it will not necessarily be in the interests of those who place low value on status to do so. Instead, we expect a sorting process to take place in the labor market, in which firms (local hierarchies of co-workers) organize themselves so that those persons who are willing to sacrifice most to have high-status positions are the ones who end up with them.

To gain some insight into how this sorting process might work, let us consider another example, again set in the context of the brickmaking industry discussed earlier. To keep matters simple, let us suppose there are only six people in a country—call them Carson, McMahon, Holmes, Quixote, Watson, and Panza—and that their only paid activity is making bricks. (Perhaps their food comes from tending their gardens.) Suppose further that each comes in contact only with those who make bricks for the same firm he does.

For each of the six, suppose that status involves only whether he is in the top half or the bottom half of the earnings hierarchy composed of his co-workers. The six differ with respect to their productivity as brickmakers, and also with respect to how strongly they feel about occupying top-half positions. Their productivity values, the maximum amounts each would be willing to pay to be in the top half, and the smallest amounts each would accept for being in the bottom half are listed in Table 3.1.

In Table 3.1, note first that Carson and McMahon share the same characteristics as the brickmakers A and B considered earlier. Watson, whose productivity is only $2 per hour, is like Carson and McMahon in that he, too, would be willing to give up at most 10 percent of what he produces in order to be in a top-half position, and would have to be given at least 10 percent more before accepting a bottom-half position. Note also that, in relative terms, Holmes, Quixote, and Panza feel more strongly about status than Carson, McMahon, and Watson do. That is, the corresponding compensation payments for the former amount to 20 percent of their respective marginal products, as compared with only 10 percent for the latter.

Each of the six has the option of working alone, in which case he would earn exactly the value of his marginal product. Or, he can negotiate an agreement to form a firm with one or more of the others. Two of the possible two-person firms, namely "McMahon & Holmes" and "Quixote & Watson," involve workers who are equally productive; and in those two, each worker would also earn exactly the value of his marginal product. (When all workers in a firm are equally productive, the need for anyone to be compensated for occupying a bottom-half position does not arise.) But any other firm of two or more persons will involve workers of unequal productive ability, and thus cannot form if each worker is paid his marginal product, for the reasons discussed earlier. Rather, these firms can form only if compensation payments flow from persons occupying top-half positions to those occupying the respective bottom-half positions.

Some of the possible firms that people might consider forming are obvious losers. There is no way, for example, that the firm "McMahon & Quixote" can be profitable, because the minimum wage Quixote would accept to occupy the bottom-half position is $2.40, while McMahon would not accept less than $2.70 to occupy the top-half position. The sum of these two minimum acceptable wage levels is thus $5.10 per hour, which is 10 cents more than the

Table 3.1 *Valuations of Top- and Bottom-Half Positions*

Brickmaker	Value of Marginal Product ($/hour)	Maximum Sacrifice for Obtaining Top-Half Position ($/hour)	Minimum Reward for Accepting Bottom-Half Position ($/hour)
Carson	4	.40	.40
McMahon	3	.30	.30
Holmes	3	.60	.60
Quixote	2	.40	.40
Watson	2	.20	.20
Panza	1	.20	.20

total value of the bricks McMahon and Quixote would produce each hour. This firm could not succeed because more money would have to be paid out in wages than it could collect from its sale of bricks.

But other possible firms do much better. As we have already seen, the firm "Carson & McMahon," with $3.65 per hour for Carson and $3.35 per hour for McMahon, produces a surplus of 5 cents per hour for each of its members compared with their working alone. Or consider, for example, the coalition "Carson & Watson," which produces an even larger surplus for each of its members. Watson would be willing to join that coalition if he were paid at least $2.20 per hour, whereas Carson would be willing to join if he were paid at least $3.60 per hour. The sum of these minimum acceptable wage levels is only $5.80 per hour, which is 20 cents per hour less than the value of the bricks Carson and Watson together produce each hour. The firm consisting of Carson and Watson could thus sustain itself indefinitely if the two were to split this surplus between them (by having Carson earn $3.70 per hour while Watson earns $2.30 per hour). At these wages, each would receive a surplus of 10 cents per hour compared with their working alone.

If these six brickmakers were left to their own devices, what collection of firms would they elect to form? What this question really asks is whether there is some collection of firms and feasible wage payments that will prevent the participants from leaving the firms of that collection to form a new firm or firms in which each person has a larger surplus. Now, there are 333 ways of dividing a group of six people into exhaustive sets of distinct groups. One way of approaching the question would be to calculate the surplus generated within each firm for each of these 333 possibilities and see whether any one collection of firms dominates the others.

Fortunately, there is an easier way of finding the best collection of firms. Think of top-half positions as being things that the six persons would like to have if they were free, but of which at most three can be made available (since each top-half position must be balanced by a corresponding bottom-half position). Because the demand for top-half positions exceeds their supply when they are free, it becomes necessary to ration top-half positions in some way. As with antique clocks, a natural way of rationing such positions is through the use of an auction.

Suppose the brickmakers choose Panza to be their auctioneer and he starts off by asking how many want a top-half position at a price of 15 cents per hour. The bidding strategy for each brickmaker in this auction is simple: If the announced price is less than the value he assigns to a top-half position (as given in Table 3.1), he bids; otherwise he does not. Here, not bidding for a top-half position at a given price amounts to agreeing to occupy a bottom-half position.

In response to Panza's call for bids for top-half positions at a price of 15 cents per hour, all six, including Panza himself, bid. So Panza raises the price and asks again for bids. By the time he has reached a price of 21 cents per hour, both he and Watson will have stopped bidding. By dropping out, they are saying, in effect, that rather than *pay* that price to occupy a top-half position, they would prefer to *receive* that price in return for occupying a bottom-half position.

For any price between 20 and 30 cents per hour, there are four people demanding top-half positions (Carson, McMahon, Holmes, and Quixote) but only two (Watson and Panza) willing to occupy the bottom-half positions needed to make this possible. Once the price reaches 30 cents per hour, McMahon too ceases to demand a top-half position and offers, in effect, to supply one by occupying a bottom-half position. Demand and supply of top-half positions are thus in balance at three each for any price between 30 and 40 cents per hour.

Once the price goes beyond 40 cents per hour, however, both Carson and Quixote cease demanding top-half positions. When those two drop out of the bidding, the supply of top-half positions (that is, the number of people wanting bottom-half positions) grows to five, while the demand for top-half positions shrinks to one. Thus, any price greater than 40 cents per hour results in an excess supply of top-half positions.

Since the demand and supply of top-half positions are in balance for any price between 30 and 40 cents per hour, let us pick some price in this range, say 35 cents per hour, and see if it is possible to accommodate everyone's wishes in an actual collection of firms. The collection of firms given in Table 3.2 does the job nicely. Although the details of the argument need not detain us here, we can easily demonstrate that no brickmakers can leave the firms in Table 3.2 and form a new firm or firms in which each does better than before.[6]

Properties of the Internal Wage Structure

In order to see more clearly some of the patterns in the wage and productivity values displayed by the three firms in Table 3.2, let us plot hourly wage rates against productivity (value of marginal product), as in Figure 3.2. Points representing workers in the same firm are connected by dotted lines. The 45° line is the locus along which a worker's wage is equal to the value of the bricks he produces. Workers above the 45° line are being paid more than the value of what they produce, whereas those below are being paid less.

Note that in each of the three firms, the higher-paid member is paid less than the value of what he produces, while the lower-paid member, in turn, is paid more. And given the way each person values his status within his firm, this outcome is perfectly stable. A new firm, for example, cannot lure Holmes

Table 3.2 *Firms That Accommodate Demands for Status*

Firm	Top-Half Member, Top-Half Member's Wage	Bottom-Half Member, Bottom-Half Member's Wage
Carson & McMahon	Carson, $3.65/hr	McMahon, $3.35/hr
Holmes & Watson	Holmes, $2.65/hr	Watson, $2.35/hr
Quixote & Panza	Quixote, $1.65/hr	Panza, $1.35/hr

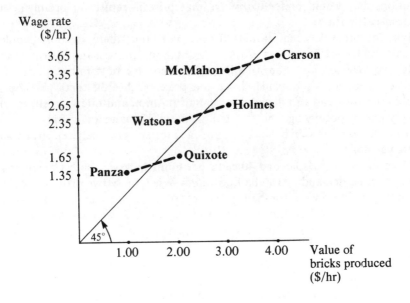

Figure 3.2 The Wage Structure When Top-Half Status Matters

away from his current firm by offering him a wage equal to the value of what he produces. After all, the top-half position he now has is worth more to him than the difference between what he is paid and the value of what he produces. By the same token, Watson's wage of 35 cents per hour more than the value of what he produces imposes no burden on the firm that employs him and Holmes. If that firm sought to increase its profits by laying Watson off, it would then also lose Holmes, who would leave to rejoin Watson under the banner of some new firm.

Of the six workers whose wage and productivity values are plotted in Figure 3.2, four—namely, McMahon, Holmes, Quixote, and Watson—faced a full range of choices in that each could have joined a firm in which he occupied a top-half, bottom-half, or equal-status position. The choices open to the remaining two—Carson and Panza—were constrained at the outset by the fact that each occupied one extreme of the productivity range. That is, since Carson was the most productive of the six workers, it was not possible for him to form any firm in which he could occupy a bottom-half position. Even though Carson did not feel strongly about occupying a top-half position (as measured by the share of his income he was willing to sacrifice to get one), the only choices open to him were to work by himself or to occupy such a position. Similarly Panza, even though willing to devote a relatively large share of his income to acquiring a top-half position, faced only the choice of working alone or occupying a bottom-half position. In the collection of firms that produces the greatest surplus for these six workers, top-half positions were allocated among McMahon, Holmes, Quixote, and Watson according to how large a fraction of his income each was willing to give up for such a position.

The internal wage structures observed in the firms in this example are qualitatively much like the wage structures we observe in practice, in that each is substantially more egalitarian than would be warranted by productivity considerations alone. To generate this outcome, the example required only two simple assumptions: (1) that people care about where they stand in the earnings hierarchies of the firms they work for; and (2) that people are free to work for whatever firms they choose. Both of these assumptions appear reasonable within the context of contemporary Western societies. Together, they yield a structure that reconciles the economist's plausible claim that labor markets are competitive with the observation that wage structures within actual firms tend to be highly egalitarian.

Thus, the economist's claim that wage rates equal the value of what workers produce in competitive labor markets is simply not true when workers care about their status in local hierarchies and are free to choose their co-workers. Under these circumstances, the egalitarian internal wage structures we observe in firms do not require us to conclude that labor markets must not be functioning competitively. On the contrary, the competitive theory of labor markets would be in trouble here if the wage structures we observed actually *did* mirror individual differences in productivity.

In the foregoing example, each person's concern about status was assumed, for simplicity, to be limited to whether he occupied a position in the top-half or the bottom-half of the earnings hierarchy of his firm. A more realistic description of people's concerns about status would recognize that it also matters exactly where one ranks in that hierarchy. Other things the same, for example, most people would consider a position in the 80th percentile of an earnings hierarchy (that is, one that outranks 80 percent of the positions in the firm) to be superior to one in the 55th percentile.

No matter how finely partitioned people's concerns about their status in local hierarchies may be, it is possible for firms to cater to those concerns. In large labor markets that encompass a wide range of productivity values and concerns about status, we should see an overlapping hierarchy of firms that offers people a rich menu of choices involving wage income and within-firm status. Figure 3.3., for example, depicts a labor market consisting of a large number of workers whose marginal products range in value from $1 per hour to $4 per hour, and which is served by the five firms whose wage schedules are shown.

In Figure 3.3, let us focus on the menu of choices confronting those workers whose marginal products have the value of $2.50 per hour. A worker who places a high enough value on status will be attracted to Firm 1. There, he will earn $2 per hour in return for being able to occupy the top-ranked position among his co-workers. In contrast, a worker who cares relatively little about local status will find Firm 5 most attractive. At that firm, he will be the lowest-paid worker, but in return he will get a wage of $3 per hour, 50 cents per hour

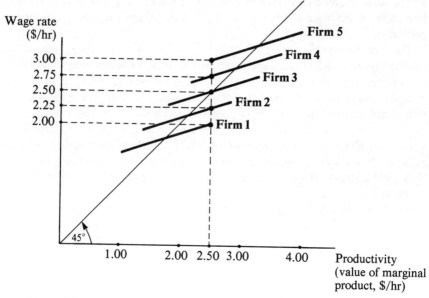

Figure 3.3 Competitive Wage Schedules When Percentile Rankings Matter

"*The salary isn't high, but the position, figuratively speaking, carries Cabinet rank.*"

more than the value of what he produces. Workers whose concerns about status lie between these two extremes will choose between Firms 2, 3, and 4, in which positions in the 75th, 50th, and 25th percentiles are available, respectively, at wage rates of $2.25, $2.50, and $2.75, per hour.

Where the scale of the labor market permits it, there will in general be an implicit market established for positions in the earnings hierarchies of firms of the sort depicted in Figure 3.3. As participants in this market, firms need know nothing about how strongly any individual worker feels about status. Firms may be thought of as posting menus (their wage schedules) of wage-status combinations they have to offer. Confronted with a collection of such menus, the worker then identifies the firm whose wage-status combination best suits him.

Viewed in this context, one's status in a local hierarchy thus emerges as a "good" very much like other goods that are exchanged in markets. As with any other such good, people who value it highly can have more of it only if they are willing to pay its price, which in this case means working for a lower wage rate. Those who least value status will elect to be sellers of status by agreeing to occupy low-ranking positions in firms that pay them more than the value of what they produce.

Do Income Comparisons Make People Worse Off?

The recognition that people may have the capacity to insulate themselves from unfavorable income comparisons by forming local hierarchies of their own choosing suggests an intriguing possibility, one curiously at odds with traditional social thought. Given individual differences in productivity, if someone had a magic wand that could make it impossible for people to carry out income comparisons, would people want her to wave it? The foregoing discussion suggests that they might not. For if people are able to insulate themselves completely from the effects of unfavorable income comparisons, then the only way an unfavorable comparison will ever take place will be in a local hierarchy in which it will have been adequately compensated for. Taking away the capacity to make interpersonal income comparisons under these circumstances would produce the same level of satisfaction among people as when the economists' decree resulted in firms composed of equally productive workers. But we saw that where income comparisons matter, and people can make them or not as they choose, everyone can achieve a better outcome. Those who value status highly can give up an amount of wage income that is worth less to them than the status they get in return. And those who do not value status highly can accept a wage premium that is more valuable to them than the status they give up to get it.

Now, as a practical matter, a person's ability to form local hierarchies does not protect him completely from unfavorable income comparisons for which he is not adequately compensated. At best, it merely reduces the frequency and importance of such comparisons. But even if *some* uncompensated, unfavorable income comparisons are inevitable, their negative effects will not necessarily outweigh the positive effects of the compensated comparisons that take place in local hierarchies. Perhaps those who favor eliminating income comparisons really mean that the world would be better if people's productive abilities were more nearly equal than they are in practice. That may be so. If we accept the distribution of people's productive abilities as given, however, and then grant them the freedom to associate with whomever they choose, it simply does not follow that their welfare would be improved by making them blind to interpersonal income comparisons.

The Class-Reunion Effect

The market for status in local hierarchies suggests an implicit tradeoff between local and global status. The person who takes a position of high rank in his firm must, as noted, accept a cut in wages. This means, in turn, that he will rank lower than he otherwise would have in those hierarchies consisting of persons outside his firm. In Figure 3.3, for example, the individual who takes a top-ranked position in Firm 1 will earn less than the person who takes a bottom-ranked position in Firm 5, even though the two have exactly the same marginal product value.

Even if people care most about their status among their co-workers, they surely also care about income comparisons outside the workplace. These broader concerns will dampen people's willingness to purchase high-ranked positions within firms. The implicit wage cut the high-ranked worker in a firm accepts is therefore a lower bound on the value he assigns to his status generally. In Figure 3.3, for example, the top-ranked worker in Firm 1 was willing to take a wage cut of 50 cents per hour in order to occupy that position, even though by so doing he reduced his rank in the external income hierarchy consisting of, say, the members of his high school graduating class. Had he somehow been capable of simultaneously moving forward in both of those hierarchies (as, for example, by moving to a poorer planet), he presumably would have been willing to take an even larger wage cut.

If comparisons outside the workplace mattered more than comparisons within, then the implicit wage cut required to be able to occupy a high-ranked position within a firm could not be very large. Large wage cuts would cause people to seek low-ranked positions in order to receive correspondingly large wage premiums, which, in turn, would advance their standing in external hierarchies. But with an excess supply of people thus trying to occupy low-ranked positions, large wage premiums would not survive for long.

Now, the degree to which hierarchies outside the firm matter to people is not completely beyond their control. And the fact that high status makes people feel good gives them an incentive to exercise their control in a specific way. In particular, people will tend to focus their attention on those hierarchies in which their own rank happens to be highest. (Some such tendency may help explain why substantially more than half of all drivers believe themselves to be more skillful than the average driver.[7]) Perhaps once a person has paid the price to acquire a high-ranked position within his firm, he can then divert his attention away from the remaining hierarchies he belongs to. Similarly, the low-ranked member of a firm can also gain by focusing as much of his attention as possible on external hierarchies.

In a fanciful mood, one might employ such notions in an attempt to predict people's likelihood of attending their class reunions. All other factors held the same, for example, the occupant of the top-ranked position in Firm 1 in Figure 3.3 might be less likely to attend class reunions than the lowest-ranked member of Firm 5. If attendees at reunions tend to be thinner, less bald, and have fewer wrinkles than nonattendees do, then perhaps they have higher incomes as well.

It may seem less far-fetched to note that the most productive members of a group appear to focus much more of their attention and energy on the group's activities than do the least productive members, who often seem to seek their satisfaction elsewhere (although what is cause and what is effect here is obviously open to question). Perhaps the lowest-paid members of firms work harder than others do on their tennis games, hoping to raise their standing among their opponents.

How strongly relative standing in the workplace matters to people will surely depend in part on the intensity with which co-workers interact. (Recall from the discussion in Chapter 2 the psychologist's emphasis on the role played by vivid information in establishing the norms people use; and the connection, in turn, between vividness and proximity.) In firms in which co-workers perform their tasks largely independently of one another, one's rank among one's co-workers should matter less than it does in a firm in which interactions among co-workers are more extensive. The door-to-door vacuum cleaner salesman, for example, should care less about the incomes of his fellow salesmen than the touring circus performer cares about the incomes of his troupemates. An important implication of the theory of markets for local status is thus that wage schedules will be flattest in those firms in which co-workers interact most intensively. The presence of extensive interactions among co-workers will tend also to limit the range of productive ability that can be accommodated within a single group. These relationships, which are depicted in Figure 3.4, will play an important role in Chapter 4, where I attempt to assess the empirical validity of this theory.

Halo Effects and Learning Effects

In the discussion thus far, I have neglected an important dimension of people's status as perceived by those outside their firms. In a world in which everyone does not know everything there is to know about everyone else, one's status in the eyes of outsiders will depend in part on the reputations of one's co-workers. If people know nothing else about a physicist, for example, than that she is a professor at MIT, they know that, among physicists in general, she must be a good one. Faced with a choice of being a low-ranked professor at a

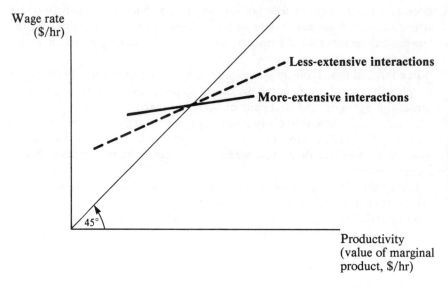

Figure 3.4 Wage Schedules and the Extensiveness of Co-worker Interactions

prestigious school or a high-ranked professor at a less prestigious school, such "halo effects" clearly enhance the attractiveness of the former option.

The attractiveness of higher quality groups is further enhanced by the possibility that people in such groups stand to learn relatively more through interactions with their colleagues. The attraction of these "learning effects" will apply to workers in all age groups, but should be particularly important for younger workers.

Like the class-reunion effect, both the halo effect and the learning effect will reduce the wage premiums workers receive for occupying low-ranked positions in their firms. Indeed, if halo and learning effects were *all* that mattered (that is, if one's rank among one's co-workers counted for naught), then the internal wage structure within firms would have precisely the opposite tilt as the ones we observe in practice. As in the wage schedule HH shown in Figure 3.5, the low-ranked worker would then have to work for less than the value of what he produces. High-ranked workers, in turn, would be paid more than the value of what they produce directly, to compensate for the fact that they contribute disproportionately to the external status of the group and to the training of its lesser ranked members.[8]

The class-reunion, halo, and learning effects thus act to offset, at least partially, the wage premiums that reflect internal status rankings within firms. Together, they serve to make the wage schedules we observe in practice steeper than they would otherwise be. Put another way, the wage schedules in actual firms would be even flatter than we find them were it not for the presence of these three effects.

The Domino Effect

Educational and demographic realities being what they are, most readers of this book will be members of the upper portion of the national income distribution. And many will occupy top-ranked positions in the groups in which they work. I suspect that many such readers will find it unpalatable to think of themselves as, in effect, willfully bribing the lowest-ranked members of their groups to provide ego support through their continued presence. It is an unflattering image, after all, to imagine oneself buying a "serotonin high" (see Chapter 2) from one's lesser ranked co-workers, much as the heroin addict exchanges cash for his own brand of chemical euphoria. It is surely true, moreover, that both the halo and learning effects suggest important ways in which the top-ranked member of a group would be better off if the lowest-ranked member were to depart. If the top-ranked member would fare better with the bottom-ranked member gone, then why on earth would he pay him a large bribe to stay on?

In order to see what forces bind the top-ranked members to their groups, we must first recognize that it is not the comparisons between occupants of the extreme positions in an earnings hierarchy that really count. Instead, it is the comparisons between the occupants of closely ranked positions that are most important. Thus, for example, the theory readily concedes that the top-ranked member might feel better off if the bottom-ranked member of his group left, *and all other things remained the same as before*. The catch, however, is that

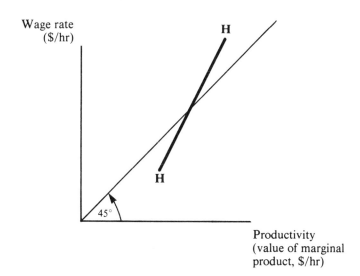

Figure 3.5 The Internal Wage Structure When Only Halo and Learning Effects Matter

all other things would *not* remain the same. In particular, the next-to-last-ranked member surely would not feel better off now that he is on the bottom. And if the labor market is competitive, as assumed, his previous wage and rank were just sufficient to make membership in the group attractive to him *before* the departure of the person who used to be last. (Why would a profit-seeking firm have paid him any more than that?) Now, though, the wage he was previously paid will no longer bind him to the group. If he is to be induced to stay on, he will have to be paid more than he was paid before. But that, in turn, would mean that other members, including the top-ranked members, would have to be paid less.

Alternatively, if the wage of the next-to-last member is not adjusted upward following the departure of the lowest-ranked member, then he, too, will find it in his interests to leave. But his departure, in turn, will make the third-to-last member's position no longer sustainable without a wage increase. And in like fashion, the entire membership would unravel, one by one, until the top-ranked member is left standing alone. He, too, will leave, since the wage-rank combination he previously enjoyed was, by assumption, just sufficient to bind him to the firm in the first place.

Through the action of this "domino effect," it thus follows that the bottom-ranked member's presence does indeed serve to benefit the top-ranked members, albeit in an indirect way. The comparisons that count favorably for the top-ranked members are those with the members who rank just below them. The presence of the latter group, in turn, depends critically on the favorable comparisons with those who rank just below them. And the whole chain of comparisons rests ultimately on the continued presence of the lowest-ranked member.

Economies of Scale and Production Complementarities

The exchange of local status is by no means the only reason that workers coalesce into firms. They may also form firms in order to take advantage of important synergies. Adam Smith was the first to emphasize the efficiency gains that follow from the division and specialization of labor.[9] The least skillful brickmaker, for example, is probably just as good at digging and carrying clay as is the most skillful one. Consequently, the two can expand their production by having the more skillful worker devote all of his time to molding, while the less skillful worker specializes in digging and carrying.

A more realistic description of production would also recognize the importance of efficiency gains from sharing common production facilities. A large kiln, for example, will normally cost less than two half-size ones. By banding together to share the cost of larger facilities, workers will produce more than if they had continued working alone.

Where such economies are important, they constitute a clear incentive for people to work together in groups. If this incentive is sufficiently strong, and people's concerns about local status sufficiently weak, it would then no longer necessarily follow that complete stratification would occur in response to a decree that wages must equal the values of marginal products. For a large enough gain in pay, a less skilled worker would agree to work with a more skilled worker, even if the two were paid in exact proportion to what each contributes to total output.

Even with substantial economies of scale in production, however, we would still not expect workers to be paid in proportion to their marginal products. As before, the highest-paid workers within firms will still reap the benefits of the status that accompanies those positions. And the occupants of the lesser-ranked positions will continue to experience the same costs as before. Even though both now stand to gain from economies of aggregation, the top group needs the bottom group just as much as when there were no such economies. Granted, the bottom group will lose out on these gains if it refuses to coalesce with the top group. But the top group will also lose out on these gains if it fails to agree to a compensation schedule that is acceptable to the bottom group.

Social scientists who study workplace behavior have often noted that wide disparities in pay between co-workers hurt employee morale and productivity.[10] The morale that suffers most is presumably that of the lowest paid workers. And these workers often risk being fired by being openly disruptive on the job. The employer's response in such instances, however, is often not to discharge the disruptive workers, but to reduce the pay disparities that precipitated the trouble in the first place.[11] I interpret this response as reflecting the employer's belief that it would not be possible to maintain the original pay scale and to replace the rebellious workers with others who would be less so. But this, in turn, says that the protesting workers would rather miss out on a share of the gains from aggregation than be insufficiently compensated for occupying positions of low rank. As I argued in Chapter 2, an inherent distaste for occupying low-ranked positions in local hierarchies may thus enhance the bargaining position of those who ultimately occupy such positions.

Status and Fairness

It is frequently said that "equity considerations" account for why the wage schedules within firms appear so much flatter than predicted by the marginal productivity theory.[12] Indeed, when pay scale adjustments of the sort described above are carried out, they are often done so in the name of "fairness." Such statements ring true for many, but raise provocative questions about just what is meant by "equity," or "fairness." It is easy to see why, in Figure 3.6, workers W and Y might find the wages they get from their firms to be equitable. After all, they are being paid more than the value of what they produce. But why should X and Z have similar feelings about the wages they receive, which are less than the value of what they contribute? Is it plausible to argue that their dedication to the ideal of equity makes them derive satisfaction from cross-subsidizing the less productive workers in their respective firms? Maybe so, but if the ideal of equity is really what X wishes to support, why doesn't he

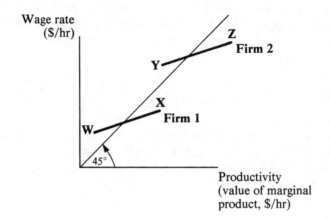

Figure 3.6 "Equity" in the Workplace

then join Firm 2? There he would earn the higher wage that Y now gets and could donate part of his extra pay to UNICEF. By so doing, he would get a lot more equity for his dollar than by remaining in Firm 1.

Suppose, though, that the wage schedules within all firms had wages set equal to the respective values of marginal products for all workers. The result would then be that the high-ranked members within each firm would be getting something valuable for free—namely the privilege of occupying their high-ranked positions. By the same token, low-ranked members within each firm would be incurring costs for the benefit of high-ranked members, without being compensated for doing so. Neither of these outcomes would be called "fair" or "equitable," as those terms are commonly used and understood. And with this understanding in mind, it makes perfectly good sense to say that a wage structure in which each worker receives the value of his marginal product is an "unfair" wage structure.

It thus appears difficult to divorce common usage of the term "fairness" from people's desires to occupy high-ranked positions in local hierarchies. Thought of in this way, a "fair" wage structure is one in which people's earnings compensate them for where they stand in their respective earnings hierarchies. These observations suggest that fairness, too, might be viewed as a good traded in the marketplace. Indeed, to the extent people have broad freedom in their choice of co-workers, friends, and neighbors, society's beliefs about fairness will be as richly and fully reflected in the structure of private market transactions as they are in political decisions regarding tax and public expenditure policies. (More on these points in Chapter 6.)

This observation, in turn, suggests that we can learn something about the value people place on equity by observing the premiums they pay or receive in return for occupying various positions in the income hierarchies of their firms.

Additional research along these lines promises high returns, for while equity has always played a major role in political decision making, we remain in the awkward position of having no consistent framework for measuring its value.

Before concluding this chapter, I should stress that, while the marginal productivity theory does not hold for individual workers within any one firm, it should nonetheless hold for each firm taken as a whole. Thus, for example, we saw in Table 3.2 that while neither Carson nor McMahon is paid the value of his marginal product, the sum of their wages is nonetheless equal to the total value of what they produce. The observation that people value their status in local hierarchies does not in any way challenge the economist's claim that the forces of competition hold each firm's profits within normal limits—the claim, that is, that workers will *on average* be paid the values of their marginal products. On the contrary, recognizing that an implicit market for status may operate alongside the competitive labor market provides, as noted, an avenue along which to reconcile the apparent inconsistency between the economist's claim that labor markets are competitive, on the one hand, and the observation that wage differences within firms do not closely reflect productivity differences, on the other.

Yet merely to say that a market for high-ranked positions could in principle resolve the inconsistency between the economist's claim and the reality we observe does not establish, of course, that it actually does so. Indeed, to prove conclusively that it does is a task well beyond reach here. We can nonetheless gain additional insight about the market for status by examining more closely the wage schedules we observe in actual firms. To what extent do wages actually deviate from the value of what workers produce in specific cases? What patterns would we expect if whatever deviations we see are in fact primarily a reflection of the positions workers occupy in their firms? And what alternative explanations might give rise to differences between what workers are paid and the value of what they produce? To these questions let us now turn.

Four

How Much Is
Local Status Worth?

Measurement Problems

The question of whether each worker is paid the economic value of what he produces might have been settled long ago if there existed simple, unequivocal measures of the economic value of what people produce. But in most cases, no such measures exist. In most firms, workers participate as part of highly complex team production processes. And in such cases, it is difficult even to define, much less measure, what any one worker contributes to what the team as a whole produces.[1]

When the output of the team as a whole can be readily measured, but when each individual's contribution is not known, competitive forces will tend to equalize individual wage rates.[2] Members of more productive teams will be paid more than members of less productive teams, to be sure. When an individual team member's contribution cannot be measured, however, competitive forces cannot reward him in strict proportion to that contribution. A firm is not in a position to reward a contribution it cannot observe.

Thus, the mere fact that individual contributions are often inherently difficult to measure is one plausible explanation for why individual workers might not be paid in strict proportion to the value of what they produce. But this explanation cannot hope to satisfy those whose own observations that pay differences understate productivity differences are what made them skeptical in the first place about the marginal productivity theory. (Would the mere assertion that ghosts are invisible be convincing to a person who had just *seen* one?) Because people can see obvious discrepancies between pay and productivity, the economist can hardly hope to persuade them that measurement difficulties account fully for why people are not paid what they are worth.

We can attempt to investigate the market for local status by examining pay differences among workers involved in complex team production processes. It will be simpler, though, if we initially focus on cases where interactions between co-workers are of only minimal importance. Such occupations as automobile or real estate sales are a good place to begin. In these settings, interactions between co-workers are not extensive, and it is therefore possible to obtain relatively precise measures of the contributions of specific employees.

The Standard Theory of Sales Commissions

What should competitively determined pay schedules for such sales workers look like in a world in which people take no interest in what their co-workers earn? That is, how is the value of what each worker contributes to his firm's net revenue determined?[3] To make matters concrete, let us consider a firm that sells some product that it gets from a manufacturer at a price of $100 per unit. If the retail price of this product is, say $110 per unit, its gross commission is then $10 per unit. We might be tempted to conclude that a worker who sells ten units of that product per week contributes $100 per week to his firm's net revenues, and should therefore be paid that amount. This conclusion, though, would fail to take into account what the firm itself contributes to the success of its sales operation.

In the case of an automobile dealership, for example, the firm could not have attracted any sales prospects without having first incurred a variety of expenses. It must maintain a showroom, keep an inventory of demonstrator vehicles, advertise its products, and so on. Having incurred these expenses, the firm attracts a pool of sales prospects, which it then distributes among its sales staff. Whether any given prospect then buys the product will depend partly on the skill of the particular salesperson to whom he is assigned. A lot of luck is obviously involved in each individual case. But over the long run, a more skillful salesperson will convert a higher proportion of his prospects into final sales. If the labor market is competitive, then the least skillful salesperson employed by the firm will sell just enough to justify the firm's paying him a wage slightly more than what he could have earned in his best alternative job.

Given this picture of the sales firm, the task of determining each salesperson's economic value is straightforward. The question we need to answer is: "How much would the firm's net revenues (excluding the sales commissions it pays) go down if a particular salesperson were to leave?"

To answer this question, first note that sales prospects are themselves valuable assets to the firm. Giving one salesperson an opportunity to try to make a sale to a prospect deprives every other salesperson of the same opportunity. If a given salesperson were to leave, whatever sales prospects had been assigned to him could then be assigned to the remaining salespersons. Granted, the efforts of the remaining salespersons would be spread thinner, but they would still manage to convert at least some of these additional prospects into final sales.

It is thus possible to think of the departing salesperson's contribution to the firm's net revenues as existing in two parts—one negative, the other positive. The negative part consists of the sales he kept other salespersons from making by taking a share of the overall sales prospect pool. The positive part, in turn, consists of the gross commissions from the sales he made. Using this interpretation, we see that a truly incompetent salesperson actually hurts the firm by taking away sales prospects that would have been more successfully served by others. On this account, no salesperson is worth hiring unless his sales exceed those that would have been made if his prospects had been divided up among the other salespersons.

The forces at work here can be seen most clearly with the help of a numerical example. Let us again suppose that the spread between the wholesale and retail prices of the product is $10. Suppose further that each of 10 salespersons is assigned 90 sales prospects per week, and that if any one salesperson were to leave, his prospects would be divided equally among the remaining 9. With each salesperson now serving 100 sales prospects per week instead of 90, it is reasonable to assume that the sales efficiency of each is reduced somewhat. But suppose that each nonetheless averages one additional sale per week (for a total of 9 extra sales per week for the remaining group). If the departing salesperson had made, say, 20 sales per week, then the firm's net revenues (exclusive of his salary) will go down not by the $200 his 20 sales would have generated, but by only $110.

By the same token, a salesperson who averages fewer than 9 sales per week actually decreases the net revenues received by the firm. A salesperson who averages only 5 sales per week, for example, would increase the firm's net revenues $40 per week by his departure. A salesperson who never makes a sale, but who nonetheless is assigned 90 sales prospects per week, costs the firm $90 per week—the commissions on sales that would have been made had his sales prospects been given instead to the others.

In this example, the weekly economic value of what each salesperson contributes is thus equal to $10 times the number of sales he makes, less $90. The traditional theory of competitive labor markets says that each salesperson should be paid according to this earnings formula, which is depicted in Figure 4.1.

If a firm were to implement the pay schedule shown in Figure 4.1, it would, in effect, charge each salesperson $90 per week for the right to keep whatever sales commissions he could generate from sales to his share of the firm's sales prospects. Thus, the salesperson who sold 20 units per week would pay the firm $90 and then keep the $200 in commissions, leaving him with net earnings of $110 per week.

Practically speaking, we would not expect to see salespersons actually making cash payments to their firms. After all, no one would accept a sales job unless he could earn more than he could in whatever alternative employment he faced. Thus, we would not see any salesperson persistently in the

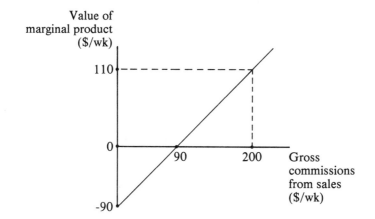

Figure 4.1 A Competitive Earnings Schedule for Salespersons Who Take No Interest in the Incomes of Their Co-workers

negative region of the earnings schedule in Figure 4.1 in any event. If the going wage in non-sales work is, for example, $110 per week, we might then see sales firms offer salespersons $110 per week plus $10 for every sale made in excess of 20 units per week. Anyone who didn't sell an average of at least 20 units per week would be discharged.

The difference of the average weekly earnings of two salespersons working under the earnings schedule shown in Figure 4.1 will be exactly the same as the difference of their average weekly gross sales commissions, just as the economist's intuition about competitive labor markets requires. Suppose this were not the case. Suppose, for example, that Dangerfield is being paid what he is worth to the firm while Madden, who sells an average of 10 units per week more than Dangerfield, receives only $50 more in earnings. Some other sales firm can then pay Madden $60 per week more than Dangerfield and in the process augment its profits by $40 per week (since Madden is worth $100 per week more than Dangerfield). As in the brickmaking example from Chapter 3, the bidding for Madden's services should not subside until his earnings are $100 per week more than Dangerfield's.

If the sales firm paid each of its 10 salespersons according to the earnings schedule shown in Figure 4.1, it would then be receiving $900 more in commission revenues each week than it paid out in salaries. Although the details of the argument need not detain us here, let us note in passing that the standard theory of competitive markets says that the retail price of the product and the number of competing sales firms would have been determined in such a way that this $900 per week would be just what the firm needed to cover its nonsalary expenses, plus a normal return on its investment.

Automobile Sales Commissions

With this picture in mind of what the standard theory says about earnings schedules for salespersons, let us look at some of the schedules sales firms actually use. I begin by considering a sample of automobile dealerships. As in the case of our hypothetical sales firm, each firm in this sample maintains a showroom and makes various other expenditures designed to attract sales prospects. Almost all of these expenditures vary positively with the number of prospects the dealer manages to attract. But having attracted a prospect pool of a given size, these expenditures will not vary with the number of car sales actually made. That is, even though replacing a bad salesperson with a good one will increase the percentage of sales prospects to whom final sales are made, it will have no effect whatsoever on the dealer's advertising, showroom, or other expenses.

Suppose, for example, that the retail price of each car is $300 more than its wholesale price, and that Montalban sells an average of one car more each week than Stewart. Since the firm's expenses depend only on the number of prospects it attracts and not on the number who actually buy cars, it then follows that Montalban is worth $300 per week more to the dealer than Stewart is. And the standard theory of competitive labor markets says, accordingly, that Montalban's pay should be $300 per week more than Stewart's.

Yet the earnings schedules I found in a random sample of 13 large automobile dealerships in Upstate New York do not coincide with this prediction at all. Whereas the slope of the earnings schedule predicted by standard theory is 1.0—meaning a $1 increase in earnings for every extra dollar in gross commissions, as in Figure 4.1—the largest slope among the earnings schedules in my sample was only .30—meaning 30 cents more in wages for every extra dollar in gross commissions. The slopes of the earnings schedules for the dealerships in the sample are shown in column 3 of Table 4.1.

Although the standard competitive theory of labor markets says that a salesperson's earnings should vary dollar for dollar with his gross commissions, the average value of the slopes in Table 4.1 is only .236. That is, for the dealerships in this sample, salespersons received an average of only 23.6 cents in additional earnings for each additional dollar of gross commissions.

Difficulty in measuring the value of what salespersons produce for their dealers cannot explain why the earnings schedules are so much flatter here than the ones predicted by the marginal productivity theory. The difference between the wholesale and retail price of a car, whatever that difference turns out to be, is exactly the amount by which the salesperson enhances the dealer's net revenues when he sells that car. The entries in column 3 of Table 4.1 tell us the share of that difference that the salesperson gets to keep. Any other expenses that are incidental to the transaction itself, such as "dealer preparation," are added onto the selling price and paid by the buyer, and thus do not compromise in any way this interpretation of the slopes of these earnings schedules. The marginal productivity theory of wages requires these slopes to be 1.0, yet they average less than one-fourth of that.

Table 4.1 *Slopes of Earnings Schedules for 13 Automobile Dealerships*

Dealership	Number of Salespersons	Slope of the Earnings Schedule
1	15	.25
2	10	.25
3	10	.20
4	14	.20
5	8	.30
6	10	.30
7	10	.25
8	11	.25
9	9	.20
10	10	.25
11	8	.20
12	14	.25
13	17	.17

Risk Aversion

While measurement difficulties cannot explain why the salespersons in these dealerships are not paid the value of what they produce, perhaps other factors can. Several economists have suggested, for example, that earnings schedules may be flatter than the ones predicted by standard theory because employees are more averse to risk than firms are.[4] At least two ideas are involved here.

One is that when workers are just beginning their careers, both they and their employers are highly uncertain about how productive each worker will prove to be.[5] Each worker realizes that, while there is some chance he will become a star, there is also the possibility he will end up a dud. But since the performances of stars and duds added together do not differ much from the average, it is possible to employ workers under contracts in which everyone's salary mirrors the average productivity of the group. The advantage to the worker of this type of contract is that it removes much of the gamble from his future.

This story is fine as far as it goes, but it does not explain why internal wage structures are as egalitarian as they are. In order for it to do so, employers would have to sign contracts with their employees binding them to remain in their jobs for long periods of time. Otherwise, firms could bid away those employees who have shown that they are worth much more than their current rates of pay. Yet binding long-term contracts of this sort are never observed in practice, and interfirm mobility is common for workers of all age groups. Without such binding contracts, a firm could never hope to retain the services of its star employees, whose high productivity levels would be needed in order for it to pay average wage rates to its duds.

The second reason offered for why workers' aversion to risk might flatten earnings schedules centers on the observation that, while each worker may know how productive he is on average, none can predict how productive he will be in any one period of time.[6] This is especially true of automobile salespeople, whose sales in any particular period depend on a host of factors beyond their control. If we assume that people prefer steady income streams to erratic ones, as seems plausible, workers may then be attracted to firms with gently sloped earnings schedules. But income smoothing can be accomplished in a variety of other ways that do not produce unearned benefits for less productive employees at the expense of their more productive counterparts. Many automobile dealers and insurance agencies, for example, provide salespersons with a steady "draw," which is adjusted periodically to maintain balance with commissions earnings over the long run. In good weeks, the firm, in effect, banks some of the salesperson's commissions, which it then returns to him during bad weeks.

Even if such devices were not available, it would be difficult to argue that workers' aversion to earnings variability could account for the flatness of the earnings schedules in this sample of automobile dealers. Most of these dealers reported that their best salespersons consistently make several times as many sales as do their least productive salespersons, and even during generally depressed years will make more sales than the average salesperson does in an average year. In terms of earnings, the best salesperson's lowest annual earnings figures averages 1.3 times the average annual earnings figures for all salespersons.

To illustrate what these responses seem to say about risk aversion as an explanation for flattened earnings schedules, let us refer to Figure 4.2, which depicts both the earnings schedule predicted by standard theory and an earnings schedule whose slope is the average of the slopes in this sample. The assumption that competition causes dealers to take in only enough revenues to cover their expenses means that the average earnings for salespersons would be the same regardless of which of these schedules was actually used. If C

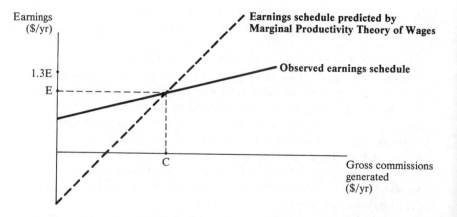

Figure 4.2 The Lowest Earnings of the Best Salesperson

represents the average annual commissions contributed by all salespersons to the dealership, and E the average annual earnings figure, then each earnings schedule must yield E in earnings for a salesperson who generates C in annual commission revenues.

Yet the best salesperson, even in his worst year, doesn't earn less than $1.3E$. This means, in turn, that his gross commissions, *even in his worst year*, will lie to the right of the point where the two schedules intersect. And for any commission level to the right of this point, the corresponding earnings figure will be higher on the steeper schedule than on the flatter one.

Now, variations in gross commissions will correspond to larger *variations* in earnings on the steeper schedule, to be sure. But the best salesperson's earnings would nonetheless be higher *every* year if he were compensated according to the steeper schedule (that is, the one implied by standard theory). To say that risk aversion makes the most productive salespersons choose the observed schedule over the steeper alternative is to say, preposterously, that these salespersons prefer a smaller income stream to one that, while more variable, is also larger, element for element. Suppose, for example, that the average gross commission and earnings values are $300 per week and $200 per week, respectively. The best salesperson's earnings in his worst year would then be $260 per week on the observed pay schedule (1.3 times the average earnings level) but more than $454 per week on the steeper schedule. The difference would be even larger in all other years. A better explanation than risk aversion thus seems needed for why the best salespeople have not been bid away from existing dealerships by dealers whose earnings schedules are steeper than the ones observed in this sample.*

Real Estate Sales Commissions

Real estate sales commissions are slightly more complicated than automobile sales commissions in that most real estate firms participate in local multiple-listing services. A typical house for sale will be listed with a particular agency and at the same time with the multiple-listing service (MLS). For a house to appear in the MLS means that all member agencies receive information on its price and other relevant characteristics, as well as an implicit invitation to show it to their clients. When a client of the listing firm purchases a house that also appears in the MLS, that firm receives all of the resultant sales commission, which is some share of the contract price of the house. Typical values for this

---

*My colleague Micky Falkson suggested the possibility that, during slack times, sales managers may give preferential treatment to their best salespersons in the assignment of sales prospects. If so, then the extent to which the top salesperson's sales exceed others' would overstate the corresponding differences in productivity. But in the sample of firms I studied, several managers stressed their practice of equal treatment in their allocations of sales prospects. Among barbers, whose wages I also attempted to study, the standard practice was in fact to give preferential treatment to the *least* successful barbers. That is, when one barber in a shop managed to establish a larger clientele than the others, shop managers would compensate for that fact by assigning "walk-ins" preferentially to other barbers. The specific details of this practice were unfortunately so ill-defined as to preclude reasonable estimates of the contributions of individual barbers.

share lie between 6 and 7 percent for residential properties. When the house is purchased by a client of some other member agency of the MLS (a "co-brokered" sale), that agency receives a share of the total sales commission, with the remaining share going to the original listing agency. Typical sharing schemes give 60 percent of the total sales commission to the selling agency and 40 percent to the listing agency.

In a large market in which many real estate firms participate in the MLS, the most common transaction involves a client of one firm purchasing a house listed by some other firm. The firm that makes the sale typically will not have expended significant resources advertising the house, and most of the costs for these transactions are borne by the selling agent herself (primarily for the upkeep of the car she uses to transport her clients). For sales in which an agent in one firm sells a house listed by another firm, then, the earnings schedule implied by the marginal productivity theory takes essentially the same form as the one it implied for automobile salespersons. That is, agents should receive all commissions generated by the sales they make, less an implicit fixed fee for their access to the agency's sales prospects.

When an agency acquires an additional listing, it incurs a number of expenses that it would not otherwise have incurred, such as advertising outlays to alert the public to the house's availability. For any given number of houses listed, however, the agency's total costs will remain the same, regardless of how many are sold by its own sales force. Thus, the case of houses sold by the listing firm may be treated in the same way as co-brokered sales. For brevity's sake, however, let us focus on the co-brokered sale, which is, as noted, the most common transaction.

How do agencies actually compensate their agents for making co-brokered sales? In an attempt to answer this question, I collected data from four large real estate agencies located in Ithaca, New York. The Ithaca real estate market is not a large one by any means. But there are, nonetheless, 32 member agencies in the city's multiple-listing service. And the Ithaca Board of Realtors reports that the majority of transactions consummated by these firms are co-brokered sales.

Firms in my sample compensate their agents by giving them a share of the gross commission the firm receives from each sale. Within each of three of the four firms, this share varied from agent to agent. The agents' shares, or the range of such shares, of the firms' commissions from co-brokered sales are listed in Table 4.2.

Whereas the marginal productivity theory says that an agent's earnings should rise dollar for dollar with his gross commissions from co-brokered sales, earnings in this sample rose only between 50 and 70 cents per dollar. Each of the firms in this sample reported that its best agents had gross commission totals that were several times those of the least productive agents, and that these differences were highly consistent over time. For the same reason we saw in the sample of automobile salespersons, aversion to risk thus does not seem a plausible explanation for the flatness of the earnings schedules in this sample. The marginal productivity theory of wages appears completely

Table 4.2 *Slopes of the Earnings Schedules for Four Real Estate Agencies*

Firm	Slope of the Earnings Schedule (share retained by agent of gross commissions from co-brokered sales)
1	.50
2	.50–.575
3	.50–.70
4	.50–.60

inconsistent with the observation that an agent who receives only 70 percent of the $100,000 he generates for his firm each year has not been bid away by some other firm willing to pay him a higher commission rate.

Specific Training and the Internal Labor Market

In addition to citing measurement difficulties and risk aversion, many economists have argued that long-run aspects of the labor contract might cause wage differences to understate individual differences in productivity. Mincer, Becker, Oi, Thurow, and others have argued that investments in on-the-job training might often produce such a tendency.[7] These arguments focus on what are called "firm-specific" investments—investments whose returns can be realized only through continued employment with the firm that makes them. Teaching an employee how to deal with the idiosyncracies of a particular firm's network of suppliers, for example, has an important firm-specific component of this sort.

In order to make its investment in specific training more likely to pay off, a firm often designs its labor contract to discourage employees from leaving to join competing firms. One way of doing this is to pay workers less than they are worth in the early stages of their tenure, then gradually increase their pay so that, beyond some point, they actually make more than what they are worth to other firms. The lure of having higher pay in the future induces workers to remain with their firms for extended periods. And this, in turn, enables firms to make specific training investments that will benefit both themselves and their workers over the longer term.

Once employees have committed themselves to an implicit long-term employment contract of this sort, however, their opportunities in the broader labor market are curtailed. As more and more of their training and experience have economic value only to their current employers, their chances of using outside employment offers as bargaining chips diminish. Their careers become increasingly confined to what Doeringer and Piore have called the "internal labor market."[8] Yet despite the inherent limitations on future mobility, many workers choose this option because of its high payoff.

Under implicit labor contracts such as those described, the employer gains a measure of discretion in setting individual wage rates. Rather than try to fine-tune his wage structure to reflect individual differences in productivity—an expensive and time-consuming process—he might instead decide to set one wage for all workers at a given career stage in a given job category. If this wage is (or will soon be) higher than what even the most productive employees could obtain from outside firms (because their specific training is not worth much to outside firms), then the auction model of competition no longer assures that wage differences will reflect differences in productivity.

Now, these are all good arguments that take into account what really happens in many employment settings. Still, it would be difficult to argue that long-run aspects of the employment contract could account for the pattern of individual wage differences we have seen. In the selling of autos, for example, knowledge about specific models of cars can be acquired in a relatively short time. After all, the next year's models arrive each October, and salespersons must begin describing their merits to potential buyers on the very same day the autos arrive in the showroom. The real difference between a good auto salesperson and a bad one stems less from differences in detailed knowledge about the product than from differences in the ability to perceive, and respond effectively to, potential buyers' concerns. Ronald Reagan would be good at selling even an inferior brand of car, but Richard Nixon would probably have trouble moving vehicles that are stylish, durable, and economical. Because

*"The minute you walked in, I said to myself, 'There's a
guy who's had it up to here with wimpmobiles.'"*

someone who is good at selling Pontiacs is thus also likely to be good at selling Dodges, the Pontiac dealer cannot assume that this employee's outside opportunities will be limited in the way suggested by the specific-training arguments.

Similar difficulties would arise in trying to argue that implicit long-term labor contracts account for the degree of wage compression we observed in the real estate industry. In real estate sales, after all, the houses that agents are trying to sell all come from essentially the same pool. A given agent is likely to be just as good at persuading people to buy houses from that pool if she works for one agency as she would be if she worked for another. Accordingly, firm-specific training simply does not appear to be an important part of the picture in the automobile and real estate industries.

Stratification among Sales Firms

My claim here is that an implicit market for local status can account for much of the earnings compression we see within sales firms. When presenting early versions of this argument to my colleagues, I was occasionally greeted by the response that many salespersons would never turn down a job with a higher commission rate just to maintain their high rank among their current co-workers. This response, however, is perfectly in keeping with the theory developed in Chapter 3. There, we saw that many workers will, in fact, accept higher wage rates in return for lower within-firm status. People who care relatively little about local status will do best if they accept those jobs that offer the highest rates of pay. In those jobs, their rank vis-à-vis their co-workers will be lower than in other jobs, but they are amply compensated for that by their higher wages.

Do sales firms stratify in the manner described in Chapter 3? That is, do we find an overlapping hierarchy of firms that presents workers a rich menu of wage-status combinations from which to choose? Unfortunately, I was unable to obtain the detailed individual earnings data that would be needed to answer this question properly. Among the people I interviewed, however, there was agreement that there is a small number of elite firms within each industry to which many of the most able salespersons eventually gravitate. In the real estate industry, for example, these firms are the ones whose listings tend to come from upscale neighborhoods, and which thus generate higher commissions for listing agents. The talented sales agent who cares relatively little about local status will find these firms most attractive. Other talented agents, however, may prefer to play more prominent roles within lesser firms.

Pay Schedules for Professors in Research Universities

A THOUGHT EXPERIMENT

If the measurement of employee productivity in sales industries lies near one end of the difficulty spectrum, then the same task for professors in research universities surely lies close to the other. The process whereby individuals and groups of professors labor to produce "knowledge" through their collegial interactions, research, teaching, and administrative duties appears so bewilderingly complex as to defy any reasoned effort to measure the specific contribution made by an individual employee.

Despite the obvious difficulties, however, many thousands of such judgments are made every year. Administrators do not throw up their hands and say, "Evaluating productivity is a hopeless task, so we pay all professors the same salary." Much as they might like to do so, the intensely competitive environment in which major universities operate will not permit it. Universities are constantly on the lookout for able new faculty members, and the pressure of competition generally results in good professors receiving higher salaries.

In such an environment, what sorts of personnel judgments must be made in order to protect a group's position in the academic hierarchy? Let us take as a working hypothesis that there is substantial overlap in the range of abilities of scholars in departments that are ranked close together in a given field. Let us suppose, in other words, that the average scholar in one department is more highly regarded than some of the scholars in a slightly better department, and less highly regarded than some in a slightly worse one. It is also safe to suppose that professors are willing to change jobs if they receive a better salary offer from a comparable institution, or are at least willing to act like they will in order to induce their deans to match outside salary offers. The limitations on mobility found in some occupations do not apply much to major universities, where a scholar's external reputation is by far his most important professional asset. Firm-specific training counts for very little in this particular market.

Suppose we assume, for argument's sake, that professors take no interest in the salaries of their colleagues. Because the market for professors' services is highly competitive, we would then expect professors to be paid in proportion to the values of their productive contributions (to the extent those contributions can be estimated). If a particular department seems stable in the academic hierarchy, we can assume that none of its members are perceptibly underpaid. If they were, some other department could have improved its position by hiring them, or should at least have bid up their salaries in the attempt.

We can use these observations to carry out the following simple thought experiment. The purpose of this experiment is to test whether professors are paid the value of their marginal products (at least within the limits of our perceptions). In this experiment, you are to play the role of salary administrator in an academic department. (If you are unfamiliar with academic personnel decisions, you can easily translate the details of the experiment to fit your own employment experience.) To carry out this experiment, first identify those two of your colleagues in a given age group whose contributions you consider the most valuable. Then identify those three colleagues in this same age group whose combined efforts make, in your view, the least valuable contribution.

If the age and salary structure of your co-workers resemble those for members of the Department of Economics at the University of Michigan shown in Table 4.3,[9] then the three in the second group will together earn more than the two in the first group do. (In most academic departments, any three people in a given age group will collectively earn more than any other two; I make no judgment here about the quality of any particular economist at the University of Michigan.) The concluding step in the thought experiment is to decide whether the absence of the top two employees would more seriously detract from your employer's mission, as you see it, than would the absence of the bottom three.

If people are paid in proportion to their marginal products, then the answer to this question should be no. An unequivocal yes to this question, on the other hand, may be interpreted as further support for the claim that the distribution of employee salaries does not parallel employee productivity.

How are we to interpret the finding that the top two would be missed more than the bottom three even though the former are paid less? The explanation I offer here is that peoples' salaries include implicit compensating differentials that reflect their standing in their group's internal hierarchy. The plausibility of this interpretation depends, as I stressed in Chapter 3, on the perspective from which we view it. From the vantage point of a department's median member, for example, the department might actually look like a more attractive environment if the three lowest-ranked members were dismissed, and their salaries used to attract the services of two outsiders who are better than any of its current members. But even if that were so, it would not necessarily be possible to sustain the new department membership without making further salary adjustments. With the departure of the three lowest-ranked members,

Table 4.3 *Experience and Salary Structure of University of Michigan Economists, 1983–84*

Faculty Member	Experience (years since Ph.D.)	Salary	Faculty Member	Experience (years since Ph.D.)	Salary
1	43	$63,000	17	18	$45,000
2	32	54,300	18	17	50,700
3	32	51,000	19	17	37,500
4	30	39,000	20	16	61,000
5	26	52,000	21	16	48,100
6	25	55,000	22	16	30,000
7	23	41,200	23	15	51,500
8	22	47,700	24	13	40,600
9	22	44,500	25	12	51,300
10	21	43,000	26	12	50,300
11	20	46,800	27	10	62,400
12	20	42,400	28	10	39,300
13	19	56,500	29	9	43,200
14	19	55,000	30	7	40,400
15	19	53,000	31	6	37,700
16	18	55,000	32	5	27,700

for example, those who had been next above them on the departmental totem pole will now find themselves at the bottom—probably not a positive change as seen from their perspective. And those who had been best paid before will no longer be so. Complaints would thus likely be heard that the previous salary structure is now "unfair." And the ripple effects of such complaints on the remainder of the department's salary structure would have to be taken into account before we could say that the department had in fact improved its position.

The interpretation I offer here is that, even where the departure of the top two professors would hurt more, such ripple effects would prevent departments from improving their rankings in the way described. Whether this interpretation is correct or not, we know that *something* prevents departments from improving themselves in this way; otherwise the salaries of top-ranked members would by now have been bid up far past their current levels.

THE VALUE OF GRANTSMANSHIP

In an effort to generate some less subjective evidence on whether salaries track productive contributions in academia, I collected data on the research grants obtained by a sample of 18 biochemists and organic chemists, all full professors at Cornell University. Research grants are important to the university's budget, and the outside grants professors bring in thus constitute one important component of their total value to the university. In this section I will investigate the extent to which this component is reflected in the salaries professors actually receive.

When a Cornell professor obtains a research grant from an outside source, the university's grant contract stipulates that the donor pay the direct costs itemized in the proposal's budget, plus some of the indirect costs of operating the university's infrastructure. This indirect cost contribution is expected to equal 49 percent of all budgeted direct costs, although contributions much smaller than that are routinely negotiated with individual donors, and many donors do not include any indirect cost contributions at all. The university is reluctant to disclose the identities of these donors, apparently out of concern that to do so might encourage other sources to withhold indirect cost contributions as well. The university's Office of Sponsored Programs made it clear, however, that the university would gladly accept an additional grant that made no contribution to indirect costs if it could do so without changing the indirect cost contributions it receives from other donors.

I assume here that the university's willingness to accept such a grant is a sensible policy. (I assume, in other words, that even those grants that make no contributions to indirect costs still contribute in other ways to the enhancement of the university.) Given this assumption, it then follows that when a professor brings a grant to Cornell, his or her contribution to the university must be at least as great as the indirect cost contribution that accompanies that grant.

For convenience, I will focus on the top three, the median four, and the bottom three grant recipients in the sample of 18 professors for the academic

Table 4.4 *Indirect Cost Income*
Generated by Cornell Organic
Chemists and Biochemists

Group	1979–80 Indirect Cost Income per Professor
Top 3	$245,000
Median 4	92,994
Bottom 3	8,575

year 1979–80. The per capita indirect cost contributions that accompanied their grants are listed in Table 4.4. University records show that the indirect cost contributions for the specific individuals involved here have been very stable over time. For the discussion that follows, I will assume that the figures in Table 4.4 represent long-run differences in the indirect cost contributions generated by these professors. The general conclusions that follow from this assumption would not be altered even if the top group's figure were half as large, and the bottom group's twice as large, as the corresponding figures in Table 4.4.

Unlike the University of Michigan, which is required by state law to make its faculty salaries public, Cornell keeps faculty salaries a carefully guarded secret. The associate dean's office was willing to reveal, however, that the salaries of organic chemists and biochemists at Cornell did not differ more than 10 percent at either end from the range of faculty salaries in chemistry at the University of Michigan.* The average salary, then, of the three best-funded professors in our Cornell sample cannot be higher than $58,025, the figure that is 10 percent more than the salary of the most highly paid full professor in the chemistry department at Michigan. The associate dean's office was also willing to reveal the ratios of the average salary levels for the three groups of professors. These two pieces of information enable us to calculate conservative estimates of the average salary differences between the three groups (conservative in that they overstate the true differences). These estimates, together with the corresponding differences in indirect cost contributions, are shown in Table 4.5.

Viewed from the perspective of the university, which has ultimate authority over faculty salary policy, the differences in indirect cost contributions shown in Table 4.5 represent one important dimension along which marginal products differ among these three groups. These marginal product differences are dramatically larger than the corresponding figures for salary differences, which, as noted, are themselves overestimates of the true salary differences among the groups.

*Ironically, I was told that salaries in biochemistry are much higher at Michigan than at Cornell because "Michigan's medical school is located right in Ann Arbor." The close interactions that ordinarily take place between highly paid medical school professors and biochemists do not develop at Cornell, whose medical school happens to be located in New York City. Perhaps we economists are destined to be the last to grasp the full significance of salary comparisons between co-workers.

It is difficult to argue that differences along other dimensions of productivity could possibly offset the observed differences in indirect cost contributions. On the contrary, these indirect cost differences probably *understate* differences in values of marginal products. As in other fields, it is presumably also true in the sciences that a scholar's ability to obtain research grants is positively related to the quality and quantity of his or her past research efforts. Prestige is one of a university's most important products, and the external recognition such scholars confer on their colleagues is surely an important part of what they contribute. The ability to generate these halo effects should command a salary premium even in the absence of accompanying research grants. Moreover, the *direct* cost portion of most grant budgets contains many expenditures —for the purchase of capital equipment and support for graduate students, to name two—that make important contributions to a department. Finally, while faculty with extensive outside research support often teach fewer courses, this fact is largely offset by funds allocated within the direct cost portion of grant budgets specifically to purchase released teaching time.

These are all points that could be investigated explicitly if I knew the names of the individuals in the specific groups in Table 4.4. Since I do not, let us be conservative and assume, contrary to the preceding paragraph, that productivity along dimensions other than grant-getting is *inversely* related to grant-getting for this sample of professors. The most conservative set of assumptions we can make is that members of the top group contribute nothing to the university except the grants they receive; that members of the bottom group earn their salaries exclusively through contributions in areas unrelated to grant-getting; and that members of the median group contribute to the university in some way other than through the grants they receive.

Given these assumptions, the marginal productivity theory of wages would say that the average value of the bottom group's contributions along nongrant-related dimensions is equal to its average salary, which we have seen is less than $40,618 per year. This implies that the difference in marginal products between professors in the top and bottom groups must be at least $195,807 (which is the difference between average indirect cost contributions for the two groups, less the average salary of the bottom group). Yet the difference in average salary levels for the top and bottom groups is no more than $17,417, or less than 9 percent of the former figure.

It might be argued that universities are reluctant to allow salaries to reflect indirect cost contributions for fear the flow of grants might suddenly be

Table 4.5 *Salary Differences Versus Differences in Indirect Cost Contributions*

Group Comparison	Average Difference in Salary	Average Difference in Indirect Cost Contribution
Top versus median	$ 4,642	$152,006
Median versus bottom	12,765	84,419

discontinued, leaving them in the always difficult position of having to negotiate reductions in existing salary levels. The professors in the top group, however, could presumably stipulate in advance that their salaries be linked explicitly to their grant totals, rather than settle for their current pay. More to the point, a competing university that offered a 50-year-old top grant-getter a mere $10,000 premium over his or her existing salary would need to see only one year of successful grant-getting before its gamble paid off. Even the most cautious university would probably be willing to take that risk.*

It is also possible that the granting agencies themselves might object if universities were to link professors' salaries by formula to indirect cost contributions. After all, the explicit purpose of indirect cost contributions is to help defray the university's overhead expenses, not to pay professor's salaries. Yet even if a constraint against an explicit link did exist, surely no granting agency would have objected or altered its awards in any way had some competing university hired one of Cornell's top grant-getters by offering a $70,000 annual salary. That such offers were not forthcoming says that some other factor must explain why indirect cost contributions are so weakly reflected in professors' salaries.

One might reasonably claim that if *all* indirect cost contributions were funneled into professor's salaries, the infrastructure on which a university's reputation so strongly depends would deteriorate. This would in turn seriously diminish the capacity of its professors to attract financial support from outside sources. Although this observation is undoubtedly correct, competitive pressures should *still* cause indirect cost contributions to be more fully reflected in professors' salaries than they are. With respect to the receipt of outside grants, many university infrastructure expenses are properly viewed as fixed costs: The costs of libraries, philosophy departments, snow removal equipment, and administrators' salaries do not change when some professor receives an additional research grant. Any university that managed to hire away one of Cornell's top grant-getters for an annual salary of $70,000 would capture at least $175,000 in additional annual funding to help defray the costs of maintaining its own infrastructure. Thus it is strongly in the interests of any one institution to bid vigorously for the services of proven grant-getters. Yet whenever such bidding has taken place, it has fallen far short of what would have been predicted by the traditional theory of wage determination. When the University of Texas recently lured the Nobel physicist Steven Weinberg away from Harvard by offering a salary of $110,000, the pressing question for the traditional theory was not why Weinberg's salary is so high, but why it is so low.

---

*A related risk is that a university might have so many grant-getters that its total indirect cost collections would exceed an amount deemed reasonable by government funding agencies. Such a university would then no longer stand to gain in the same way that others would by hiring a prolific grant-getter. But Cornell was not, and does not expect to be, confronted with the problem of too many grants. The problem for even the most well-funded universities has rather been their failure to attract sufficient indirect cost support for the research programs they carry out.

I argued in Chapter 3 that an implicit market for status within each firm causes the distribution of earnings to be compressed relative to the distribution of marginal products. Yet it is difficult to assert that all major grant-getters at a university could feel so strongly about occupying a high-status position that they would willingly sacrifice hundreds of thousands of dollars per year. Why don't the proven grant-getters who care little about status leave their current posts for jobs in which their status is lower but their income is closer to the value of what they contribute? One answer to this question is that it may not be possible to organize a university that consists *only* of top grant-getters. For a university to achieve genuine distinction it needs strong perfor-

"Maybe our problem is too many chiefs."

Drawing by Mal. Copyright © 1981 Saturday Review, Inc. Reprinted by permission of the artist.

mance not only in the sciences, but in the arts and humanities as well. If we assume that grant-getting possibilities outside the sciences are relatively limited, it then follows that top grant-getters simply cannot be paid their marginal products without earning vastly more than most other university faculty members. Those at the very top of a population's productivity distribution may be forced, then, by the lack of a viable work-alone option into spending much more for status than they would if a broader menu of choices were available.

Variations in the Price of Status

In Chapter 3, I argued that the importance workers attach to their relative standing within their firms will be greatest where interactions between co-workers are most extensive. Other things equal, as co-workers work in closer contact with one another, we should see the slope of the earnings schedule become flatter, or see the degree of earnings variability become more limited. (Reduced earnings variability is, of course, one *consequence* of having a flatter earnings schedule, but it can also be achieved by limiting the range of productive abilities included within the firm.)

I offer no scientific evidence here that automobile salespersons have closer ties to their co-workers than do real estate salespersons. But we do know that the former work in close physical proximity with one another, while many of the latter work primarily out of their own homes and spend the bulk of their working hours visiting houses with prospective clients. As I noted in Chapter 2, both the psychologist's model of perception and the sociologist's description of the reference group stress the role of exposure and proximity as determinants of what we focus most closely on.

On the basis of these considerations, then, the implicit price of status should be higher among people who sell automobiles than among those who sell houses. As we have already seen in Tables 4.1 and 4.2, the slopes of the observed earnings schedules are indeed substantially smaller for automobile than for real estate salespersons. Concerning the range of earnings variations within groups, the information I was able to gather is relatively more fragmentary. But what I could get confirms the prediction that the salary range within a work group decreases with the degree of contact that occurs between the group's members. For the three of the four real estate firms from the sample (the relevant information was not available for the fourth), the maximum annual earnings figure averaged 5.7 times the minimum annual earnings figure for full-time salespeople. Among auto dealerships, the corresponding ratio was only 3.1.

In a similar vein, we can argue that research professors in the sciences interact more intensively with one another than do co-workers in either of the two sales occupations discussed above. In addition to working in close physical proximity to one another, professors in the sciences commonly engage in collaborative research projects. They frequently co-author books and articles, are often members of the same administrative committees, and frequently cooperate in supervising students. Moreover, job turnover is much less frequent among full professors than among automobile and real estate salespersons. This means that professors stay in contact with one another as colleagues over a longer period of time than do people in those other occupations.

For the research professors in the Cornell sample, we saw that the top earners received less than 50 percent more than the bottom earners. We saw further that salaries of professors might go up by as much as 9 cents for every extra dollar they contribute to the university's net revenues, but probably go up much less. These observations are also consistent with the notion that the price of status is highest in groups whose members interact most intensively.

We also have information on two other relationships that bear on the question of how the closeness of contact between co-workers affects earnings variability within firms. The first concerns the closeness of contact between co-workers in union, as opposed to nonunion, firms. In his classic book, Hirschman has argued that the union's grievance and other administrative procedures facilitate enduring relationships between co-workers in unionized firms.[10] Mincer has found that the average length of job tenure is indeed substantially greater for union workers.[11] If these findings mean that union workers interact more extensively with their colleagues than nonunion workers do, as seems plausible, they suggest that wage schedules should be flatter in union firms. A large literature supports the finding that rates of pay do, in fact, vary much less between co-workers in union than in nonunion firms.[12]

The second piece of additional information involves the closeness of contact between co-workers in the military. To the extent that military personnel live together in groups more or less sequestered from the civilian population, they are uniquely isolated from comparisons with people other than their co-workers. To a much greater degree than for the civilian worker, the military person's co-workers, friends, and neighbors will all tend to be drawn from the same closed group of people. This means that military pay scales should be much more compressed than civilian pay scales, just as in fact, they appear to be.[13]

The foregoing observations hardly settle the question of how the price of status depends on the closeness of contact between co-workers. Still, if my closeness-of-contact rankings for the various groups are acceptable, these observations have a certain measure of statistical force. Suppose we let X_1, X_2, X_3, X_4, X_5, X_6, and X_7 represent the slopes of the earnings schedules for real estate salespersons, auto salespersons, research scientists, nonunion workers, union workers, civilian workers, and military workers, respectively. The theory developed in Chapter 3 then implies that the following relationships will hold: $X_1 > X_2 > X_3$, and $X_4 > X_5$, and $X_6 > X_7$. These are exactly the relationships we do observe, and the likelihood of this particular pattern having occurred purely by chance is less than 1 in 20.*

The Implicit Price of a Top-Ranked Position

A firm's earnings schedule may be used to calculate the difference between the wage its top-ranked worker earns and the value of what he produces. In Figure 4.3, if *EE* represents the earnings schedule for a firm, this difference will be the amount by which the top-earner's spot on the right-most part on the earnings schedule lies below the 45° line (which tells what his earnings would have been had he been paid the value of what he contributes).

For the automobile dealerships in my sample, the best salesperson's earnings were 67 percent higher than those of salespersons on average. If markets are competitive, average sales earnings, in turn, must be equal to the average value of what all salespersons contribute to the firm. For a dealership in which earnings increase with marginal products at the rate of 23.6 cents per dollar (the average rate observed in this sample), these figures imply that the top-ranked salesperson is paid almost 57 percent less than the value of his marginal product. For real estate agencies in my sample, the best agents earned twice as much as the average agent earned. When an agent's earnings increase at the rate of 59 cents for every extra dollar of gross sales commissions (the average rate for the steepest earnings schedules in each firm in my sample), the best-paid agent will receive almost 26 percent less than the value of his marginal product. For full professors in biochemistry and organic chemistry at Cornell, finally, we saw that the best-paid faculty members

---

*In a nonparametric framework, which seems natural here, the null hypothesis would be that $X_1, \ldots, X_7$ are independently, identically distributed. Under this null hypothesis, the probability of the observed pattern having occurred by chance would then be .042.

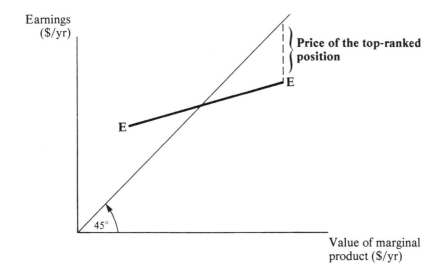

Figure 4.3 The Implicit Price of the Top-Ranked Position in an Earnings Hierarchy

received salaries that are less than one-fourth as large as the value of only one component of what they contribute to the university, which translates in dollar terms to a difference of nearly $200,000 per year.

Whether these amounts may be interpreted as the implicit prices for top-ranked positions depends on why the slopes of the observed wage schedules are as gentle as they are. I argued that risk aversion does not materially flatten those slopes, because firms have at their disposal other, better means for smoothing employees' earnings. I also argued that internal labor market considerations are not important in the occupations whose wage schedules I have examined here. The flatness that we observe, then, may be primarily a manifestation of the market for local status discussed in Chapter 3. If so, the amounts by which the values of the top-earners' marginal products exceed their respective wages may be interpreted as the implicit prices of occupying those top-ranked positions. Any other factors besides status that contribute to the flattening of observed wage schedules would cause the implicit prices of top-ranked positions to be lower than these amounts.

As noted in Chapter 3, however, the price a person pays for status in any one local hierarchy is itself a lower bound on the total value he attaches to status generally. In order for a person to occupy a high-ranked position among his co-workers, he must work for less than the value of what he produces. This in turn reduces his rankings in both the global hierarchy and in any other local hierarchies to which he may belong. As I argued in Chapter 3, the halo and learning effects also act to make the wage schedules we observe within firms steeper than they would otherwise be. For these reasons, too, the implicit wage reductions observed for the top-ranked members of firms may underestimate the value of a broader sort of status.

Still, the estimates of the implicit prices of top-ranked positions in the firms examined here suggest that the value of even this one component of status may be very large. To the extent that these estimates have any meaning, they contradict the claim that status in local hierarchies is of only passing importance. On the contrary, these estimates are consistent with the view that people's concerns about local status are very powerful indeed.

The evidence I have discussed here obviously does not prove conclusively that concerns about relative standing account for why wage structures are so much flatter than traditional theories predict. I have tried to show, however, that the various alternative explanations that have been offered cannot account for the degree of wage compression we observe in actual firms. To be sure, other factors, yet to be discovered, may also play important roles.

Still, I hope it is fair to say that the theory developed in Chapter 3 does not appear any *less* plausible in light of the evidence we have seen. And this evidence is but a small part of the much larger mosaic that has led me to believe that people's concerns about relative standing play a pivotal role in their behavior. Let us now return to the continuing task of filling in this broader picture.

Five

Further Indications of the Value of Local Status

High-Priced Consultants and Breakaway Executives

In the task of producing oil, an unusually talented geologist may literally be worth several times his weight in gold. He is certainly much more valuable than is, say, the chief executive of the large multinational oil company that will ultimately extract the oil from the earth.

One might expect that these geologists would be most effectively utilized as fully integrated members of the technical staffs of these large oil companies. After all, if anything were to be gained from their interactions with the many other well-informed professionals already in these organizations, an integrated relationship would seem to benefit all parties concerned. In fact, however, the most talented finders of oil often operate as independent contractors.

In a world in which people took no interest in the incomes of their co-workers, it would make little sense for firms to pass up apparently obvious gains through integration. But if people care about what their co-workers earn, then it is not at all surprising that an oil company might find it difficult to pay a technical staff member much more than its chief executive officer and other senior management personnel.

In the same vein, we observe that many firms apparently would rather maintain ongoing relationships with costly consulting organizations than hire the same consultants directly. A variety of reasons might explain why firms thus continue to incur heavy overhead billings that seem avoidable. But the recognition that status in local hierarchies has high value suggests that one of the firm's motives may simply be to isolate its own internal wage structure from costly ripple effects that would be stimulated by internal placement of these highly paid consultants.

Similarly, concerns about relative standing may often preclude certain incentive devices from corporate pay schemes. Suppose, for example, a junior corporate officer comes up with a patentable idea that will greatly reduce the cost of producing an item, thus saving the company $10 million annually. If each employee's pay could be determined in isolation, the employee would probably give the patent to the firm in return for a payment reflecting its market value. Because a payment of such size would greatly upset the balance of the internal wage structure, however, he may have to start a new firm in order to exploit his innovation. To do so, he will have to duplicate many facilities already present in his old firm. But the cost of doing that may be substantially less than the costs of redressing the imbalances that would be created if he were paid his due and remained with his old firm. Where existing structures prevent an able frog from becoming the biggest in his current pond, it may pay him, and the rest of society as well, simply to start a new pond.

Spinning Off the Ailing Division

Just as it may often pay for the most productive contributors to break away from a given hierarchy, it may also occasionally benefit a hierarchy to shed its least productive members. Consider, for example, the following scenario involving first the growth, then the contraction, of a conglomerate enterprise. This scenario involves a number of separately owned firms, each of which produces a different type of product but all of which engage in many similar activities, such as economic forecasting, marketing surveys, research and development, brand name promotion, maintaining distribution networks, raising capital, and so on. Because these firms perform many of the same activities, they decide to cut costs by merging into one large conglomerate. In its early days, the firm realizes the expected high profitability made possible by the cost-saving consolidation.

One effect of the merger is that the work force, which was once an independent collection of local hierarchies, has become one large, consolidated local hierarchy. And as in any local hierarchy, there may be pressures to limit the range of earnings within it. Whatever the earnings ratio between the highest-paying firm and the lowest-paying one may have been before the consolidation, the theory developed in Chapter 3 says that this ratio must now become smaller. If the gains from consolidation are sufficiently large, however, employees of the top-paying firm before the merger may nonetheless find their absolute earnings increased.

Now suppose one of the divisions in the conglomerate falls on hard times. Because of a change in consumer tastes, its product is no longer as in demand as before. The textbook response would be for the firm to lower both the price of its product and the wages of its workers. If demand picked up at the new, lower price, and if wages did not fall enough to prompt workers to leave, the firm would have weathered the storm.

In the context of the consolidated firm, however, the task of keeping the ailing division afloat by reducing wages promises to be much more difficult. The workers in the ailing division now regard themselves as part of the larger hierarchy, within which wage rates other than theirs are not falling. As a result, they may refuse to accept a wage cut, and the consolidated firm may be unable to restore profitability.

To prevent the division from shutting down, management may pursue the following alternative, suggested by the theory developed in Chapter 3. It may simply spin the division off, making it once again a separately owned company. No longer part of the larger, more prosperous hierarchy, workers in the ailing division might then be more willing to make wage concessions. After all, people are less willing to tolerate hardships when others in the same boat do not bear an equal share of the burden. Although the new company would lose many of the real economic gains it had reaped by associating with the conglomerate, its savings in labor costs might easily offset those losses.

If external market forces, rather than bad management, are the cause of the ailing division's difficulties, there is no reason to discharge the division's current management after the spin-off. On the contrary, there will be clear advantages in retaining the current management, since it is already well-acquainted with the division's workings. Indeed, the spin-off might take a form of the so-called "leveraged buy-out" in which the parent company provides financing for the sale of the division to its current managers. As more and more divisions of conglomerate companies have fallen on hard times in recent years, such leveraged buy-outs have become increasingly common.[1] The strong interest workers take in the incomes of their co-workers makes it easy to see why spin-offs of this form might make economic sense.

"See? It's not as if you were the only one."

In this example, note that I have implicitly extended the concept of the local hierarchy beyond the group of people with whom the worker associates in close physical proximity. Indeed, the various divisions of conglomerate firms are often located in different cities, which means that workers in one division may never even meet those in other divisions. But as I stressed in Chapter 2, direct exposure is not the *only* factor that governs whose income people care about. Employees in the various divisions of a conglomerate firm apparently see themselves as competing with one another for a share of a common economic pie, and, in a certain sense, they surely are. It is this knowledge that might reasonably account for the strong interest they apparently take in one another's incomes. Once the ownership connection between divisions is severed, however, this competition no longer exists. Whatever concerns it had spawned may be expected to focus elsewhere.

Limitations on Piece-Rate Earnings Schemes

Armed with the view that status in local hierarchies may be a thing of considerable value, we can make sense of a vast literature that documents the widespread existence of attempts to limit the earnings of a firm's most productive workers. Consider, for example, the results of a survey of sales commission plans, summarized in Table 5.1, in which the National Industrial Conference Board reports that 54 out of the 100 plans studied imposed ceilings above which a salesperson's earnings could not rise, *regardless of his sales output*.[2] Equivalent pay ceilings are described in a large literature that discusses the widespread practice, in both union and nonunion firms, by which workers impose strong sanctions against their co-workers who exceed informal production quotas.[3] Instances are even reported in which firms themselves take steps to limit the amounts workers produce. McKersie, for example, reports the case of a General Electric plant that abandoned an incentive pay experiment despite its strong effect on productivity, because it caused some production workers to earn more than their supervisors.[4] He also tells of a large manufacturing firm that refused, for similar reasons, a union's request to increase the speed of the production assembly line.[5]

Within the framework of the traditional marginal productivity theory of wages, observations such as these appear completely incoherent. Unable to

Table 5.1 *Incentive Compensation Ceilings by Type of Selling Activity*

	Total Plans	Sales Engineers	Type of Selling Activity	
			Direct Contact	Promotional Selling
Have no ceiling	46	17	20	9
Have ceiling	54	16	20	18
Total	100	33	40	27

Source: National Industrial Conference Board (1970), p. 79.

answer the question "Why don't new firms bid the most productive employees away from their current firms?," economists as a group have tended to ignore limitations on piece-rate earnings. But if economists have been oblivious to what goes on in the world around them, their critics are vulnerable to the equally serious charge of offering logically inconsistent interpretations of the facts they have recorded.

One such interpretation says that workers impose production quotas in the belief that high productivity will prompt firms to lower the piece-rate. They will then be left with no more income than before, in return for having expended a greater amount of effort.[6] No one denies that many workers hold this belief. The flavor of workers' views toward management's motives is perhaps nowhere better captured in this literature than in the following passage from a diary kept by the sociologist Donald Roy during the 11 months he worked as a drill press operator in a steel fabricating plant. In the passage, an experienced worker (Starkey) counsels a new man on the job (Tennessee) on the ways of doing battle with their mutual antagonist, the time-study man, who establishes the pay rates for the various jobs they perform.

"Another thing," said Starkey, "You were running that job too damn fast before they timed you on it! I was watching you yesterday. If you don't run a job slow before you get timed, you won't get a good price. They'll look at the record of what you do before they come around and compare it with the timing speed. Those time-study men are sharp!"

"I wasn't going very fast yesterday," exclaimed Tennessee. "Hell, I was going as slow as I could without wearing myself out slowing down."

"Well, maybe it just looked fast because you were going so steady at it," said Starkey.

"I don't see how I could of run it any slower," said Tennessee. "I stood there like I was practically paralyzed!"

"Remember those bastards are paid to screw you," said Starkey. "And that's all they think about. They'll stay up half the night figuring out how to beat you out of a dime. They figure you're going to try to fool them, so they make allowances for that. They set the prices low enough to allow for what you do."

"Well, then, what the hell chance have I got?," asked Tennessee.

"It's up to you to figure out how to fool them more than they allow for," said Starkey.

"The trouble with me is I get nervous with that guy standing in back of me, and I can't think," said Tennessee.

"You just haven't had enough experience yet," said Starkey. "Wait until you have been here a couple of years and you'll do your best thinking when those guys are standing behind you."[7]

Such conflicts between workers and management are often viewed as games that pit management's greed against the ingenuity of the worker. As William F. Whyte writes:

Thus, a game could be played not only against time but against personalized opponents. The operator watched the clock as he expended his skill and energy, but sometimes the otherwise guileless face of the timepiece on the wall took on the crafty features of the time-study man.[8]

The structure of this game assumes that the only way management finds out if a piece-rate has been set too high is observing workers making exceptionally high earnings. To be sure, there is often a great deal of uncertainty as to what a reasonable piece-rate should be. And we do know of cases in which managements have instructed their industrial engineers to reevaluate a piece-rate whenever earnings exceed a given amount.[9] Such a policy would obviously create the impression among workers that it could be self-defeating for them to be too productive on a given task, and could help explain why they might put pressure on one another to limit output.

Yet, by itself, the fear by workers that management will simply cut the rate if they produce too much does not adequately explain why workers would thus limit the amounts they produce. To suppose that management has no other way of discovering that a piece-rate has been set too low is to credit management with none of the same ingenuity demonstrated by workers in their skirmishes with the time-study man. Surely management has independent ways of finding out what normal people are capable of producing on the machines installed in its factory. Why, for example, couldn't management evaluate production times by hiring several outsiders to run a job for a period of, say, one month, setting a high piece-rate and guaranteeing that they can keep whatever they earn during that period? If management feared that outsiders would face pressures from permanent workers in the plant, the same experiment could be performed off the premises.

Similarly, the worker's fear that management will discover piece-rates are too high cannot account for why workers would impose production quotas on themselves even when they realize that management *knows* they can produce more than they are currently producing. Management observes, for example, that quotas are often met by the most productive (or even all but a few) employees well before their shifts are over. In the forge shop of one auto parts company, the employees normally worked only six hours per day before reaching their self-imposed quota, whereupon they stopped working and spent the remainder of their shift idly passing time.[10] Donald Roy estimated that his co-workers in the steel fabricating plant deliberately wasted some 36 percent of their time, often in full view of their foremen, in order to stay within their quotas.[11] In another case, most employees reached their quotas in seven hours, whereupon they played cards in the restroom, prompting some of their wives to complain to management about their gambling losses.[12] In an electrical appliance plant, piece-rate workers averaged 200 percent of the normal production quota, but during a strike supervisors found they could easily produce 300 to 400 percent of that same quota.[13] Given these examples, it is difficult to insist that the principal reason workers impose production quotas upon themselves is to fool management.

Furthermore, management appears to have it well within its power to write contracts with workers that would guarantee the piece-rate for a specified period.[14] If management knows, or even suspects, that fear of a rate change is holding down production, then why doesn't management sign an agreement with workers to allay that fear? It might be argued that workers believe that management would always find some way to weasel out of such a contract. But this argument doesn't explain why management doesn't simply *reduce* the existing piece-rate, thereby forcing workers to step up production to maintain their current earnings.

It has also been argued that workers observe voluntary quotas on piece-rate tasks because failure to do so would expand production so greatly that many would be laid off.[15] This argument has at least two serious weaknesses. First, most firms compete with other firms that produce similar products, which means that the lower prices made possible by higher productivity would enable them to enlarge their market shares. For firms that produce only a small fraction of total industry output, there would thus be no layoff danger whatever to workers who exceeded existing production quotas. Second, and even more telling, we have no persuasive reasons to believe that the most productive workers in existing firms would be willing to accept substantial pay cuts in order to protect their less productive counterparts from being laid off. If a new firm were to offer the most productive workers in existing firms a chance to increase their earnings substantially, is it reasonable to suppose that they would refuse on the grounds that their leaving might cause some of the less productive workers to become unemployed?

Although worker-imposed production quotas for piece-rate tasks are, as noted, encountered in both nonunion and union firms, their prevalence and intensity is greater in the latter.[16] It has been argued that union workers impose stronger piece-rate quotas because they know they will be handicapped in their bargaining with management if management sees that many workers can achieve high earnings at the current piece-rate.[17] (Presumably the proponents of this argument would concede that nonunion workers would have similar motives for imposing quotas but would simply be less effective in doing so because of their lower level of organization.)

But this argument is also flawed. Although it is easy enough to see why collectively bargained rates might be higher than those in nonunion agreements, it is not at all clear why the visibility of some workers with high earnings would make union workers more inclined to impose production quotas. As noted, management probably already knows that many workers are capable of exceeding such quotas. And if management knows what workers are capable of producing, why should union workers be any more likely than nonunion workers to handicap themselves in this way? As bargaining chips, these quotas make as little sense in one case as in the other.

Let us next consider cases in which ceilings on piece-rate earnings arise not from the workers' initiative but from the firm's. (I have in mind the cases mentioned earlier in which earnings caps were imposed on sales commissions plans, and in which firms abandoned incentive pay schemes that had boosted productivity substantially.) One argument given for such practices is that they are needed to maintain adequate quality standards.[18] According to this argument, where quality standards are costly to monitor, letting workers' earnings rise in proportion to the quantity of goods they process will lead to shoddy workmanship, which will ultimately compromise profitability.

Although there often are legitimate difficulties in assuring desired quality levels, it is not at all clear how a cap on piece-rate earnings would improve matters. If workers are inclined to cut corners because they know it is too costly for the firm to inspect their work, we would then expect sloppy workmanship with or without earnings quotas. As we have already seen in the case of worker-imposed earnings quotas, limitations on earnings often result simply in a reduction of the total time people work. Having reached their daily earnings quota at 3:00 P.M., why would workers spend the next two hours increasing the quality of each piece? Where quality control truly is a problem, a much more direct solution would be to examine a small random sample of each person's work and impose penalties where quality falls below standard. It might even make good sense to sample more intensively from the items processed by workers with unusually high earnings totals, under the plausible assumption that high rates of output might be a signal of careless work. But simply to put a cap on earnings is a ridiculously roundabout means of approaching the problem of quality control.

While none of the foregoing explanations of piece-rate quotas is completely without merit, it is nonetheless fair to say that, as a group, they leave much to be desired. Once the importance of status in local hierarchies is introduced, however, we can easily explain such quotas, whether they be imposed by firms or by workers themselves.

Profit-seeking firms may choose to abandon piece-rate systems despite the extra output they stimulate if the high earnings realized by the most productive workers create costly ripple effects throughout the lower reaches of their wage structures. Similarly, when top-ranked positions in local hierarchies are highly valued, the most productive people in an organization may be perfectly willing to accept pay ceilings, if the alternative is to play a lesser role in some other organization that did not constrain earnings.

The greater incidence of production quotas in union firms also begins to make sense when we consider the co-worker group is likely to be relatively more important to union workers. As noted in Chapter 4, the union member's average length of tenure with his firm is substantially longer than that of his nonunion counterpart.[19] Because the importance of a local hierarchy grows with the length of a person's involvement in it, as I argued in Chapter 4, the implicit price of a top-ranked position will be higher for union than for nonunion workers. The closer the ties among co-workers, the greater the pressure will be to limit differences in their earnings.

Before leaving the subject of earnings quotas, I should note that many of the able scholars who have contributed to the industrial pay literature appear well aware that concerns about status affect earnings. Indeed, Sylvia Shimmin devotes much of her book on piece-rate earnings plans to the role of status in the workplace.[20] Similarly, William F. Whyte has written:

[R]estriction of output under some circumstances contributes to the stability of relations among individuals in the work group. A group is not simply an undifferentiated aggregate of associating individuals. Groups have their own structures, with leaders and followers and varying levels of status or prestige separating them.[21]

Even some economists have recognized that other things besides marginal productivity seem to play a role in determining wages. The venerable Sir John Hicks, for example, has written:

There has . . . always been room for wages to be influenced by non-economic forces—whether by custom . . . or by any other principle which affects what the parties to the wage bargain think to be just or right. Economic forces do affect wages, but only when they are strong enough to overcome these social forces.[22]

With these same "social" forces apparently in mind, Pencavel has suggested that piece-rate pay schemes tend to produce disparities in pay that "induce discontent among employees," which is then "followed by uncooperative and unaccommodating work behavior."[23] Similar analyses have been offered by Doeringer and Piore and by Thurow.[24]

All of these observations suggest that concerns about relative standing may indeed weaken piece-rate pay schemes. But in so doing, they have left unanswered the critical question of why new firms haven't organized to bid for the services of those employees who are paid less than what they are worth. Lacking a satisfactory answer to this question, economists as a profession have refused to accept the possibility that concerns about relative standing could have any significant bearing on wages.

In Chapter 3, I argued that there is a disarmingly simple explanation for why the best workers aren't bid away. By observing that status is a reciprocal phenomenon and that workers are, in large measure, free to isolate themselves from unfavorable income comparisons, we saw that paying each worker the value of his marginal product would result in a highly fragmented workplace, one in which firms must be composed of equally productive workers. In such an environment, no one suffers low status among his co-workers. But, by the same token, no one enjoys high status, either. When people value status differently, it is possible to produce a better result for everyone. Those who value status highly can transfer some of their income to others who agree in return to occupy the lower-ranked positions that make high status possible. The resulting internal wage structures are compressed in relation to the productive contributions of individual workers. Yet this pattern provides no opening whatever for the most productive workers to be bid away by new firms offering to pay them the value of what they produce.

In a preview of an argument I develop in much more detail in Chapter 7, I note briefly here another mechanism by which people's concerns about position might help to account for earnings quotas. This mechanism involves the possibility that piece-rate workers become caught up with one another in earnings "rat races." In my discussions of the market for status so far, I have considered only those productivity differences among workers that result from differences in ability. In most jobs, however, workers' productivity will depend not only on their ability but also on the amount of effort they expend. Under pay schemes in which workers' earnings are linked explicitly to the amounts they produce, it will thus be possible for them to increase their earnings by expending additional effort. Indeed, the hope of encouraging additional effort undoubtedly plays an important role in the firm's decision to adopt piece-rate schemes in the first place.

In a world in which workers took no interest in the incomes of their co-workers, people would choose how much effort to expend by weighing the gains from extra effort (in terms of extra earnings) against the costs of extra effort (in terms of increased fatigue, strain, and so on). And the economist would nod approvingly that the resulting effort levels represent the best possible outcome. If workers care about relative income, however, effort levels chosen in this way will no longer be optimal. A works harder and gets ahead of B, which then induces B to work harder to restore his position. But in the end, this expenditure of additional effort does not alter the rank ordering of co-workers' incomes. As Fred Hirsch put it:

> *There is an "adding up" problem. Opportunities for economic advance as they present themselves serially to one person after another, do not constitute equivalent opportunities for economic advance of all. What each of us can achieve, all cannot.*[25]

The problem is that the return to effort appears misleadingly large to each individual worker. To the extent that the prospects of moving forward in the co-worker earnings hierarchy is one of the payoffs people hope for when they expend extra effort, the result will be that workers as a group will labor too intensively. From their collective vantage point, a cap on earnings might thus serve to limit the speed of the treadmill on which they find themselves.

How Income Affects Demands for Status

If status is like most goods, people will demand more of it as their incomes rise. Yet the total proportion of high-ranked positions available to the members of any population is by definition fixed. As with land or any other resource whose supply is fixed, increases in demand (whether induced by rising incomes or by any other factor) lead inexorably to increases in price. Thus, we may expect that if demands for status rise with income, then the implicit price one must pay in order to occupy a high-ranked position (or the premium one receives for occupying a low-ranked position) will rise hand-in-hand with income. Putting this another way, we may expect the slopes of the earnings schedules observed within firms to become flatter as income levels rise over time. And the data we have are consistent with this prediction. McKersie, for example, reports that during the twentieth century a steady flattening of the slopes of incentive pay schedules has taken place in the United States.[26]

One direct consequence of flattened earnings schedules is the reduced amount by which a person's pay varies with the effort he expends. There occurs, in effect, a reduction in the reward workers receive for making extra contributions to their group's output. As a result, people may direct less effort toward their productive tasks. (As noted, such an outcome may even have been sought deliberately in some cases.) The possibility thus emerges, albeit highly speculative, that the much-decried reduction in productivity growth that has occurred in recent years may in part be an indirect consequence of the rising price of status.

Now, the possibility that rising demands for status could result in persistently *reduced* levels of aggregate output calls to mind Yogi Berra's observation that a certain St. Louis restaurant is "so crowded that no one goes there anymore." Effort reductions stemming from flattened earnings schedules are by their nature self-limiting. Once the level of effort falls to the point where output per person begins to decline, the ensuing income reductions would then be accompanied by *reduced* demands for status. Reductions in the demand for status, in turn, will reduce the price of status, which means that earnings schedules will begin reverting to their earlier, steeper form. With the reward for effort thus reinstated, the cycle would begin anew. But implicit in this process lies the potential for an extended period of low productivity growth.

The question of how the slopes of earnings schedules compare, at a given moment in time, across firms with different average productivity levels raises an important question about the extent to which workers are free to choose their co-workers. In the brickmaking example in Chapter 3, I assumed for the sake of simplicity that workers could group themselves into firms in any way they chose. Where people within firms essentially work independently of one another, as in that example, the implicit price of a high-ranked position in each firm must be the same, regardless of the firm's average productivity level. If that were not the case, someone would be paying more than necessary for the privilege of ocupying a high-ranked position. If, for example, a low-ranked member in a highly productive firm received a larger premium than a low-ranked member in a second, less productive firm was getting, then the latter worker could offer to occupy a low-ranked position in the first firm for a smaller premium than its current occupant receives. In this fashion, the premiums for positions of a given rank would adjust until they were equal across firms of different average productivity levels.

In most actual firms, however, there is a great deal of interaction among co-workers, and it will not ordinarily be feasible for an employee from an unskilled group to assume a low-ranked position in a group of highly skilled workers. Even if interactions were not important, the presence of such a worker would probably not be perceived by the group members as having enhanced their status in any meaningful sense. To have high status in a local hierarchy means to occupy a high-ranked position among people who might reasonably be thought of as peers. If the unskilled worker's skill level is significantly below the skill levels of others in the group, he may simply not be considered part of the group for purposes of internal status calculations. To suppose otherwise would be to suppose that the demand for status could be well-satisfied by hiring a derelict.

If it is difficult to form groups of disparately skilled workers, then the implicit prices of high-ranked positions need not be the same for all groups. On the contrary, the need for a certain degree of productive homogeneity within each group permits the price of a high-ranked position in one group to remain higher or lower than in another group. Because demands for status rise with income, the slopes of the earnings schedules for groups with high average productivity levels should be flatter than for groups with low productivity levels, as depicted in Figure 5.1.

In practice, it does in fact appear that the closest we ever come to seeing pure piece-rate pay schemes is in the wage schedules of impoverished immigrant sweatshop workers and farm laborers. By contrast, piece-rate pay schemes of any sort are almost unheard of in the upper reaches of the labor market. Granted, it is more difficult to measure individual contributions to output in highly skilled groups. This by itself would make it harder to

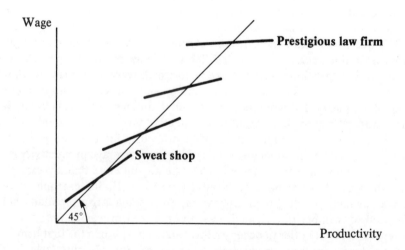

Figure 5.1 Earnings Schedules When Demands for Status Rise with Income

implement piece-rate schemes for such groups. Just the same, one can get a reasonable idea of individual productivity differences even in complex team production processes. And as I argued in Chapter 4, the slopes of earnings schedules in such cases do not even come close to reflecting these differences, and may not even be linked directly to productivity at all. At Cravath, Swaine, and Moore, for example (perhaps the most prestigious law firm in the United States), partners with eight years of experience or more in that rank all receive $855,000 per year regardless of the number of hours they bill.[27]

Nonpecuniary Elements of Compensation

I have focused up to now on how concerns about status affect the structure of monetary compensation. It is clear, however, that interpersonal comparisons also focus on various nonmonetary job characteristics.

Consider, for example, the case of job titles. Being vice president of a company once meant being next in line to the person in charge of the whole organization. But no longer. Of the 1100 employees of a large advertising agency in New York City, for example, 150 have the title of vice president. The same agency has 11 senior vice presidents, and, above these, 11 executive vice presidents. In one large New York City bank, most management employees who avoid offending anyone become vice presidents after five years of service with the firm. This bank has several hundred vice presidents, 50 senior vice presidents, and 10 executive vice presidents. Why so many titled positions?

Using the analysis of the monetary wage structure in Chapter 3, we can easily show why a firm with several vice presidents might do better than an otherwise identical firm with only one. To illustrate, let us consider an earlier day in which each of numerous identical firms had a president and only one vice president. What happens in such an environment if someone then establishes a firm with a president, an executive vice president, and vice presidents for both production and marketing? Because the title of vice president confers greater status than do the existing titles of marketing or production director, some marketing and production directors from incumbent firms will be willing to work for the new firm at a salary less than they currently enjoy. The fundamentally reciprocal nature of status suggests that, while these titles confer advantage to their recipients, they simultaneously reduce the status of those subordinate employees whose job descriptions have not changed. In large markets, however, we know there will be at least some people willing to pay enough for the titles to offset the losses they cause subordinates. We may expect, then, that some successful firms will have multiple vice presidents and will pay these executives less, and their lower staffs more, than will firms with only one vice president.

Concerns about status appear to affect group titles as well. At Cornell University, for example, there is a unit called the "Theoretical and Applied Mechanics Department." People in this department specialize in mechanics, which is a branch of physics. Since there are only two kinds of mechanics— theoretical and applied—any curious person quickly wonders why these people

"I don't know, Al. On the one hand, there's no doubt
that it's a make-work, dead-end job, but, on the other
hand, it's also a vice-presidency."

do not simply call themselves the "Mechanics Department." It would be hard to prove conclusively that their reason for not doing so is to avoid being mistaken for people who repair automobiles. Yet none of the faculty members in the Theoretical and Applied Mechanics Department to whom I have put this question has been able to offer any other coherent rationale for their conspicuously uneconomical choice of a department title.

Titles are free for the giving, but many nonsalary compensation items cost real resources to provide. Obvious tax motivations underlie the provision of certain fringe benefits, such as life and health insurance. But why would a firm spend large sums providing job-related amenities for some employees rather than give them an equivalent salary increment, which they could then spend or not, as they saw fit, on those same (tax-deductible) amenities? Why, for example, do chaired professorships in universities carry with them sizable research budgets rather than salaries that are larger by the amounts of those budgets? One possible explanation is that the provision of nonsalary compensation items may be an expedient device for rewarding relatively productive employees without stimulating excessive ripple effects throughout the lower end of the wage scale. If salary levels are the primary focus of co-worker interpersonal comparisons, it may well be cheaper, for example, for a university to give a chaired professor a $60,000 salary and a $60,000 research budget than to provide only a salary of, say, $75,000, which might satisfy the professor equally well as the larger combined package.*

Why are workers more tolerant of a co-worker's lofty title or costly fringe benefit than they would be of his higher salary? After all, titles are printed on one's door, visible for all to see, whereas salaries, even if known, come in sealed envelopes. A possible answer may be that the maintenance of a collegial environment involves interactions not only between co-workers themselves, but between their families as well. Tensions arise when some members of a group can afford to take frequent vacations and send their children to private schools while others cannot. Differentiation through the use of job titles and certain fringe benefits, rather than through salaries, would limit such tensions.

The use of nonpecuniary devices to reduce compensation costs is an art perhaps nowhere more finely developed than in the bureaucracies of various governments. As anyone who has ever served in the federal government knows, there exists an extremely broad range of ability and dedication among the ranks of upper-level civil servants. Some routinely put in 70-hour work weeks, while others accomplish little more each day than a careful reading of the *Washington Post*. Yet the presence of salary ceilings has all but completely eliminated any differences in the monetary compensation these bureaucrats receive. What appears to hold the package together is a variety of strategically employed nonmonetary compensation items. Of these, a bewildering array of titles is perhaps the most conspicuous. Such labels as "division chief," "bureau director," "associate office director," or "deputy assistant secretary" mean little to outsiders, but to insiders they convey important information about where those who hold them stand in the Washington hierarchy.

But titles are only the beginning. The General Services Administration, which supplies office furnishings to federal bureaucrats, has established "use standards" in its Federal Property Management Regulations. The stated purpose of these standards is to assure that the bureaucrat's office and equipment permit him to "conduct his normal business in an efficient manner and with a reasonable degree of dignity."[28] What constitutes a reasonable degree of dignity depends, of course, on one's position in the bureaucracy. Top-level executives get "executive" wood furniture, middle management get "unitized" wood furniture, while all others make do with contemporary steel, general steel, or general wood furniture. Top bureaucrats get dictionary stands and water carafes, while others do not. (Those with dictionary stands are allotted four square feet of office space to accommodate them.) Higher-ups get wooden waste baskets, while those lower down get ones made of steel. At the very highest levels, offices come with their own bathrooms, and the plumbing fixtures tell a lot about where their occupants stand in the Washing-

---

*One might argue that the university's reason for offering the research budget instead of additional salary is to stimulate the production of additional research. At least in the sciences, however, most faculty members distinguished enough to occupy a chair would have no difficulty in securing sufficient external support for their research efforts. To the extent that guaranteeing internal support for these chaired professors discourages some of them from applying for external funds, the direct costs of this practice are even higher.

ton pecking order. Those whose bathrooms measure 45 square feet or more and have a shower, toilet, wash bowl, and vanity are definitely near the top of the heap, while those with only a toilet and sink have not quite made it. Conference rooms, kitchens, television sets, carpets, and a host of other signals alert callers as to just whom they are dealing with.

The government has even thought to extend the trappings of rank, so visible in the office, to the executive's home neighborhood. Those executives who have gotten near the top of Washington's ranking scheme will be picked up at their homes in the morning and delivered back in the evening by a government-owned, chauffeur-driven car. Sleek black custom limousines are reserved for a small elite, while those further down are transported in tan or gray, fuel-efficient, mid-size, production cars.

Viewed from the outside, there is something vaguely absurd about all of these distinctions. To many taxpayers, the expenditures required for the government to maintain them must seem a poor use of scarce public funds. These distinctions, however, apparently play a vital communications role in the workings of the bureaucracy. And their net effect may very well be to reduce the government's total compensation expenses, not increase them.

Relative Standing and the Economics of a Fair Price

There are certain entertainment events that are always sold out well in advance of when they occur. Tickets for Michael Jackson concerts, championship prize fights, the Super Bowl, the Wimbledon finals, and the World Series never last long at the box office.[29] Often they cannot be obtained through official outlets even well in advance of the event unless one is willing to stand overnight in a line or endure some other gross inconvenience.

Yet anyone willing to pay the price can always get tickets to these events simply by purchasing them on the so-called black market. It is not uncommon to see black market prices for such tickets to be large multiples of their original prices. Tickets to the 1984 Super Bowl that were supposed to sell for $60, for example, changed hands privately at prices up to $600.[30] Why, in such cases, do promoters not simply set aside large blocks of tickets, which they could then sell at the inflated prices now being received by ticket scalpers? Why do they repeatedly give away such a large part of the purse that appears to be theirs for the taking?

Why, similarly, is it impossible to find a hotel room during these entertainment events in the cities that host them? And why is it impossible to get a table at the most popular restaurants without calling several days in advance?

The traditional theory of competitive markets finds such observations unintelligible. This theory predicts that when something is consistently and predictably in short supply, its price must rise. Yet in circumstances such as the ones mentioned, prices do not rise. Or, if they do, it is not by enough to discourage the queues of eager would-be buyers.

Such observations are not nearly so puzzling, however, in a framework in

Drawing by Gini Curl.

Figure 5.2 Contrary to the economist's standard supply and demand model, the prices of certain scarce goods persist below market clearing levels.

which people take a strong, if often unstated, interest in the incomes of the people and organizations with whom they engage in market transactions. To see why, it is helpful to look carefully at just what takes place in a voluntary market transaction. When one party sells something to another, it is presumed that both parties benefit. The gain to the buyer will be the difference between what economists call his "reservation price" and the price he actually pays. His reservation price is defined as the most he would have been willing to pay for an item, rather than do without it entirely. By the same token, the gain to the seller is the difference between the prices she gets and her own reservation price, which, in turn, is the lowest price she would have been willing to accept, rather than forego the sale. The total surplus available to be divided up between the buyer and the seller is thus the difference between their respective reservation prices. If, for example, the buyer's reservation price for an item is $10 and the seller's reservation price is $6, there is then a $4 surplus.

In Chapter 2, I suggested that the concept of the local hierarchy embraces not only those with whom one associates on a close and continuing basis, but also any others with whom one might reasonably be viewed as competing for resources. To the extent that buyers and sellers compete for shares of whatever surplus exists when they consummate a transaction, each may thus be thought of as a member of the other's local hierarchy. The question of how the surplus is to be divided will thus play a role in determining whether or not the transaction will be consummated. This view contrasts with the position of standard economic theory, which holds that (strategic bargaining considerations aside) a transaction will take place if and only if the buyer's reservation price exceeds the seller's.

Thaler has produced experimental evidence suggesting that how the surplus is to be divided does, in fact, strongly influence people's decisions about whether or not to engage in particular transactions.[31] He asked two groups of experimental subjects to imagine themselves on a hot beach, feeling a deep thirst that would be nicely quenched by a cold bottle of beer. They were told to imagine that they have a friend, whom they trust, who offers to go and get them a bottle of beer. One group of experimental subjects was told that the friend will buy the beer from a resort hotel; the other that he will buy it from a supermarket. People in the two groups were told to write down the maximum price they would be willing to pay for the beer. The median response for subjects in the resort hotel group was $2.65. That is, the median subject in that group told his friend to return empty-handed if the hotel charges more than $2.65 for the bottle of beer. By contrast, the corresponding median response for the supermarket group was only $1.50. Thaler has obtained similar responses in numerous replications of this experiment. Even though people's desires for the cold beer presumably run equally strong in both groups, people in the supermarket group insist that they would rather do without the beer than pay the same price that people in the resort hotel group would gladly pay.

Thaler explains this anomaly by saying that people have an aversion to paying what they perceive is an "unfair" price for any item.[32] A fair price, in turn, he argues is linked to the buyer's perception of what it costs the seller to offer the product. Because a resort hotel has higher costs than a supermarket does, a fair price for a beer it sells will thus be higher than for one sold by a supermarket.

Why should aversion to paying an unfair price lead people to do without something even when it is really worth more to them than that price? One possible answer is that people may benefit strongly from an aversion to being taken advantage of, even if it occasionally causes them to pass up otherwise attractive opportunities (see Chapter 2). Viewed in this light, a fair price is a price that does not greatly alter the relative standing of the two parties to the transaction. Perhaps most people would resent paying a grocer $2 for a bottle of beer, knowing that the grocer would thus be gaining ground at their expense. It is not only the price itself, then, but also its effect on relative position that the buyer seems to care about.

People's aversion to seemingly unfair transactions appears to have broad implications for the prices they pay for goods and services. Consider, for example, the case of haircuts. Many barbershops are extremely crowded on Saturdays but not very busy during the rest of the week. For such barbershops, traditional economic theory insists that the price of a haircut should be higher on Saturdays than on other days. And some barbershops do, in fact, offer discounts for haircuts during weekdays. Yet most barbershops charge the same price for a haircut no matter what day of the week it is. My conversations with a handful of barbershop owners suggest they fear that many of their customers would be offended if they charged higher prices on Saturdays— and would then take their trade elsewhere, not only on Saturdays, but on other days of the week as well. In the customer's eyes, the cost of producing a haircut on Saturday does not appear different from the cost of producing one on weekdays. Many of the customers who cannot come during the week apparently would prefer to wait in line at a crowded barbershop than to be served promptly in a barbershop that they feel is overcharging them—even though, in the abstract, the time they would save at the latter barbershop would be worth much more to them than the extra cost of the haircut there.

Similarly, when the owner of a popular restaurant sets his price dramatically higher than what his patrons perceive to be his costs, many of these patrons are apparently offended and take their trade elsewhere, even though they might well have been willing to pay that price had it been more in line with the restaurateur's expenses. In the case of premium entertainment events, people who pay a ticket scalper $200 for tickets that originally sold for $20 often express contempt for the scalper, and even vote for laws making ticket scalping illegal. But there is no question that, for many of them, it is well worth paying the $200 in order to avoid missing the event. Management, however, cannot charge these same people $200 without offending many of them, and risking their future business. The ticket scalper, by contrast, has nothing comparable at stake and is therefore in a position to suffer the buyer's resentment with relatively greater impunity.

Building on the observation that the buyer's perception of a fair price relates closely to the firm's costs, Thaler has suggested that firms can sometimes boost their prices by making it appear that their costs have gone up.[33] For example, he cites the instance in which hoteliers require guests to book rooms for a mimimum of several days surrounding the day of a popular event. Buyers who would resent being charged $300 for a room on the Saturday night before the Super Bowl (and refuse to patronize any hotel chain that charged such a high price) are apparently much more willing to pay $400 for the same room from Thursday through Monday, even though they still make use of the room only on Saturday. Many of these rooms would have been empty on the other nights anyway, and thus cost the hotelier little to offer. But including them in the package seems to make buyers feel they have gotten their money's worth.

Viewed within the framework of the economist's standard model, pricing practices of this sort appear altogether bizarre. But by recognizing the importance of people's concerns about relative standing, we see that these

"We're earmarking $16,500,000 of our net profits to finance a nationwide public-relations compaign to correct the current impression that we're making too much money."

practices are in fact consistent with the economist's view that people and firms act in purposeful, self-serving ways. To insist that people care little about relative standing is to focus on a world that does not exist.

I have confined the discussion thus far to cases in which people's concerns about relative standing might influence the structure of private market transactions. Of course, the nature of these transactions does not prove that concerns about relative standing cause them to take the particular forms they do. But a picture nonetheless emerges from this discussion that is consistent with the claim that people care deeply about where they stand in their various local hierarchies. And in later chapters, I will discuss evidence that further supports this claim.

That concerns about status might influence the structure of voluntary private transactions is not, on its face, a controversial notion. In the next chapter, however, I argue that these concerns spill over into the public arena as well, where they become very controversial indeed.

Six

Why Redistributive Taxation?

The Fairness Argument

Most countries have redistributive tax and expenditure systems. The existence of these systems is often rationalized by appealing to commonly held notions of fairness. Since well-to-do members of society are better able to afford the costs of government, it is said that taxes should claim a larger share of their incomes. As Cordell Hull put it to the House of Representatives in 1913, a progressive tax on income would "equalize existing tax burdens, requiring every citizen to contribute to the government in proportion to his ability to pay."[1]

In other circumstances, such fairness arguments tell us very little about the actual sacrifices one group is willing to make on behalf of another. A strong fairness argument can be made, for example, that inhabitants of the earth should be free to live in whatever country they choose. In spite of this argument, most well-developed nations have tightly controlled borders. And among those who seek to immigrate, strong preference is often shown to persons of wealth and high educational attainment. These restrictions contradict traditional fairness notions. Yet they persist because citizens of developed nations believe that their abandonment would lead to increased crowding and sharply reduced incomes.

Without denying the existence of genuinely charitable impulses, we may note that people's willingness to exploit their power to enhance their own well-being seems widespread—sufficiently widespread, in any event, to make us question whether the ideal of fairness really explains why countries so consistently redistribute income. In this chapter, I explore an alternative approach to explaining redistributive fiscal systems, one very similar to the one I took in Chapter 3 to explain competitive wage structures. In this approach, transfers from rich to poor emerge as a necessary feature of a particular social contract that creates significant advantages for rich and poor alike. In order to call attention to the essential differences between this approach and existing approaches to the theory of distributive justice, I begin by briefly reviewing the contributions of John Rawls and Robert Nozick.

Rawls and Nozick on Distributive Justice

In *A Theory of Justice,*[2] Rawls has developed an illuminating framework for thinking about what constitutes a fair distribution of income. He begins by imagining people in an "original position" behind a "veil of ignorance," which prevents them from knowing anything about their skills, talents, or material wealth. From behind this veil, they are asked to decide what the distributional rules of society should be once the veil is lifted. Rawls notes that the natural impulse of a cautious person is to choose strict equality in the distribution of income. But he argues that this impulse is tempered by the realization that such a scheme would greatly reduce the total output available to be shared. After all, economic goods do not fall like manna from heaven; people must take risks and expend effort to produce them. If the total economic pie were shared equally, the size of any one person's slice would be virtually unaffected by his own contribution to it. Under these circumstances, why would people bother to take risks and expend effort for the purpose of enlarging the pie?

Drawing by Mankoff. Copyright © 1981 The New Yorker Magazine, Inc.

Rawls concludes that people in the original position will permit some inequality for the purpose of maintaining economic incentives. But they will do so only as long as it raises the income of society's least well-off member. Rawls argues, in effect, that people in his original position will adopt the most cautious strategy available. Many writers have objected that persons behind Rawls's veil of ignorance might be willing to take a more daring position than that.[3] If greater inequality would raise the incomes of all but, say, the poorest 5 percent of the population by a sufficiently large amount, many might prefer that option to the one put forward by Rawls.

But that is a minor detail. I take Rawls's main point to be that people deciding distributional questions behind a veil of ignorance would opt for considerably greater equality than would emerge under completely unregulated conditions. And this claim seems indisputably to capture an essential element of the way people would actually behave. The appeal of Rawls's framework is that people resolve the distribution issue before they know their endowments of talent, ability, health, energy, charm, and the like. To the extent that these endowments are essentially a matter of luck, Rawls has made a persuasive case that redistribution is required in the name of fairness. That, of course, does not explain why we actually see redistributive policies enacted into law, for laws are enacted not behind a veil of ignorance, but with reasonably full knowledge of their probable consequences for specific individuals.

Nozick, in his *Anarchy, State, and Utopia,*[4] counters Rawls by saying that the decisions people would make from behind a veil of ignorance are not sufficient to determine what constitutes a fair distribution of income. After all, such decisions take no account of actual *processes* by which incomes are generated. If we focus only on the result of the distribution process, Nozick argues, we are forced to conclude that two identical income distributions are equally just no matter what processes may have produced them. One that resulted through fraud and thievery, for example, would have to be considered just as fair as another that resulted from free exchange.

Nozick then offers persuasive arguments for his "entitlement theory" of distributive justice, which rests on the following premise: If we start from an initial income distribution that we agree is fair, and move to a new one through a process of free and voluntary exchange, then the new distribution is also fair. Those who find this premise reasonable will encounter difficult questions should they then attempt to defend the Rawlsian view of distributive justice. As Nozick writes:

It is not clear how those holding alternative conceptions of distributive justice can reject the entitlement conception of justice in holdings. For suppose a distribution favored by one of these nonentitlement conceptions is realized. Let us suppose it is your favorite one and let us call this distribution D_1; perhaps everyone has an equal share, perhaps shares vary in accordance with some dimension you treasure. Now suppose that Wilt Chamberlain is greatly in demand by basketball teams, being a great gate attraction. (Also suppose *contracts run only for a year, with players being free agents.) He signs the following sort of contract with a team: In each home game, twenty-five cents from the price of each ticket of admission goes to him. (We ignore the question of whether he is "gouging" the owners, letting them look out for themselves.) The season starts, and people cheerfully attend his team's games; they buy their tickets, each time dropping a separate twenty-five cents of their admission price into a special box with Chamberlain's name on it. They are excited about seeing him play; it is worth the total admission price to them. Let us suppose that in one season one million persons attend his home games, and Wilt Chamberlain winds up with $250,000, a much larger sum than the average income and larger even than anyone else has. Is he entitled to this income? Is this new distribution, D_2, unjust? If so, why? There is no question about whether each of the people was entitled to the control over the resources they held in D_1; because that was the distribution (your favorite) that (for the purposes of argument) we assumed was acceptable. Each of these persons chose to give twenty-five cents of their money to Chamberlain. They could have spent it on going to the movies, or on candy bars, or on copies of* Dissent *magazine, or of* Monthly Review. *But they all, at least one million of them, converged on giving it to Wilt Chamberlain in exchange for watching him play basketball. If D_1 was a just distribution, and people voluntarily moved from it to D_2, transferring parts of their shares they were given under D_1 (what was it for if not to do something with?) isn't D_2 also just? If the people were entitled to dispose of the resources to which they were entitled (under D_1), didn't this include their being entitled to give it to, or exchange it with, Wilt Chamberlain? Can anyone else complain on grounds of justice? Each other person already has his legitimate share under D_1. Under D_1, there is nothing that anyone has that anyone else has a claim of justice against. After someone transfers something to Wilt Chamberlain, third parties still have their legitimate shares; their shares are not changed. By what process could such a transfer among two persons give rise to a legitimate claim of distributive justice on a portion of what was transferred, by a third party who had no claim of justice on any holding of the others before the transfer? . . .*[5]

In Nozick's framework, whether a person's talents and skills are a matter of luck or not, they are an essential part of his being. He is entitled to do with them what he will. He may be moved by Rawls's arguments to share the fruits of his talents but cannot be forced by the state to do so without violating his rights. Nozick has offered, in effect, a detailed and thoughtful defense of the distributional scheme put forward by such free-market proponents as Milton Friedman, who writes:

The ethical principle that would directly justify the distribution of income in a free society is: to each according to what he and the instruments he owns produces.[6]

Nozick elaborates only slightly on this principle, to allow for gifts and other voluntary transfers:

From each according to what he chooses to do, to each according to what he makes for himself (perhaps with the contracted aid of others) and what others choose to do for him and choose to give him of what they've been given previously (under this maxim) and haven't yet expended or transferred.[7]

Nozick continues:

This, the discerning reader will have noticed, has its defects as a slogan. So as a summary and great simplification (and not as a maxim with any independent meaning) we have: "From each as they choose, to each as they are chosen."[8]

As persuasive as Nozick's arguments may be to those who value individual liberty highly (and to those who have a lot of talent and wealth), they do not seem to provide a very good *description* of what governments actually do. As noted at the outset, most societies have redistributive tax systems and take many other specific steps to transfer income from rich to poor. Indeed, the theory articulated by Rawls seems to fit much better than Nozick's the actual pattern of governmental tax and expenditure programs we observe in the world. Granted, Nozick did not offer his entitlement theory as a description of reality. Even so, because what actually happens differs so consistently from the recommendations that follow from his arguments, we are faced with something of a puzzle. Albeit imperfectly, the well-to-do and talented appear to be doing what they *ought* to do (according to Rawls's theory of fairness, at least), instead of what it appears in their narrow interests to do.

Now, the rich and talented obviously do not have unlimited power to structure society's rules to their own liking. Yet neither can the poor forge a society whose rules are all stacked against the rich. On the contrary, the balance of power in practice is likely to favor the wealthy. Why, then, have those who bear the burden of redistributive taxation cooperated with such programs to the degree they seem to have? Would they, if they could, form separate societies in which the beneficiaries of redistributive taxation are excluded? Let us now turn to these questions.

An Alternative Theory of Redistributive Taxation

As did Rawls, I approach the distributive justice question with the help of a simple thought experiment. Specifically, I suppose that a representative group of people with no previous commitments has just emerged from a large ark in the wake of a flood that has destroyed all existing property and social arrangements. They are faced with the task of forming a new society or group of societies. In confronting this task, each person is assigned the following in-alienable right:

No society shall form except by the voluntary agreement of each member to associate with every other member of that society and to abide by such rules and procedures as its members may agree to adopt.

Given this right, the decision to form a society resembles the decision to enter into a marriage contract. The agreement can be consummated only with the explicit consent of all parties concerned. The framework outlined here is thus a libertarian framework, insofar as no person may be compelled under any circumstances to do anything against his wishes.

I also assume that land is homogeneous and is allocated in equal-sized parcels to each person once societies form, with members of each society receiving contiguous parcels. Each society's state border is the perimeter of its collection of contiguous parcels, and all of its laws apply to whoever chooses to live within its borders.

It is only for convenience that I assume here that landholdings start out equally divided. Because people's abilities differ, there will soon emerge corresponding differences in wealth holdings if members of a society are allowed to trade freely with one another (as in Nozick's Wilt Chamberlain example). Thus, the usual questions of distributional equity will arise with essentially the same force here as they would have if I had instead assumed some dispersion in the initial distribution of land and other material wealth holdings. (More on this point in Chapter 9.)

Within the framework set out above, the task facing these hypothetical people is different in at least two important respects from the one set out by Rawls in *A Theory of Justice*. There, people did not have the option of forming smaller groups on their own.[9] They also would not have had any particular reason to, operating as they were behind Rawls's veil of ignorance. Here, by contrast, people can form separate societies. Moreover, they have full knowledge of their tastes and abilities, and thus can easily determine when a particular set of social rules will prove contrary to their narrow interests. The most able individuals among them may feel it their duty to join a society of others less well-endowed than themselves. But they may not be compelled to do so without violating their rights.

Some readers may complain that, by allowing the talented to form separate societies of their own, the very structure of this exercise guarantees an unfair outcome, in the sense defined by Rawls. To be sure, it is possible to argue that a truly fair system might impose some obligation on the talented to remain and share the fruits of their talents. Yet what if the less talented persons decided to form a separate society on *their* own? Shouldn't *they* be granted that right? And if they *are* granted that right, can the relatively more talented then be denied a parallel right? By what standard of fairness could we insist that one group be granted that right but not the other?

I raise these questions here not to insist that freedom of association should be clearly acceptable to everyone as a just moral principle. Readers will obviously have their own views on that issue. Instead, I raise them to call attention to the fact that the social contracting exercise I am about to discuss has a dual purpose. I will attempt to establish, first, that *if* one believes that freedom of association should be granted at the society formation stage, it then becomes very difficult to deny the moral legitimacy of redistributive taxation. For, as I will argue, such tax structures would almost surely emerge as the result of purely voluntary choices made by self-interested parties endowed with very powerful initial rights. I intend in part, therefore, to criticize the libertarian position by its own terms.

My second purpose is the positive one stated at the outset—a quest for further insight into why redistributive taxation is so widespread. I will argue that *any* tax structure, redistributive or not, may be viewed as an implicit distributional contract that applies to all of a society's members. If this contract is to succeed, it must create mutual advantages for all involved. Otherwise, social fragmentation will result, the high costs of which are experienced in parallel ways by rich and poor alike. I will argue that the natural desire to avoid these costs helps account for why redistributive taxation is so often encountered in modern societies.

To gain insight into what sorts of societies people might form when they have the option of choosing their own associates, it is necessary to make some assumptions about their abilities and tastes. In order to focus on distributional questions at all, it is obviously necessary to assume that people's abilities differ significantly. As for tastes, I again assume that satisfaction depends on both absolute and relative income.

Given freedom of association, individual differences in productivity, and the importance of income and rank, what kinds of societies will these hypothetical ark passengers sort themselves into? The similarity between this question and the one I discussed in Chapter 3 (about how people with such characteristics would sort themselves into private firms) is readily apparent. Indeed, if one's firm were the only hierarchy one cared about, the two questions would be formally identical. People would sort themselves into firms according to how much they were willing to pay for high-ranked positions, and the functional equivalent of a redistributive income tax would be observed in the wage structure of every firm, just as described in Chapter 3. The most productive people in each firm would be paid less than the value of what they produce, while the least productive people would be paid more.

Now, some libertarians might disdain the preference structure that produces this outcome. But within their framework, they would find no legitimate grounds to object, since everything would have been completely voluntary. Actually, libertarians and others who profess to take no interest in their associates' incomes would make out very well here. They could receive wage premiums for occupying low-ranked positions in firms, which, by their own account, would not bother them.

For most people, however, it is safe to assume that the firm is not the only hierarchy in which relative standing matters. When other hierarchies besides firms are important, we must consider an additional layer of complexity in the sorting process, one in which the members of one firm consider the terms on which they would be willing to associate with the members of other firms. (In fact, these two sorting decisions are not independent; they would have to be considered simultaneously in a more formal discussion. I treat them here as if they could be handled sequentially, which greatly simplifies matters and does not alter in any way the point I wish to illustrate.)

To make the discussion concrete, suppose that people have initially sorted themselves into two types of firms—one involving workers of low average productivity levels, and the other involving workers of high average productivity levels. Suppose, more specifically, that the people here earn their living by farming and that there are two types of farms: Type P farms, in which farmers grow an average of 100 bushels of grain per year, and Type R farms, in which farmers average 200 bushels of grain per year. Each type of farm must decide whether to participate in the same society with the other.

Now suppose, as in Chapter 3, that some external power imposes the constraint that transfer payments between the two types of farms not be allowed. Let us suppose, that is, that the distributional maxim recommended by Friedman is imposed here, not person by person as Friedman intended, but farm by farm: A farm's total income is whatever it produces, no more, no less. Once this constraint is imposed, we get the same type of result that the analogous constraint produced in Chapter 3. Two separate societies would form, one composed only of Type P farms, the second with only farms of Type R. Why should the Type P farmers join a society in which they will be second-rank citizens?

But, as before, there is no reason to suppose such fragmentation would occur if redistributive transfers were not prohibited. To see why, suppose that each person would be willing to pay up to 20 percent of his income to be in the top half of his society's income hierarchy, and would have to be given at least that same amount to accept bottom-half status. If transfer payments can be freely made, having a single society in which farmers of Type R average 165 bushels per year while those of Type P average 135 will be better for everyone than the alternative of two separate societies. Granted, a single society in which R farms average 200 and P farms average 100 would be better still from each R's point of view. But this, as noted, is not feasible—the P farms by assumption would rather live separately than earn 100 bushels per year in a society in which they make up the bottom half of the income hierarchy.

If people value both status and material goods, and if they are free to form societies with whomever they wish, then transfer payments (which are equivalent to a redistributive income tax schedule) are necessary for the achievement of the most-preferred social structure. Hardly a burden on the high-ranking members of the various societies, redistributive taxes are rather the means without which these members would be unable to achieve their favored positions.

Now, the idea that the rich would gladly pay the poor for their continued presence may strike many readers as implausible, not to say utterly absurd. But I am not claiming here that the very rich derive satisfaction by comparing their circumstances to those of the very poor. Nor, for that matter, are the poor likely to be troubled much by direct comparisons with the very rich. As Bertrand Russell once put it, "Beggars do not envy millionaires, though of course they will envy other beggars who are more successful."[10] The comparisons that count for people are the ones with others most like themselves. The rich do not compare themselves directly with the poor, but they do compare themselves with people of similar means. And among the well-to-do, as among less favored groups, it will be preferable to have high rank rather than low rank. Group A, which is rich, benefits from its comparison with Group B, which is also rich, but slightly less so. Group B, in turn, benefits from its standing in relation to Group C, which has slightly less income than it does. The chain of such comparisons stops with the lowest-ranked group on the income scale. As with the domino effect discussed in Chapter 3, the presence of the lowest-ranked group thus benefits the highest-ranked group indirectly: It constitutes the foundation of a chain of comparisons whose highest links are of direct value to Group A.

Some readers may still insist that they would never voluntarily give up a substantial portion of their income "merely" to occupy a high-ranked position in the social hierarchy. Perhaps those high-income readers who do not consider their current high relative standing that important will find it illuminating to consider a simple thought experiment. In this experiment you are to imagine yourself in the following situation: As a high-income resident of the United States, you are suddenly confronted with an opportunity to be transported to a much richer planet. The trip is to be free of charge, but with no option to return. You are a genuine standout here on Earth. You earn $100,000 per year and live in a tastefully decorated home in a quiet, fashionable neighborhood. Your children are enrolled in the best schools and are very popular among their classmates. You are happily married to a person you hold in high esteem, who regards you likewise. You are a person of integrity, a highly respected expert in your profession, and are in good health. You enjoy peace of mind and the admiration and affection of a large group of friends, who regard you as one of the most charming and caring people they know.

On the new planet your income would be $1,000,000 per year. But instead of being near the top of the income scale as you are here, you would be at the bottom. The home you would be able to afford there is much larger and better appointed than the one you live in here. Yet it is located in a marginal neighborhood, one that people urge their children not to venture into. You would pursue the same occupation there as you do here. But the people on the new planet are so skilled that they regard your profession in the way we think of repetitive, assembly tasks here. The schools your children would go to there compare very favorably with the ones they go to here, but among schools on the new planet they are thought to be ill-equipped and poorly staffed. Although your children will amass more knowledge in those schools than they do in the ones here, they will struggle there on the academic borderline, instead of bringing home A's as they do here. Although your children are much sought after by their classmates here, you will discover on the new planet that most parents attempt to steer their children to more suitable playmates. You will recount the same anecdotes there as you do here, but your friends there will regard them as simple and boring, instead of clever and erudite as your friends here regard them. Although your spouse will love you equally there as here, you know that, once there, he or she cannot fail to notice how the achievements of others surpass your own.

Confronted with this thought experiment, someone who decides to remain on Earth rather than move to the splendid new planet reveals that his high-ranked position here is worth at least $900,000 per year to him. (Most of those who *would* take the trip probably never made it as far as Chapter 6 of this book.*) Now, saying that a high-ranked position in society is a thing of real value is exactly the same as saying that a low-ranked position imposes real costs. And if one can imagine giving up valuable resources in order to avoid being in a low-ranked position, one ought to be able to imagine making sacrifices (in the form of high taxes) to be in a high-ranked position. The gains and losses from status in any hierarchy are simply two sides of the same coin.

This social contracting exercise is in several important respects a highly stylized one. What can it tell us about the role of redistributive taxation in the societies we actually observe? What happens if, as is always the case in practice, there is much less freedom of mobility than assumed? If people are stuck in the societies they are born into, why would the rich then feel any need to make compensation payments to the poor? Is it proper to levy taxes on them to facilitate the formation of hierarchies they may have no interest in joining? What about the wealthy person who takes no interest in what others earn? Can it conceivably be a legitimate use of state power to tax that person just because other people envy his standard of living? And even if many people want to make transfer payments to facilitate associations outside the work-place, why can these transfer payments not be made on a purely voluntary basis? Why must the state use the force of law to carry them out? Let us consider these and related questions.

Voluntary Private Compensation Agreements

Suppose, for the moment, that most of the well-to-do *want* to make compen-sating payments to the poor, for the reasons discussed above. Why can such payments not be carried out voluntarily, as they are in the case of private firms? Recall that in private firms, it is simple for the relatively more pro-ductive employees to compensate the relatively less productive employees for the unfavorable positions they occupy in the firm's earnings hierarchy. Indeed, such compensation payments take place automatically without any employees ever having to lift a finger. Firms simply announce earnings schedules that

---

*One might argue that millions of impoverished American immigrants have made a very similar sort of move to the one contemplated in this thought experiment. But there is at least one critical difference. While the immigrants may be willing to accept temporarily a position at the bottom of the economic order, they have every reason to believe that in time there will be opportunities to advance. For the thought experiment to bear on the question it addresses, such opportunities must be assumed away.

implicitly incorporate these payments, and then let workers choose positions along these schedules.

Once we leave the confines of the firm, however, it becomes more troublesome to carry out such compensation payments privately, but still possible to do so. For example, within social circles it is possible for those with relatively high incomes to absorb more than a proportional share of the group's joint expenses and nonfinancial burdens. Those with the largest homes may do most of the entertaining or be expected to entertain more lavishly. Or perhaps they are asked to perform a disproportionate share of the most burdensome committee assignments. Developers may even construct self-contained neighborhoods in which membership is required in neighborhood associations that have progressive fee schedules.[11]

But such devices have clear limits. When the members of one Type R farm make payments to induce the members of a Type P farm to remain in their society, the Rs reap a benefit for themselves, but at the same time they create a benefit for all other Type R farms in that society. R's desire to purchase a favorable position in the social hierarchy from P thus presents the same set of difficulties we encounter in trying to provide any public good. Each group in society may want, for example, to enjoy protection from crime; yet each group knows that, if other groups finance a police force, it will then get to enjoy that protection for free. Where free-rider problems of this sort are sufficiently important, people will find it attractive to empower the states they form to mandate taxes to provide various public goods. Every R farm may be willing to pay for high status but each knows that if other R farms compensate the P farms it will then get high status for free. High standing in the social hierarchy is thus no different from any other public good. In order for people to have the amount of it that they really want, it may be necessary to act collectively.[12]

If redistributive taxes are to play a role within the libertarian framework set out in this discussion, then, it will be that of trying to mimic the compensation payments people would negotiate for themselves if only free-rider problems and other practical difficulties did not prevent them from doing so. The implicit role of the tax structure here is to secure cohesion and stability in the many formal and informal income hierarchies in which people would ideally like to participate outside the workplace. Given the nature of people's preferences, we have seen that, without such transfers, freedom of association results in what for many is a wastefully high degree of social fragmentation.

Individual Rights in the Face of Imperfect Mobility

Even if people were free at the outset to sort themselves into societies according to how much status they were willing to pay for, various rigidities would soon set in. Dialects would emerge, homes would be built, children would be born, networks of friends would develop, and a host of other commitments would be acquired. Such commitments would stand in the way of new societies forming if the terms of the original distributional agreement were ever to prove no longer attractive. With extensive commitments a part of the picture, we may note that it is one thing for a private firm to redistribute income through its internal wage structure but quite another for a national government to do so under force of law. One is free to leave one's firm to seek more suitable terms of employment elsewhere. But the costs of voting with one's feet to protest a national government policy are much more substantial. In view of this distinction, can we say that the interests of those who want redistributive tax structures are "legitimate"? There are surely some high-income people who would rather not join groups in which they are required to compensate others whose incomes are lower than their own. With redistributive taxation they are, in effect, denied that option.

We can clearly object to redistributive taxation on the grounds that some people have no desire for the state to supply favored positions in the social hierarchy as a public good. But this objection, by itself, is not sufficient, for the same objection can be raised concerning virtually any public good. Why would people join societies whose governments are empowered to collect taxes to build roads on which they know they will never travel? They do so in the expectation, or hope, that the *overall package* of public goods will be more attractive than the alternative in which unanimous support was required before proceeding with any project. When constitutions are drafted (or amended), then, there is no real loss of freedom entailed in granting elected representatives the power to levy taxes for the provision of public goods. As James Buchanan put it in *The Limits of Liberty:*

If . . . individual rights are defined as rights to do things with respect to some initial set of endowments or goods, along with membership in a collectivity that is empowered to act by less-than-unanimity rules, and, further, if these rights should be mutually accepted, it becomes inconsistent and self-contradictory for a person to claim his "rights" are violated in the mere working out of the collective decision rules that are constitutionally authorized.[13]

When society employs redistributive taxation, there will obviously be costs imposed on groups that object. Yet the completely reciprocal nature of the problem means that the alternative is to impose costs on those who want redistributive tax structures—namely, the wastefully high social fragmentation that results when we do not redistribute. The essential question, then, is whether one set of costs is more important to escape than the other.

The libertarian's answer to this question is often framed in terms of inviolable individual rights. In the libertarian's eyes, no other individual has a more just claim to the product of human effort than the person who actually expends that effort. As Michael Levin recently put it:

I understand the government's right to collect funds for purposes like national defense. This is part of the general welfare: it protects all of us. But Mr. Jones is lying in the ditch and he's starving. I didn't put him there, it's no fault of mine, and let's say it's no fault of his. Nevertheless, taking money from me to give to

Mr. Jones doesn't increase the general welfare. It increases Mr. Jones's welfare and decreases mine. Now, where does the government or any other party acquire the right to force me to give my money to Mr. Jones?[14]

To tax the rich to provide benefits to the poor does indeed deny the right of the rich to retain the full fruits of their labors. And if this right could be protected without cost, all societies would surely do so. But, again, rights are reciprocal in nature. To affirm the right to keep the full fruits of one's labor is to deny the right of others who desire redistributive taxation. Both rights cannot be upheld simultaneously. So a decision must be made as to which of these rights is to be sacrificed.

It is natural to consider moral arguments in trying to reach such a decision. And at least some of these arguments seem to favor the libertarian position. Many cultures, after all, embrace moral teachings that say it is wrong to envy another's material possessions, and we deeply admire people whose self-esteem does not seem to depend very strongly on how large their incomes are in relation to those of others. With these observations in mind, we may wonder whether one person's wish to have high status is as worthy of our moral respect as another's wish to keep the full fruits of his labors. Similarly, perhaps the poor should simply tolerate whatever feelings of relative deprivation they may experience in the presence of the rich.

I argue in succeeding chapters that moral condemnation of concerns about relative standing serves a practical purpose, because it helps suppress many harmful actions that are motivated by these concerns. Moral sanctions against concerns about position also help us to control the concerns themselves. If we are taught to be hostile toward them, we will be better able to suppress them, which is especially useful in circumstances where there is little we can do to alter the conditions that trigger them. After all, it is a clear waste of time and energy for people to be unhappily preoccupied with the inevitable fact that others earn more income than they do.

Yet these moral norms, by themselves, do not imply that concerns about relative standing are a morally unacceptable basis for redistributive taxation. We have moral norms, for example, that urge us to be tolerant of life-styles that differ from our own, yet that does not prevent us from passing laws that prevent others from killing and eating those animals we normally think of as pets. The justification for such laws centers, at least in part, on the question of which party would suffer more if denied its way. And, as discussed in Chapter 1, society seems to have decided that there are clear limits to the tolerance we can demand of pet lovers. Assigning positive moral value to tolerance does not mean that the costs of being tolerant should be ignored.

Similarly, assigning negative moral value to concerns about relative standing does not mean that the costs of having low standing in the income hierarchy are not legitimate costs. Nor does it mean that it is morally improper to structure one's environment with those costs in mind. A low-income parent may feel considerable anguish at not being able to provide the same educational advantages for his own children as most other parents provide for theirs. And in many instances, the power of introspection to neutralize these feelings will be limited. As we saw in Chapter 2, having low status may even impose measurable biochemical costs on people. People should, and presumably do, take whatever efforts they can to avoid these costs. But there may be physical limits to the degree to which they can will them away. The fact that society urges us to suppress our concerns about position does not mean that these concerns have no legitimate role in public policy decisions.

Nozick explicitly recognizes that the social urge to equalize income may have something to do with people's concerns about relative standing.[15] But he argues that steps taken to equalize income simply will not work because of human nature:

People generally judge themselves by how they fall along the most important dimensions in which they differ *from others. People do not gain self-esteem from their common human capacities by comparing themselves to animals who lack them. ("I'm pretty good; I have an opposable thumb and can speak some language.") . . . Self-esteem is based on differentiating characteristics; that's why it's self-esteem.*[16]

If the state succeeded in equalizing incomes, Nozick argues, people would then focus upon whatever other dimensions along which they differed, and the problem of some people having low self-esteem would be just as serious as before. He concludes:

The most promising ways for a society to avoid widespread differences in self-esteem would be to have no common weighting of dimensions; instead it would have a diversity of different lists of dimensions and of weightings. This would

enhance each person's chance of finding dimensions that some others also think important, along which he does reasonably well, and so to make a non-idiosyncratic favorable estimate of himself. Such a fragmentation of common social weighting is not to be achieved by some centralized effort to remove certain dimensions as important.[17]

Nozick's call for a diverse set of dimensions along which to seek affirmation and build self-esteem has obvious merit. And it may very well be that once income comparisons are downgraded, other invidious comparisons will take their place. After all, people do seem to have hierarchies of needs, and when the highest-priority need is met, the next-ranking need is then felt with the same intensity as the one before.[18] Yet these observations surely do not mean that people should take no actions to deal with their most pressing needs. If a man who is worried about his health realizes that once his health problem clears up he will begin worrying about his leaking roof, does that mean he should not bother seeing a doctor? As we have already seen in the behavior of participants in the labor market, people may feel strongly enough about the stress caused by unfavorable income comparisons to devote substantial resources toward reducing it. To say their efforts serve no useful purpose gives little credit to their judgment. Granted, income transfers may not solve the problem of low self-esteem for many people. Still, they do enable one's children to enter the world on more nearly equal footing with the children of one's associates, and this is something people seem to feel very strongly about.

Nozick initially argues on practical grounds against using concerns about relative standing as a basis for equalizing incomes. But the ultimate basis for his opposition rests on moral considerations. He argues, for example:

Even if envy is more tractable than our considerations imply, it would be objectionable to intervene to reduce someone's situation in order to lessen the envy and unhappiness others feel in knowing of his situation. Such a policy is comparable to one that forbids some act (for example, racially mixed couples walking holding hands) because the mere knowledge that it is being done makes others unhappy. The same kind of externality is involved.[19]

In some ways, at least, the externalities are of the same kind, just as the smoke from a campfire in the desert is the same kind of externality Consolidated Edison produces when it burns coal to generate electricity for Manhattan. Similarly, when one three-year-old unjustly accuses another of being a "meany-crabby-witchface," he creates the same kind of externality a journalist creates when he falsely charges a banker of corruption.

Although all of these externalities are alike in kind, they differ greatly in degree. And it is the degree of damage caused, not the kind of externality, that triggers state involvement. When the damage caused by a disparaging remark is small, for example, we rely on the victim to take his own evasive measures.

Once a certain threshold of damage is crossed, though, we turn to the legal system.

Similar considerations apply to the externality discussed by Nozick. Some people undoubtedly would claim that to witness an interracial couple holding hands in public causes them great anguish. To such people, the nonracist's impulse is to respond that people have a *right* to hold hands in public, even where the enforcement of that right causes anguish to other people. And, indeed, people do have such a right. But *why* do they have it? Why is the right to hold hands more worthy of our moral respect than the right to be free from sights that cause discomfort? The answer is surely at least partly rooted in very deep beliefs we hold about the sorts of adjustments people are capable of making. Granted, the racist might honestly feel profound discomfort today at the sight of the interracial couple. Still, we feel strongly that it is much more within his power to adjust than it would be for people to adjust to being told that they are not allowed to hold hands in public. People's attitudes about others holding hands are not indelibly stamped on them at birth. Moral pressures can and should be used to mold such attitudes in ways that enable people to coexist peacefully. But no amount of cultural conditioning could hope to extinguish the injury people experience at being denied basic rights that others are freely granted.

As in the case of attitudes about holding hands in public, people can also control, to at least *some* degree, their concerns about relative standing. And in an attempt to help people control these concerns, most cultures have adopted a moral posture that views them with disapproval. This posture, however, does not mean that the costs of being near the bottom of the economic ladder are too small to warrant government intervention. On the contrary, the evidence we have seen from the wage structures of private firms suggests that these costs are very large indeed. Granted, they are similar in kind to other types of costs against which we would never allow the state to intervene. But that, by itself, does not settle the question of whether the government should redistribute income.

In *A Theory of Justice*, Rawls goes to great lengths to construct a rationale for equalizing incomes that is independent of concerns about relative standing. He believes such concerns are not even rational, let alone morally legitimate. Speaking of his hypothetical decision makers behind the veil of ignorance, he writes:

> *Throughout I have assumed that persons in the original position are not moved by certain psychological propensities. A rational person is not subject to envy, at least when the differences between himself and others are not thought to be the result of injustice and do not exceed certain limits.*[20]

Rawls's concern here, which most people undoubtedly share, is that a malicious envy should not stand in the way of policies that would cause every person's wealth to grow.[21] Yet he concedes the inevitable and profound discomfort people feel in the presence of large, visible differences in holdings:

A person's lesser position . . . may be so great as to wound his self-respect; and given his situation we may sympathize with his sense of loss. Indeed we can resent being made envious; for society may permit such large disparities in goods that under social conditions these differences cannot help but cause a loss of self-esteem.[22]

A considerable body of evidence suggests that what counts for people is much less their absolute level of income than where they stand in relation to others. There are good reasons for believing, moreover, that this attitude does not arise out of malicious feelings toward others. Rather, as discussed in Chapter 2 (and as will be discussed further in the next chapters), concerns about position are so deeply felt because having high relative standing is *instrumental* in helping people to achieve the objectives they care most deeply about.

Once we grant the relationship between people's relative standing and their ability to achieve goals we acknowledge are important, we cannot insist (and Rawls would not insist[23]) that their concerns about relative standing are not rational. Nor can we insist that it is not rational to take positive steps to alleviate those concerns. Granted, there will be occasions in which the best response to these concerns will be simply to attempt to ignore them. But where this is not possible, it is surely not irrational to consider isolating oneself from the source of those concerns, even if one must experience some reduction in income in order to do so (see Chapters 3, 4, and 5). The importance to each animal of finding an ecological niche in which it can prosper is clearly recognized by those who study animal behavior.[24] It is not obvious why the concerns that motivate people to undertake similar efforts are so often viewed with disdain.

But let us suppose, for argument's sake, that we are willing to disregard the concerns, however strongly felt, of those who do not wish to occupy low-ranked positions in society's income hierarchy. We are still left with the concerns of those high-ranked members who, quite apart from considerations of status, may wish to associate with others of lower rank. Perhaps their vision of the good life involves having associations with persons of varied interests and abilities. As we have seen, however, if the poor are told they must tolerate whatever feelings of relative deprivation they may experience in the presence of the rich, they are still able, even within the confines of a single society, to limit their association with the rich. Moreover, even if it is sometimes possible to facilitate associations by carrying out compensating transfers privately, free-rider problems and other practical difficulties will give rise to demands to redistribute income through collective means. By what moral principle can demands such as *these* be branded as illegitimate? Or less legitimate than the demands of those who oppose redistributive taxation? Why should the opponents of redistributive taxation get something valuable for free (namely, high-ranked positions in the income hierarchy) just because the cost of forming new societies is prohibitively high? And what of the interests of those who, having read Rawls, feel it would be unfair to live in a society in which people are paid strictly in proportion to what they produce? How is the position of a person who opposes redistributive taxation different from the position of a person who insists that his taxes not be used to help construct a particular road because he has no intention of ever driving on it?

Whenever one group's demands conflict with another's and neither side has decisive moral arguments in its favor, practical guidelines are needed to reach a compromise. Given that there will be serious costs no matter which policy is chosen, coherent arguments can be made for selecting the policy that most closely resembles the compromise people would have worked out for themselves had circumstances permitted them to do so. No one can judge better the costs of a policy than the people who will have to live with it. And it will often be possible to learn more about how people assess these costs by watching what they do than by listening to what they say.* If the associations of co-workers in private firms may be thought of as voluntary, the evidence we have seen indicates that those who oppose redistributive transfers bear most of the burden of compromise in private negotiations. If they cannot escape compromise in the labor market, where they have complete freedom to choose their associates, then why should they be protected by the state from having to make similar compromises outside the labor market?

Economies of Scale and Enlightened Self-Interest

Thus far, I have attempted to show that redistributive transfers would be part of a voluntary social contract even if no productive efficiency gains resulted from forming large, heterogeneous societies, rather than small, homogeneous ones. Such efficiency gains, though, are likely to be plentiful. As I argued in Chapter 3, they will result in part from the increased scope for the specialization of labor that is inherent in large populations. Skilled people working alongside less skilled subordinates together will produce more than the sum of what each would produce alone. There may also be important efficiency gains at the national level from sharing such common public costs as defense. (More on these points in Chapter 11.)

These economies of aggregation constitute an important reason for forming large, heterogeneous societies, quite apart from considerations related to status. But if concerns about relative standing are as powerful as they appear to be, it may be impossible to sustain the high degree of social interaction necessary to exploit economies of aggregation without having redistributive taxation. Senator William Peffer argued as much when, in defense of the proposed Sixteenth Amendment,† he said that taxes levied on incomes "would help to counteract the menace to republican institutions created by the

---

*I will point out in Chapter 10, however, that we *sometimes* learn more about what people want by listening to what they say than by watching what they do.

†The Sixteenth Amendment, passed February 25, 1913, gives Congress the power "to levy and collect taxes on incomes from whatever source derived."

centralization of wealth."[25] If, as a practical matter, a large heterogeneous society cannot be sustained without redistributive transfers, it is then difficult to argue that such transfers constitute a real burden on those who finance them. On the contrary, the net incomes of even the most productive workers might well be smaller in the relatively more fragmented societies that would result without redistributive transfers. If so, the moral force of the libertarian's complaint that such taxes rob people of their liberty is weakened further.

Fairness Revisited

The libertarian might concede that such taxes are expedient, given the kind of world we live in. But he might also insist that, for all their expediency, redistributive transfers are nonetheless unjust. This response, however, is open to question once the connection between fairness and relative standing is clearly recognized. In Chapters 3 and 4, I argued that having high standing is a thing of value that can exist only when others suffer the cost of having low standing. And we feel comfortable saying that a person should not receive for free something whose value arises from a cost borne by another person. Other things of value are not generally available free of charge, and it is not clear why high-ranked positions in society's income hierarchy should be any exception.

The libertarian might be on solid footing if he claimed only his right to the full fruits of his labors. But it is not clear that he is also entitled to claim a high-ranked position in the social hierarchy for free. If the first claim could be separated from the second, there would be no difficulty. The two, however, cannot be separated. When a highly productive person receives the full fruits of his labors, he necessarily receives a high-ranked position for nothing. And even if he insists that that position is of no personal value, it still imposes real costs on those whose presence makes it possible. If an otherwise just claim cannot be enforced without simultaneously enforcing a second claim that is not obviously just, we cannot presume that the first claim is just.

Michael Levin thus misses something important when he insists that he is not responsible for the poor man being poor. The poor man is not poor because he has low income in any absolute sense. On the contrary, the poor in this country today have higher incomes by far than the rich had a century ago. They are poor only because they are embedded in a social network in which most other people have larger incomes than they do. As a man with a relatively high income, then, Michael Levin *is* responsible for the poor man's being poor, just as the poor man is responsible, albeit indirectly, for Levin's *not* being poor.

Thus, it appears that a fairness argument of sorts can be offered after all as an explanation of why societies have redistributive taxation—a fairness argument with positive content. But it is very different from the kind of fairness argument put forth by Cordell Hull during the congressional debate prior to the passage of the Sixteenth Amendment. And it is different, too, from the fairness argument of Rawls.

The fairness argument I offer here requires no altruism from the well-to-do, as does Hull's. Nor does it require that the rules be passed before people discover what their abilities are, as does Rawls's. Instead, it says that no social contract is sustainable unless it is fair, in the sense of creating parallel benefits for all who are part of it. I have attempted to show that redistributive taxation is an essential element in a fair social contract, even one that is not negotiated behind a veil of ignorance.

If this particular fairness argument is unfriendly to the libertarian position, it is also not without cost to the traditional liberal position, for it suggests limits on the extent to which the liberal urge to equalize incomes can be satisfied. High-ranked positions in the social order are things of value, to be sure. Yet their value is not unbounded. A social contract that lacks redistributive transfers surely is unfair to the poor, in spite of what the libertarians say. But beyond some point, further attempts to equalize incomes will produce a social contract that is unjust to the rich, notwithstanding the protests of traditional liberals. The rich are not entitled to high-ranked positions for free, but neither may they be forced to pay more for them than they are worth. Between the extremes in which the social contract is demonstrably unjust to one group or another, there will inevitably exist a bitterly contested middle ground in which some of the poor feel unjustly exploited by the rich, and vice versa.

In making the arguments developed in this chapter, I did not intend to claim that the income distribution we currently have in the United States is just. That distribution was obviously not arrived at under the conditions of perfect mobility assumed here. The bargaining power of the less well-to-do is clearly constrained by their inability to form separate societies of their own. Indeed, since restrictions on mobility prevent the poor from withholding high-status positions from the rich, one might well ask why the rich would bother to compensate the poor at all.

The fact that the poor may lack the practical capability to form a separate country does not mean that they are completely powerless to bargain over the terms of the social contract. Even within the confines of a single society, individuals and groups have substantial power to isolate themselves from others. And even where a certain degree of interaction cannot be avoided, the poor may still have considerable control over the terms on which that interaction takes place. After all, it is in the interests of those who benefit most from such interaction for it to take place in a peaceful and orderly manner. If the rich refuse to compensate the poor as part of a distributional contract, it is by no means clear that they can then count on having a climate of peaceful interaction.

Having failed to win the voluntary cooperation of the poor, the rich could then only hope for a system of laws that would impose penalties on those who refuse to interact peacefully. But as discussed in Chapters 2 and 5, people will often endure various penalties in order to avoid participating in transactions they believe to be too one-sided. Passing and enforcing laws that require cooperation is not the same as persuading those who are governed by them that the rules are fair. And where people regard the rules as unfair, they may very well refuse to cooperate with them, even if the result is a reduction in their standard of living.

In order to sustain the social order on peaceful terms, it has more than once proved necessary for the well-to-do to relinquish substantial control over the fiscal decisions of government.[26] It is thus clear enough that the less well-to-do have *some* bargaining power under current circumstances, if not as much as they would have had under conditions of perfect mobility. But it is by no means obvious that that bargaining power is sufficient to assure a just outcome in the sense defined here.

A second complication is that, even if there were perfect freedom of mobility, there would still be no single income distribution that the theory developed here could identify as being just. As discussed in the example of poor and rich farms, there will normally be surplus value created whenever a heterogeneous society is formed. In that example, the poor would have joined the rich, provided they were able to earn at least 120 bushels per year; and the rich, similarly, would have joined the poor, provided they received at least 160 bushels per year. With a total available production of 300 bushels per year, there were thus 20 bushels per year of surplus value created when the rich and poor formed a single society. The theory discussed here tells us nothing novel about what justice requires with respect to the distribution of such a surplus.

In the inevitable struggle to capture a larger share of whatever social surplus does exist, it is natural to expect each side to attempt to claim the moral high ground. Spokespersons for low-income groups will insist, for example, that the rich lack compassion for the plight of the poor. They will point out, correctly, that the rich often attribute a naively large share of their good fortune to cunning and industry, and an unrealistically small share to luck.

BEGLEY

And they will remind us that even industry and cunning are largely a matter of genetic and environmental happenstance, for which one is not entitled to claim personal credit.

For their part, spokespersons for the rich will insist that the poor lack motivation and discipline; and that to support the poor will in the end only further undermine these essential traits of character.* The same spokespersons will call to mind images of the poor using tactics of coercion and intimidation

"Otis, shout at that man to pull himself together."

in their struggles to confiscate ever more income from the rich. Perhaps they will cite accounts such as Tom Wolfe's of a late-sixties meeting between ghetto youths and a San Francisco antipoverty bureaucrat.[27] The youths are carrying big wooden sticks, and they are there to "mau-mau the Flak Catcher" about summer jobs:

"Hey, Brudda," the main man says. He has a really heavy accent. "Hey, Brudda, how much you make?"

"Me?" says the Flak Catcher. "How much do I make?"

"Yeah, Brudda, you. How much money you make?"

---

*I argue in Chapter 12 that specific design features of the particular transfer programs we use in this country seem almost as if they were chosen for the very purpose of weakening work incentives. But such perverse design features are by no means an essential property of transfer programs generally.

. . . [*the Flak Catcher's*] *mouth shimmies back into the terrible sickening grin, and then you can see that there are a whole lot of little muscles all around the human mouth, and his are beginning to squirm and tremble . . .*

"How much, Brudda?" . . .

"Well," says the Flak Catcher, "I make $1,100 a month."

"How come you make so much?" . . .

"Wellllll"—the grin, the last bid for clemency . . . and now the poor man's eyes are freezing into little round iceballs, and his mouth is getting dry . . .

"Listen, Brudda, Why don't you give up your paycheck for summer jobs. You ain't doing shit." [28]

No social contract can eliminate all of the acrimony from the ongoing distributional debate. But there seems little doubt that the terms of the social contract play an important role in determining the amount of tension in that debate. And it is surely not necessary to morally endorse coercive tactics to understand why that might be so.

Having begun with a framework that might well be called hyperlibertarian in terms of its initial assignment of individual rights, I have reached conclusions that differ sharply from the libertarian position as put forward by Nozick. I agree with Nozick that basketball team owners have the right to bid for Wilt Chamberlain's services, and the right as well to demand that customers who wish to see him play deposit extra money in a box with Chamberlain's name on it. Nozick is also correct in saying that each fan who attends Chamberlain's games finds trading 25 cents in exchange for that privilege an individually attractive proposition. But that does not mean that the overall effects of such trades would meet with the collective approval of basketball fans. On the contrary, fans might strongly object to the disparity in incomes created by the very payment schemes they participated in voluntarily. Yet by staying home, the individual fan would have no perceptible effect on the amount of income Chamberlain receives, just as the individual driver who stays home has no perceptible effect on the amount of smog in the Los Angeles basin. The fan does not signal by his presence at the game that he approves of the distributional consequences of his actions, any more than a person who drives to work signals that he approves of air pollution.

As Mancur Olson emphasized in *The Logic of Collective Action*,[29] individual incentives and collective desires are often sharply in conflict. When they are, individual behavior tells us little about the outcomes people truly seek. People who want cleaner air may be forced to take collective steps if they wish to alter the consequences of their individual actions. They may seek laws, for example, that limit automobile exhaust emissions. Similarly, the people who comprise Chamberlain's audience may desire some collective voice regarding the disposition of the ticket prices they pay. The society they are all part of may, for reasons such as I have discussed here, tax some of what is in the box with Chamberlain's name on it and give it to others. If so, then Chamberlain has a just claim only to the after-tax portion of the money fans place in the box. (By the same token, though, once the specified taxes are paid, no one has any further just claims against Chamberlain's remaining earnings, no matter how large they may be.) Following the framework set out in this discussion, we may say in general that one is entitled to keep not the full fruits of one's labors but only whatever share thereof is specified under society's distribution rules.

Conflicts between individual incentives and collective desires arising out of concerns about relative standing are by no means limited to the question of redistributive taxation. On the contrary, in the succeeding chapters I attempt to show that they pervade numerous other important aspects of economic and social interaction as well.

Seven

The Positional Treadmill

Individual Versus Collective Rationality

Biologists teach us that the physical characteristics and even the behavior of a species evolve in such ways as to give individual members of the species the greatest reproductive advantage. The fact that a particular characteristic or behavior might prove harmful to the species as a whole matters less in the evolutionary scheme of things. If a trait helps individual members compete more effectively against their own kind in the contest to see who can leave the most offspring, natural selection will favor it.[1]

This principle is clearly illustrated by what happens when one dog confronts another in a so-called "conflict situation." In such situations, each dog must decide whether to fight or defer to its opponent. One of the most important factors in this decision is the relative size of the two dogs. Dogs that adopt the prudent strategy, "Defer if my opponent is significantly larger than I am, otherwise fight," will leave greater numbers of offspring than will those that fight no matter what.

The advantage inherent in this strategy has resulted in an interesting evolutionary sleight-of-hand. A complex collection of neurological hardware has evolved that causes the hair on each dog's back to stand on end when the dog is confronted by a rival. This mechanism causes dogs to appear larger, and any strain of dog that lacked it would get into too many fights to be able to compete successfully in the reproductive contest.

As effective as the hackle-raising mechanism is from the standpoint of any individual dog, however, there is something inescapably futile about it when viewed from the perspective of the species as a whole. When the hair on each dog's back stands on end, the rank ordering of the dog population by size is precisely the same as it would have been if no dog had raised its hackles. In any conflict, the decision of whether to fight or defer would have the same outcome either way. From the point of view of the species as a whole, then, hackle-raising mechanisms are a waste of effort. Dogs would have been much better off if this neurological capacity had been spent on the development of, say, greater visual or olfactory acuity, or some other ability that would help them to acquire food. Yet dogs are stuck with their hackle-raising mechanisms because it would not benefit any *individual* dog to devote this neurological capacity instead to the support of keener eyesight. Other dogs would "discount" the size of such a dog, the same way they discount the size of other dogs. They would have no way of knowing that its hair was not standing on end. Some dogs who would otherwise have deferred to this dog would thus instead choose to fight with him. Excessive fighting is not in the interests of any dog, and this disadvantage would soon relegate nonhackle-raisers to the evolutionary scrap heap.

Similar anomalies are often present in interactions between people. In his wonderfully insightful book, *Micromotives and Macrobehavior*, Schelling describes the following paradoxical observation: Hockey players, given a choice, will seldom wear helmets; yet, when questioned privately, they will usually insist that they favor rules requiring them to do so.[2] Why this apparent contradiction? Hockey players care about both their safety and winning hockey games. Ever so slightly, the wearing of hockey helmets reduces the effectiveness of individual hockey players, perhaps by restricting vision or hearing. Or, where the wearing of helmets is left optional, the decision to wear one may also make it more difficult for a player to intimidate opponents psychologically. Whatever the reason, a player who does not wear a helmet creates some small competitive advantage for his team—an outcome he likes— at the expense of a slightly higher risk of serious injury—an outcome he doesn't like. If the former weighs more heavily in his mind than the latter, as it appears to for most athletes in highly competitive sports, then he will play without a helmet.

But such decisions are clearly maladaptive when viewed from the perspective of hockey players as a group. The Bruins remove their helmets to gain advantage over the Flyers, who then restore the competitive balance by removing theirs. In the process, all players suffer increased exposure to risk of injury, while neither side gains anything of much value.

The Prisoner's Dilemma

Both hackle-raising dogs and helmetless hockey players confront examples of what has been called the "prisoner's dilemma." The classic illustration involves two prisoners, A and B, who are guilty of a serious crime. They are each told that if one confesses while the other remains silent, the one who confesses will be set free while his accomplice will be given the maximum sentence, say, 30 years.

Figure 7.1 Hackle-raising serves the interests of individual animals, but accomplishes nothing for the animal kingdom as a whole.

If both confess, they will receive an intermediate sentence—say, 5 years. If neither confesses, the state has only enough hard evidence to convict them of a minor offense, for which they will receive but a short sentence—say, 1 year. The prisoners are not allowed to communicate with one another. The choices and sentences confronting them are summarized in Table 7.1.

In considering his own choice, A has no idea whether B has confessed or not. If B has confessed, A clearly does better if he, too, confesses, for then he will get only 5 years instead of 30. On the other hand, if B has remained silent, A still does better to confess than not, since he will then go free rather than spend a year in jail. In other words, no matter what B does, A can get a better outcome by confessing. The same must hold true for B. The apparently inescapable result is that A and B, following what they rationally perceive to be their own best interests, will each choose to confess. In return each will receive a 5-year jail term. But both A and B would have realized a clearly superior outcome had they each instead chosen to remain silent. Then each would have gotten only a year in jail, which is clearly preferable to the 5-year sentences they ended up with.

We are tempted to think that the prisoner's dilemma could have been resolved easily had A and B only been allowed to communicate with one another, for then each could have agreed on the jointly optimal strategy of remaining silent. But if the stakes are high enough, simple communication is not necessarily enough. Suppose A and B promise one another to remain silent. How does B know A will keep his word? If A breaks the promise while B keeps it, A will go free instead of having to spend a year in jail. A knows that B realizes this. So perhaps A fears that B, anticipating A's defection from their agreement, will decide to defect himself. Unless A and B are both bound by an ethical code that enables them to trust one another, some sort of enforcement mechanism is necessary to ensure that the promise is kept. (The various brutal enforcement mechanisms employed by organized criminals have a certain chilling logic when viewed as attempts to resolve the prisoner's dilemma.)

One critical difference between humans and other animal species is the degree to which humans are able to resolve such prisoner's dilemmas. Endowed with superior communicative and cognitive skills, people need not settle for the individualistic or evolutionary outcome to the same extent that animals must. Hockey teams, for example, can elect to play in leagues that require all

Table 7.1 *The Prisoner's Dilemma*

		B	
		Confess	Remain Silent
A	Confess	5 years for A 5 years for B	0 years for A 30 years for B
	Remain Silent	30 years for A 0 years for B	1 year for A 1 year for B

players to wear helmets, as the NCAA does. With league rules in effect, players do not have to trust one another, and the prisoner's dilemma vanishes. The "arms race" is another example of the prisoner's dilemma, which makes it clear why closely matched antagonists often sign arms control agreements. If it were not for the difficulty of coming up with effective enforcement mechanisms, many more such agreements would undoubtedly exist.

In many prisoner's dilemma games, contestants are competing for what in the end must be a fixed number of favored positions in some hierarchy. Dogs seeking to appear larger than their rivals, hockey players trying to enhance their team's chances of winning, nations trying to achieve military superiority— all are involved in contests in which the payoffs depend much less on performance against some absolute standard than on performance in relation to the competition. When the stakes in such contests are high, each contestant may face irresistible pressures to make heavy investments that in the end turn out to be mutually offsetting. I argue in this chapter that competitors for favored positions on the economic totem pole find themselves in the midst of high-stakes prisoner's dilemmas much of the time, and that the main purpose of many of our legal, organizational, and regulatory structures is to support cooperative solutions to these contests—to slow the "positional treadmill."

Safety Regulation as a Solution to a Prisoner's Dilemma

In the United States and in most other industrial countries, numerous laws restrict private labor contracts. In this country, for example, the Occupational Safety and Health Act prescribes minimum safety standards that *must* be observed, even when both employers and employees insist they would prefer to waive them.

On both sides of the political spectrum, discussions of such "paternalistic" laws call forth assertions of absolute moral authority. Commentators on the right, for example, protest that safety standards abridge the liberty of a worker to choose the higher rates of pay that are possible when less stringent (and less costly) safety standards are maintained.[3] The left counters that it is morally wrong—or, in its parlance, "unconscionable," or even "obscene"—for the government to permit unsafe conditions in the workplace.[4]

The antecedents of paternalistic legislation can be traced back to an era when company towns were much more prevalent than today. Such laws were intended to curb unfair exploitation of workers by employers who enjoyed a decisive bargaining advantage.[5] But the left's impassioned defense of the continued existence of these statutes puzzles many practical-minded economists, who believe that labor markets are, for the most part, well-informed and structurally competitive.

To the market-oriented economist, the question of whether a firm should have a particular safety device is no different in principle from the question of whether a firm should have an air conditioner. Safety devices, like air conditioners, cost money to install and yield benefits to employees. The question of whether firms should have them ought to be settled in the same way in both cases. Suppose, for example, that a person must choose between working for one firm that has an air conditioner and another that does not. In competitive labor markets, wages will be lower in the first firm by an amount that reflects the costs of installing, running, and maintaining the air conditioner. If the climate is hot or if the worker is particularly sensitive to heat, he probably will choose the firm with air conditioning. The extra comfort will be worth the sacrifice in wages. Otherwise, he will forego cool air and take higher wages instead.

The crucial point in the economist's argument is that if workers desire a particular amenity in the workplace, then they, not the employer, will have to bear its cost. As Henry Ford put it earlier in this century, "It is not the employer who pays the wages—he only handles the money. It is the product that pays the wages."[6] After all, wages are paid from revenues from the sale of products, and the amount a consumer is willing to pay for the product is not influenced by whether workers have air conditioning. Other things the same, competition assures that workers who are willing to work without air conditioning will receive wages that are higher, by an amount equal to the cost of the air conditioning, than the wages received by those who work in air-conditioned firms.

This same argument holds when people are faced with a choice between one firm that has safety devices and a second firm that does not. Those workers who place a high value on safety will accept the necessarily lower wage rates offered by the first firm. Those who don't will instead take the higher-paying but riskier jobs the second firm has to offer. If the labor market is competitive, those who opt for safety devices will, like those who choose air conditioners, have to sacrifice in wages only the amount necessary to cover the added costs. Firms that cut wages by more than that would risk having their workers bid away by competing firms, whereas firms that cut wages by less would fail to earn a competitive rate of return.

Viewed within the economist's framework, laws that mandate minimum safety standards will thus either have no effect, or else a perverse effect, on the people they are intended to help. Those who would have chosen in any event to work for firms that offer high safety levels will not be affected by the safety standards. But those who would have preferred the riskier, higher-paying jobs will now be forced to buy enhanced safety levels that to them are just not worth the price.

Numerous criticisms can of course be leveled at the economist's simple account of why unregulated markets produce the right level of safety. One is that people may not always have all of the necessary information to make intelligent choices about safety. To be sure, the lack of information is an important problem in many safety decisions. Yet it cannot explain why we regulate even those health and safety risks that are widely known and reasonably well understood by workers. The coal miner knows, for example, that, unless costly precautions are taken, he is likely to contract black lung disease after 30 years in the mine. His father and grandfather probably both died from it, as did a host of other people whose histories he knows well.

Whatever sensible reasons there may be for regulating mine safety, the need to protect the miner from the consequences of his own ignorance does not appear to be one of them.

Perhaps the most common objection to the economist's claim that unregulated competitive markets will produce the right amount of safety is that labor markets are not really competitive. The miner may know that working in the mine will kill him, but he may have no choice. After all, the mine may be the only employer in the area. Workers with families and other commitments are not able to move freely in search of a more favorable labor contract.

I argued in Chapter 3, however, that it is not necessary for *all* workers to be willing to move in order for the labor contract to become workably competitive. I noted also that labor mobility is, in any event, much higher than is generally assumed. And I pointed out, finally, that the rates of return on capital we observe in practice are not compatible with the claim that firms have the power to exploit workers appreciably. The mine may indeed be the only employer in the area, but its profits are still not likely to be very high—not high enough, certainly, to support the charge that it grossly underpays its workers.

Even if the firm *did* possess a certain degree of market power in its dealings with the worker, however, it *still* would have no reason to provide too little safety. Suppose, for example, that the cost per year per worker of a certain safety device is $10. Suppose also that workers would each be willing to forfeit $11 per year in order to have it. No matter how much market power it may have over the worker, the firm could still enhance its profits by $1 by installing the safety device. On the other hand, if workers were only willing to forego $9 per year in wages to have the safety device, the firm will not install it. And if workers would rather retain the $10 in wages than have the safety device, why *should* the firm provide it?

To these arguments, the economist's critic may respond that the safety device is really worth more to the worker than what he is able to pay for it in his current state. After all, the exploitative firm may already have cut his wages to the bone. But if exploitation were the problem, an even better approach would be for the government to see to it that the worker gets additional income, and then let him decide for himself whether the additional safety equipment is worth what it costs to install. Either a minimum wage law or a cash transfer to the poor would be a more direct solution to the problem here. (More on minimum wage laws below; more on cash transfers to the poor in Chapter 12.)

Many noneconomists apparently feel offended on moral grounds by the economist's claim that workplace safety is, at bottom, an economic issue. Perhaps they feel that the workplace should be made as safe as technology allows, with the cost factor kept out of the picture entirely.[7] Yet when pressed to its logical limits, such a view leads to troubling contradictions.

Consider, for example, its implications for the question of pedestrian safety. Assuming the world will last indefinitely, some pedestrians will be run over and killed at each urban intersection. Most, perhaps all, of these deaths could be prevented by walling off our streets and building pedestrian overpasses, as we already have done in some busy spots. Yet, given our limited resources, would most people find it sensible to fence off *all* streets and build overpasses over *all* busy intersections? Or would they rather devote the same scarce public funds to other pressing purposes, such as cancer research, day care centers, and scholarships? In view of these alternative needs, most of us reluctantly conclude that our best option is to continue to enforce the traffic laws and urge people to be careful when they cross unprotected intersections.

Suppose we agree that weighing the costs of safety measures (in terms of the alternative uses to which the same resources could be put) against the benefits of such measures (in terms of the expected number of deaths and injuries they will prevent) makes moral sense in the case of pedestrian overpasses. Why shouldn't the same framework be used to determine the best menu of safety levels in the workplace? By so doing, those who place a high value on safety can accept the sacrifice in wages necessary to pay for it. Similarly, those who place a lower value on safety can earn higher wages in return for the increased risks they accept.

Whatever merits such considerations may seem to have, none of the economist's arguments will carry much weight among those who believe that people are simply incapable of making intelligent decisions on their own. To be sure, people often appear to fail to perceive their own interests clearly, to discount the future too heavily, and in other ways to act inconsistently with Rawls's description of a rational person.[8] (More on this point in the next section.) Many of those who hold this view of human behavior may find it easy to justify having the state make certain important decisions on the individual's behalf.

Others, however, will find such views troubling on several accounts. They may acknowledge that making mistakes is an inescapable part of being human. But they will reject the view that many of a person's most important actions are consistently at odds with his own interests. More important, even where systematic behavioral "errors" can be identified, they will feel people nonetheless have an inherent right to make mistakes, provided they do not interfere with the legitimate interests of others.[9] This perspective might permit the state to impose safety requirements that prevent people from causing injury or expense to others. But it would not recognize the individual's incompetence as legitimate grounds for the state to take from him the power to make decisions regarding his *own* safety.

Conflicting views of this sort raise some of the thorniest issues ever encountered by those who take an interest in trying to define the proper role of government. I consider such conflicting views in detail in Chapter 11, where I take up the paternalism question in earnest. These issues need not be settled, however, for us to see why demands for safety regulation might emerge even in an environment composed of perfectly competitive firms and fully informed, fully rational workers.

To illustrate, let us consider the following example in which two neighbors with similar tastes and abilities—call them Hatfield and McCoy—face a choice between working in a safe mine or in an unsafe mine. The market for miners' services is assumed to be competitive. In the unsafe mine, workers are exposed to some harmful substance that will shorten their lives by 15 years. In the safe mine, this substance is removed by filtering devices. Wages in the unsafe mine are $250 per week. In the safe mine, they are only $200 per week, which reflects the cost of the filtering devices. Both Hatfield and McCoy are fully informed about these facts. And, like most of the other hypothetical persons discussed in this book, they care about the size of their incomes, both in an absolute sense and in relation to the incomes of others. Given their concerns about relative standing, the attractiveness of each choice to either one of them depends on the particular choice taken by the other. In Table 7.2, the four possible choices are represented in the form of a 2 × 2 matrix similar to the one used to summarize the prisoners' alternatives. The entries in each cell indicate how each alternative is ranked by Hatfield and McCoy.

Let us focus first on the decision as viewed from the perspective of McCoy. The relationship between McCoy's concerns about relative standing and the assumed ranking of the four alternatives is as follows. The upper left and lower right cells both represent alternatives in which Hatfield and McCoy have the same income levels. The fact that McCoy prefers the latter to the former means that the additional safety, taken by itself, is worth more than $50 per week to him. But McCoy prefers the upper right cell to both of these alternatives, because in that cell he has more income both absolutely and in relation to Hatfield. When McCoy moves from the lower right to the upper right cell, the extra income he gets is not, in its own right, sufficient to compensate him for the attendant reduction in safety. It is the fact that this income moves him ahead of Hatfield that tips the balance. Similar considerations account for why McCoy prefers the upper left cell to the lower left one. He would gladly pay $50 for the extra safety he gets in the lower left cell if he could do so without falling behind Hatfield in the process. McCoy ranks that combination of choices lowest because it results in Hatfield's having more income than he does.

Because of the way McCoy feels about the various alternatives, it is clear that, regardless of what choice Hatfield makes, the "best" option available to McCoy is to work in the unsafe mine. By so doing, he will achieve his most-preferred outcome should Hatfield decide to work in a safe mine (as opposed

Table 7.2 *Mine Safety When Relative Income Matters*

		Hatfield	
		Unsafe Mine $250/week	Safe Mine $200/week
McCoy	Unsafe mine $250/week	Third best for each	Best for McCoy Worst for Hatfield
	Safe mine $200/week	Best for Hatfield Worst for McCoy	Second best for each

to his second-best outcome had he instead chosen to work in the safe mine). Similarly, by choosing the unsafe mine, McCoy achieves his third-best outcome in the event Hatfield also chooses the unsafe mine. This is better than the fourth-best outcome McCoy would get by choosing a safe mine when Hatfield chooses an unsafe mine. In short, no matter what Hatfield does, McCoy does better by choosing the unsafe mine. Because the two men have similar tastes, the choice of an unsafe mine is also a "dominant strategy" for Hatfield.

Hatfield and McCoy are thus confronted with another variant of our standard prisoner's dilemma. Faced with these dominant strategies, the self-interested Hatfield and McCoy will each work in an unsafe mine. This means that each will achieve an outcome that is only third best out of the four possible. Both can agree, however, that it would be better for both to work in a safe mine.

Thus, as in the hockey helmet example considered earlier, individual rationality and collective rationality need not coincide in the selection of workplace safety levels. Just as each individual hockey player saw it in his narrow interests to play without a helmet, so Hatfield and McCoy see a compelling advantage in working in the unsafe mine. But when the dust settles, so to speak, each person's advantage is nullified by the parallel actions of others. It will therefore pay them to enter, if they can, into a binding agreement that commits them to work in a safe mine. Such an agreement might take the form of an Occupational Safety and Health Act that requires certain minimum safety standards for mines.

Now, some might object that since the concerns felt by Hatfield and McCoy about their relative standing are not rational in the sense that Rawls defines the term (see Chapter 6), the real reason for safety regulation here, too, is the irrationality of man. But, as noted in Chapter 6, it is difficult to sustain the claim that concerns about relative standing are irrational. In an evolutionary context, it would be difficult to argue that people would *not* have developed a way of looking at the world that makes exchanging longevity for higher current income irresistibly attractive. Higher current income makes it possible for a person to give his children greater advantages, enabling them to compete more effectively against the children of others. If our preferences were forged in the crucible of natural selection, then being able to provide extra advantages for our children should indeed taste sweeter than the contemplation of an extended old age. After all, no matter how pleasant an extended retirement period might seem in the abstract, it is less important than seeing to it that the next generation is safely launched. The home computer companies are betting on this proposition when they show us television advertisements that depict a dejected young freshman as he disembarks from a train, having just flunked out of college. We are told that the boy might have made it had his parents only provided him with the learning stimulus of a personal computer.

Yet when everyone's parents work in the unsafe mine, the advantage each parent sought to provide for the next generation serves only to protect against falling behind in the contest. When everyone has a home computer, the contest to see who makes it will simply be decided by other differences. As with the hockey helmet example, the ultimate outcome of the contest is left unaffected.

If Hatfield and McCoy were the only two citizens of the hypothetical country in which this safety law was passed, we may presume that no libertarians would find fault with the law. After all, it does not restrict anyone in a way in which he does not want to be restricted. But practically speaking, we could never expect unanimity in favor of such a law. Suppose, for example, that Hatfield and McCoy favor it for the reasons discussed, while others who do not care about relative standing oppose it. They complain, correctly, that it would deny them the right to make their own judgments about how much safety to purchase. This objection has obvious force, and I consider it in detail in Chapter 11. For the moment, let us simply concede its legitimacy, while noting that the desire to have safety standards may be motivated by legitimate concerns as well.

Relative Standing and the Faulty Telescopic Faculty

Pigou and other economists have written about man's "faulty telescopic faculty"[10]—the tendency many people have of devoting too little concern to the future consequences of their actions. Even Milton Friedman himself, a champion of the view that people act rationally for the most part, has argued that people behave as if the world were going to exist for only three more years.[11] (The behavior on which Friedman's argument is based long pre-dates the threat of nuclear annihilation, and so cannot be explained on that account.)

As an apparent illustration of the faulty telescopic faculty, consider the following excerpts from Mary Williams' account of the tasks performed by the "glow worm," the term used in the nuclear power industry for workers who clean up radiation spills.[12]

Each day when Tom Geer goes to work it's with the satisfying thought that he will labor only 10 minutes and be paid for 12 hours. . . . The catch—and of course there has to be one—is the job site. Mr. Geer does his work in an atmosphere so radioactive he can stay only minutes before, in industry parlance, he "burns out."

. . . Yeah, there's a risk," says Mr. Geer, who is 32. "We know we can't go back to the company 20 years from now if we've got cancer."

"But," he adds, "We need the money."

Workers receive a bonus of several hundred dollars every time they burn out, and there is apparently no shortage of workers willing to accept as much radiation exposure as employers will pay them for.

"Last year I think I got over 4,000 millirems," says Mr. Geer. "I like to work till I get my limit. If you don't reach your limit, you're wasting your time."

The acceptance of such terms of employment may appear to signal a careless, if not totally irrational, disregard for the future. Yet if concerns about relative standing are an important motivating force for individuals, such behavior need not be *individually* irrational at all. The forward move in the income hierarchy it enables may be more than enough to compensate for the future damage it will cause. After all, Geer's children will be raising families of their own well before the effects of his radiation exposure come home to roost.

But every such forward movement in the income hierarchy must create offsetting backward movements for others. From the collective standpoint, then, a major part of the reward each individual perceives from radiation exposure is completely spurious: Everyone cannot move forward simultaneously in the income hierarchy. It is not necessary, therefore, to assume that people are irrational to see why society might wish to set limits on radiation exposure. Man's telescopic faculty may not be faulty at all. Rather, the problem here may be that what is individually rational makes little sense from the collective vantage point. Camus's remark that "Real generosity toward the future consists in giving all to what is present" may indeed represent an attitude toward which people are prone.[13] And such an attitude may be genuinely adaptive from the individual point of view. Yet people might nonetheless rationally seek to limit the consequences of the behaviors summoned forth by that attitude.

Contingent Commodities

Consumption decisions regarding "contingent commodities" have many of the same properties as consumption decisions whose consequences will be felt only at some distant point in the future. By contingent commodities I mean any commodity whose payoff to the consumer depends on some uncertain event occurring. Insurance is one example, as is any other good whose effect is to create a slight reduction in the odds of suffering a loss.

The tendency to devote too few resources to contingent goods is illustrated by the following example, in which A and B must decide between two lawnmowers with different safety features. The first lawnmower is the standard model, which each year mutilates the feet of thousands of suburban residents as they mow their lawns. Most of these accidents involve some degree of carelessness by the persons operating the mowers. The second lawnmower is virtually idiot-proof. No matter how careless the operator is, the mower has so many protective features that it is almost impossible for it to cause serious injury. The second lawnmower costs $200 more than the first. For people like A and B, who exercise reasonable care while mowing, the odds of becoming involved in an accident are only, say, one ten-thousandth per year.

Let us assume that in a world where relative standing didn't matter, both A and B would prefer the safer lawnmower despite its higher purchase price. But once we introduce concerns about position, this intrinsic preference will not necessarily cause them to buy that mower. Although each dreads the thought of an accident, both nonetheless realize that the odds of one occurring during the life of the first mower are very small. (If the mower lasts 10 years, the odds are less than 1 in 2500.)

So if A picks the less safe mower while B picks the safe one, A is very likely to end up with more free cash than B—enough, say, to send his child to a summer computer camp he would otherwise have been unable to afford. B may find it distressing to watch A jr. head off to computer camp while B Jr. languishes around the neighborhood, merely having fun. If the prospect of seeing his family in a disadvantaged position is sufficiently troublesome to him, B will also buy the less safe mower. He knows that in the event of an accident he will lose ground relative to A; but when the odds of an accident are sufficiently small, it will nonetheless be individually rational for him to take that risk.[14] When viewed from the perspective of the collective interest of A and B, however, part of the payoff to taking such a risk is illusory. As before, the advance in position that each seeks does not materialize because of the mutually offsetting effects of their actions.

Recognizing that concerns about relative standing alter the payoffs from participating in risky activities changes our understanding of what it means to "play it safe." Consider, for example, a person who is faced with the decision of whether or not to accept some gamble whose probability of payoff is very high. If that person were unconcerned about her relative standing, the "safest" strategy available to her would be to refuse the gamble, no matter how favorable the odds. When relative standing matters, however, this is no longer necessarily the safest strategy. If similar gambles are available to others, she would jeopardize her position in the queue by refusing the gamble, hardly a safe step to take when relative standing is important. The concept of playing it safe is thus one that has its traditional meaning only when viewed from the perspective of the collective. The safest available strategy is for *everyone* to refuse to gamble. But it may be a risky strategy indeed for any one person acting individually to do so.

Minimum Wage and Overtime Laws

Few statutes have been so widely denounced by any group as minimum wage laws have been by economists. And if one accepts the economist's claim that labor markets are workably competitive, then minimum wage laws do raise difficult questions. If an employer and an employee agree on a given wage, why should the state then prevent them from consummating their transaction? If it makes sense to do that, why doesn't it also make sense for the state to set a minimum price below which I am not allowed to sell my used television set? Is the market for used television sets any more competitive than the market for unskilled workers?

Because a profit-seeking firm will hire fewer workers when the going wage goes up, one effect of minimum wage laws is to cause unemployment among unskilled workers. Numerous studies document this effect.[15] Yet it seems all but impossible to imagine Congress repealing the minimum wage statutes in the near future (although there have been serious proposals to relax minimum wage standards for teenagers). If labor markets are as competitive as economists think, why do we keep minimum wage laws on the books?

Similar questions may be posed regarding overtime laws. The so-called Fair Labor Standards Act requires that covered employees be paid 50 percent more than their normal wage rates for all time worked beyond eight hours per day. One possible reason for this requirement is to encourage employers to hire more workers, thus spreading the available work more equitably. This objective might make some sense during a period of deep depression. But the notion that there is a limited amount of work to be done and that this amount needs to be rationed is in many ways a curious one.[16] If people do additional work, they will earn extra income. Why doesn't this income generate demands for the additional goods they produce? Even if demand were deficient, there would be more direct and productive ways of attacking unemployment. We could, for example, reduce taxes or increase public spending. And during periods of reasonably full employment, overtime laws seem almost bizarre. According to the traditional theory of competitive labor markets, society's welfare will go down whenever the state blocks a voluntary employment transaction. If someone wants to work a ninth hour at the same or even a lower wage than he was paid for the previous eight, how does the state help him by making it illegal to do so?

Coherent answers to such questions begin to take shape once we view the worker's leisure versus income choice in the same way we viewed his safety versus income decision. Suppose, for example, that there are no overtime regulations and that Hatfield and McCoy have preferences over income and leisure as described in Table 7.3. As in Table 7.2, the entries in the cells represent the ranks they assign to the various alternatives.

As in the safety example, the two men both have an individually dominant strategy here, which is to work 12 hours per day. And, again as before, these dominant strategies lead to an outcome that both regard as inferior to the feasible alternative in which each earns less but works only 8 hours per day. Under these circumstances, both will support a law that constrains the number of hours they work.

Instead of requiring overtime premiums, why not have an outright ban on overtime work, as in the earlier instance where risky activities were prohibited?

Table 7.3 *Income-Leisure Tradeoff When Relative Income Matters*

		Hatfield	
		12 hours per day Total pay = $225	8 hours per day Total pay = $150
McCoy	12 hours per day Total pay = $225	Third best for each	Best for McCoy Worst for Hatfield
	8 hours per day Total pay = $150	Worst for McCoy Best for Hatfield	Second best for each

Because of the uncertain product demand levels that confront many firms, a ban on overtime might prove much more costly than a simple overtime premium. An overtime premium discourages firms from offering overtime most of the time, but nonetheless allows some degree of production flexibility. These considerations raise the more general question of what form collective restrictions should take if ever there are circumstances in which they can be justified. I return to this question in Chapters 11 and 12. In those chapters, I argue that there are strong reasons for avoiding an outright ban on even those activities whose consequences for other people are extremely costly.

Minimum wage laws can be explained within the same framework used to explain safety and overtime laws. Because firms generally try to keep their costs as low as possible, we can easily see how Hatfield and McCoy could become embroiled in a competition in which each offered to cut his wage slightly in order to sell more labor than the other. Suppose they are initially working for the same employer for 40 hours per week at $3 per hour. McCoy, who wants to provide additional advantages for his family, then cuts his wage to $2.95, hoping to expand his work week from 40 to, say, 50 hours. If Hatfield refused to take a similar cut, their employer would then gladly substitute McCoy's services for Hatfield's and McCoy would have achieved his objective.

If relative standing is as important to Hatfield as to McCoy, however, Hatfield will agree to the same wage cut. When he too offers his services for $2.95, the employer's incentive to substitute one for the other will be gone, and there might be little more work for the two than before. Given the clear possibilities for such a competition to get out of hand, it is hardly surprising that the two might want to act collectively to limit the damages. Similar considerations might help us understand why most employers offer "paid" vacations, which, in effect, keep workers from becoming caught up in similar competitions regarding vacation time.

Demonstration Effects in Consumption

In Upstate New York the winters are long and cold, and since the Arab oil embargo of 1973 it has made economic sense to install heavy layers of insulation in the walls and ceilings of homes. Nonetheless, most people on my street in Ithaca had not installed insulation in their walls as of 1982.

But that summer, one resident at the end of the block hired a contractor to pump cellulose into the walls of his home. Before long, I hired the same contractor to do likewise, and the following summer four neighbors at my end of the block all had crews working on their homes.

In his bitterly satirical *Theory of the Leisure Class*, Thorstein Veblen first called our attention to the central role such demonstration effects play in shaping our behavior.[17] The things we buy cannot be predicted very well without first knowing what our associates have bought. Whether or not we have a swimming pool, for example, depends less on our income, the climate, how much swimming pools cost, and the like, than on how many of our neighbors have pools.

Yet demonstration effects by their very nature apply with greater force to some kinds of goods than to others. We may know very well, for example, what makes of cars acquaintances drive or the kinds of clothes they wear. But we are much less likely to know how much they save or what they spend on insurance. If demonstration effects stimulate the amounts people spend on goods that can be readily observed, it then follows as a matter of simple arithmetic that they *reduce* the amounts spent on goods that are not readily visible. People's incomes are only so large, and when more income is devoted to the purchase of one type of good, less can be spent on other types.

To explore the welfare consequences of demonstration effects, it is first necessary to digress briefly on how consumers would allocate their incomes in the absence of these effects. To do this, let us put Crusoe on a deserted island and examine his decision of how much to save. To keep the problem simple, let us assume that Crusoe knows he has exactly 30 more years to live and that infirmities will prevent him from working during the last 10. He grows grain for a living, and his only reason for saving is to provide for his old age. Saving in this context means storing grain for future use. Assuming he wishes to consume the total amount of grain he produces in equal parts during each remaining year of his life, the solution to Crusoe's simple savings problem is for him to save one-third of the grain he produces during each of his 20 remaining productive years.

Now let us add Friday to the island, and assume that the satisfaction each man gets depends not only on his own "intrinsic" needs (that is, the needs he would have if he were the sole resident of the island), but also on how the amount he consumes compares with the amount consumed by the other. Relative savings levels matter less to them because savings, unlike current consumption, are not readily observed.*

To make the problem concrete, let us suppose that each of the two considers the following two savings options: (1) save one-third of each year's grain production; and (2) save one-sixth each year. Given their concerns about relative consumption, the attractiveness of each option depends, as in the safety and leisure examples, on which option is chosen by the other. The decision here thus has the same structure we saw in those earlier decisions. And, if concerns about current relative consumption levels are sufficiently strong, each will save only one-sixth of his current income, even though what results is less appealing than the alternative in which both save one-third. As in the earlier examples of the same form, individual and collective preferences are in conflict. Crusoe and Friday will thus find it attractive to enter into an agreement binding them to the higher savings rate.

---

*One might be tempted to argue that relative savings levels should be just as important as relative current consumption levels, because savings affect future relative consumption levels. As noted in the earlier discussion, however, there are good reasons for believing that future relative consumption levels are intrinsically less important than current relative consumption levels. After all, in the struggle to launch the next generation, it is current, not future, spending levels that count most. I argue below, moreover, that spending a greater fraction of one's current income will not necessarily lessen one's future standard of living.

Such an agreement could take a variety of forms. Among people who work for the same firm, employers could withhold part of each year's salary and disburse the accumulated funds in monthly payments when the worker retires. Such employee pension plans are common in industrialized countries. These plans have the advantage of not being unduly coercive, insofar as it would be possible to organize a firm that did not force people to save if such a firm seemed likely to appeal to a significant number of workers. At the other end of the coerciveness spectrum, we find governmentally imposed savings programs, such as the Social Security system. With very few exceptions, the Social Security system does not give workers the option of not participating. It is thus vulnerable to the charge, often leveled, that it deprives people of the right to decide for themselves how much to save. Let us grant the legitimacy of this criticism and defer until Chapter 11 the question of whether those who wish to require others to save may have legitimate interests of their own.

The dichotomy between observable and unobservable budget categories is not limited to the distinction between savings and goods. Various other expenditures, such as premiums for insurance and payments for medical checkups, are also by their very nature outside the normal scope of interpersonal comparisons. Where such comparisons are important to people, they are likely to buy too little insurance and spend too little on preventive health care. I argue in the next chapter that these observations may help account for why most employers require their employees to participate in company-sponsored insurance plans. They may also help explain why some companies provide incentives for employees to make greater use of preventive medical services. And they may even help explain why many societies require a physician's prescription before dispensing certain types of drugs. Some drugs that are currently available only by prescription could apparently be taken safely without a physician's advice *most* of the time. So it is easy to see how, in the absence of prescription laws, some families might be tempted to prescribe such drugs for themselves, thereby avoiding a costly physician's visit; and how other families, in turn, might feel pressure to do likewise in order to keep pace with community consumption standards; and why, finally, the community might favor laws requiring *all* families to seek competent medical advice before taking certain drugs.

Ability Signaling

In societies in which economic and social interactions between people are pervasive and important—that is, in every known human society—information about people with whom we might interact has obvious value. It determines, for example, the people we consider as potential mates, the employees we hire, those whose company we seek, and so on. Many of the most important decisions ever made about us depend on how strangers see our talents, abilities, and other characteristics.

But, as Robert Half once put it, "There is something that is much more scarce, something rarer than ability. It is the ability to recognize ability."[18]

People's various talents and abilities are not like numbers tattooed on their foreheads, there for all the world to observe at a glance. Their assessment is a subtle and complicated task, which to accomplish with reasonable accuracy requires a heavy investment of time and effort. Time and effort, however, are valuable for other purposes as well, and so we are led to seek ways of economizing on the evaluation process.

To see what sorts of shortcuts might emerge, let us consider a population in which people's abilities are known to differ substantially, but in which any specific individual's abilities cannot be observed directly. Though exceptions abound in specific cases, a person's various abilities will in general be positively correlated.[19] Thus, for example, we predict a higher-than-average score on the verbal section of the Scholastic Aptitude Test when we already know that a person has scored much better than average on the math section. Similarly, those persons who are highly endowed with the productive abilities that firms seek are likely to be better endowed with other abilities as well.

In a competitive labor market, there will be a strong positive correlation between people's productive abilities and their incomes. Similarly, when there is broad dispersion in income, there will be a strong positive correlation between one's income and the amount one consumes. In turn, there will be a similarly strong positive correlation between the total amount one consumes and the size of various observable components of one's consumption: the size and location of one's home, the quality of one's automobile or wardrobe, the clubs to which one belongs, and so on. When a person's ability level cannot be observed directly, these items tell us something about his total income and, by extension, about his level of ability. When people saw Walt Frazier driving the avenues of Manhattan in his Rolls Royce, they may not have known exactly what his income was, but they could be reasonably sure he wasn't poor, and that, whatever his job was, he was probably very good at it.

Now, it is clear that such signals will often be very weak. When someone we know very well shows up with an expensive new car, for example, we are not suddenly led to believe that his ability is much higher than we previously thought. On the contrary, if we know that the car is beyond his budget, we may question his judgment in having bought it.

But where important decisions involving people we do not know well are concerned, it is clear that even weak signals of ability can make a decisive difference. Close employment decisions are an obvious example. First impressions count for a lot during job interviews, and placement counselors have always stressed the importance of quality attire and a good address in the job-search process. Even when the employer *knows* how good an employee is, he may still care a great deal about how that employee comes across to others. This will be especially true in jobs that involve extensive contact with outsiders who do *not* know how good the employee is.

Judging from the spending behavior of single young people, we appear forced to conclude that *they* believe that their marriage prospects hinge critically on what clothes they wear and what cars they drive.[20] At first glance, this seems curious. After all, by the time most people marry, they presumably know one another well enough for such seemingly petty matters not to count for much. Even so, many potential mates were probably rejected out of hand during the courting process for seeming "unsuitable." The trappings of success surely do not guarantee that a person will marry well. But they do strengthen the chances of drawing a second glance. And to win any game, one must first be a player in it.

The importance of consumption goods as signals of ability will be different for different occupations. Earnings and the abilities that count most among research professors are not very strongly correlated, and professors think nothing of continuing to drive a 10-year-old automobile if it still serves them reliably. But only in a very small town, where people know one another well, might it not be a mistake for an aspiring young attorney to drive such a car in the presence of his potential clients. Good lawyers generally earn a lot of money, and people with a lot of money generally drive fashionable new cars. The potential client who doesn't know better will assume that a lawyer with a battered car is not much sought after. If you were on trial for first-degree murder, would you feel comfortable hiring a lawyer who arrived at the court house in a rust-eaten car, wearing a tattered suit? Even if you knew he was extremely competent, the jury, who would not have this knowledge, might discount his arguments because of the impression he conveys.

Because important outcomes hinge on the signals implicit in observable consumption goods, it simply does not follow that people who save "too little" money or buy too little insurance will fare worse than others. On the contrary, curtailing the *proportion* of income devoted to inconspicuous consumption

*"Look at it this way: If I weren't a very good lawyer,
could I practice in a clown costume?"*

might even enhance a person's earnings to such a degree as to raise his actual *level* of consumption of unobservable goods.[21] As with the dog whose hackles do not stand on end, a person who fails to keep pace with community consumption standards may cause others to underestimate where he stands vis-à-vis the field.

Although emphasizing observable consumption may be highly adaptive from the individual's point of view, it is clearly maladaptive from the standpoint of the population as a whole. One individual's forward move in any hierarchy can occur only at the expense of backward moves by others. If some individuals spend extra money on observable goods, others who do not do so will then be perceived as having lower ability than they really have. So in self-defense they too spend more on observable goods. In the process, one person's "offensive" signal is canceled by another's "defensive" signal. And in the end, too many resources are devoted to conspicuous goods. Under these circumstances, it is hardly surprising that people might seek collective restrictions on their spending behavior.

The ability-signaling rationale for imitative behavior suggests that a person's incentives to spend extra money on observable goods will be inversely related to the amount and reliability of independent information other people have about his abilities. The more people know about someone, the less he can influence their assessments of him by rearranging his consumption pattern in favor of observable goods.[22]

Stable environments with long-standing social networks will have more such information than do less stable environments, and for this reason we would expect people to devote larger budget shares to unobservables in the former than in the latter. Perhaps this helps explain why consumption patterns in small towns exhibit a certain sanity that big-city consumption patterns seem to lack. The wardrobe a professional person "needs" in Ithaca, for example, costs less than half as much as the one that same person would need in New York City. Differences between urban and rural consumption patterns may spring less from fundamental differences in the personal values held by the two groups than from differences in the payoffs they face from consuming observable goods.

In the same vein, people who move frequently should have lower budget shares for unobservable goods than do those who stay put. Similarly, budget shares for unobservables should be higher for married than for unmarried persons. Once one has found a mate, the payoff to further investment in ability signals may be greatly reduced.

Because independent measures of a person's ability become more numerous and reliable as he grows older, budget shares for unobservables should increase with age. This observation coincides with our observation that peer pressures are most troublesome for the young. It suggests that maturation may not result exclusively from people acquiring greater wisdom and experience as they become older. To be sure, people do learn from the mistakes they make. But what may be more important is that as people get older and establish a track record, their efforts to impress outsiders will yield ever smaller returns.

As that happens, their spending will be governed less and less by their desire to influence others. Young people's emphasis on conspicuous consumption may well spring less from their lack of wisdom and experience than from the particular payoff structure they face.

Vividness and Arousal Revisited

In the preceding section I argued that imitative consumption behavior might make sense even within the coldly cognitive framework of the market economist. But there is clearly an important dimension of such behavior that is not at all related to people's attempts to signal their abilities to others. This dimension has to do with the psychologist's arousal mechanism discussed in Chapter 2. There, we saw, for example, that a person's motivation to seek food springs from a variety of sources, most of which are noncognitive. The taste of food, the way it looks and smells, and even the application of electrical stimuli to specific brain sites all can trigger the impulse to eat, even when we know that it would be better not to eat. In restaurants that bring a dessert trolley around after dinner, patrons are more likely to order dessert than in restaurants that do not. A person is also more likely to order dessert if others at the same table do so. Ability signaling clearly has nothing to do with any of this.

A variety of consumer demands may spring from a motivational structure of much the same sort that governs our appetites for food. Even if we know, for example, that an acquaintance has both a stylish automobile and a hefty savings account, we can still see one and not the other. Whether the dessert trolley comes around or not, the diner *knows* that dessert is available if he wants it. But he is more likely to order dessert if he also sees it. His information is more vivid in one case than in the other. The stimulus to purchase a car may for essentially similar reasons be greater than the stimulus to save.

Rational calculations do govern consumption decisions much of the time, just as economists stress. But other forces also seem important for even the most determinedly hard-headed consumers. We process information with our brains, not with computer hardware. And we do the best we can to promote our purposes with the neurological capacities we have. Yet most people are either unable, or find it not worth the effort, to base all of their judgments on strictly cognitive considerations.

Consider, for example, the curious practice by which some people deliberately set their watches five minutes ahead. When asked, they will usually say they do so as a means of prodding themselves to get to appointments on time. Yet most of these people surely "know" what the correct time is, even though their watches are fast. Still, when it is really only 6:55, their eyes will physically record an image that says 7:00. The impact of the visual image may very well be completely discounted by the determined cognitive centers of the forebrain. But the same image is nonetheless transmitted into the nether reaches of the limbic system of the brain, where it is less subject to conscious control. There, it evidently elevates the arousal level, however slightly. And the wearer of the fast watch is thus prompted—much, perhaps, to his own amusement—to get moving toward his destination.

In the same way, the wearer of an elegant suit of clothing may not really fool anyone at all, in a cognitive sense, into thinking he has higher ability than he actually has. Yet the suit may still influence important judgments and behaviors in very subtle, noncognitive ways. And whatever influence the suit has will depend less on its quality in any absolute sense than on how it compares with the suits that others wear.

Fred Hirsch, in his penetrating book, *Social Limits to Growth*, emphasized the important distinction between "positional" and "nonpositional" goods (see Chapter 1). Positional goods, in Hirsch's scheme, are goods or jobs whose characteristics "are either (1) scarce in some absolute or socially imposed sense or (2) subject to congestion or crowding through more extensive use."[23] The consumption decisions I have discussed in this chapter have all had to do with goods in Hirsch's first category, and particularly with those that are scarce in a socially imposed sense.

In my scheme, the identifying feature of such goods is that they confer some advantage in launching the next generation. Goods that are readily observed have this property, because of their function as signals of ability. So do activities whose payoffs are concentrated in the present. The higher wage earned by the person who cleans up a radiation spill will influence the outcome of a competition that will have been long since decided by the time the mortgage against his health comes payable. Viewed from the perspective of the population as a whole, savings, insurance, leisure time, safety devices, and a host of similar nonpositional goods will tend to be underconsumed, even by fully rational participants in perfectly competitive markets. And it is this tendency that suggests an alternative explanation for why both private firms and the government might take the numerous steps they do to restrict the ways in which people allocate their time, their incomes, and even their lives among the various alternatives they face. Traditional attempts to explain these restrictions have stressed both imperfections in the competitive process and people's shortcomings in being able to perceive and act effectively on behalf of their own interests. The alternative theory I propose here is that these restrictions represent attempts to slow the positional treadmill, and have little to do with such imperfections.

But merely to observe that our concerns about relative standing create prisoner's dilemmas does not prove that those concerns are what cause us to regulate behavior in the ways discussed. As with my earlier claim that an implicit market for status accounts for the egalitarian wage structures we observe within firms, establishing causality is here, too, an elusive task. As before, my approach will be to derive specific predictions from the relative-standing model and see how they check out against observable aspects of people's behavior. To this task let us now turn.

Eight

Collective Protection of Inconspicuous Consumption

In this chapter, I investigate whether concerns about relative standing actually influence the way people allocate their incomes, and whether people, in turn, counteract such influences by implementing collective agreements.

Experience has taught economists never to approach such tasks with high expectations. Economics differs from the hard sciences in that economists generally have no way of performing controlled experiments against which to test their theories. We are forced instead to look for so-called "natural experiments," instances in which some fortuitous change in circumstances may provide an opportunity to study relationships of interest. The result is that no single empirical exercise is ever likely to rule out alternative explanations of a phenomenon. For any proposed explanation of a particular pattern of events, it is almost always possible to imagine several alternative causes. Under these circumstances, opinions on the validity of a theory depend strongly on how well its predictions coincide with actual behavior in a variety of disparate situations. And even more so than in the hard sciences, the attractiveness of a theory in economics will depend on its logical plausibility.

With these considerations in mind, my strategy here is to examine how concerns about relative standing appear related to observed spending behavior in numerous settings. I will also give careful scrutiny in each instance to the alternative explanations that have been offered for the same behavior.

The Allocation of the Consumer's Income

In Chapter 7, I argued that concerns about relative standing cause people to devote fewer resources to safety, leisure, and a variety of less readily observed budget categories, such as savings and insurance. This happens because the prospect of advancement in the consumption hierarchy acts as an implicit subsidy to the consumption of positional goods.

This subsidy is present for consumers of all income levels, but the logic of traditional economic theory suggests that its effect is strongest for low-income consumers. To see why, it is first necessary to summarize briefly what the traditional theory says about how consumers allocate their incomes.

The fundamental premise of traditional consumer theory is that people allocate their incomes across various budget categories so as to maximize their utility, or satisfaction. This premise simply states the economist's belief that people make consumption decisions in purposeful, self-serving ways. When utility has been maximized, the extra satisfaction obtained from the last dollar allocated to each budget category must be the same for all categories. (Suppose the satisfaction obtained from the last dollar spent on clothing were larger than the corresponding value for entertainment. The consumer could then increase his satisfaction by devoting a dollar less to entertainment, a dollar more to clothing.)

Traditional theory says that, beyond some point, the extra satisfaction, or "marginal utility," one receives from consuming an additional unit of a good begins to diminish. For a thirsty person, the first few swallows of water are the sweetest; for a hungry person, the first few bites of a beefsteak the most satisfying. Thus, a high-income person, who already has a lot of status, will experience a relatively smaller increase in satisfaction from a gain in status than will a low-income person, who starts with relatively little.*

People of all income levels may take a variety of actions to enhance their rank, or at least their apparent rank, in the hierarchies to which they belong. They may, as noted, work longer hours, take greater safety risks, and spend a greater portion of their incomes on readily observed consumption goods. For two reasons, the increased satisfaction all of these activities provide will generally be higher for low-income persons. First, just as the poorly fed person derives more satisfaction than others from additional food, so too will the low-ranked person derive greater satisfaction from an advance in the rankings.

The second reason is that any given positional expenditure will generally produce a larger change in rank for low-income than for high-income persons.

---

*As I stressed in Chapter 3, a person's perception of his own status does not depend only on how his income compares with incomes in the population at large. A low-income person, for example, may have relatively high income, and correspondingly high status, within a restricted local hierarchy. But for the members of even the most tightly-knit local hierarchies, external income comparisons will carry some weight. In a statistical sense, then, a person whose income is low relative to the incomes of population members at large will be more likely than others to have low status.

This happens because people are bunched together more closely nearer the bottom of the economic ladder. For a low-income person, there are many people with consumption levels only slightly higher than his own, so even a small increase in positional expenditure will appreciably increase his rank. But in the upper reaches of the income distribution, where incomes are more spread out, the same expenditure increase will not affect rankings by much. A hundred dollars more spent on clothing, a hundred dollars less saved—all such expenditure shifts will produce larger advances in the ranking for persons near the bottom of the economic hierarchy than for those near the top.

The differential return to activities that enhance status implies that the extent to which people devote too few resources to nonpositional goods depends on their position in the overall distribution of income. And this observation, in turn, suggests a specific way of testing whether concerns about relative standing do indeed influence the way people allocate their incomes. In particular, it suggests the following hypothesis:[1]

> H1:   The amounts people spend on nonpositional goods will increase less rapidly with income than they would if people were not concerned about relative standing.

The obvious difficulty in testing this hypothesis lies in specifying how expenditures would vary with income if people were not concerned about relative standing. Traditional consumer theory distinguishes several possible relationships between income and the amount spent on a good. Those goods for which expenditures rise more than proportionately with income are often designated as luxury goods. Travel abroad is an example. Those goods for which expenditures rise less than proportionately with income are often called necessities. Food fits this definition. Unfortunately, for present purposes, traditional theory offers few quantitative predictions about where specific goods or expenditure categories ought to lie along this necessity-luxury continuum.

But one very important exception occurs in the case of savings, which traditional theory predicts should be precisely on the dividing line between a luxury and a necessity. That is, traditional theory predicts that savings should rise proportionately with income, which means that the *share* of income that a person saves does not depend on the level of his income at all. By contrast, the alternative theory presented here says that savings should rise more than proportionately with income. For the case of savings, then, Hypothesis H1 may be restated in the following testable form:

> H1': The share of income a consumer saves should rise with his level of income.

Let us examine why traditional theory makes the prediction it does in the case of savings, and whether, in turn, that prediction is supported by the savings patterns we observe.

Savings Versus Income

The share of GNP that is saved varies slightly from year to year. Over the long term, however, that share has been remarkably constant, just as the traditional theory seems to require.[2] At the same time, we observe that, every year, high-income families save larger fractions of their incomes than low-income families do. The latter observation supports the alternative theory embodied in hypothesis H1'.

Since incomes have been growing steadily over time, there is thus an apparent paradox: Although the rich save higher shares of their incomes than the poor do each year, the share of national income that is saved has not risen steadily over time. Instead, it has remained approximately constant. For many years economists struggled to resolve this apparent paradox.

Duesenberry's proposed solution in 1949[3] was essentially the same as the one offered here—namely, that demonstration effects weigh relatively more heavily on people with lower incomes, causing them to consume relatively higher fractions of their incomes. This sense of relative deprivation is not diminished by across-the-board changes in absolute income, and Duesenberry thus saw no reason for aggregate income growth to alter the share of income consumed over time.

Duesenberry's explanation was persuasive to many and seemed an intuitively plausible description of how people actually behave. Yet it is perhaps an understatement to say that many economists felt uncomfortable with what they regarded as a sociological theory of consumption. To many economists, the notion of consumers being strongly influenced by demonstration effects must have seemed troublingly inconsistent with the reasoned pursuit of self-interest, if not completely irrational. It is hardly surprising, therefore, that the economics profession later so warmly embraced the "life-cycle hypothesis" of Brumberg and Modigliani,[4] and the related "permanent income hypothesis" of Friedman.[5] Without relying on vague constructs borrowed from other branches of the social sciences, these theories provided clear *a priori* reasons, carefully grounded in utility-maximizing behavior, for the observed patterns of savings rates in time-series and in cross-section data. With the emergence of the life-cycle and permanent income theories, Duesenberry's relative income hypothesis has been relegated to a historical footnote in most modern economics textbooks. At least two leading texts (Sargent, 1978, and Gordon, 1979) do not even mention Duesenberry's work at all.[6]

Both the life-cycle and permanent income hypotheses begin with the observation that the primary motive of saving is to smooth the consumption stream during one's lifetime. In years of high earnings, more will be saved, so that consumption standards will not have to fall in years of low earnings. In a random sample of persons taken in a given year, we will thus see people whose current incentives to save differ markedly. Those in their peak earnings years will save more than will those in the early stages of their careers or those who are already past retirement. Someone who has had an unusually lucky year will save a high fraction of his income as a hedge against an unlucky year in the future, when he will save much less, or perhaps even dissave. But both of these theories insist that the share of income saved over the life cycle does not depend on income.

Qualitatively speaking, the life-cycle and permanent income theories of consumption do predict exactly the patterns of time-series and cross-section savings rates we observe in actual data. And there is no question that the phenomena addressed by these theories are important. But these theories simply cannot account fully for the positive relationship between savings rates and incomes we observe in cross-section samples of individuals. The life-cycle and permanent income theories of savings both claim that if the influence of life-cycle differences and transitory earnings could be eliminated, we would then see high-income persons saving the same fractions of their incomes as low-income persons do. In study after careful study, however, this prediction has failed.

Mayer, for example, has argued that one way of eliminating the effects of transitory earnings variations is to look at average savings rates across occupations.[7] For example, even though some attorneys will have higher incomes than normal in any given year, others will have unusually low incomes. In a large sample of attorneys, therefore, the surpluses of those who had good years will largely cancel the shortfalls of those who had bad years. Mayer observed that, according to the permanent income hypothesis, the average savings rate for an occupation should thus be independent of its average income level. He then gathered data on average savings rates and average income levels for different occupations in numerous Western countries during various periods in the twentieth century. The correlations he found between occupational savings rates and occupational income levels are summarized in Table 8.1. For virtually every country for which the necessary data were available, Mayer found occupational savings rates positively correlated with average income levels by occupation. This finding is flatly inconsistent with Friedman's permanent income hypothesis.

Watts has gone a step further by studying the savings behavior of groups of individuals who represent similar heterogeneous cross-sections of the population with respect to age.[8] In so doing, Watts eliminates not only transitory earnings effects, by focusing on group averages, but life-cycle effects as well. A sample of Watts's findings is reproduced in Figure 8.1. Watts notes that, although many factors obviously affect savings rates, there is a significant positive relationship between savings rates and lifetime incomes.

Perhaps the most damaging evidence against the life-cycle and permanent income theories is that from a recent study by Diamond and Hausman.[9] Using data that record the spending and savings behavior of the same group of individuals over a multi-year period, these researchers find that, even after accounting for permanent income and life-cycle effects, savings rates still rise substantially with incomes. They write:

[O]ur most important finding is the extent to which the savings to permanent income ratio rises with permanent income. Not only does the level of savings

Table 8.1 *Correlations between Savings Rates and
Incomes across Occupations*

Country	Date of Study	Correlation between Occupational Income Levels and Savings Rates
Switzerland	1912	Positive
Finland	1920–21	Positive
Sweden	1923	Positive
Czechoslovakia	1925–26	Negative
Denmark	1931	Positive
Sweden	1933	Positive
The Netherlands	1935–36	Positive
Switzerland	1936–37	Positive
Switzerland	1937–38	Positive
United States	1948	Positive
United States	1949	Positive
Switzerland	1949	Positive
Urban United States	1950	Positive
Switzerland	1951	Positive
The Netherlands	1951	Positive
Great Britain	1951–52	Positive
Switzerland	1952	Positive
Great Britain	1952–53	Positive
Portugal	1953–54	Positive
Great Britain	1953–54	Positive
Denmark	1955	Positive
Sweden	1955	Positive
Great Britain	1955–56	Positive
Portugal	1955–56	Positive
Sweden	1957	Positive
Israel	1957–58	Positive
Norway	1958	Positive
United States	1958–59	Positive
Japan	1960	Positive

Source: Mayer (1966), Table 1.

*(wealth) rise with permanent income, but it does so in a sharply non-linear
fashion. . . . [for permanent incomes below $4770 per year, the savings-
permanent income ratio rises by 3.3% for each extra $1000 of permanent
income;] beyond $4700 it rises by 5.7% for each extra $1000 and beyond
$12,076 it rises by 14.2%. These results strongly confirm . . . that a simple
linear relationship between savings and permanent income is not supported in
our data.*[10]

Numerous other authors have presented evidence that savings rates are
positively related to life-cycle and permanent income.[11] In his review of this
evidence, Mayer wrote:

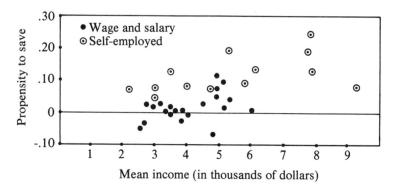

Figure 8.1 Lifetime Average Propensities to Save and Mean Incomes
Source: Watts (1958), p. 140.

[O]f all the many tests which have been undertaken by friends of the [permanent income, or life cycle] hypothesis, not a single one supports it. . . . I therefore conclude that the . . . hypothesis is definitely invalidated.[12]

The evidence on this relationship is so strong and so consistent that it would appear difficult for proponents of the permanent income and life-cycle theories to continue to insist that savings rates are unrelated to income.* Yet these claims persist in all major undergraduate and graduate texts in macro-economics.

I have argued here that, unlike the permanent income and life-cycle theories, a consumption theory that incorporates people's concerns about relative standing is able to account for the observed positive relationship between savings and income. Granted, the permanent income and life-cycle theories have made important contributions to our understanding of consumer behavior. Long-run considerations matter to most consumers, and anyone who ignores that will make systematic errors when trying to predict savings rates. But in view of the empirical evidence, the extent to which these theories have supplanted Duesenberry's relative income hypothesis must be seen as yet another testament to the power of economists' *a priori* beliefs. This outcome is both unfortunate and ironic, for, as we have repeatedly seen, concerns about relative standing are perfectly compatible with the economist's view that people pursue their own interests in a rational way.

---

*Some authors have attempted to reconcile the life-cycle and permanent income hypotheses to the savings rate data by arguing that the rich bequeath larger shares of their lifetime wealth to their heirs than do the poor.[13] Yet the aggregate ratio of bequests to national income has not risen hand in hand with national income, as a consumption theory based on absolute wealth would require. If, on the other hand, the bequest motive depends on relative wealth, then the permanent income and life-cycle theories are almost indistinguishable from Duesenberry's relative income theory.

An Alternative Interpretation of the Role of the Trade Union

I argued in Chapter 7 that two people with identical incomes can engage in cooperative consumption agreements that enhance their welfare. The same principle applies when there are many persons with different incomes. In such situations, people can make their rank in the observable consumption hierarchy appear higher than it actually is by saving a smaller proportion of their income. Yet when others in the income hierarchy do likewise, everyone's rank stays the same as before. To escape this positional spending treadmill, people may find it attractive to participate in collective agreements that increase the consumption of nonpositional goods.

Such agreements are easier to carry out with some people than with others. For example, collective consumption agreements will probably be much easier to implement among co-workers than among friends and neighbors. Firms can easily arrange for a certain share of each worker's salary to be automatically put into a pension account. Working out similar arrangements with friends and neighbors, however, would entail greater practical difficulties.

Each person has his own personal reference group, and the extent to which co-workers make up this group varies from person to person. At one extreme, the chronically unemployed person will not have any co-workers at all in his reference group. Toward the other end of the spectrum, the person who has been employed for a long time at the same firm will have a personal reference group that is more heavily composed of co-workers. These differences in the composition of personal reference groups have important implications for the way people allocate their incomes between positional and nonpositional goods.

Suppose, for example, that A and B both care about where they stand in their respective 100-member reference groups, and that each is able to make collective consumption agreements only with his own co-workers. Suppose further that 80 out of the 100 members of A's reference group are his co-workers, while the corresponding figure for B is only 20. Given these differences, A's budget share for nonpositional goods should be larger than B's. After all, if B cares mostly about where he stands relative to his friends and neighbors, then payroll savings plans and the like will be of little use to him. In general, as the share of a person's reference group with which it is practical to implement consumption agreements increases, the budget share devoted to nonpositional goods should increase as well.

To examine this prediction empirically, we must uncover some variation in the extent to which individuals can form such agreements. Several considerations suggest that trade union members are better positioned in this respect than are their nonunion counterparts. First, as noted in Chapters 4 and 5, the average length of job tenure is much higher for union members. If we assume that the bonds of friendship mature with time, this difference will cause the union member's personal reference group to be more heavily composed of co-workers. Second, a similar tendency should emerge as a result of union firms being larger, on the average, than nonunion firms. The more co-workers a person has, the more likely it is that some of them will share his values and interests. Finally, the union's administrative apparatus may facilitate an exchange of information between co-workers that makes it easier for them to form consumption agreements.

These considerations suggest the following testable hypotheses:

H2:   Budget shares devoted to pensions should be higher for union members than for nonunion members.

H3:   Budget shares devoted to insurance should be higher for union members than for nonunion members.

H4:   Budget shares devoted to paid vacations should be higher for union members than for nonunion members.

H5:   Budget shares devoted to workplace safety should be higher for union members than for nonunion members.

UNION VERSUS NONUNION COMPENSATION ITEMS

Using data from the Bureau of Labor Statistics' Expenditures for Employee Compensation Survey, Richard B. Freeman has examined the effect of collective bargaining on various fringe benefits in the compensation package.[14] After first employing a statistical procedure to eliminate the effects of income differences between union and nonunion workers, Freeman estimated the effect of collective bargaining on eight components of voluntary fringe benefits. His results are reproduced in Table 8.2. The entries in column 3 of this table represent the effects of unionism on the fringe items listed. The first entry in that column means, for example, that union workers receive an average of 4.8 cents per hour more in life, accident, and health insurance benefits than do nonunion workers with the same income levels.

Table 8.2 *The Effect of Collective Bargaining on Specific Fringes, All Private Industry, 1967-72*

Fringe	Cents per Hour Spent on Fringe	Coefficients (and Standard Errors) for the Effect of Collective Bargaining on Cents per Hour Spent on Fringes
1. Life, accident, and health insurance	10.1	4.8 (0.2)
2. Vacation	8.3	1.6 (0.2)
3. Overtime premiums	10.1	−0.5 (0.4)
4. Pension	9.4	3.9 (0.4)
5. Holidays	5.2	0.8 (0.1)
6. Shift differential	1.1	0.3 (0.1)
7. Sick leave	1.1	−0.5 (0.1)
8. Bonuses	1.8	−1.4 (0.3)

Source: Freeman (1981), Table 4, p. 503.

Note that collective bargaining has its largest impact on fringe items 1 and 4. Union workers devote almost 48 percent more to insurance benefits than do nonunion workers with the same income levels. Similarly, union workers devote over 41 percent more to pensions. These findings strongly support hypotheses H2 and H3. Hypothesis H4, which says that union workers will devote a larger share of total compensation to "paid" vacations, is supported by Freeman's estimates for fringe items 2 and 5.

Freeman's estimates of the effects of collective bargaining on shift differentials and overtime premiums offer a mixed message for the theory of collective bargaining proposed here. On one hand, union members have higher shift differentials (e.g., premiums for working at night), which is consistent with the notion that cooperation helps workers resist the temptation to gain position by working at night for higher wages. (By this interpretation, the greater willingness of nonunion workers to work at night results in their getting a smaller shift premium.) On the other hand, Freeman reports that overtime premiums are smaller for union workers than for nonunion workers, which does not support the view of union objectives offered here. But the union/nonunion difference is less than 5 percent of the total devoted to this fringe item, which is not statistically significant. Overtime premiums, moreover, are largely dictated to employers by the provisions of the Fair Labor Standards Act, so we shouldn't see large union/nonunion differences in this item in any event. Sick leave is also smaller for union than for nonunion workers, although the difference here, too, is small.

Note, finally, that "Bonuses" (item 8 in Table 8.2) are substantially smaller for union workers than for nonunion workers with the same incomes. For purposes of the consumption theory proposed here, bonuses are equivalent to wage income insofar as both come in the form of cash. Bonuses therefore represent a portion of the compensation package that is left free from any collective allocation pattern the respective groups may wish to promote. Accordingly, this theory predicts that bonuses will be larger for nonunion workers than for union workers who have similar income levels. And Freeman does find that bonuses for nonunion workers are four and one-half times those of their union counterparts.

Needless to say, there may be other explanations for the pattern of findings we see in Table 8.2. Freeman's own explanation assumes that older workers, who play a decisive role in the collective bargaining process, have comparatively high demands for fringe benefits. The union firm must therefore cater to these workers in the design of its compensation package. The nonunion firm, by contrast, is forced to tailor its fringe benefits to the tastes of younger workers, who are relatively more willing to move to another firm if they don't get what they seek. Let us consider the merits of this alternative explanation.

Freeman's argument says, in effect, that the nonunion firm forces older workers to take fewer fringe benefits than they really want. (If it gave the older workers what they wanted, it would then lose its mobile younger workers to other firms that offer a larger share of the compensation package in the form of cash.) But why is it necessary to force *all* workers to consume the same fringe package? Firms can, and almost always do, link many compensation items by formula to the employee's length of tenure. In union and nonunion firms alike, wages, as well as pensions and vacations, are explicitly linked to tenure. Other fringes, such as life and accident insurance, are often linked to total compensation, which, as noted, is also highly correlated with tenure.

Assuming that demands for fringes differ by age group, and that firms can tailor their fringe benefits to the demands of different age groups, let us explore the consequences for a firm of failing to do so. Suppose, for example, the workers in a nonunion firm were willing to trade income for vacation time in the manner shown in Table 8.3. The entries in Table 8.3 take into account Freeman's assumption that older workers assign higher value to vacation time than younger workers do. Let us assume the marginal products of younger workers and older workers are $150 and $175 per week, respectively, and that vacations can be taken only in multiples of one week. Given the entries in Table 8.3, it is easy to see that the "best" amount of vacation time for younger workers would be one week per year. They would willingly sacrifice up to $200 in pay for the first week of vacation, but the firm would lose only $150 worth of output by granting it. The second week of vacation, however, is worth only $100 to younger workers, yet still costs the firm $150 in lost output. So the second week of vacation should not be taken by younger workers. Parallel reasoning shows that three weeks is the best amount of vacation time for older workers.

Why, then, would this firm offer older workers only one week of vacation per year (saying "We can't help it, that's what the younger workers want")? Both older workers and the firm would do better by increasing the vacation time of these workers to three weeks per year. By so doing, the older workers would, by assumption, be willing to accept as much as a $500 yearly pay cut (the difference between the $900 they would be prepared to give up for three weeks of vacation and the $400 they would give up for one week). Yet the extra cost to the firm (in terms of lost output resulting from the longer vacations) would be only $350 per year per worker. A package in which older workers got, say, $375 less in wages per year in return for two weeks of extra vacation time would thus leave both the older workers and the firm better off than before.

Table 8.3 *Willingness to Pay for Vacation Time, Younger Versus Older Workers*

Total Vacation Time per Year	Maximum Acceptable Income Sacrifice ($/year)	
	Younger Workers	Older Workers
1 week	200	400
2 weeks	300	700
3 weeks	350	900
4 weeks	425	1000

Applied to the union firm, Freeman's argument similarly requires union members to be willing to ignore obvious opportunities for mutual gain. Suppose Freeman's older union workers forced all company employees to take three weeks of vacation per year. By so doing, they would be making younger workers consume two additional weeks of vacation that are worth only $150 per year to them, but that cost $300 per year in lost output. If younger workers were allowed to cut back their vacation time from three weeks to one week per year, $150 of net gain would thus be produced. That $150 could be distributed among older and younger workers however the union saw fit. Freeman's explanation seems unable to account for why union members and the owners of nonunion firms would insist on constructing fringe packages in the manner they do.

Mincer finds a pattern of union/nonunion compensation differences similar to the one found by Freeman, for which he offers yet another explanation.[15] Mincer argues that union workers are fearful that if they raise wages too high, firms will then find it profitable to limit the number of hours employees may work.* He then contends that union workers try to frustrate this strategem by demanding a larger share of their compensation in the form of fringe benefits. Fringe benefits, he explains, act as lump sums in the compensation schedule— even if the firm curtails hours, it must still pay out the same fringe benefits as before. By thus restructuring its compensation package, the union reduces the firm's incentive to curtail hours worked.

This is a very curious strategy for a union to implement. Any union that had sufficient bargaining power to implement such a strategy presumably also would have enough power to demand and get a lump sum cash benefit appended to its weekly salary formula. Shifting part of its compensation into this form would produce the same change in incentives as would shifting compensation into fringe benefits. But having the income in the form of cash would give workers greater latitude in their consumption decisions, and, in Mincer's framework, would lead therefore to higher utility levels for union workers. That they fail to take advantage of this simple opportunity means that Mincer's argument cannot adequately account for the observed differences between union and nonunion compensation packages.

Several people have suggested to me that tax considerations might account for the observed differences between union and nonunion fringe shares. Since income in the form of fringe benefits is nontaxable, there are obvious gains from taking income in this form rather than in cash. But these tax advantages are present for both union and nonunion workers. And since we know that union workers devote a larger share of compensation to fringe benefits than do nonunion workers with the same income level, the difference cannot logically be the result of tax incentives.

---

*Mincer doesn't say, but the reason that unions don't simultaneously bargain with firms to prevent such hours reductions is perhaps that unpredictable variations in product demand (which are unobservable by workers) make it inefficient to do so.

UNION VERSUS NONUNION WORKPLACE SAFETY LEVELS

Unfortunately, little reliable information exists on what firms spend to promote health and safety in the workplace. We are thus forced to search for an alternative means of testing the hypothesis that union members devote comparatively large shares of total compensation to safety. One additional way the hypothesized difference ought to show up is in the wage premiums the two groups receive for performing risky tasks. Union workers, like nonunion workers, are willing to accept greater risks in return for higher wages. But if union workers are better able to express safety demands cooperatively, it then follows that, for a given level of income and risk, the wage premium for performing risky tasks should be higher for union workers.

In their widely cited 1976 paper, Thaler and Rosen report the results of a statistical study that is well-suited for testing this hypothesis.[16] In their study, they employ data on 907 male household heads taken from the 1967 *Survey of Economic Opportunity*, together with industry/occupational mortality rates obtained from the *1967 Occupation Study of the Society of Actuaries*, to assess the effect of exposure to risk on individual wage rates. Using these data, Thaler and Rosen estimate that the union worker must receive a risk premium that is $8.08 per week higher than the premium required by an identically situated nonunion worker for accepting a one-thousandth increase in the annual probability of death. This difference amounts to a substantial fraction (often more than one-half) of the total premiums workers receive in return for performing risky tasks.[17]

To be sure, other explanations than the one advanced here may help account for this difference. As Thaler and Rosen themselves speculate, the tastes of union workers may simply be different from those of nonunion workers. Or perhaps unions disseminate information about job risks to their members, who are then in a better position to make informed decisions about risks. This possibility seems especially worth investigating in the current environment, as we are just beginning to discover the long-term consequences of exposure to hazardous chemical substances in the workplace. The Thaler-Rosen data on wage and risk rates, however, are drawn from occupations and from a period in time for which the most clearly perceived differences in job safety conditions had to do with differences in the incidence of injuries and fatalities on the job. Information of this sort should have been about equally visible to both union and nonunion workers.

One other important possibility is that union and nonunion workers have the same preferences regarding safety and wage income but may weigh the preferences of older, more risk-averse employees differently during the bargaining process. Viscusi explains higher union safety levels along these lines.[18] This explanation parallels Freeman's explanation of why the fringe share of the compensation package is higher for union workers, and it suffers, therefore, from the same difficulties. In almost every firm, there is a menu of tasks to be performed, not all of which are equally risky. Where such a menu exists, risk-averse older workers can be accommodated by simply assigning them to the relatively safe tasks. There is thus no apparent reason for Viscusi's older union workers to require their younger co-workers to purchase uneconomically large quantities of safety. If older workers really control union decision making, they would presumably allow younger workers to perform the risky tasks those workers would choose for themselves. The cost savings could then take the form of higher wages, distributed in whatever way union members see fit. The failure of these older workers to do so suggests that some factor other than age-related preferences must explain higher union safety levels.

Perhaps the older workers are behaving paternalistically (and altruistically, too, since it costs them money) toward the younger union workers. But altruism cannot account for the parallel implications of Viscusi's argument for behavior in nonunion firms. For why would nonunion firms inflict uneconomically large risk burdens on risk-averse older workers? In Viscusi's framework, both the firm and the older worker could do better by shifting older workers to less risky tasks.

GOALS OF THE TRADE UNION MOVEMENT

The differences between union and nonunion compensation packages suggest an alternative interpretation of the economic role of the trade union movement. Early accounts of the movement stressed the role of unions as a force for neutralizing the excessive market power of firms. In his 1903 history of the American labor movement, for example, John Mitchell wrote:

In its fundamental principle trade unionism is plain and clear and simple. Trade unionism starts from the recognition of the fact that under normal conditions the individual unorganized workman cannot bargain advantageously with the employer for the sale of his labor. Since the working man has no money in reserve and must sell his labor immediately, since, moreover, he has no knowledge of the market and no skill in bargaining, since, finally, he has only his own labor to sell, while the employer engages hundreds or thousands of men and can easily do without the services of any particular individual, the working man, if bargaining on his own account and for himself alone, is at an enormous disadvantage.[19]

More recent accounts of the role of the union paint a somewhat broader picture. Hirschman, for example, stresses the valuable contribution unions make by organizing procedures for the redress of worker grievances.[20] Other authors have stressed the union's role in making the workplace more democratic.[21] And few would deny that labor relations have made significant strides since Mitchell's day, in form if not always in substance. Still, the view of the union as a countervailing force against exploitation continues to be prominent in modern accounts.[22] As already noted, for example, Freeman and Viscusi stress market power in their discussions of safety and fringe benefits.

In the alternative interpretation suggested here, by contrast, the firm's market power plays no role. Even if labor markets were perfectly competitive, workers who negotiate individually might nonetheless sell various aspects of their services too cheaply. When concerns about relative standing loom large,

Drawing by Ed Arno. Copyright © 1971 Saturday Review, Inc. Reprinted by permission of the artist.

"I am afraid this is not a propitious time for a raise, Adams. Or, as my father would have said, why the devil should I give you a raise? Or, as my grandfather would have said, GET THE HELL OUT OF HERE!"

for example, the individual bargainer will accept a safety risk that the collective bargainer would not. And this would be true even if the total economic pie available for workers were fixed at the outset by the forces of competition. No matter that labor markets may be just as highly competitive as economists insist; there might nonetheless be sensible reasons, quite apart from the prospect of an increase in total compensation, for workers to determine the distribution of compensation collectively.

In proposing this alternative interpretation of the trade union's objectives, it is not necessary to abandon the conventional view that trade unions arose, at least in part, to oppose the almost unspeakably degrading working conditions encountered during the early phases of industrialization. On the contrary, the trade union movement surely derived much of its moral force from the widespread existence of such working conditions as those described in Upton Sinclair's account of life in the meat-packing factories of Chicago at the turn of the century:

Some worked at the stamping machines, and it was very seldom that one could work long there at the pace that was set, and not give out and forget himself, and have a part of his hand chopped off. There were the "hoisters," as they were called, whose task it was to press the lever which lifted the dead cattle off the floor. They ran along upon a rafter, peering down through the damp and the steam; and as old Durham's architect had not built the killing-room for the convenience of the hoisters, at every few feet they would have to stoop under a beam, say four feet above the one they ran on; which got them into the habit of stooping, so that in a few years they would be walking like chimpanzees. Worst of any, however, were the fertilizer-men, and those who served in the cooking-rooms. These people could not be shown to the visitors,—for the odor of the fertilizer-man would scare any ordinary visitor at a hundred yards, and as for the other men, who worked in tank-rooms full of steam, and in some which there were open vats near the level of the floor, their peculiar trouble was that they fell into the vats; and when they were fished out, there was never enough of them left to be worth exhibiting,—sometimes they would be overlooked for days, till all but the bones of them had gone out to the world as Durham's Pure Leaf Lard.[23]

The owners of the factories of that era enjoyed a material standard of living that was as lavish as the worker's was wretched. Their capital investments were large enough to produce very generous incomes, even if the rate of return on those investments never exceeded a perfectly competitive rate. Perhaps it was all but inevitable that this juxtaposition of the owner's wealth and the work-man's poverty would establish, in most people's mind's, the existence of an exploitative relationship between the owner and the worker. Granted, there may be a strong tendency for owners to exploit workers whenever they have the power necessary to do so. But the presence of market power is not logically necessary for an account of why workers so often labored under such poor conditions. In the presence of strong concerns about position, persons with relatively few skills may bargain individually for just such conditions, even when the labor market is as strongly competitive as all available evidence suggests (see Chapter 3). But when bargaining as a group, those same workers may distribute their total compensation in a very different way.

The Structure of Military Compensation

Most military personnel live together in groups that are more or less se-questered from the civilian population. The personal reference groups of military workers will thus consist almost entirely of their co-workers. To an even larger extent than are union workers, then, military workers are well-positioned to implement cooperative consumption agreements. The relatively high degree of isolation of military personnel from non-co-workers suggests the following testable hypotheses:

H6: Budget shares devoted to savings should be higher for military personnel than for civilian workers.

H7: Budget shares devoted to insurance should be higher for military than for civilian workers.

To test Hypothesis H6, let us compare military retirement plans with those of private and government civilian workers. The figures in Table 8.4 represent total expected lifetime pension payments exclusive of Social Security payments. Military personnel and most private sector employees are eligible for Social Security payments at age 62, whereas federal government civilian employees receive no Social Security payments. Although this difference distorts the comparisons in Table 8.4 in favor of federal government civilian workers, military personnel nonetheless have far and away the most liberal pension coverage in absolute terms of any of the three groups considered. In terms of the share of after-tax income replaced by the various pension plans (this time including Social Security), the military worker again fares best with a 97.7 percent replacement ratio, as compared to 73.5 percent for civil service workers and even lower ratios for most private sector workers.[24]

Concerning other unobservable fringe elements, the military requires its personnel to carry life insurance, whereas civil service employees have no such requirement (though coverage is made available to civil servants at subsidized rates). Many private sector employers provide employees with automatic life insurance coverage. Medical insurance coverage is by any standard more

Table 8.4 *Lifetime Value of Military and Private Pension Provisions, in 1978 Dollars*

	20 Years of Service		30 Years of Service	
	Value[a]	Age Annuity Begins	Value[a]	Age Annuity Begins
U.S. military				
Officer level	$240,000	43	$590,000	53
Enlisted level	190,000	39	280,000	49
Typical private				
Executive level	40,000	62	135,000	62
Nonexecutive level	15,000	62	45,000	62
Federal civil service				
Executive level	90,000	60	465,000	55
Nonexecutive level	25,000	60	155,000	55

Source: The President's Commission on Military Compensation, April 1978, p. 31.

[a]See notes in Source for details of calculations.

extensive in the military than in other sectors. Military personnel on active duty receive "free" unlimited health care, including dental and optometry services, whereas private and civil service medical benefits are limited in most cases to some form of major medical insurance coverage.

As with other evidence considered earlier, numerous alternative explanations can of course be offered for these features of the military compensation package. Especially where life insurance and medical benefits are concerned, for example, it is tempting to suggest that these are related in some way to the inherent riskiness of military life. Still, benefits could have been restricted to cover only deaths and injuries sustained in combat or in combat training. Yet they were not.

Perhaps the structure of military compensation reflects some tendency toward paternalistic regulation of employee behavior that is for various possible reasons more pronounced in the military than elsewhere. Yet we have evidence that the heavy tilt toward deferred compensation in the military has had adverse consequences on the military's efforts to recruit new personnel.[25] If the degree of existing deferred compensation also ran counter to the preferences of most current career military personnel, why would the military then set up its pay scheme this way? Under these circumstances, a more front-loaded compensation structure would simultaneously reduce costs and raise morale. Simple incompetence may of course account for suboptimal features in the military compensation package. Or, as I suggest here, the current package may not be suboptimal at all.

A Speculation on the Japanese Labor Contract

Of the myriad differences between Japanese and American employment practices, there is one in particular that stands out: Whereas in the United States it is common for people to work for numerous firms during their careers, most Japanese workers remain with a single employer throughout their working lives. As James Abegglen described the Japanese practice in his influential book, *Management and Worker:*

When comparing the social organization of the factory in Japan and the United States one difference is immediately noted and continues to dominate and represent much of the total difference between the two systems. At whatever level of organization in the Japanese factory, the worker commits himself on entrance to the company for the rest of his working career. The company will not discharge him even temporarily except in the most extreme circumstances. He will not quit the company for industrial employment elsewhere. He is a member of the company in a way resembling that in which persons are members of families, fraternal organizations, and other intimate and personal groups in the United States.[26]

The Japanese worker's association with his co-workers is one not only of long duration, but also of close physical and social proximity during nonworking hours. Even in large cities, for example, most plants provide company housing for at least a third of their employees.[27] With these arrangements in mind, we can assume that the reference group of the typical Japanese worker is much more heavily composed of his co-workers than is the case for the typical American worker.

One other salient feature that differentiates employment practices in Japan from those in the United States concerns the provision of a variety of in-kind employee benefits. Although the share of total compensation devoted to fringe benefits in the United States has grown substantially in recent decades, such benefits remain small compared to those in Japan. In Japan, it has become increasingly commonplace for large firms to provide total living environments for their employees. The following account by Abegglen of the benefits, beyond simple housing and dining facilities, provided in a large textile plant is by no means atypical:

The public bath, a popular institution in Japan, is provided and maintained in the factory area at no cost to the workers. Since the company maintains a well-equipped and well-staffed dental and medical center, the worker's medical expenses are almost nil. Athletic facilities exist in considerable number, and the dormitory has an extensive and active club system to provide entertainment. The worker is most likely to spend his holidays at the mountains or beach dormitory maintained by the company, for which he will be charged a small fee. . . . He will also receive financial aid in the event of illness, death, or other misfortune. His income increases with marriage, of course, and will increase still more as children are born. His children may attend the company school. . . . In short, nearly every detail of his life is interpenetrated by the company's facilities, guidance, and assistance.[28]

In addition to receiving greater in-kind benefits than his American counterpart does, the Japanese worker also saves more than twice as much.[29]

Now, I am far too ignorant of the details of life and culture in Japan to do more than speculate here about the possibility of a causal connection between the differences in employment relationships and the differences in the ways workers dispose of their income in the two countries. Still, two propositions appear clear: (1) Co-workers seem to play a more important role in the lives of Japanese than of American workers; and (2) co-workers are the easiest group with whom to implement cooperative consumption agreements. Given these two propositions and the theory developed in Chapter 7, the differences we see in the American and Japanese compensation packages are of just the sort we would predict.* Whether such a causal connection really exists and, if so, how important it is are questions that must be taken up by scholars well-acquainted with Japan.

---

*In addition, the intrafirm wage structure is generally much more compressed in Japan than in the United States,[30] which is consistent with the prediction that follows from the theory of compensating wage differences developed in Chapter 3.

As I have stressed, no one particular piece of evidence discussed in this chapter proves conclusively that concerns about position systematically distort the composition of consumption spending. Indeed, readers are well-advised to be especially skeptical any time the author of a proposition examines it with evidence of his own choosing. Guard as the researcher may against it, there is always the danger of falling into the pattern of inference Francis Bacon so aptly described when in 1620 he wrote:

The human understanding when it has once adopted an opinion draws all things else to support and agree with it. And though there be a greater number and weight of instances to be found on the other side, yet these it either neglects or despises, or else by some distinction sets aside and rejects, in order that by this great and pernicious predetermination the authority of its former conclusion may remain inviolate.[31]

In my choice of cases to examine, perhaps I have fallen victim to the subconscious bias that Bacon described. In any event, I hope I have made my case that the prevailing explanations for the phenomena examined here are themselves seriously flawed. (Perhaps their authors, too, were subject to Bacon's bias.) The permanent income and life-cycle hypotheses of consumption, for example, are flatly inconsistent with the relationship between savings and lifetime income found in numerous careful studies. Even more troubling, the traditional explanations for union/nonunion differentials in workplace safety levels and in fringe shares of the compensation package appear to rule out utility-maximizing behavior on the part of unions and cost-minimizing behavior on the part of nonunion firms. The interdependent choice framework proposed here, by contrast, can account for these differentials in a simple, straightforward way, one completely in harmony with the economist's traditional characterization of the behavioral objectives of individuals and firms.

Much more empirical work obviously needs to be done on all of these issues. Still, it appears fair even at this stage to say that the framework offered here provides a more coherent, parsimonious explanation of the observations in question than alternative studies do.

Nine

The Left's Critique of Capitalism

The market system is the celebrated child of the political right. Conservatives admire the almost astonishing quickness and flexibility with which it responds to people's demands; the way it encourages self-reliance; the way it calls forth technological progress and economic growth; and, in particular, the way it rewards thrift, initiative, and hard work.

But critics on the left see the market system through a much less flattering lens. In the marketplace, they see first a system in which the strong exploit the weak. Firms with market power take unfair advantage of workers whose opportunities are limited. The so-called voluntary employment contract is seen as yet another capitalist fiction, since a reserve army of unemployed stands ready to replace any worker who complains that his wage is too low, his hours too long, his factory too unsafe, or his working conditions too alienating and stultifying.

Critics from the left also see the market system as promoting, indeed almost depending on, the sale of products that serve no social need. They see manipulative advertisements that cajole people into spending their incomes on gas guzzling cars with retractable headlights, while the environment decays and children lack good books to read.

These critics see, finally, that the market system's rewards are not in proportion to need or even to merit. People whose talents and abilities differ only slightly often earn dramatically different incomes. And reward bears almost no relation to the social value of the work that is done: The lawyer who helps his corporate client exploit tax loopholes takes home several hundred thousand dollars annually, while the person who struggles to teach our eighth graders algebra is paid a pittance. As seen by critics on the left, rewards in the market system are doled out not according to need or merit, but according to power and privilege.

An impartial observer might be tempted to attribute these conflicting views to the fact that the market system favors the personal values and abilities of conservatives. On the average, conservatives do, in fact, earn more than liberals do. Yet the earnings distributions of the two groups overlap too much for this explanation to be completely persuasive. There are plenty of rich liberals, and even more poor conservatives.

Most people, of course, are at neither extreme of the political spectrum. Those in the middle presumably see the real truth about the market system as lying somewhere between the views offered by the extreme camps. In this chapter, I argue that the most fruitful interpretation is *not* to think of the marketplace as being some convenient middle ground between these two extremes. The marketplace I portray here has both the positive qualities put forth by its defenders as well as the catalogue of ills for which it has been attacked. I will argue, however, that the left has in almost every instance offered the wrong reasons for why market outcomes go awry. Let us begin by examining the left's claim that working conditions are excessively stultifying.

Alienation in the Workplace

Adam Smith was the first to observe formally that the division and specialization of labor are generally accompanied by greatly enhanced productivity.[1] Smith made his "point" by describing the division of labor in a pin factory:

One man draws out the wire, another straightens it, a third cuts it, a fourth points it, a fifth grinds it at the top for receiving the head; to make the head requires two or three distinct operations. . . . I have seen a small manufactory of this kind where only ten men were employed . . . [who] could, when they exerted themselves, make among them about twelve pounds of pins in a day. There are in a pound upwards of four thousand pins of a middling size. Those ten persons, therefore, could make among them upwards of forty-eight thousand pins in a day. Each person, therefore, making a tenth part of forty-eight thousand pins, might be considered as making four thousand eight hundred pins in a day. But if they had all wrought separately and independently, and without any of them having been educated to this peculiar business, they certainly could not each of them have made twenty, perhaps not one pin in a day. . . .[2]

Smith's observation accounts for why the typical person does not devote 10 percent of his time to auto manufacturing, 5 percent to growing food, 25 percent to building housing, .0001 percent to performing brain surgery, and so on. By concentrating on one task and learning to do it well, we can cooperate with others who have become similarly specialized, which greatly increases everyone's standard of living.

But it is easy to see that specialization also has certain costs. In his 1936 classic, *Modern Times*, Chaplin gives us an amusing, if disturbingly real, look at the psychological damage inflicted on the worker whose only task—all day, every day—is to tighten the nuts on two bolts as they pass mockingly before him on an assembly line. The human nervous system performs best when exposed to variety, and too much of the same thing quickly results in a sense of boredom and ennui. As Karl Marx wrote more than a century ago, when the process of automation was still very much in its infancy:

> [A]*ll means for the development of production transform themselves into means of domination over, and exploitation of the* [workers]*; they mutilate the laborer into a fragment of a man, degrade him to the level of an appendage of a machine, destroy every remnant of charm in his work and turn it into hated toil. . . .*[3]

There is thus a fundamental tension involved in increasing the specialization of labor. When labor becomes more specialized, we get more output—something we like—but at the same time we deprive ourselves of the stimulus of variety—something we don't like. Between the extremes of, on the one hand, performing all of life's tasks for oneself and, on the other, performing only a tiny fraction of one task all of the time, there presumably lies some point that represents an optimal balance. At that point, the satisfaction from the extra output we get from a slight increase in specialization is exactly counterbalanced by the dissatisfaction from the accompanying reduction in variety. The optimal specialization point will differ from person to person. But wherever it happens to lie, it will fall short on both dimensions people care about here—namely, stimulus and productivity.

Critics of the market system believe that producers' hunger for profits causes them to force workers to move far past the optimal stopping point on the specialization scale. This charge falls on receptive ears among those who feel that the workplace *has* gotten too specialized; and that producers really care primarily about profits, and only secondarily, if at all, about whether workers get enough stimulus on the job.

But the producer's relentless search for profits is not sufficient reason to conclude that specialization has proceeded too far. Proponents of the market system have never pretended that employers feel an unselfish concern about their employees. On the contrary, the true elegance of the marketplace (as seen by its proponents) is that it provides workers with a fair and efficient work package precisely *because* employers seek relentlessly to enhance their profits.

Suppose that we grant the left's claim that the gains from having greater variety would outweigh the added costs. Why then doesn't some new firm, motivated by its greedy search for profits, offer less specialized jobs? Such a firm could, by definition, reduce wages by an amount greater than the output lost from its decreased specialization. In the process, it would earn higher profits than existing firms do. Given that excess specialization means profit opportunities for new firms, where are these firms?

The critic on the left may respond that firms conspire with one another to thwart the competitive process. The defender of the marketplace readily concedes that the antitrust records are filled with instances in which firms agree to fix prices, to stay out of one another's markets, and so on. But trying to limit competition and succeeding at it are two different things. As noted in Chapter 3, the history of cartels is one of gross instability. The number of outsiders not involved in anticompetitive agreements is too large, and the gains to insiders from cheating on such agreements are too great for the competitive process thus to be systematically and persistently frustrated.

Even if there were only one firm in the world, however, it would still not pay for that firm to divide tasks excessively. If a slight increase in variety would be worth, say, $10 per week to the worker, but would result in only a $5 drop in output, why would the firm insist on maintaining the degree of specialization at its current level? If, on the other hand, increased variety would be worth, say, only $5 per week to the worker, but would result in a $10 drop in output, then reducing the degree of specialization will serve only to make both the firm and the worker worse off than before.

Democracy in the Workplace

Related complaints are heard that alienation in the workplace runs high because the workplace is insufficiently democratic. Owners and managers tell workers what to produce and how to produce it, thus robbing them of that sense of participation that is so essential to their psychological well-being. We are even told that alienation is so severe that it actually reduces productivity. As Bowles, Gordon, and Weisskopf write:

Workers in more participatory workplaces are not only more productive but also much more satisfied with their jobs. We could apparently increase hourly output by at least 15 percent without pushing workers harder or exposing them to greater workplace hazards. This waste elimination would come from greater work commitment, not speedup. It would capitalize on all of the worker effort currently WASTED in capitalist enterprises through working to rules, through slowdown and shirking, through direct worker resistance. . . . If production workers controlled their own conditions of work, the returns in economic effectiveness would be enormous.[4]

In a very thoughtful analysis of social relationships in the workplace, Herbert Gintis attempts to explain why the firm is reluctant to take advantage of these potential gains in productivity.[5] Gintis concedes that increasing worker participation will produce gains for the employer in the short run. But he argues that participation itself will transform the worker's consciousness in a way that will later prove harmful to the employer. As Gintis puts it:

"I'm hoping to find something in a meaningful, humanist, outreach kind of bag, with flexible hours, non-sexist bosses, and fabulous fringes."

The profit maximizer must take into account in his choice of work organization, job staffing, and wage differentials, the effect of his or her actions on the consciousness of the workers. *Since the labor exchange depends on the preferences of workers in addition to their capacities, since the employer-employee relationship tends to endure over many production periods and since the experience of workers in the production process will affect their consciousness, the simple one-product firm faces a joint-product production function: The inputs are raw materials and workers with a certain consciousness and the outputs include both the good produced and the "new" workers with transformed consciousness. Many of these "new" workers will be inputs at the next stage of production. . . . [F]orms of work organization which tend not to reproduce worker consciousness appropriate to further profits will not be introduced, however strongly desired by workers and however materially productive.*[6]

By "worker consciousness appropriate to further profits," Gintis and other writers mean an attitude that makes workers willing to carry out their employer's wishes.[7]

Now, it is clear enough that a work force with ideas of its own about what products should be produced could prove detrimental to the employer's interests. But the crucial point critics on the left overlook here is that workers cannot harm the owners of the firm without simultaneously hurting themselves.

Suppose, for example, a group of auto workers were given greater control over workplace decisions. And suppose that, as a result of a consciousness transformation of the sort described by Gintis, these workers decided to produce automobiles that coincided with their own vision of true human needs. There would be no more bright synthetic finishes and aluminum alloy wheels. Instead, the resources previously consumed by such frills would go into the production of sturdy, reliable, basic transportation machines.

In some instances, workers might be lucky, and find that their vision of a desirable car coincided exactly with what buyers wanted. But success here would not be guaranteed. After all, this is exactly what the firm itself is currently trying to do with the help of trained marketing professionals. Granted, firms often misjudge the whims of the buying public.* But since their survival depends on being able to market their products, firms invest considerable resources toward keeping such errors to a minimum. We have no persuasive reason to expect that workers with little training or experience in marketing would outperform seasoned professionals in this area. And if workers produced cars that few people wished to buy, then the firm's profitability would indeed be at stake. Also at risk, however, would be the jobs and wages of the workers themselves. Worker-managed firms are not exempt from the laws of the marketplace. Firms that sell few cars simply could not support a large work force at high wages.

When interpreted in this way, Gintis' argument differs little from the market economist's. Any party is free to organize a firm that offers whatever degree of worker participation it wishes. To the extent that a high degree of participation prevents a firm from marketing its products successfully (whether because of altered consciousness or any other reason), there is then an identifiable cost associated with increased participation. Workers who value participatory environments highly will elect to bear that cost, while others will gravitate toward more conventional firms. And by the market economist's standard, at least, this is just as it should be.

Critics on the left may respond that such arguments do not take into account the critical distinction between the ownership class and the underclass. To survive, the ownership class must maintain strict control over the deployment of its assets, and over the very class structure itself. Giving workers some say in these matters sets a dangerous precedent that in the future can serve only to undermine the position of the ruling elite.

---

*And they also often fail to predict sudden dramatic shifts in input prices, as in the spring of 1979, when oil prices suddenly doubled. The ensuing slump in auto sales is often cited by critics as evidence of domestic auto industry mismanagement. Such critics apparently feel that Detroit should have long since introduced a full line of small, fuel-efficient cars, as the Europeans and Japanese had done years earlier. It is far from clear, however, that ineptitude on the part of domestic producers was responsible for the superior performance of their foreign rivals during the early 1980s. Foreign producers have always faced stiff taxes on gasoline and even on vehicle horsepower, and so had little real choice but to offer small, fuel-efficient cars all along. Americans wanted such cars, too, once the price of gasoline soared. But there is no reason to suppose that a full line of such cars would have been a profitable marketing strategy prior to the unanticipated events of the spring of 1979.

For this response to make sense, however, there must be an extraordinary degree of class solidarity among the ruling elite. After all, the nature of power relationships in society surely does not depend significantly on the employment practices of any one firm. Whether a given firm grants additional control to workers or not, the fundamental nature of power relationships in society remains the same, just as the level of smog in Los Angeles is virtually unaffected by the actions of any particular driver. Does the left ask us to believe that each firm refrains from exploiting lucrative profit opportunities, even though no single firm's actions would have any real effect on the class structure?

Suppose, for argument's sake, that we grant the existence of such an extraordinary degree of self-restraint among the ownership class. What would then prevent workers from organizing firms of their own in which specialization and democratization are set at whatever levels they see fit? In Marx's day, the left might have responded that workers could never raise the necessary capital to do so. Receiving only a subsistence wage, workers were, in effect, forever alienated from the means of production. Echoes of this claim are still heard today, but it is imprudent for the left to base its case on such a weak premise. Most workers in developed countries obviously earn much more than a subsistence wage. Even if bankers tried to discriminate against workers who tried to form businesses, serious practical difficulties would stand in their way. Banks find it profitable, for example, to make signature loans and second mortgage loans to their customers without asking what the funds are to be used for. Are we to suppose that they would discontinue this practice once word got out that people were using the loans to start thriving new businesses?

Although worker-controlled firms might be forced to begin on a small scale, the inability of workers to raise the necessary capital cannot account for the shortage of such firms. After all, most conventional businesses themselves start on a small scale. And despite numerous difficulties, those with a better way of doing things manage to prosper and grow. Indeed, there are numerous worker-controlled firms that begin operation each year, and although many of them fail, some manage to survive. Moreover, many conventional firms have experimented profitably with granting greater worker participation in workplace decision making. Banks would not long resist the opportunity to make profitable loans to firms in those industries in which worker participation has proved successful.

For the market-oriented economist who reviews these arguments, the question of whether there are the "correct" amounts of specialization and worker participation amounts to a nonissue. Those workers who like to attend meetings at which workplace decisions are discussed at length will choose to work for firms that offer such meetings. If having meetings reduces output, wages will be lower in these firms; otherwise they will be the same or higher than in conventional firms. Those who would rather play softball or stop for a beer on the way home than become involved with the various decisions that confront an enterprise can continue to work for the types of firms we see today. By this view, the left's complaint that there is too much alienation in the workplace simply reflects its failure to understand that we cannot have our cake and eat it too. We can have high variety and low wages, or we can have low variety and high wages; but we cannot have both.*

The Role of Concerns about Relative Standing

Once we recognize the importance of people's concerns about relative standing, however, we can see how even a perfectly competitive labor market might produce excessive specialization; and how, at the same time, it might present too few opportunities for workers to participate in important workplace decisions. The line of reasoning here parallels the argument in Chapter 7 about how concerns about position lead to an excessively risky work environment.

As before, suppose workers care about their wages, in both an absolute and relative sense, and about some other dimension that adds quality to their lives, this time a stimulating and democratic working environment. Since participation and variety have costs (in terms of the output losses that accompany them), it is possible for each worker to increase his wage by agreeing to accept less variety and participation. Doing so produces two rewards: (1) an increase in wages, which is valued for its own sake; and (2) an advance in standing vis-à-vis other workers who do not make such a trade. As in the earlier analysis of the safety choice, the first of these rewards is real. But for workers taken as a whole, the second is illusory. If everyone accepts reduced variety and participation, the rank ordering of earnings is the same as it would have been had no one accepted these sacrifices. Because relative standing matters, workers deciding on the quality of life in the workplace face the same sort of prisoner's dilemma that hockey players face when left free to decide whether to wear a helmet. When deciding as individuals, they will therefore opt for too little variety and participation in their working lives.

The distortions involved here are not minor. If concerns about position outweigh concerns about income levels per se, as all evidence suggests, it follows that the primary motive for individuals to accept greater fragmentation of workplace tasks is entirely spurious. This suggests that individually chosen levels of workplace variety and democracy will be substantially smaller than those that would have been chosen collectively.

As we have already seen in Chapters 7 and 8, similar claims by the left that firms exploit workers by making them work for low wages, in unsafe conditions, and for inhumanely long hours can be similarly reconciled with the market economist's insistence that labor markets are well-informed and structurally competitive. In all of these instances, recognizing the importance of relative standing enables us to accommodate the conservative's view that

---

*This statement readily concedes that if participation levels were *sufficiently low*, output might rise with greater worker involvement. All it says is that, *beyond some point*, further increases in worker participation will reduce output.

Drawing by Gini Curl.

Figure 9.1 Concerns about position lead to excessive fragmentation of workplace tasks.

markets respond efficiently to the demands of individuals. At the same time, it allows room for the liberal's view that market allocations fall short along many important dimensions.

If a person's co-workers were the only local hierarchy in which position mattered, it would be a relatively simple matter to solve prisoner's dilemmas of the sort described here. Workers could decide collectively on the environmental and compensation packages they wanted, and then seek firms willing to hire them on those terms. To be sure, such collective agreements among co-workers undoubtedly already go a long way toward rationalizing the compensation package.

But one's co-workers are generally not the only hierarchy that is important. If the workers in firm A settle on a low-quality, high-wage package, they are then able to provide advantages for their children that outstrip those provided by workers in firm B, who have settled on a high-quality, low-wage package. Under these circumstances, the workers in firm B may also feel compelled to opt for higher wages and reduced environmental quality. Thinking along these lines, we can see why workers in the two firms might want the state to mandate less-alienating conditions in the workplace, much as coal miners support mine-safety standards.

Such a demand would raise the same sort of questions we confronted in Chapter 7. Although individually made decisions regarding workplace quality may produce unsatisfactory outcomes for many people, governmentally imposed standards will be equally unsatisfactory for many others. Many people simply do not want to become more actively involved in management decisions. It would be hard to persuade these people that their lot would be improved by government standards that would both lower their wages and make them attend meetings to discuss management issues. As in Chapter 7, let us note here the kernel of legitimacy in both of these opposing views, and leave for Chapters 11 and 12 the question of how such conflicts might be resolved.

The Impersonal National Retail Chain

It has become increasingly common to see locally owned retail businesses fail and their locations taken over by large, national retail chains. In explaining why the local business failed, its owner will often say that "revenues were better than ever but were still not high enough to cover rapidly escalating rents." Large chains, with their so-called "deep pockets," are said to outbid the locally owned firms for scarce prime commercial locations.

In the wake of such transitions, we often hear angry complaints from the left of yet another instance of the market's failure to reward small-scale enterprises that provide personal service and show a true sense of involvement with, and commitment to, their patrons. "Rich" national chains are accused of using their superior financial resources to drive out the smaller firms that everyone really prefers.

The economist has never been able to make sense of such arguments. In a competitive market, one firm outbids a second for a prime location because it can put the location to better use, not because it has greater financial resources. The economist argues, with the facts on his side, that the large chain's ability to outbid the smaller firm results from its superior efficiency. Faced with a choice between locally provided service at one price and chain-outlet service at a lower price, the economist argues, consumers seem overwhelmingly to choose the latter. They might like to have both lower prices *and* locally owned businesses. But, as before, this is not one of the possible options.

By taking people's concerns about relative standing into account, however, we can see why consumers might individually decide to shop in the large retail chain, even though collectively they might prefer to see the earlier environment preserved. When one shopper pays higher prices for his Gucci shoes than others do, his relative standing in the consumption hierarchy declines. Preventing this decline may, to the individual, be more important than supporting a local business enterprise. But the collective ranking of the alternatives might easily be the opposite.

In this situation, too, the difficulty in resolving conflicting interests is readily apparent. Some people see no advantage whatever in shopping at locally owned stores, and community attempts to keep the national chain out will obviously infringe on their legitimate desire to pay as little as possible for the goods they buy.

The Manipulative Advertiser

In the capitalist's economics textbook, the consumer is sovereign. He or she has preferences that arise largely internally. The consumer is faced with a menu of different goods at different prices, and these preferences dictate which goods are bought. But social critics on the left, and even some economists, insist that purchase decisions are less the result of intrinsic preferences than of the producer's success at manipulating the consumer. In John Kenneth Galbraith's view, the chain of causality is often precisely the opposite of the "accepted sequence" described in standard economics textbooks.[8] His "revised sequence" has producers first decide what goods are cheapest and most convenient for them to make, and then persuade consumers to buy them:

It follows that the accepted sequence is no longer a description of the reality and is becoming ever less so. Instead the producing firm reaches forward to control its markets and on beyond to manage the market behavior and shape the social attitudes of those, ostensibly, that it serves.[9]

Thus, in Galbraith's scheme, we do not really need stylish automobiles or roll-on deodorants. We are merely bludgeoned into thinking we do by an endless repetition of advertising messages. A persuasive case can indeed be made that, however mindless they may be, advertising messages do influence purchase decisions. If they did not, how could anyone then explain why a profit-seeking company would spend millions of dollars each year trying to educate consumers that "relief" is spelled "R-O-L-A-I-D-S"?*

But it is a slip of logic to conclude that, because most successful companies advertise, advertising must therefore alter purchase decisions in a way that harms consumers. If General Motors can attempt to persuade the consumer to buy its product, so also can Ford. Suppose GM picks a car to promote because that car is the cheapest, most convenient one for it to produce, even though that car is unresponsive to any "real" consumer needs. Ford can then offer a rival car, which although it costs more to produce, responds to the buyer's own desires. GM and Ford will presumably be equally effective in promoting their respective products, and will incur roughly the same costs in doing so. The consumer, then, will be confronted with conflicting campaigns about two products whose prices reflect the difference in their production costs. Thus faced with a choice between two products, one of which better

---

*Nelson (1974), Klein and Leffler (1981), and others have argued that the mere fact that a product is advertised at all creates a presumption that many consumers will find it a good purchase. The argument is that, once the firm has invested heavily in good will through its advertising outlays, it will then be reluctant to jeopardize that investment by frustrating the buyer's expectations.

responds to his own needs but costs a little more, how is the consumer any less sovereign than in standard economics textbooks?

People talk with one another about which products are good buys. They read *Consumer Reports*. They experiment with a variety of products. They take 30-day free trials, and in countless other ways sift through the competing claims of producers. Promotional puffery undoubtedly misleads some people some of the time. But is there really any reason to believe that consumers would

Drawing by Mankoff. Copyright © 1977 Saturday Review, Inc. Reprinted by permission of the artist.

"Of course, the mileage you get on the road will depend on how and where you drive and other varying factors such as wind direction and velocity."

choose between privately produced products any more effectively than they do now if advertisements were banned altogether?*

The left has not offered a convincing case that profit-seeking firms manipulate consumers into buying the wrong kinds of privately produced goods. Even so, many people perceive a sharp discrepancy between the mix of goods people actually buy and the mix that appears best to serve their most important human needs. There are obvious pitfalls in using one's own values to determine what goods other people should buy. Still, it is sometimes difficult to avoid thinking that the nation as a whole would be better off if each family were to spend, say, $100 per year less on automobile styling features and $100 per year more on design changes that make cars more crashworthy. And consumers themselves make just such a judgment, in fact, when they voice their approval of various automobile safety regulations.

As we have by now seen repeatedly, misallocations of just this sort can result, even in perfectly competitive markets, whenever concerns about relative standing loom large. Where the specific products people buy have a significant impact on their relative standing, either in reality or merely as perceived by others, rational spending behavior from the individual standpoint can be very different from what is rational for society as a whole. There are good reasons that aspiring young professionals want to be seen driving the best cars, living in the best neighborhoods, belonging to the best clubs, and so on. (And there are even stronger reasons that the poorest members of society wish not to be seen driving the most dilapidated cars or living in the most rundown housing.)

Consider, for example, the following scenario. A young IBM executive, who prides herself on being a no-nonsense consumer, surveys the housing market carefully. She concludes, correctly, that the mobile home provides much more housing space per dollar than do conventional homes. Suppose that, by placing several mobile home modules together, she can purchase the square footage she needs for only 50 percent of the cost of a conventional home. She is indifferent between the two types of housing, and if her own views were all that mattered, she would unhesitatingly purchase the mobile home. Yet her job requires her to entertain frequently, and she fears, with good reason, that many of her clients will feel uncomfortable attending cocktail parties in a mobile home park. No matter how disdainful she may feel toward the attitudes of those clients, does it follow that she is acting irrationally if she then buys the conventional home? Would her own narrow purposes have been better served had she instead purchased the mobile home?

In situations where what really counts is not what we consume per se, but how our consumption compares with the quality and quantity of the goods

---

*The real distortion that results from advertising, if any, seems much more likely to involve decisions between public goods—such as parks, transit systems, and environmental beautification —and private goods. Because consumers are flooded with information about privately produced goods, they may very well tend to consume too few public goods, much as Galbraith himself earlier argued in his *Affluent Society*.[10]

consumed by others, an equilibrium emerges in which we invest too heavily in positional goods. And this occurs quite apart from whatever advertising messages we may be exposed to. To suppose that our consumption patterns would suddenly become more sensible if producers stopped bombarding us with advertising messages is to ignore the severe penalties that have always confronted people who failed to keep pace with community consumption standards.

Power, Privilege, and the Distribution of Income

In most market economies, the distribution of pretax incomes is very skewed. In the United States, for example, the top 5 percent of all income earners receive roughly 15 percent of each year's net national income.[11] In decrying this high degree of inequality, critics from the left often complain that it results from the powers and privileges that come with membership in the upper social classes. Yet inherited wealth is only a minor cause of income inequality. The distribution of labor earnings alone, for example, is itself highly skewed (the top 5 percent of all earners receive more than 10 percent of all earned income). Moreover, much of the dispersion in wealth holdings is the result of acquired wealth rather than of inherited wealth.

"So now they have fire. That still doesn't make either of them more interesting as <u>people</u>."

In part, the dispersion in the distribution of earned income results from differences in access to educational opportunities and favored networks of contacts, just as critics on the left charge.[12] And there is no denying that the penalties imposed on people who fail to receive adequate nourishment and other support early in life are severe. But in countries such as the United States, students who arrive intact into the public schools—even those from poor families—are given strong opportunities to complete a university level education. Moreover, although contacts undoubtedly matter in many instances, we must bear in mind that firms incur substantial financial penalties whenever they fail to fill positions with the best-qualified applicants. Firms struggling to survive in an intensely competitive environment simply cannot often afford to pass up well-qualified applicants in favor of demonstrably inferior ones.

Where nonlabor earnings are involved, we see much more dispersion than in the distribution of labor earnings. But here, too, the claim that inequality results primarily from special privilege is difficult to sustain. Business is a gamble, and every year thousands of firms go bankrupt. Of the firms that ultimately survive, many do so only after suffering protracted losses. It makes little real sense to insist, after the fact, that the survivors then owe their wealth to some ill-deserved power or privilege. It is easy to argue, of course, that the recipients of substantial inherited wealth have done nothing in particular to "deserve" their good fortune. Yet proposals for confiscatory estate taxes have consistently drawn sharp objections, even from those with relatively low income.[13] Many people apparently feel very strongly about maintaining the right to bestow on their children a share in whatever material wealth they may someday happen to enjoy.

As economists reflect on the foregoing arguments, their reaction to the left's complaints about power and privilege is likely to be much the same as their reaction to the left's complaints about alienation and exploitation. People have various talents, they will say, and they are free to choose what they do with them. Their choices will obviously influence the incomes they earn. For the left then to complain that income inequality is primarily the result of arbitrary privileges seems, to the economist, merely to signify the left's refusal to acknowledge these perfectly defensible sources of inequality.[14] These are, after all, the very sources of inequality that Rawls so eloquently defended in his *A Theory of Justice*.[15]

Many people find it hard not to sympathize with the economist's critique of the left's arguments about power and privilege. Still, it is hard to escape the feeling that differences in people's incomes often vastly overstate the differences in social benefits that result from the work they do. Here, too, an appreciation of the role of relative standing suggests a possible avenue along which the conflicting claims might be reconciled.

The story is told of two campers who encounter a grizzly bear in the woods. At the sight of the bear, one camper hurriedly takes off his hiking boots and puts on his running shoes. "Why are you bothering with those?" the second camper asks. "Don't you know there's no way a man can outrun a bear?" The first camper responds, "I don't have to outrun the bear. All I have to do is outrun *you*." In the labor market no less than in the wilderness, a person's fate will often depend much less on his ability in any absolute sense than on how his ability compares with the abilities of others.

Consider, for example, the following scenario.[16] Firm A and Firm B are antagonists in a $1 billion lawsuit. Suppose that, on its merits, the case is so close that the winner will be whichever firm manages to hire the best lawyer. Assume also that there are only two lawyers, Smith and Jones, and that Smith is ever so slightly, but nonetheless perceptibly, better.

Under these circumstances, Smith finds himself sitting in the driver's seat. Whichever firm hires him will win the suit and will thus be $1 billion better off than it would have been had it not hired him. If the two firms do not collude, we would then expect the fee for Smith's services to be a figure close to $1 billion. (Suppose Firm A offered Smith only $900 million; rather than lose the suit, Firm B would presumably then offer Smith $901 million; and so on.) Jones's fee, on the other hand, cannot exceed zero. Whichever firm fails to hire Smith is going to lose the suit anyway, so there is no point in even hiring Jones.

In this example, the two firms did not care at all about the absolute quality levels of their lawyers' services. The talents of each lawyer could have been halved and the details of the example would have worked out precisely in the same way. The discussion in Chapter 7 suggests that similar circumstances may often arise in the labor market. Consider, for example, those instances in which buyers stand to gain a lot by consuming the best product in a given class. In such instances, the employee who is responsible for making that product the best in its class gives his firm sole access to an important segment of the market. Although the skills that person brings to his task may be only marginally higher than the skills of others engaged in similar tasks, his income may nonetheless be many hundreds of times larger.

With the stakes as high as they are, large corporations are forced by competitive pressures to seek out the best tax accountants. But the high six-figure incomes of the most able tax experts serve no collective purpose—either public or private—of commensurate value. If all corporations invested one tenth of what they do now on searching out tax loopholes, their competitive positions would then be roughly as they are now. What corporations would lose in higher tax payments, the population at large would gain, dollar for dollar, in the form of lower tax payments (since government revenue requirements are unaffected by any of this). Thus, the net effect would be to make everyone but tax experts better off than before. And tax experts themselves would suffer only the difference between what they had earned previously and what they can now earn in whatever task they are next-best suited to perform. (This is but one of many arguments for simplifying the tax code.)

In circumstances where the stakes of the game are high, and the game has something of a winner-take-all character, as in these examples, differences in rank between the principal actors take on critical significance. The distribution of income that emerges in such cases will almost always be dramatically skewed. No matter how small the differences in talents between the principal actors might be in absolute terms, those at the top of the heap will tend to capture a disproportionate share of the total gains. As Sherwin Rosen recently described this phenomenon in the case of full-time concert soloists:

The market for classical music has never been larger than it is now, yet the number of full-time soloists on any given instrument is also on the order of only a few hundred (and much smaller for instruments other than voice, violin, and piano). Performers of first rank comprise a limited handful out of these small totals and have very large incomes. There are also known to be substantial differences in income between them and those in the second rank, even though most consumers would have difficulty detecting more than minor differences in a "blind" hearing.[17]

As with the earnings of soloists, so also with the earnings of leading tax experts. Such earnings levels are often the unintended result of purely voluntary, self-serving transactions that occur between fully informed adults in perfectly competitive markets. They don't necessarily have anything to do with power, privilege, or coercion. Yet there is something decidedly less than optimal about them. If what buyers care about is the rank of a product, then how are they helped by a competition in which absolute quality levels escalate, along with the salaries of those who determine them?

Even many economists will doubtless find something disturbingly inequitable about the income distributions that emerge under these circumstances. It is one thing to say that the person who makes 40 bricks per hour should be paid twice as much as the one who makes 20. But it is quite another to say that two people whose talents are almost the same should be paid such wildly divergent amounts.* People in Rawls's original position would surely reject such a distribution scheme. The libertarian may insist that people are nonetheless entitled to keep whatever incomes they acquire from voluntary transactions. As I argued in Chapter 6, however, such entitlements, in some cases, may be circumscribed by other members of society, who have a legitimate collective voice in those transactions.

All of the examples in this chapter fit the same general pattern. The critic from the left first expresses the view that some feature of the market system is undesirable, then explains that it results from a fundamental imbalance in economic power relationships. Firms with market power are said to force workers to perform fragmented tasks under unsafe, undemocratic conditions

---

*Note here the contrast between the effects on wages of (1) people's concerns about how their own wages compare with the wages of co-workers, and (2) people's concerns about how the products they buy compare with those bought by others. The first concern works through the supply side of the labor market to flatten the relationship between wages and marginal products within each firm (see Chapter 3). But the second concern works through the demand side of the labor market to *heighten* dispersion in the distribution of marginal productivity relative to the underlying distribution of ability.

in exchange for unconscionably low wages. The market-oriented economist has good reasons in every instance for believing that these power imbalances are a figment. And for this reason there is little real communication between critics on the left and the orthodox economics community. We have seen, however, that once people's concerns about relative standing are taken into account, many of the left's complaints can be reconciled with the economist's view that product and labor markets are competitive.

Having identified real problems, but having ascribed them to spurious causes, the left has found it difficult to formulate policy remedies. Citing firms with excessive power as the heart of the problem, the left has sought to transfer power from the firm to the presumably benevolent state. But the real difficulty here does not lie in the power of firms to exploit people. Instead, it stems from our tendency to engage in unproductive competitions among ourselves. And as I argue in Chapter 12, the policy interventions suggested by these two views of the problem are dramatically different.

Ten

Why Do Ethical Systems Try to Limit the Role of Money?

The Man from the South

In a short story entitled "Man from the South," Roald Dahl describes a macabre wager that raises a number of provocative ethical questions.[1] The narrator is seated alone at a hotel poolside patio table when he is joined by a small, elderly man who is a stranger to him. The elderly man speaks with a Spanish-sounding accent and is wearing a white suit. Presently they are joined by a young couple—he an American naval cadet, she an English tourist—both strangers to the two men. A stiff breeze is blowing, and when the American lights a cigarette, the little man in white comments on what an extraordinarily effective lighter he has. The American boasts proudly that his lighter never fails. At this, the little man animatedly proposes that the group go to his hotel room so that he and the seaman can carry out the following wager: The seaman is to attempt to light his lighter ten times in succession. If it fires successfully each time, he will then take possession of the stranger's new Cadillac sedan, which is parked next to the hotel. If the lighter fails to fire even once, though, the man will cut off the seaman's left little finger with a cleaver.

Both the narrator and the woman voice their strong opposition to the wager. But the American is sure of his lighter and nervously accepts. The following passage picks up the narrative shortly after the group has arrived in the stranger's hotel room.

192

We stood there, the boy, the girl, and I, holding Martinis in our hands, watching the little man at work. We watched him hammer two nails into the table, about six inches apart. He didn't hammer them right home; he allowed a small part of each one to stick up. Then he tested them for firmness with his fingers.

Anyone would think the son of a bitch had done this before, I told myself. He never hesitates. Table, nails, hammer, kitchen chopper. He knows exactly what he needs and how to arrange it.

"And now," he said, "all we want is some string." He found some string. "All right, at last we are ready. Will you pleess to sit here at de table," he said to the boy.

The boy put his glass away and sat down.

"Now place de left hand between dese two nails. De nails are only so I can tie your hand in place. All right, good. Now I tie your hand secure to de table—so."

He wound the string around the boy's wrist, then several times around the wide part of the hand, then he fastened it tight to the nails. He made a good job of it and when he'd finished there wasn't any question about the boy being able to draw his hand away. But he could move his fingers.

"Now pleess, clench de fist, all except for de little finger. You must leave de little finger out, lying on de table.

"Ex-cellent! Ex-cellent! Now we are ready. Wid your right hand you manipulate de lighter. But one momint, pleess."

He skipped over to the bed and picked up the chopper. He came back and stood beside the table with the chopper in his hand.

"We are all ready?" he said. "Mister referee, you must say to begin."

The English girl was standing there in her pale blue bathing costume right behind the boy's chair. She was just standing there, not saying anything. The boy was sitting quite still, holding the lighter in his right hand, looking at the chopper. The little man was looking at me.

"Are you ready?" I asked the boy.

"I'm ready."

"And you?" to the little man.

"Quite ready," he said and he lifted the chopper up in the air and held it there about two feet above the boy's finger, ready to chop. The boy watched it, but he didn't flinch and his mouth didn't move at all. He merely raised his eyebrows and frowned.

"All right," I said. "Go ahead."

The boy said, "Will you please count aloud the number of times I light it."

"Yes," I said. "I'll do that."

With his thumb he raised the top of the lighter, and again with the thumb he gave the wheel a sharp flick. The flint sparked and the wick caught fire and burned with a small yellow flame.

"One!" I called.

He didn't blow the flame out; he closed the top of the lighter on it and he waited for perhaps five seconds before opening it again.

He flicked the wheel very strongly and once more there was a small flame burning on the wick.

"Two!"

No one else said anything. The boy kept his eyes on the lighter. The little man held the chopper up in the air and he too was watching the lighter.

"Three!"

"Four!"

"Five!"

"Six!"

"Seven!" Obviously it was one of those lighters that worked. The flint gave a big spark and the wick was the right length. I watched the thumb snapping the top down onto the flame. Then a pause. Then the thumb raising the top once more. This was an all-thumb operation. The thumb did everything. I took a breath, ready to say eight. The thumb flicked the wheel. The flint sparked. The little flame appeared.

"Eight!" I said, and as I said it the door opened. We all turned and we saw a woman standing in the doorway, a small, black-haired woman, rather old, who stood there for about two seconds then pushed forward shouting, "Carlos! Carlos!" She grabbed his wrist, took the chopper from him, threw it on the bed, took hold of the little man by the lapels of his white suit and began shaking him very vigorously, talking to him fast and loud and fiercely all the time in some Spanish-sounding language. She shook him so fast you couldn't see him any more. He became a faint, misty, quickly moving outline, like the spokes of a turning wheel.

Then she slowed down and the little man came into view again and she hauled him across the room and pushed him backward onto one of the beds. He sat on the edge of it blinking his eyes and testing his head to see if it would still turn on his neck.

"I am so sorry," the woman said. "I am so terribly sorry that this should happen." She spoke almost perfect English.

"It is too bad," she went on. "I suppose it is really my fault. For ten minutes I leave him alone to go and have my hair washed and I come back and he is at it again." She looked sorry and deeply concerned.

The boy was untying his hand from the table. The English girl and I stood there and said nothing.

"He is a menace," the woman said. "Down where we live at home he has taken altogether forty-seven fingers from different people, and he has lost eleven cars. In the end they threatened to have him put away somewhere. That's why I brought him up here."

"We were only having a little bet," mumbled the little man from the bed.

"I suppose he bet you a car," the woman said.

"Yes," the boy answered. "A Cadillac."

"He has no car. It's mine. And that makes it worse," she said, "that he should bet you when he has nothing to bet with. I am ashamed and very sorry about it all." She seemed an awfully nice woman.

"Well," I said, "then here's the key to your car." I put it on the table.

"We were only having a little bet," mumbled the little man.

"He hasn't anything left to bet with," the woman said. "He hasn't a thing in the world. Not a thing. As a matter of fact I myself won it all from him a long while ago. It took time, a lot of time, and it was hard work, but I won it all in the end." She looked up at the boy and she smiled, a slow sad smile, and she came over and put out a hand to take the key from the table.

I can see it now, that hand of hers; it had only one finger on it, and a thumb.[2]

Markets for Fingers, Kidneys, Babies, and Sex

Many ethical systems would find the terms of the little man's proposal unacceptable, even if the car *had* been his to bet. But *why* are these terms unacceptable? To some people, this question may appear bizarre. Just as it makes little sense to ask why the color blue is blue, some see it as pointless to inquire why certain acts are wrong and others right. By this view, ethical values spring somehow from within, and there is little point in trying to fathom rational reasons for them.[3] Some things are wrong and we simply know it.

Many moral philosophers have argued, however, that ethical norms are simply adaptations to various environmental circumstances.[4] When an ethical system forbids lying or stealing, for example—as virtually all ethical systems do—we can easily see why such norms might produce a better outcome for everyone.

For purposes of discussion here, let us adopt the view that ethical norms have adaptive significance. With this view in mind, I will try to discover the adaptive significance of an ethical sanction against the proposal made by Dahl's man from the South, and of sanctions applied in other circumstances that similarly limit the range of things that can be bought and sold for money. Why, for example, do we consider it unethical for a couple to have and sell a baby to some other couple who desperately want one but cannot have one of their own? Why, similarly, would it be considered unethical for a person to sell one of his kidneys to a person who will die unless he gets a kidney transplant? And why is prostitution so strongly frowned on in many ethical systems?

Daniel Callahan, director of the Hastings Center, a group of scholars who study medical ethics, has been quoted as saying, "In theory there ought to be no laws that would stop competent adults from selling whatever they want. But the potential for abuse is just too great."[5] What specific sorts of abuse does society have in mind when it prevents "competent adults from selling whatever they want"?

All of the transactions in question have in common the structure that one party—call him A—wishes to transfer some part of himself to the control of another party—call him B—in exchange for a monetary payment or the equivalent. If A *wants* to sell—or, in this case, risk selling—his little finger to B in return for a new Cadillac, why should society try to stop him? If the wager is also attractive to B, and if no third parties are adversely affected, then who is it we are trying to protect?

An objection to the wager might be raised on the grounds that A merely *thinks* the Cadillac is a good trade against his finger, but that, after the fact, he will think differently. To protect him against the possibility of feeling regret, we therefore discourage such wagers. Yet surely there is *some* price high enough that the likelihood of A's regretting the exchange would be negligible. If the proposed trade would *still* be considered unethical at that price—as, in many systems, it surely would—then protection against regret cannot be the only reason for society's disapproval.

Perhaps society disapproves of such wagers because it feels people should learn to respect the human body. Magnificent as it is, the body still requires care in order to function properly. A society that lets people sell body parts for cash might thus have trouble teaching its children prudent health habits. Even so, there are obvious advantages to be had by selling a little finger for a huge sum of cash, should someone else happen to be foolish enough to pay for it. The distinction between selling a noncritical body part, on the one hand, and the need to get proper rest, diet, and exercise, on the other, is not a difficult one. Would the fact that an occasional person might make an apparently rational decision to sell his little finger *really* compromise our efforts to train our children to take care of themselves?

Perhaps third parties are in some way adversely affected by the sale of the finger. Having one's finger cut off is, after all, a gory business, and those who later see the stump may experience feelings of great agitation and disgust. But suppose what was involved had been the sale of a little toe, not a little finger, and that the seller always wore shoes, so that no one ever had to see the remains of his wound. Would the transaction *then* be considered an ethical one? By many people, surely not.

Alternatively, the purpose of the ethical sanction may be to prevent B from squandering his money. Since society reckons no legitimate gains can possibly come from buying someone else's little finger, perhaps it wants to instill values that would discourage such purchases. This argument seems to have more force than the others but is still less than compelling. It is not clear, for example, that many people would want to engage in such transactions even in the absence of ethical sanctions against them. Nor is it clear that there would be any real *social* gain from an ethical sanction imposed on this account. Whatever sum B loses by making such a foolish purchase would be gained by A, and it is not obvious that A's gain would be insufficient compensation for B's loss. Society might even take comfort in the knowledge that people like B are penalized financially when they participate in such transactions.

Moral objections to the sale of babies and transplantable organs raise even harder questions. For unlike the transaction involving the seaman's finger, these transactions produce results we strongly favor. Surely most people would approve if a man's life were saved by a kidney transplant that would otherwise have been impossible. And, similarly, most people would be pleased by the outcome, if not the means by which it was achieved, in which an otherwise childless couple can experience the joys of loving and raising a child.[6]

Perhaps because we sympathize so strongly with the childless couple, society has not yet curtailed an emerging practice whereby some such couples have managed to sidestep state laws prohibiting the sale of babies. This practice goes by the name of "surrogate motherhood" and involves a contract between a fertile woman and a couple in which the wife is unable to bear children. The contract calls for the fertile woman to become pregnant through artificial insemination with the husband's semen and to turn over the infant to the couple for adoption shortly after its birth. The terms of these contracts vary, but almost all require the couple to cover all medical and related expenses, and most also stipulate that a "fee for service" be paid to the surrogate mother. According to Nancy Reame, a University of Michigan researcher who counsels surrogate mothers, a typical fee for service is $10,000. But it is not uncommon to see fees of $20,000 or even higher. The practice of surrogate motherhood is growing rapidly. In late 1983, Reame reported that two years earlier there were "only two programs in the country to bring potential mothers together with infertile couples; today there are 20." Reame also reported that between 75 and 100 surrogates are now carrying babies under written contracts.[7]

Some groups have raised moral objections to surrogate motherhood quite apart from the commercial aspects of the practice. The Catholic Bishop's Committee for Pro-Life Activities, for example, has called it a "pretty seedy business . . . a kind of technical adultery and premeditated child abandonment."[8] Most of the opposition to surrogate motherhood, however, has focused narrowly on the fee for service. The state legislature in Michigan, for example, is considering a law that would make surrogate motherhood explicitly legal but the fee for service unlawful.

Just as there is an excess demand for adoptable infants, recent advances in medical technology have created a burgeoning demand for transplantable human organs. More than 6000 people, for example, are waiting for kidney transplants, another 4000 for cornea transplants.[9] Predictably, these conditions have spawned commercial attempts to mediate exchanges between donors and recipients. Ellen Goodman reports the case of a Virginia physician who "set up a business to broker human kidneys. Under this scheme a person who needed the money could literally sell a kidney to a person who needed the organ, and the doctor would get a fee for services."[10]

As in the case of surrogate motherhood, commercial transactions involving the sale of transplantable organs have drawn sharp ethical criticism. Tennessee Senator Albert Gore, for example, has said, "Our system of values isn't supposed to allow the auctioning off of life to the highest bidder."[11] In October 1983, Gore introduced legislation in Congress that would prohibit the sale or purchase of transplantable organs. Echoing Gore's refrain, Ellen Goodman has lamented the growing irony in the Joan Baez folk lyric, "If livin' were a thing that money could buy, the rich would live and the poor would die."[12]

Some of the sharpest objections to the sale of babies and organs are, as noted, rooted in an ethical distaste for the inherent inequality of the market process. Yet such distributional objections can be dealt with in a simple way: The community at large can set aside a store of funds with which to provide poor people access to essential resources. After all, this is precisely what we already do in the Medicaid program. Given that the needs of the poor can be met, we cannot use the burden of payment as grounds for preventing private markets for adoption and organ transplantation.

Another possible reason for taking steps to curb the sale of babies is to protect the biological mother from the emotional anguish she will almost inevitably suffer upon separation from her baby. Nancy Reame reports that even though the surrogate mothers she counsels make every effort to distance themselves emotionally from the fetuses they carry, the actual separation itself is always traumatic. Reame also reports, however, that most mothers express no lasting desire to get their babies back.[13] Despite extensive counseling, unanticipated regrets may still be an important problem for some surrogate mothers, particularly those who have never given birth to a child before. This problem might be addressed by restricting surrogate motherhood to those women who have already borne children. In addition, a waiting period could be employed before the final adoption takes place, just as such waiting periods are already employed in the adoption procedures of many states. But in the end, it is of course impossible to eliminate all possibility of regrets. And there is no reason to believe that people would want the state to try to do so, even if that could somehow be accomplished.

Perhaps one of society's reasons for wanting to prevent the sale of babies is that it feels a human life is "too precious" to be sold. According to this line of reasoning, allowing babies to be bought and sold would diminish people's perception of the value of human life, with all the obviously undesirable consequences that would entail. But why should something that sells for a price, and a high price at that, be valued less than something that is merely given away? When one pays a high price for a house, does one value and respect it less than if one had gotten it for free? When one pays a fee in the adoption process, is there any reason to believe adopted children will be valued less than if there had been no fee?

Or, perhaps the selling of babies is the object of ethical sanctions because it so closely resembles the buying and selling of slaves, which is ethically repugnant for obvious reasons. Granted, both instances involve the exchange of cash for a human being. But the similarity in the two transactions ends there. In every other respect, the selling of babies bears no resemblance whatsoever to the sale of slaves. Unlike the slave, the baby who is sold is in no way deprived of his natural liberty. We have no reason to suppose that a couple who so desperately want a child as to be willing to pay a high price for one would be any less likely than other parents to love and care for the child.

The questions we encounter in trying to explain ethical sanctions against the sale of babies are very similar to those we must face in trying to explain sanctions against the sale of transplantable organs and prostitution. If these transactions affect only the direct participants, and if the terms of the transactions are mutually attractive to those participants, why then do we impose such sanctions?

Since virtually every other question in this book has had "concerns about relative standing" play an important role in its answer, the alert reader will have correctly guessed that I believe these concerns are in some way involved here, too. In particular, for the same reason we saw in Chapter 7 for limiting safety risks in the workplace, it may also be in society's interest to impose the ethical sanctions discussed above.

To illustrate, let us consider a simple choice problem similar to those discussed in Chapter 7. Imagine two couples, the Smiths and the Joneses, who are the poorest in society. To reduce their poverty, both couples consider having and selling babies. As in the earlier examples, the two households care not only about their absolute incomes but also very much about how their incomes compare with the incomes of others. Under these circumstances, the couples confront a prisoner's dilemma of precisely the same form as those encountered in Chapter 7. As before, the individually rational decision for both couples is to have babies and sell them. If one couple failed to do so while the other did, it would fall that much farther behind in the income hierarchy. But once both sales are made, the original relative positions are restored. The two couples are still the poorest, but they have now also endured an emotionally wrenching experience that failed to achieve its most important objective.

Just as it may make sense to demand restrictions that keep us from selling our safety and our labor too cheaply in the workplace, so it may also make sense to limit the extent to which we are able to market other important aspects of ourselves. It is easy to see how a young couple struggling to raise a down payment to buy a home in a better neighborhood might be sorely tempted to have and sell a baby. But their forward move in society's queue would create backward movements for their former neighbors. Those neighbors would then feel heightened pressure to take steps of their own—if not selling a baby or a transplantable organ, then perhaps taking a riskier job—as a means of restoring their relative positions.

This is not to say that the poor would *necessarily* regard such transactions as being contrary to their collective interests. (More on this point below.) But neither can we say that those transactions would win collective approval *just because* the people who participate in them do so voluntarily.

The skeptical reader may feel that I am using people's concerns about relative standing to explain too much here. Equipped only with a hammer, I insist on viewing every problem as a nail. To be sure, it does *sound* strange to say that concerns about relative standing could account for ethical sanctions against the sale of babies and transplantable organs. Perhaps it will be useful, therefore, to review the premises that must hold in order for this claim to be plausible.

There is actually only one premise that must hold—namely, that people's relative economic standing contributes significantly to their sense of well-being. This premise implies that a large share of the benefit perceived by the seller comes from the forward movement in the income hierarchy made possible by the cash he or she receives. But the laws of simple arithmetic say that such forward movements must always be accompanied by backward movements on the part of others. Although third parties do not *appear* to be involved in these transactions, they nonetheless *are* involved, by virtue of the effects the transactions have on where they stand in the income hierarchy. Under these circumstances, the sum of the payoffs perceived by the individual sellers will be significantly larger than the aggregate social gains that result once the transactions are consummated. Put another way, from the point of view of society as a whole, the payoffs facing each potential seller are misleadingly attractive. Ethical sanctions against such transactions make them less attractive than they otherwise would be: People who engage in them suffer the very real cost of social disapproval. And if the problem is that the payoffs perceived by individuals were too high to begin with, this constitutes a step in the right direction. To reject this conclusion requires us to reject the basic premise from which it logically follows.

These arguments do not mean, needless to say, that concerns about relative standing are the only, or even the most important, reason for the ethical sanctions in question. Nor do these arguments imply that there should necessarily be *legal* sanctions against any of the transactions discussed here. On the contrary, there are many similar transactions against which the imposition of legal sanctions would seem utterly absurd.

One such transaction was called to my attention during my stay as chief economist at the Civil Aeronautics Board during the late seventies. The board had proposed a regulation that would require airlines to offer cash payments to people who voluntarily relinquished their seats on overbooked flights. These people would also get an additional cash bonus if the airline then failed to get them to their destination within four hours of their originally scheduled arrival time.

The idea behind this regulation was that some people's needs to arrive on time are more urgent than others'. To the board, it seemed that passengers themselves should determine how urgent their needs were by deciding whether a cash payment was sufficient compensation for giving up their seats. Those with important schedules to keep would not have to volunteer. Others, whose time was more flexible, could adjust their schedules in return for a cash reward. Sorting people out in this way seemed more sensible than simply accommodating passengers on a first-come, first-served basis, which was the airlines' standard practice at the time.

A consumer action group promptly objected to the board's proposal on the grounds that it would result in poor people always being the ones to give up their seats on overbooked flights. They were concerned, evidently, that "if seats were a thing that money could buy, then the poor would wait while the rich would fly." One suspects that the poor, for whose interests this group purported to speak, were not consulted before this objection was filed. Had they been, they would almost surely have rejected this attempt to "protect" them against picking up some extra cash for waiting a few hours in an airport. If a national referendum could have been held on this regulation, rich and poor alike probably would have voiced strong approval of it. But even if the proposed regulation won unanimous support, relinquishing a seat would still appear misleadingly attractive to individuals, for the same reasons discussed in the earlier examples. If the *terms* on which people were willing to relinquish their seats were decided collectively, the cash payments might well be higher than when people resolve the same issues individually. The net gains from such exchanges are often extremely large, however, and it would make little sense to prohibit them for fear the free market terms of trade might not be *exactly* right.

The difference between the sale of airline seats and the various sales discussed earlier is one of degree rather than of kind. Where the gains to buyers are very large (in the airline case, the value to travelers with tight schedules of arriving on time) in relation to the costs borne by sellers (here, the inconvenience of waiting a few hours to people who aren't in a hurry), we do not bother to interfere. Our posture is often very different, however, when the stakes are higher and the balance between gains and losses closer.

Ethical Objections to Cost-Benefit Analysis

The fundamental principle of cost-benefit analysis is that, when faced with a choice between alternatives, we should choose the one whose total benefits most exceed its total costs. Beneath its superficially pleasing, commonsensical ring, this principle embodies an implicit claim that it can distinguish between right and wrong courses of action. It is not surprising, therefore, that it has been the subject of enormous controversy among moral philosophers, both professional and amateur.[14]

Virtually every critic of cost-benefit analysis mentions distributional issues.[15] Even in cases where the total benefits of a proposed action substantially exceed its total costs, it will usually make at least *some* people worse off. A and B will gain when a dam is built, but C will lose. Understandably wary about weighing the gains of some against the losses of others, critics correctly insist that there is no way to be sure that, from a moral perspective, C's loss is not more important than the gains to A and B. Yet surely this does not imply that a dam should never be built whenever some party would be adversely affected. No society could seriously consider taking only those collective actions that produce clear gains for each and every citizen. Costs and benefits are reciprocal phenomena. To forego a benefit is a cost, just as to avoid a cost is a benefit. Not building a dam to prevent C's loss means *causing* a loss for A and B.

Nor can we presume that avoiding a cost is generally more important than acquiring a benefit. Suppose, for example, that C strongly opposes the dam because it threatens the snail darter or some other rare form of aquatic life. A and B, on the other hand, strongly favor the dam because it will provide low-cost, pollution-free power to low-income people in the valley. Why should our desire not to harm C necessarily take precedence here over our desire to help A and B?

Cost-benefit analysis tries to identify the most favorable balance between gains and losses. Economists can, and often do, integrate distributional considerations explicitly into cost-benefit analysis[16] (although I argue in the next chapter that case-by-case adjustments for distributional concerns can produce unintended consequences when the losses to indivduals are relatively small). And the political process generally assures that the voices of adversely affected parties will not be drowned out by the economist's flurry of cash flows, discount rates, and present values. Serious proponents of cost-benefit analysis do not advocate it as a substitute for making difficult moral judgments. Instead, they see it as a tool to be considered alongside such judgments.[17]

Critics of cost-benefit analysis are also correct in pointing out that, distributional and other moral concerns aside, there are often enormous practical difficulties in measuring the costs and benefits of any proposed public action. How, for example, does one measure the benefit of preserving a breathtaking panorama? Or the cost of a cough provoked by elevated concentrations of nitrous oxide in the air? Economists are quick to concede these difficulties, but usually insist that there is no better alternative than to attempt to estimate, as best we can, the pros and cons of our various options.

What puzzles economists most is the position taken by critics who say that even if distributional concerns and measurement difficulties could be worked out, there would *still* be profound ethical objections to the application of cost-benefit analysis in certain areas. There have been especially strident objections of this sort concerning environmental, health, and safety issues. Let us explore these objections.

Some critics claim that it is morally repugnant to assign monetary prices to such things as people's safety and the cleanliness of the air. And in the legislation it has passed, Congress has largely sided with these critics. Various environmental and health and safety laws require the workplace to be made as safe, and the air as clean, as technology allows, short of forcing widespread factory closings.[18] That Congress has passed such legislation is taken by most economists to mean that Congress, or at least the constituency it is trying to please, simply doesn't understand the basic economic issues involved in making environmental, health, and safety decisions.

To be sure, there appear to be sensible reasons for the economist's frustration when Congress refuses to adopt a cost-benefit approach for the legislation in question. It is simply not possible, after all, to have either a completely clean environment or perfectly risk-free working conditions. To make the environment cleaner than it is now requires us to incur costs, such as for the installation of smokestack scrubbers or the purchase of high-priced, low-sulfur coal. We naturally adopt the cheapest pollution-reducing steps first, and the cost of each successive reduction is larger than the one before. At the same time, successive reductions in pollution produce successively smaller benefits, as measured by the monetary sums people would be willing to pay for them (with adjustments, where necessary, to reflect distributional concerns). The economist reasons, with seemingly impeccable logic, that once the cost of an additional unit of cleanliness reaches the level of benefit we get from that extra cleanliness, further increments in cleanliness will not be worth it. Just as it makes sense to tolerate a certain amount of dirt in our homes (does anyone clean his own home six times a day?), so it also makes sense to say that there is some less-than-complete level of environmental clean-up that is optimal. To make the air any cleaner than that level would require us to incur costs that exceed the extra benefits we would reap.

If both the costs and the benefits are measured correctly, it is thus difficult to see how any other approach to environmental questions could do as well as the simple cost-benefit analysis. In particular, the legislation's call to make the air as clean as possible seems destined to do worse. To the economist, at least, opposition of this particular sort to cost-benefit analysis is utterly baffling. On what kinds of ethical concerns might it be based?

One possible concern is suggested by the following hypothetical scenario. A young child has fallen into an inaccessible abandoned mine shaft. There has been a partial cave-in and the city's engineers calculate that the required excavation and other rescue costs will total $8 million. The mayor is about to deploy the municipal rescue squads when he is stopped in the corridor by the city's chief economist. The economist informs him that, for the $8 million it will cost to rescue this child, the city can maintain eight mobile coronary care units, which will save an average of 16 lives per year. The mayor, a true believer in cost-benefit analysis, then calls off the rescue squads, grabs the municipal bullhorn, and shouts into the mine, "Sorry kid, we'd like to save you but the costs are simply too high."

The fact that we cannot imagine such a chain of events may for many critics constitute all the evidence necessary to prove that cost-benefit analysis rests on a bankrupt moral foundation. Yet almost no experienced practitioner of cost-benefit analysis would ever recommend that the child in the mine not be rescued. There is a critical distinction, as Schelling has pointed out,[19] between what he calls "identified lives" and "statistical lives." The child in the mine is an identified life. We know who he is. Pictures of him are flashed into our living rooms on the evening news, we are shown his anguished family as he lies trapped in the mine, and so on. When we undertake the rescue effort, we attempt to save this identified life. By purchasing mobile coronary care units, however, we save statistical lives. Although we know that some people will almost certainly die next year if we lack such facilities, we don't know who these people will be. When we buy a mobile care unit, we thus purchase, in effect, a very slight reduction in the probability that any one of us will die next year. To be sure, such reductions in risk are of obvious value to us as a community. Even so, what we are willing to give up to achieve them is much smaller than the sacrifice we would make to save an identified life. The memory of having walked away from a child who could have been rescued would haunt a community for generations.

Cost-benefit analysis does not require us to spend the same to save identified lives as we spend to save statistical lives. In the psychologist's terms discussed in Chapter 2, the information we have concerning identified lives is *vivid*. Our information about statistical lives is, by comparison at least, extremely pallid. Vivid information excites a deeper level of concern, and it is only to be expected that our most deeply felt concerns will summon our strongest reactions.

This is not to say, however, that it would be ethically improper for monetary costs *ever* to enter the decision process where identified lives are involved. Consider, for example, Thaler's hypothetical "eating disease": "The disease has only one symptom: The victim's appetite and food intake requirements double each day."[20] Before very many days pass, a person afflicted with this disease will require more calories per day than can be produced on the planet during a year. Beyond some point, failure to pull the plug on a person with the eating disease would thus permit him to threaten the survival of the entire community. The policy decision to terminate such a patient would obviously not be an easy one. Yet it appears preposterous to argue that ethical considerations would never permit this decision.

The alternative explanation I wish to explore here suggests that opposition to the use of monetary values, per se, is not why critics are reluctant to see cost-benefit analysis applied to environmental, health, and safety matters. Rather, their reluctance may stem from a simple but fundamental theoretical flaw in the way those monetary values are measured. This flaw can be illustrated clearly with an example showing how economists measure the benefits of environmental noise reduction.

Instead of asking people how much they would be willing to pay for noise reduction, economists feel more comfortable trying to infer from people's behavior the value they place on a quiet environment. One technique for doing this has been to examine the price differentials between comparable houses in neighborhoods with different noise levels.[21] Suppose, for example, that neighborhood A is 10 decibels quieter at every moment than neighborhood B, and that houses in neighborhood A each sell for $500 more than comparable houses in neighborhood B. If all people in the community had the same incomes and were equally sensitive to noise,* the economist would then conclude that the benefits of a 10-decibel reduction in the noise level would be $5000 per family. To estimate the benefits of a project that would reduce environmental noise by 10 decibels in all neighborhoods, the economist would then multiply $5000 by the number of families affected by the project. And his critic would inevitably complain that it is ethically objectionable thus to assign a monetary value to enhanced environmental peacefulness.

As in the many similar instances already discussed, however, the economist leaves out a critically important element of the way people choose between competing alternatives. People care not only about the amount of income they have and about how quiet their neighborhood is, but also about how large their incomes are relative to those of their peers. Suppose Smith and Jones rank the various combinations as shown in Table 10.1.

Given these rankings, the individually rational action for each person is to buy a home in the noisy neighborhood. Seeing only this outcome, the cost-benefit analyst reasons that, since Smith and Jones each *could* have bought a home in the quiet neighborhood but *didn't*, the additional quietude must be worth less than $5000 to each of them. But this conclusion is wrong. Had Smith and Jones decided collectively on the matter, the rankings in Table 10.1 show that each would have instead bought a home in the quiet neighborhood.

---

*The effects of differing incomes can be easily accounted for statistically. But the problem of adjusting for sensitivity to noise is more difficult, because sensitivity to noise is such a highly subjective phenomenon. If all the residents of neighborhood B, and some of the residents of neighborhood A, were deaf, for example, we would expect comparable houses in the two neighborhoods to sell for roughly the same price. (If houses in neighborhood B sold for less, some of the deaf residents from neighborhood A would then seek to move to neighborhood B, thus bidding prices up there.) Under such circumstances it would be foolish to conclude that the nondeaf residents of neighborhood A would derive no benefit at all if noise levels were somehow suddenly reduced there. But here, too, technical adjustments could be made to reflect the fact that all people are not equally sensitive to noise.

Table 10.1 *Understating the Value of Environmental Noise Reduction*

	Jones	
	Noisy Neighborhood Price = $X	Quiet Neighborhood Price = $X + $5000
Smith Noisy Neighborhood Price = $X	Third best for both	Best for Smith Worst for Jones
Quiet Neighborhood Price = $X + $5000	Worst for Smith Best for Jones	Second best for both

And since they would prefer homes in that neighborhood to ones costing $5000 less in the noisy neighborhood, the correct conclusion here is that the extra quietude is worth *more* than $5000 to each of them.

The economist's most favored methods for measuring benefits are all based on the theory of revealed preference. This theory says that when a person buys one combination of goods when he could have bought another, he reveals by

Figure 10.1 Standard techniques of cost-benefit analysis understate the value of peace and quiet.

his action that he prefers the first combination to the second. This is a truism where individually defined preferences are concerned. But it is false when there are important interdependencies between people.

We have seen good reasons for believing that people's relative economic standing is extremely important to them. We thus have good reasons for also believing that the methods economists use will systematically underestimate the benefits people receive from increased levels of health, safety, and environmental quality. Economists infer benefits by watching what people spend in the consumption decisions they make as individuals. These amounts, however, must add up to less than what the community as a whole would be willing to spend, for the reasons repeatedly given. Accordingly, it does not follow that we always learn more by watching what people do than by listening to what they say.

It is thus unnecessary to conclude that critics oppose the application of cost-benefit analysis to environmental, health, and safety issues because it violates widely accepted ethical principles. Instead, their opposition may stem, at least in part, from the economist's failure to see that individual behavior understates the benefits in question. Confronted with an analytical tool that consistently offends, but unable to pinpoint its specific weakness, the critic responds in frustration by attacking the tool on ethical grounds.

Ethical Objections to Buying Education in the Marketplace

No developed nation relies primarily on the private enterprise system to educate its children. There are, as I will discuss momentarily, a number of obvious practical reasons for the state to play a central role in education. But even if these practical reasons were absent, many people feel it would be wrong to rely primarily on profit-seeking institutions to provide educational services. In Michael Walzer's recent discussion of the role of the state in education, for example, he remarks that "[*I*]*n principle*, educational goods should not be up for purchase . . ."[22] (emphasis added). Equal access to educational opportunity is something most people appear to feel very strongly about. And this feeling is perhaps the principal source of ethical reluctance to rely more heavily on the marketplace in the sphere of education.

Despite this ethical concern, critics of state-provided education have advanced a number of persuasive arguments for greatly expanding the share of educational services provided by the marketplace. These critics have attacked both the practical and the ethical reasons behind direct state provision of educational services. Their arguments, as we will see, are not to be dismissed lightly. On the contrary, they have been getting increasingly serious attention in high policy circles. But we will also see that there is a serious drawback inherent in greater reliance on private schools. This drawback has to do, naturally, with people's concerns about the relative standing of their children.

There are, as noted, several important practical reasons that the state should play a central role in the educational process. One is that education has powerful externalities—or "neighborhood effects," as Milton Friedman calls them. When a child is educated, the child obviously benefits directly. But so also do the other members of society, since the child becomes a more useful person with whom to interact. Private decisions about educational investment will tend to stress the former benefit and exclude the latter. The level of schooling will tend to stop where the personal benefits of additional education are in balance with the private costs. But the community at large has an interest in seeing the level of education pushed farther than that—to the point where personal *plus* external benefits of further additions balance out the costs.

A related reason for state involvement in education is the desire of the community to help foster a sense of common heritage and shared values. People making private decisions about educational services would inevitably tend to rely on others to assure that these values are maintained. After all, their personal rewards would be greatest if they concentrated on those types of training that have direct payoffs in the labor market.

Another possible reason for a state role in education is that in some locations there may be too few children to establish a workably competitive market for educational services. In other cases where it is far cheaper for only one producer to serve a market, we often see either state-provided services or state-regulated services. Just as the state regulates local telephone companies and provides postal service directly, so it is possible to envision a useful role for the state on this account, too.

Thus, we have at least several practical reasons, plus the ethical concern that children of the rich not be unduly advantaged, favoring a central role for government in the sphere of education.

In his 1962 book, *Capitalism and Freedom*,[23] Milton Friedman acknowledges the obvious force of all of these concerns. Yet he argues that none constitutes a valid reason for educational services to be provided *directly* by the state. As he wrote more than two decades ago:

> [B]oth the imposition of a minimum required level of schooling and the financing of this schooling by the state can be justified by the "neighborhood effects" of schooling. A third step, namely the actual administration of educational institutions by the government, the "nationalization," as it were, of the bulk of the "education industry" is much more difficult to justify on these, or, so far as I can see, any other, grounds. The desirability of such nationalization has seldom been faced explicitly. Governments have, in the main, financed schooling by paying directly the costs of running educational institutions. Thus this step seemed required by the decision to subsidize schooling. Yet the two steps could readily be separated. Governments could require a minimum level of schooling financed by giving parents vouchers redeemable for a specified maximum sum per child per year if spent on "approved" educational services. Parents would then be free to spend this sum and any additional sum they themselves provided on purchasing educational services from an "approved" institution of their own choice. The educational services could be rendered by private enterprises operated for profit, or by non-profit institu-

tions. The role of the government would be limited to insuring that the schools met certain minimum standards, such as the inclusion of a minimum common content in their programs, much as it now inspects restaurants to insure that they maintain minimum sanitary standards.[24]

Friedman's educational voucher plan appears to offer several advantages over our current system. One is that the quasi-competitive scheme promises a higher quantity of educational services per dollar.[25] State-run educational systems, like other state bureaucracies, are hardly paradigms of efficiency. Evidence has been accumulating that, in areas where governments have sought bids for the private production of services previously provided by the state, as with fire protection and sanitation services, costs have gone down dramatically. And these cost reductions have not been accompanied by reductions in the quality of service.[26] Granted, most municipal fire marshalls are spirited and dedicated public servants. Even so, they are bound to see advantages in large scales of operation per se. Large scales of operation will not be similarly attractive to the owner of a profit-seeking fire company, who will inevitably be much more concerned about costs than his municipal counterpart is. (Have those people who doubt that private firms are generally run more efficiently than public firms ever made a purchase in a state-owned liquor store in Pennsylvania? Do they remember the last time they had to deal in person with the Department of Motor Vehicles?)

The voucher plan would also afford greater possibilities for diversity than seem possible under state-provided education. Although forced to follow state curriculums, private institutions would have greater incentives to respond to parents' wishes than state-run schools do. Parents who particularly value, say, exposure to the performing arts, could choose a school specialized in that area.

Similarly, the incentives for schools to recruit and retain the best possible teachers would be stronger under the voucher plan than under the current system. Granted, most public school teachers are competent and dedicated. Yet it is nonetheless true that the fate of an employee is nowhere less dependent on performance than in a government bureaucracy such as a public school system. The occasional incompetent or mean-spirited teacher is often protected in the public schools, but does not survive for long in a school that has to compete for its students.

Another attraction of the voucher system is that it would be fairer than the existing system in at least one important respect. Under the current system, parents who send their children to parochial schools are forced to pay twice for the educational services they receive. They pay once through their school taxes, then again through tuition. The constitutionality of this practice has been long debated. But no matter how the courts may ultimately rule on this question, there seems little doubt that the current system imposes serious financial burdens on many parents. These burdens would be sharply reduced if we switched to an educational voucher system.

*"And then, after many years of business failures, Bertram
finally made his fortune selling signs to the postal system
that said, 'Sorry, this window closed.'"*

Perhaps some people are concerned that once educators became infected by
the profit motive, they would become prone to corner-cutting and cease to
look out for the well-being of students. Of the voucher system, Walzer says,
for example, that "[I]ts greatest danger, I think, is that it would expose many
children to a combination of entrepreneurial ruthlessness and parental indifference."[27] Without discounting such concerns completely, we may note that a
private school that was tempted to reduce its standards as a means of becoming
more profitable would not necessarily be able to do so. Schools, after all, even
private ones, do not perform their services under a cloak of complete secrecy.
Parents often visit schools, and most gather impressions from their children
about what goes on during the school day. Private schools develop reputations
the same way other private firms do. It is thus by no means clear that Adam
Smith's invisible hand would function any less effectively in education than in
spheres traditionally reserved for the marketplace. Whatever shortcomings
the profit motive may cause, these do not appear to have kept wealthy parents
from sending their children to private schools.

It has been said that if parents were able to choose their children's schools,
the school system would then become excessively stratified. Stratification, in
turn, would prevent a "healthy intermingling of children from decidedly
different backgrounds."[28] To a very substantial degree, of course, this intermingling has already been curtailed by the stratification of residential neighborhoods. Because most children continue to be assigned to schools in their
own neighborhoods, it is thus easy to see that a voucher plan might increase
intermingling, rather than reduce it.

But even if intermingling did not occur naturally under a voucher plan,
diversity in school enrollments could be achieved in much the same way as it is
in some school districts today. Those who favor busing, for example, could
advocate busing programs for schools run under a voucher system. Society
can regulate such schools in the same ways that it regulates the public schools
we have today.

One effect of the current system is to limit variability in expenditures per
pupil. Although wealthy school districts can raise school tax revenues more
easily than can poor ones, most states use equalization formulas to keep
expenditures from varying too sharply across school districts. If parents
were given vouchers to which they could then add their own funds for
purchasing educational services, however, greater variations would surely
emerge in the amounts spent per pupil.

As noted earlier, the prospect of such variations accounts for much of the
ethical resistance to private markets for education. Yet there are effective
ways of equalizing opportunities without having the state monopolize the
production of educational services. The current system employs a cross-
subsidy whereby families who pay high school taxes help defray the costs of
educating children from families who pay low school taxes. In much the same
way, it would be possible to provide cross-subsidies under the voucher system.
The size of the voucher, for example, could be made inversely related to
family income. Alternatively, the income tax could be made more steeply

progressive to assure that low-income families could educate their children according to community standards.

If, as I believe, the combined weight of these objections to the voucher system is insufficient to counterbalance its numerous benefits, why then don't we have such a system? Or, if we move to a voucher system in the end, how can we explain why we have resisted it as long and strenuously as we have? One answer is that a voucher system might easily cause an undesired escalation of the total resources devoted to education. To see why this might occur, it is first necessary to discuss briefly how education affects people's success in the labor market.

Education is an investment that does not yield equal returns for all people. Those who are motivated, intelligent, and able to concentrate effectively get more out of an extra year of education and additional educational quality than do those who are not similarly endowed. Because of such differences in payoffs, it is worthwhile for motivated, intelligent people to invest more heavily in education.

Not coincidentally, employers look for many of these same skills and traits in the workers they hire, quite independently of the actual amount of education the workers may have. But traits such as intelligence, perseverance, energy, motivation, the ability to concentrate, and the like are much harder to observe than the amount and quality of education to which people have been exposed. Because there is the noted positive correlation between these traits, on the one hand, and educational attainment, on the other, employers have found it useful to set minimum educational standards for their employees.[29] And they find that it pays to do this even when those educational qualifications, by themselves, have nothing whatsoever to do with specific job tasks. Thus, when a firm requires applicants for a janitorial position to have a high school diploma, its rationale is not that the person hired will need to perform trigonometric calculations or recall lines from Shakespearean plays. Instead, it is that the firm knows that people who fail to finish high school are likely to be sorely deficient in other important traits.

When the overall level of educational attainment increases, the level of schooling below which we find the least productive members of the labor force also increases. In the early part of this century it was possible to enter a career in banking with a high school diploma, but today a master's degree is virtually required. This change reflects much less the increased complexity of banking tasks than the simple fact that educational levels have risen so much during this century. Given the importance of this "signaling" role played by educational attainment levels, the penalties for not keeping pace with community education standards can obviously be severe.

The severity of these penalties, coupled with the single-minded concern most parents feel about seeing their children do as well as possible in the world, suggest that an educational rat race of unprecedented proportions might be unleashed if we were to switch to the voucher method of financing education. Slots in the best universities are by definition limited in number. In the end, they are rationed to those students who perform best along com-

"Attention, please. At 8:45 A.M. on Tuesday, July 29, 2008, you are all scheduled to take the New York State bar exam."

petitive admissions criteria. Even under the current system, which forces them to pay twice for doing so, some parents feel compelled to send their children to expensive private schools for fear that they would otherwise fail to land one of these scarce slots. But the current system provides substantial insulation from these pressures for most middle- and low-income parents. After all, with private school tuition levels as high as they are, parents can provide numerous other important advantages for their children with the money they save by keeping them in the public schools. And with so many good students thus induced to remain in the public schools, being a public school student has not become synonymous with having low ability.

Under a voucher system, by contrast, the incentives would be radically altered. By spending slightly more on their child's schooling, parents could improve their child's chances slightly. And it is certain that some parents would quickly respond to this lure. For other parents, failure to follow suit would then mean seeing their children move backwards in the educational hierarchy, an outcome few parents would tolerate if they had the resources to prevent it.

The prospect of such escalating expenditure levels provides a plausible reason for sticking with something like the present system, despite its manifold shortcomings. These same considerations may thus help us understand the adaptive significance of ethical sanctions against widespread reliance on private markets to provide educational services.

Let me stress that I have not argued that people should be forbidden to sell body parts or babies, or kept from purchasing private education for their children. Rather, I have tried to point out that when people are strongly concerned about relative standing, the collective return from engaging in such transactions will be markedly less than the sum of the apparent returns confronting each individual. Under these circumstances, actions that reduce individual returns will be beneficial to society. The social disapproval that stems from having the ethical sanctions we have discussed has precisely this effect. For this reason, among others, these sanctions may have proven useful.

Eleven

Freedom of Association, Economies of Scale, and the Limits of Governmental Paternalism

A wag has said that fundamentalists oppose having sex standing up because they fear it might lead to dancing. But the opposition that many religious groups express toward dancing is, in their own eyes at least, no laughing matter. And many of these groups spare no effort to prevent their children from becoming corrupted by what most other people see as a perfectly harmless pastime.

We do not question the right of these groups to hold their views. Yet we would never seriously consider a proposal for *legal* sanctions against dancing. Any such proposal would be altogether out of keeping with the legal and philosophical traditions of this country.

At the same time, governments routinely pass laws that prevent people from acting as they please. Many of these laws are completely uncontroversial. State laws requiring drivers to keep right, for example, do not provoke complaints that Leviathan has usurped yet another inalienable natural right. When people bump into one another too frequently in the course of pursuing their own interests, little real harm is done, and much is often gained, by setting up various rules. As Rousseau observed in *The Social Contract*, "[W]e can be both free and subject to the laws since they are but registers of our wills."[1]

Between the extremes of clearly acceptable and clearly unacceptable laws, there is a tense middle ground on which the government's right to restrict the behavior of its citizens will forever be heatedly debated. Some believe strongly, for example, that the state has a moral duty to prevent senseless highway deaths by requiring safety airbags to be installed in all automobiles. Yet others insist that the state may not legitimately deny people the freedom to decide such matters for themselves.

It is easy to see why people might argue in these terms about controversial legislative issues. Yet the ritualistic incantation of agreeable, but mutually incompatible, moral platitudes provides little practical guidance for policy-makers who must choose between specific alternatives. I will try here to develop a practical framework for thinking about the difficult choices that arise when moral imperatives conflict. I will focus specifically on the question of what actions the state may legitimately take to restrict the behavior of its citizens.

Mill's Statement

On the limits of the power of the state over the individual, John Stuart Mill's classic statement in *On Liberty* could hardly have been less equivocal:

> [*T*]*he sole end, for which mankind are warranted, individually or collectively, in interfering with the liberty of action of any of their number, is self protection. The only purpose for which power can be rightfully exercised over any member of a civilized community, against his will, is to prevent harm to others. His own good, either physical or moral, is not a sufficient warrant. He cannot rightfully be compelled to do or forbear because it will be better for him to do so, because it will make him happier, because, in the opinions of others, to do so would be wise or even right. These are good reasons for remonstrating with him, or reasoning with him, or persuading him, or entreating him, but not for compelling him or visiting him with any evil in case he do otherwise. To justify that, the conduct from which it is desired to deter him must be calculated to produce evil to someone else. The only part of the conduct of anyone, for which he is amenable to society, is that which concerns others. In the part which merely concerns himself, his independence is, of right, absolute. Over himself, over his own body and mind, the individual is sovereign.*[2]

Although Mill's position has been often criticized,* it continues to have appeal. Recently it has achieved new support from the arguments presented on its behalf by Nozick, in his *Anarchy, State, and Utopia.*[3]

For the sake of discussion, I adopt Mill's position as my own here and explore what concrete limits to state action are implied by it. I approach the problem in this way because I believe it can be shown, even within Mill's highly individualistic framework, that the boundaries of legitimate state action are not as severe as those set out by the classical libertarian. If so, then the same conclusion should be acceptable also to those whose philosophical orientation is less individualistic than Mill's.

---

*Indeed, Mill himself took many positions that are implicitly hostile to the libertarian position. The term "Mill's position," as used here, represents the position taken by Mill in the above-quoted passage from *On Liberty*.

A Simple Social Contracting Exercise

In an attempt to gain additional insight into where the boundaries of legitimate state action lie, I again employ the framework used in Chapter 6 to assess the legitimacy of redistributive taxation. To recapitulate briefly, this framework makes use of a hypothetical group of people who have just emerged from an ark in the wake of a flood that has destroyed all existing property and social arrangements. They are faced with the task of forming a new society or a new group of societies. As before, each person has an inalienable right that protects him from having to join any society against his wishes. Subject to the constraints implied by this right, societies are free to adopt whatever rules and procedures their members see fit. Each society is again granted a contiguous parcel of land, and its rules and procedures apply to all who choose to live within its borders.

This simple social contracting exercise is very much in the tradition established by Hobbes, Locke, Rousseau, Kant, and others,[4] despite my assumption here that people start with the same material wealth holdings. (As discussed in Chapters 6 and 9, differences in people's innate abilities will quickly produce substantial wealth differences whenever people are allowed to trade freely with one another.) In all social contracting exercises of this sort, the basic assumption is that people can and will form societies in ways chosen to promote their own interests.

As will presently become clear, the framework I use here has in some respects a distinctly utilitarian flavor. This will be most apparent in my claim below that rich and poor alike will empower the states they form to use cost-benefit analysis for a broad class of social choice problems. Yet this framework is nonetheless decidedly nonutilitarian: The assumed right of freedom of association protects each individual from being subjected to a rule whose only selling point is that the benefits it creates for others exceed the costs it would impose on him.* The proponents of such a rule can implement it only with his consent or by forming a separate society. They may not *force* an opponent of the rule to join with them in that society.

Before I go into the details of the analysis, it will be helpful first to sketch the major points in the argument. I begin by noting that, although it is possible to form numerous separate societies, each with rules tailored closely to the idiosyncrasies of its members, such social fragmentation nonetheless entails important costs. I will argue that, in order to limit these costs, people find it useful to empower the states they form to restrict their behavior in various ways.

---

*It would undoubtedly be possible for an experienced philosopher to construct a utilitarian justification for granting each individual the assumed right of freedom of association. Such a justification might, for example, be grounded on the observation that people who are forced to participate in society against their wishes are liable to wreak havoc in various ways. But I have no such justification in mind in asserting that right here. Rather, the freedom to choose one's associates may be thought of as a natural right, one that springs from a deeply felt innate desire to control one's own destiny.

I next discuss the use of cost-benefit analysis in deciding which classes of restrictive rules would be adopted. I argue that, although cost-benefit analysis works well for a broad class of important issues, there are nonetheless specific, practical reasons dictating limits on its use. People will choose to define rights for themselves that cannot be abridged, no matter how favorable the consequences of doing so might be in a particular circumstance.

I then consider what this hypothetical contracting exercise has to say about the limits of state action when people are *not* free to choose the societies in which they live. After all, once societies form, it is not practical for people to regroup whenever conditions change slightly. In this context of restricted mobility, I discuss how the state might assess a proposal to restrict behavior in some way that is not expressly prohibited by its constitution. I conclude by exploring how the analysis applies to restrictions motivated by concerns about relative standing.

With this broad outline of the discussion in mind, let us turn now to the details of the specific arguments.

Economies of Scale at the Society Level

In thinking about the sorts of societies our hypothetical people might form, it is tempting to propose some version of Nozick's utopias, so numerous and richly varied as to be able to accommodate the preferences of anarchists, socialists, welfare statists, advocates of nuclear power, and astrologists alike.[5] After all, as Nozick asks:

Is there really one *kind of life which is best for . . . Wittgenstein, Elizabeth Taylor, Bertrand Russell, Thomas Merton, Yogi Berra, Allen Ginsburg, Harry Wolfson, Thoreau, Casey Stengel, The Lubavitcher Rebbe, Picasso, Moses, Einstein, Hugh Hefner, Socrates, Henry Ford, Lenny Bruce, Baba Ram Das, Gandhi, Sir Edmund Hillary, Raymond Lubitz, Buddha, Frank Sinatra, Columbus, Freud, Norman Mailer, Ayn Rand, Baron Rothschild, Ted Williams, Thomas Edison, H. L. Mencken, Thomas Jefferson, Ralph Ellison, Bobby Fischer, Emma Goldman, Peter Kropotkin, you, and your parents [?]*[6]

A compelling practical reason that the people in our exercise might *not* form numerous small societies, each with rules carefully tailored to their own tastes, is that it would be very costly to do so. All other things the same, large societies are more productively efficient than small societies. In the debates during the Constitutional Convention, for example, the decisive arguments favoring a large federation focused on scale economies in defense and in the establishment of an advantageous international trade position.[7] There are also other important economies of scale because of the many fixed costs incurred in forming any nation-state—the establishment of a uniform currency, transportation and communication networks, and institutions for enforcing laws and contracts, to name but a few. (Imagine having to show a passport and exchange Connecticut dollars for New York dollars every time one drove from Greenwich to Manhattan; or the cost of the two states having to maintain separate militias to prevent each from encroaching on the other's territory.) In addition, many private markets perform much more efficiently at large scales, and security concerns warn against relying too heavily on trade with other nations. Perhaps most important of all, there are very high costs, both monetary and emotional, associated with moving between societies. Since our descendants will be born into whatever societies we create, we increase the risk of forcing these costly moves on them if we structure our social rules too narrowly.

Life in Hobbes's state of nature was "solitary, poor, nasty, brutish, and short."[8] As has often been stressed in the social contract literature, it was so, in part, because of the predatory actions people took against one another in the absence of a clearly defined system of property rights.[9] But surely it was also so because of the inability of people in the Hobbesian jungle to reap the benefits of important economies of scale.

This is not to say that all small states are necessarily less efficient than large states. Small states with highly skilled labor forces, such as Sweden, often produce more output per capita than do much larger states. But once the underlying differences in state characteristics, plus the costs of maintaining a defense posture sufficient to assure genuine political independence, are taken properly into account, we again see clear scale advantages.

There is thus a fundamental tension that confronts our hypothetical people as they sort themselves into societies. On one hand, the formation of homogeneous societies is attractive because the rules of each society can be chosen to suit the preferences of its members. On the other hand, a society whose rules are tailored to a particular set of preferences will by nature attract a smaller number of citizens, and therefore have a smaller disposable income per citizen, than an alternative society whose rules are less narrowly tailored.

By way of illustration, a similar tension confronts the person trying to decide whether to live alone or with a roommate. Joint living helps keep costs

Figure 11.1 Compromises are necessary in order for diverse constituencies to live under a single constitution.

down, but it also limits a person's freedom to do as he or she pleases. Suburbanites, too, face such a tension when they choose between building a pool of their own or joining a club whose members share the costs of a pool.[10] (The fact that, in practice, many societies might form would not mean there are no further economies of scale to be reaped at the society level—any more than the fact that many people build pools of their own would mean there are no further economies of scale in the construction of swimming pools.) The rest of this chapter will focus on the search for a fruitful strategy for coping with the inescapable tension between the desire to reap economies of scale and the desire to do things our own way.

A Generalized Unanimity Criterion

It will be helpful here to express some of the foregoing points in the context of concrete examples.[11] In these examples, I consider the case of two individuals, A and B, who must decide whether to live separately or to share an apartment. Living separately, each will have an income, net of rental payments, of $200 per week. But if they share living quarters each will have a net income of $300 per week. By joining together, the two thus reap a total "scale surplus" of $200 per week. Suppose for the moment that both A and B are trumpet players and that each occasionally likes to practice after 11:00 P.M. while the other wants to sleep. If they lived separately, this would cause no difficulty. If they shared an apartment, though, they would cause one another great discomfort—so great, in fact, that each would prefer to live alone, even though this means having $100 less per week.

But living alone and living together with unwanted noise are obviously not the only two options available to A and B. They could, for example, agree that no trumpets be played in their shared apartment after 11:00 P.M. If the extra $100 per week each would get by living together is sufficient to outweigh this inconvenience, the natural outcome will then be for them to share an apartment in which late-night trumpet playing is forbidden by rule. Since A and B would both favor this rule, we may assume that libertarians would not object, even though the rule occasionally prevents someone from doing as he pleases. To the extent that forcing a person to listen to late-night trumpet noise may be viewed as causing harm to that person, as seems reasonable, this rule also seems clearly acceptable within Mill's framework.

Let us now alter the structure of the example slightly by supposing that B does not play the trumpet and would rather live alone than be subjected to trumpet playing after 11:00 P.M. A, for his part, would also rather live alone than give up playing the trumpet after 11:00 P.M. These new assumptions appear at first to assure that A and B will live separately. Yet they might still elect to live together. By saying that he would prefer to live alone than to be disturbed late at night, B says, in effect, that late-night quietude is worth at least $100 per week to him (that is the amount of extra income he foregoes by living alone). Let us suppose, for the sake of discussion, that silence at night is actually worth $160 per week to B. In addition, suppose A would be willing to forego late-night trumpet playing in return for a payment of no less than $120 per week. The relevant net incomes and valuations for this version of the example are summarized in Table 11.1.

Given the information in Table 11.1, it is again possible for A and B to agree on sharing an apartment in which a rule forbids trumpet playing after 11:00 P.M. Consider, for example, an agreement that bans late-night trumpet playing and gives $360 per week of their $600 joint income to A, the remaining $240 per week to B. (For simplicity's sake, I ignore considerations of relative standing here. This complication could easily be incorporated without altering the point of the example.) The rule against late-night trumpet playing, combined with the proposed division of income, enables A and B to live together under circumstances that each prefers to the alternative of living alone. B has $40 per week extra income under the proposed scheme, and since the rule protects him against late-night trumpet playing, he is thus clearly better off joining A. A, too, prefers this arrangement to living alone: He has an additional $160 per week in net income, which is $40 more than the $120 per week he requires to give up his occasional late-night trumpet playing. A would clearly have preferred to have $300 per week while continuing to be able to play his trumpet after 11:00 P.M. But this outcome is prevented by B's freedom of association. B simply would rather live alone at $200 per week than listen to A's late-night trumpet playing and have $300 per week.

Table 11.1 *Separate Versus Shared Living Quarters*

	Net Income		Willingness to Pay for	
	Separate Apartments	Shared Apartment	Right to Play Late at Night	Quiet Late at Night
A	$200/wk	$300/wk	$120/wk	—
B	$200/wk	$300/wk	—	$160/wk

Some people will find it strange that B should have to pay A for not playing his trumpet. It may seem, after all, that B has an inherent right to peace and quiet late at night. But because A and B have freedom of association, the noise problem here is inescapably a *shared* one. A does not have to live with B, nor does B have to put up with late-night noise. If A plays late at night, then B loses, either by joining and listening, or by living separately and paying higher rent. If A does not play, however, then *he* loses. The completely reciprocal nature of the problem makes it clear that *some* burden of adjustment will have to be borne, whether there is a rule against late-night trumpet playing or not. The shared interest of A and B here is in seeing that this burden of adjustment be kept as small as possible.

If we assume that interested parties can negotiate costlessly with one another, the foregoing example suggests the following "generalized unanimity criterion" for deciding whether a restriction should be imposed:

If what those who favor the restriction would be willing to pay in order to have it exceeds what those who oppose it would be willing to pay to avoid it,

and if the scale surplus (i.e., the gain from the association) is sufficient to compensate those who lose from the restriction, then the restriction should be implemented; otherwise it should not.

The generalized unanimity criterion is, in effect, a simple cost-benefit test with a side provision that eliminates rules that would cause groups to break apart. On its face, this criterion would appear to meet the objections of the libertarian critic of state-imposed rules. After all, the failure to implement any rule that satisfied this criterion would result in an outcome that all parties would find inferior to the alternative of implementing the rule. Whenever a restrictive rule generates greater benefits than costs, and negotiation is costless, its proponents can always contrive transfer payments that, in effect, buy off the opposition.

Distributional Considerations

In the preceding examples, A and B entered negotiations from a position of equal economic strength. The incomes of interested parties, however, obviously will not always be the same. If they are not, one might then object to this "negotiated settlement" framework on the grounds that it provides an "unfair" advantage to people with high incomes.[12] Yet this objection makes even less sense than the consumer group's objection to the auction in which volunteers were paid to relinquish seats on overbooked commercial airline flights (see Chapter 10). Granted, when volunteers are induced to give up their seats by means of a cash compensation payment, low-income persons are more likely to come forward than high-income persons are. And where such decisions are made individually, the poor might indeed sell their seats too cheaply. (Although, as argued in Chapter 10, that is hardly cause to prevent people from engaging voluntarily in such transactions.) But the negotiated settlements I describe here are *collective* settlements, ones that cannot be implemented unless they are supported unanimously. Given that the poor cannot be forced to participate in these transactions, how could such settlements possibly affect their interests adversely?

Suppose, for example, that a rich person, R, and a poor person, P, are considering what procedures to use for making collective decisions should they form a society. P's concern, understandably, is that R's greater means will enable him to prevail in most instances if net willingness to pay governs social decision making. Suppose P calls for issues to be resolved by a one-man, one-vote tally (i.e., with two people, a unanimity rule). P's proposal would, in effect, give him veto power over any rule or project. P could block any proposal, no matter how strongly R might favor it, no matter how weakly he himself might oppose it. Needless to say, this is an unfavorable proposition from R's point of view. Unless there are other strong reasons for him to join P, R is likely to withdraw on this account, thus depriving them both of whatever scale surplus they could have shared.

But there is a better outcome readily available to both R and P. Suppose the scale surplus from their association is $100 and that R is willing to pay $50 to have a particular rule, which P, given his modest means, is willing to pay only $10 to avoid. The most efficient outcome, and one to which both would readily agree, would be for P to let R have the rule in exchange for a payment between $10 and $50. Any payment in this range would make both R and P happier than if the rule were not implemented.

Now, some may complain that, while it might make sense in principle to proceed in this fashion, once societies actually form the poor will lack sufficient bargaining power to force the rich to agree to the necessary compensation payments. But if that were really so, why would the poor then be any more likely to win a veto power that is even *more* costly to the rich? Or, assuming they had somehow managed to secure such a veto power, why couldn't they then bargain with the rich for an attractive set of transfers in return for their agreement not to exercise it?

In the absence of satisfactory answers to these questions, we appear forced to conclude that concern for the well-being of the poor is not a compelling reason not to use the generalized unanimity criterion in the types of social decisions discussed above. Yet it is clear enough that policy alternatives *are* often chosen that would have been decisively rejected within a cost-benefit framework. The decision to regulate prices and ration the supply of gasoline during the crude oil shortage of 1979 is a case in point. Prices and supplies were regulated in the name of keeping gasoline available to the poor. The result was an inordinately wasteful patchwork of cancelled trips and queues of angry motorists at gasoline stations. By virtually any reckoning, it would have made more sense to have allowed prices to rise to market-clearing levels, and then transfer additional income to those hardest hit.

I argue in the next chapter that we did not do this because the specific devices we use for transferring money to the poor create substantial costs of their own. (I will also describe alternative transfer mechanisms that would avoid most of these costs.) For the moment, however, I wish only to note that *if* resources could be costlessly and voluntarily transferred between the haves and have nots, then the use of cost-benefit analysis in public decision making would encounter no serious objections on distributional grounds.[13] Those who find even this claim troublesome may regard the following discussion as being addressed to the class of collective actions that have either neutral or favorable consequences for low-income people. Mine safety laws, which are supported by most miners, might be one such example.

Choosing Societal Rules When Negotiation Is Not Costless

In the examples with costless negotiation considered above, a state that implemented unanimously supported behavior-restricting rules (where the achievement of unanimity may be facilitated by compensation payments between individuals) would be chosen unanimously over an otherwise identical state that did not. As a practical matter, of course, negotiation generally will not be costless. Especially where large numbers of people are involved, negotiations would clearly be too cumbersome to carry out on a case-by-case basis. If it is not always practical to negotiate compensating payments of the sort discussed above, then what should a state's posture be toward behavior-restricting (paternalistic) rules that satisfy the generalized unanimity criterion, but that would nonetheless create uncompensated losses for some individuals? Let me stress that we are looking for a general policy for dealing with such rules, not for a way of settling whether any one particular rule, viewed in isolation, is desirable.

To keep the discussion concrete, let us focus on a comparison of two alternative states: State 1, which permits the passage of nonunanimously supported rules, and State 2, which never permits such rules. While negotiation and transfer payments are prohibitively costly to carry out on an issue-by-issue basis, let us suppose for the moment that policymakers know what individuals would be willing to pay in order to have or to avoid any particular rule. These willingness-to-pay figures may include not only the value an opponent of a prospective rule places on being able to continue the activity it would prohibit, but also any premium he might wish to add to reflect his general distaste for having his options restricted. The *net value* of a prospective rule is the algebraic sum of all of these individual willingness-to-pay values.

To postpone an obvious complication, suppose for the moment that State 1 will not consider for passage without compensation any rule that causes *major* loss of property, safety, or other freedom for any individual. A "major" loss is defined as one in which an individual's willingness to pay to avoid the rule exceeds some threshold fraction of his wealth. State 1 adopts all other rules with positive net value and refuses to adopt those with negative value. State 2 adopts only those rules that are supported unanimously.

As an illustration of how the social decision rules in State 1 might work, consider the following example. Suppose there are three people, two who are well-to-do, call them R_1 and R_2, and one who is not, call him P. The amounts these three would be willing to pay to have or avoid each of three proposed rules are shown in Table 11.2. Negative entries indicate opposition to a rule.

In State 1, which employs the net value criterion, Rules 1 and 2 pass, while Rule 3 does not. None of the rules passes in State 2, since none has unanimous support. The rules passed in State 1 provide net benefits to all three parties (100 each for R_1 and R_2, 10 for P). P votes with the winning side in two of the three cases, as do R_1 and R_2.

The way this particular example was structured, there is no tendency for the set of rules that is passed to favor either the rich or the poor. The pattern of preferences shown in Table 11.2 may be called "unsystematic," in the sense that no individuals tend more than any others to be on the losing side of an issue. Other examples can of course be constructed in which the positions taken by the rich will differ systematically from those taken by the poor. But, as already discussed, the greater purchasing power of the rich can be taken into account in such cases by transferring money to the poor. The rich would readily agree to such transfers, if the alternative were to be denied their way on issues they feel strongly about. And similar compensation arguments can be made concerning any other group whose interests are likely to be adversely affected by collective action.

In order to simplify matters, let us focus here on rules over which people's preferences are unsystematic, in the sense defined above. It is easy to show that among such potential rules, ones that have positive net value will, on the average, be favored by a majority of persons. If the total number of rules to be considered by State 1 is indefinitely large, it then becomes all but mathematically certain that the net value of the set of rules passed will be positive for *each individual*. That is, for the set of rules passed under the net value criterion, we can be all but certain that each person will consider the benefits from the rules he favors to outweigh the costs of the rules he opposes. Moreover, although there will be good rules and bad rules as seen by any particular person, we can be as close to certain as the number of potential rules permits (the more rules, the more nearly certain) that each individual will favor a majority of the rules that State 1 would adopt.

It follows directly that our hypothetical people would unanimously choose to live in State 1, despite the fact that for each of them there will be many rules in State 1 that have adverse personal consequences. As the example was structured, it is worth it to *every individual* to put up with some unpleasant

Table 11.2 *Net Value Criterion Applied to Three Rules*

Individual	Willingness to Pay for		
	Rule 1	Rule 2	Rule 3
R_1	200	− 100	− 50
R_2	− 100	200	− 50
P	20	− 10	− 5
Net value	+ 120	+ 90	− 105

rules in order to have other rules viewed as beneficial. Provided the necessary transfers can be made, a similar set of conclusions applies even to classes of rules that systematically favor specific groups.

This rather stylized example illustrates that even those states that allow behavior-restricting rules that are opposed by substantial minorities (or, indeed, even by a majority) may be unanimously preferred to states that allow only unanimously supported rules. In policy discussions about specific rules, therefore, the mere observation that a particular rule denies certain freedom of action is not sufficient, by itself, to make passage of the rule undesirable. Such a judgment can be made only in the larger context in which people's feelings about the desirability of general classes of rules are taken into account.

Some might still object to cost-benefit analysis here on the grounds that it requires us to make interpersonal utility comparisons. The application of cost-benefit analysis to a single issue, without compensation, would indeed require us to weigh one person's gain in satisfaction against another's loss. And it is quite correct to say that we have no satisfactory analytical basis for making such comparisons.[14]

But such interpersonal comparisons need not be made at all in the framework discussed here. In this framework, the cost-benefit test is applied to a large *class* of issues, in conjunction with general compensation payments made as part of a broader social contract regarding the distribution of income (see Chapter 6). Under such circumstances, we can assure that each person achieves a better outcome than he would under any other feasible decision criterion. In this limited domain, then, the cost-benefit test operates, in effect, as a unanimously supported social welfare function—a device for deciding which of the alternatives should be chosen by the community as a whole.[15] Viewed within the constitutional framework discussed here, the cost-benefit test thus sidesteps many of the thorny issues that arise in social choice problems in which people are assumed able to assign only ordinal rankings (and not measures of intensity of preference) between various alternatives.[16]

In their widely cited *Calculus of Consent*, Buchanan and Tullock make a similar point regarding the outcome of a constitutionally authorized voting procedure:

An interpersonal comparison of utilities, of a sort, does enter into the analysis here, but note that the individual is not required to compare the utilities of A and B. He is required only to compare his own anticipated gains in utility in those situations in which he is in the decisive group with his anticipated losses in situations in which he is in the losing coalition. This calculus is made possible by the chain of separate choices that is anticipated. Moreover, since this calculus is possible for each individual, constitutional decisions to allow departures from unanimity at the level of specific collective choices may command unanimous consent.[17]

If the *procedures* that a society adopts must be unanimously supported by its citizens at the outset, then the *results* of those procedures are socially optimal by definition. And this will be true even though those procedures applied to specific cases may produce adverse consequences for many people. These observations tell us more about the kind of society our hypothetical people would *not* want to form than about the type of state they would most like to live in. Still, it is a useful starting point to have established that collective restrictions of individual behavior are not something that people with powerful rights would be determined to rule out under all circumstances. It hardly needs repeating, however, that the circumstances under which collective restrictions were seen to be *unanimously* attractive were very limited. In particular, (1) rules with "major" consequences were ruled out; and (2) policy-makers were assumed to know individual willingness-to-pay values.

The consequences of relaxing these assumptions help provide a coherent account of the circumstances under which the use of cost-benefit analysis may be inappropriate for social decision making.

Rules with Major Consequences

When rules with major consequences are ruled out and certain other conditions met, people will choose unanimously to live in a state that permits collective restriction of specific individual actions rather than in one that flatly prohibits any such restriction. But what constitutes a rule with "major" consequences, and why should such rules be removed from consideration in any event?

When rules that impose large costs on individuals are not excluded, the positive net value criterion assures only the *expectation* of a positive outcome for each individual. It does not exclude the possibility that the net outcomes of the set of rules passed may be strongly negative for many individuals. Average outcomes are not all we care about. Most people are willing to make sacrifices in order to avoid or reduce the risk of experiencing a genuinely unfavorable outcome. This willingness accounts, after all, for why most people buy various commercial insurance policies whose premium payments exceed expected benefit payments.[18] These observations suggest that most people will want to limit the damage that any particular collective action may impose on any individual. One way of doing this is simply to refuse to consider any rule that would have major adverse consequences for any person.

A less draconian approach is to provide direct compensation to especially hard-hit victims of a generally beneficial rule, as, for example, when individuals are paid for the property the state uses to construct a conveniently located right-of-way. In many cases, however, the damage caused by collective action does not lend itself to the objective measurements we would need for any practicable compensation scheme. How large, for example, is the injury imposed on a Hindu living in the United States who is denied the option of protecting sacred animals from slaughter? For some, the injury must be very large. Yet how can we measure it? It is difficult to imagine a mechanism for compensating victims of such an injury that would not give people strong incentives to misrepresent their preferences, a problem to which we will return momentarily.

Since direct compensation will not always be practical, aversion to risk might thus lead our hypothetical people to draft a constitution that enumerates specific rights. For some issues, these rights would, in effect, rule out the use of cost-benefit analysis in social decision making. Such rights would prevent collective action from imposing major losses on any person no matter how much the action's aggregate benefits might exceed its aggregate costs.

Our hypothetical people could of course avoid injuries of this sort by simply forming separate societies, each composed of those who favor and oppose the same sets of rules. If each society were large enough to exploit potentially available scale economies, and if migration between societies were costless, the problem would thus be neatly solved. But, as discussed at the outset, it is clearly impractical for each dissatisfied minority to form its own separate society. (Still, the advantages of social structures that grant latitude for geographic diversity in the legislative process should be apparent.)

Criteria for setting limits on risk exposure from collective action are thus essentially constitutional questions. The resolution of these questions will define the very boundaries of the societies our hypothetical people form. Where force and coercion are ruled out, as assumed here, a society literally cannot be formed except by a collection of persons who have reached basic agreement on these criteria. Once these people are granted the preliminary right of freedom of association, the protection of other specific individual rights in the societies they form must flow ultimately from their own preferences. With freedom of association, no society will be constituted in a way in which people enjoy rights and privileges that its members do not *want* them to enjoy.

The role of economies of scale in this process is to enhance the bargaining power of any large group that can reach substantial agreement on how society should be set up. After all, any large majority can generate scale economies of its own, which a small minority cannot do. Scale itself is an asset for any society. And where people are free to choose their own associates, control over the fruits of that asset will naturally reside in the hands of any large group that is able to achieve consensus.

Yet the majority's power on this account is far from absolute. Any minority that feels strongly enough about a specific issue can form a separate society in which it does things its own way and accepts the material costs of smaller scale. But where economies of scale are extremely powerful, the costs to a minority of remaining separate may of course be substantial.

The willingness of the majority to bestow certain rights on individuals and minorities stems from many sources. Feelings of empathy and compassion may move them to assert various basic rights. Or they may do so for more narrowly self-interested reasons. For example, by building constitutional safeguards for individual rights, members of the current majority limit the degree to which they may themselves be damaged in the future, when they may no longer be in the majority. Or, as noted, the majority may accept limits on its powers in order to attract various minorities to share the material advantages of a larger society. Minority rights may also be protected because the majority prefers diversity for its own sake. Society may actually enjoy the presence of its eccentric sons and daughters, or at least may not be willing to see them bear excessive costs imposed by rules tailored too closely to the tastes of the majority.

It hardly needs saying, however, that there are limits to the majority's willingness to protect minorities from the adverse consequences of collective action. In some circumstances, these adverse consequences may be simply too great to be offset by the scale advantages of joining the larger society. When this is the case, it will, as noted, make sense for both the majority and the minority alike to form separate societies.

In our simple contracting exercise, then, societies will not necessarily limit the potential harm caused by collective action to some threshold fraction of the wealth of any potential member. When people want strongly enough to escape the consequences of some behavior that others value highly, they may choose to form societies in which that behavior is prohibited. And they may do so even though in the process they create the risk that some of their descendants may be forced to migrate away from those societies. On what grounds might people be denied the freedom to act in this fashion?

One possible objection is that restrictive rules may someday strongly injure persons who have not yet been born. The interests of future generations, after all, are not directly represented at the moment when the rules are drafted. Granted, people will usually try to represent the interests of their own descendants. But if the costs of migrating out of the society into which one is born are sufficiently high, such an objection may nevertheless have considerable moral force. Yet what if our hypothetical people believe almost all of their descendants will favor the restriction as strongly as they do? Would it then clearly be better to prevent those descendants from having it? Here again, the dilemma posed by the reciprocal nature of restrictive rules is painfully apparent.

Suppose, for example, that some of our hypothetical people come from a cultural tradition that views monogamy as an essential aspect of the institution of marriage, while others feel just as strongly that polygamous marriage is the only acceptable form. If the two groups freely pursue their respective marriage practices within a single society, it is all but inevitable that many sons from one group will come in close contact with daughters from the other. And some of them will fall in love and insist on marrying, despite the great difficulties that will result from trying to meld these two disparate cultural forms. Such marriages will cause great pain to the families of both groups and, when passions fade and practical issues come more clearly into focus, probably even to the couples themselves. Much of this suffering could be avoided if these two groups were to form separate societies in which each permitted only its own form of marriage contract.

One might argue that it is the responsibility of families and larger ethnic and religious groups, and not of the state, to provide guidance for the young as to whom they should marry. Indeed, it is precisely this more tolerant course that many societies have chosen with respect to a broad range of less extreme religious freedom issues. But what about issues, such as different marriage customs, in which there are no available avenues for adaptive coexistence that

"Your young fellow, Gina—is he Italian?"

do not involve extreme and protracted emotional trauma? And what of cases such as the one discussed in Chapter 1, in which a society of pet lovers finds itself unable to adjust to the fact that people in its midst are killing and roasting pets? On what grounds could we insist that people should not be free at the outset to form separate societies in order to avoid such trauma? (Bear in mind that I am still talking about hypothetical people with no previous commitments here. For an *existing* society in which people already have extensive commitments, the conditions under which it would be acceptable for a majority to impose *new* restrictions would be very different. More on this point below.)

Difficulty in Measuring Willingness to Pay

One difficulty in reconciling a restriction on marriage practices with Mill's statement about the proper bounds of state action lies in how we interpret what he may have meant by "harm to others." Clearly Mill *cannot* have meant that the need to adjust to hostile cultural practices causes no pain or suffering. As Wolff, for example, writes:

[T]o a truly devout Christian, a physical blow counts for much less than the blasphemy of a heretic. After all, a physical blow affects my interests by causing me pain or stopping me from doing something that I want to do. If the existence of ungodly persons in my community tortures my soul and destroys my sleep, who is to say my interests are not affected? Since Mill himself assigns the pleasures and pains of the soul a superior rank over those of the body, he is hardly in a position to deprecate the spiritual suffering which the atheist by his mere existence inflicts on the devout.[19]

Wolff goes on to say:

Naturally, we wish to reply that I take a legitimate interest in the safety of my person, while my interest in the private practices of my neighbors, however strong, is not legitimate. . . .[20]

Wolff's response must strike a resonant chord in all those with even a trace of libertarian sentiments. Yet how can the distinction he draws be consistent with the negotiated settlement framework discussed earlier for deciding whether or not to ban late-night trumpet playing? After all, if the blasphemer would be willing to pay, say, only $10 to blaspheme, while the devout would pay $50 for him to desist, what outcome would *they* prefer? Provided the scale surplus of their association is more than $10, the blasphemer would gladly agree to desist in return for a payment of at least $10. The devout, in turn, would gladly provide such a payment. Any other arrangement would be unambiguously worse for both parties. And since neither party would prefer a different result, it hardly makes sense to insist here that the principle of freedom requires giving the blasphemer his right to speak.

Yet consider the practical difficulties in doing anything else. How, for example, is the willingness to pay to blaspheme to be assessed? Or to avoid blasphemy? We clearly cannot ask the two how much they would be willing to pay, for the incentives to misrepresent these values are simply too great for us to believe them (in the blasphemer's case, at least, if not the devout's). Nor are there likely to be any observable market phenomena that reflect, directly or indirectly, these willingness-to-pay values. We have no trustworthy hedonometer, and the use of a truth serum would hardly be practical, much less ethically defensible.

More important, it is very likely that neither party even *knows* what he would be willing to pay for the specific right at issue. One might, for example, be willing in the abstract to agree not to blaspheme, but what personal costs would that impose? Would every thought have to be reviewed before being found suitable for speech? What toll would such a review exact on the normal flow of verbal communication? Furthermore, the presence of the blasphemer might, for example, cause great discomfort to the devout at first, but if given no alternative, he might discover effective ways of adjusting. He might learn to avoid the blasphemer, he might develop compassion for him, and even derive pleasure from trying to reeducate him, or he might simply tune him out. The relevant willingness-to-pay value is the one that takes into account his most effective adaptation to the blasphemer. But the devout is hardly likely to recognize that accommodation if he has never had to seek it out.

In cases where willingness-to-pay values are inherently difficult to fathom, it may simply be impractical to resolve conflicts on a case-by-case basis. Thus, while conceding that it would be desirable to curb some forms of speech if the relevant willingness-to-pay values could be measured, our hypothetical people might find they cannot discriminate effectively between harmful speech and beneficial speech. As a result, they may decide simply to permit all speech. Or they may decide to prohibit only certain extreme forms of speech for which, by consensus, costs to the listeners highly exceed gains to the speakers—as, for example, when states impose restrictions against extreme displays of public profanity.

So in this *practical* sense we might call the devout's interest in the private practices of his neighbor "illegitimate." By so doing, we place the burden of adjustment on him, for, as best we can tell, he is the one more able to adjust. This will not always be the case. When it is not, then the "right" thing to do, *in principle* (or at least what both parties would *want* to do), would be for the blasphemer to adjust. But because we are usually unable to identify the right course of action in specific cases, we place the burden of adjustment on the party who, *on the average*, is better able to handle it. Most of the time this happens to be the listener, rather than the speaker.

Concerning the question of whether the protection of speech under the First Amendment sometimes does more harm than good, consider the following example, recently described in a letter written to a newspaper advice columnist. The author of the letter wrote to confess, and apologize publicly for, a cruel action he had taken many years earlier. As a high school student, he and several friends had leafed through the school yearbook and found a picture of the girl they agreed was the ugliest in their class. With his friends eagerly listening in, he then telephoned the girl and told her of her selection. In his letter, the man said that the girl responded to this message with a pained, inarticulate moan, the memory of which had haunted him for the ensuing 20-odd years.

Surely no sentient person would claim that the "benefits" the boys received from their prank could possibly have offset the anguish it caused that girl. A cost-benefit test would have unequivocally ruled against the remark in question. Yet the First Amendment protected his right to make it, and it did so properly. There is simply no practical way to write a law to prevent the damage caused by such a remark without creating even more serious problems.

This description of why our hypothetical people might protect speech acknowledges that some speech may produce more harm than good, and might, in principle, therefore be worth preventing. It is thus at odds with one of Mill's arguments for the protection of speech, in which he emphasized a distinction between the "inner sphere" and the "outer sphere":

But there is a sphere of action [the inner sphere] in which society, as distinguished from the individual, has, if any, only an indirect interest; comprehending all that portion of a person's life and conduct which affects only himself, or if it also affects others, only with their free, voluntary, and undeceived consent and participation.[21]

Hayek has also written of a "protected sphere,"[22] and similar concepts have been discussed by Gramsci[23] and others.

   These writers place what persons think and say in the inner, or protected, sphere, which is beyond the reach of the state to control or prohibit. Yet certain forms of speech surely affect others, producing real harm that is difficult or impossible for them to avoid. The alternative rationale for protecting speech suggested here disavows the tenuous and arbitrary distinction between such inner and outer spheres. Instead, we have a hybrid between a natural rights defense and a utilitarian defense. It is a natural rights defense in the sense that freedom of association guarantees that no individual may be deprived, against his consent, of his right to speak. It is a utilitarian defense in the sense that it argues that people might *prefer* not to protect all types of speech in the various societies they form. In addition to the right to speak, each individual has the right not to be forced to listen. These rights cannot be exercised simultaneously. Sensible choices regarding such conflicting rights will often involve utilitarian devices for assigning weights to the options people face.

Sen's Paradox

This hybrid defense of free speech helps shed light on Amartya Sen's claim that liberty and the unanimity principle that underlies cost-benefit analysis are incompatible.[24] Sen illustrates the conflict he has in mind with the following example:

There is a book (e.g., Lady Chatterly's Lover) *which may be read by Mr. A ("the prude") or Mr. B ("the lascivious") or by neither. Given other things, these three alternatives define three social states, a, b, and o, respectively. Consider now the following possibility. The prude A most prefers o (no one reading it), then a ("I'll take the hurt on myself") and lastly b ("imagine that lascivious lapping it up"). The lascivious prefers most a ("it will give that lily white baby a nice shock"), then b ("it will be fun"), and last o ("what a waste of a good book").*[25]

The rankings A and B assign to the three alternatives are summarized in Table 11.3.

   If society feels people should be granted the right to read whatever books they choose, Sen argues, it then follows that society should prefer outcome *b* to outcome *o*. (After all, B wants to read the book.) Similarly, since A does not want to read the book, outcome *o* must be socially preferred to outcome *a*.

Table 11.3 *Preference Rankings over Three Alternatives*

	Best	Second Best	Third Best
Mr. A	*o*	*a*	*b*
Mr. B	*a*	*b*	*o*

(B doesn't read the book in either of these outcomes.) Yet both Mr. A and Mr. B agree that outcome *a* is preferable to outcome *b*. And to say that outcome *a* is unanimously preferred to outcome *b* implies, in the language of cost-benefit analysis, that *a* is socially preferred to *b*. Now, if *b* is socially preferred to *o*, and *o* is socially preferred to *a*, and *a* is socially preferred to *b*, it then follows that *b* is simultaneously socially better *and* socially worse than *a*, which is obviously impossible. Thus, we have the inconsistency Sen identifies between unqualified rights on the one hand, and the unanimity principle that underlies cost-benefit analysis on the other.

Such difficulties do not arise if the right to read books is thought of as having emerged from a social contracting exercise of the sort discussed in this chapter. Suppose A and B are negotiating with one another about whether to form a society, and the question arises whether people shall be granted the right to read whatever books they choose. And suppose the two agree on a constitution in which book censorship is expressly forbidden. In the framework of our social contracting exercise, that means that both A and B prefer that package to any alternative package that was available to them. Once the decision to guarantee people the right to read whatever they choose has been made, their feelings about any particular book are simply not relevant in determining the social ranking of the alternatives enumerated by Sen. Their affirmation of the right to read is a statement about the undesirability of censorship generally, not as its effects might be calculated in any particular instance.

The Tax Alternative to Outright Prohibition

The discussion thus far has assumed that when some people oppose an activity that others favor, society faces an all-or-nothing choice between banning the activity outright, on the one hand, or freely permitting it, on the other. But there are often practical alternatives for restricting people's activities that stop far short of outright prohibition.

Economists have long argued, for example, that it is much more efficient to tax pollution than to ban it outright.[26] One reason is that an outright ban on all pollution would be extremely costly. Pollution can be cheaply eliminated from some production processes, but for others the cost would be prohibitive. The benefits to society of curtailing pollution must be weighed against the costs, and, as noted in Chapter 10, the best available outcome will almost surely entail *some* pollution. Emissions taxes would automatically concentrate pollution reduction in the hands of those who can accomplish it in the least costly way. Those who cannot avoid the use of polluting processes will pay higher taxes, whereas others will escape taxation by switching to clean, low-cost alternatives. This is a cheaper way of reducing pollution than to require all parties to curtail pollution by equiproportional amounts.

Using a parallel line of reasoning, we can see that it will often prove more attractive to tax "offensive" behavior than to ban it outright. As in the case of pollution, society will often realize great benefit even when it stops short of eliminating offensive behavior completely. Moreover, given the existing diversity of preferences, it will be much more costly for some people to curtail any given behavior than it will be for others. The socially optimal level of any offensive behavior will thus usually be greater than zero. By taxing the offensive behavior rather than banning it, society concentrates the responsibility for curtailing that behavior in the hands of those who assign least value to pursuing it.

Although taxes have important advantages over simple prohibition, policy-makers have often avoided them for fear of burdening the poor. This concern can easily be dealt with, however, by simply returning the proceeds of the tax in lump-sum amounts to every taxpayer; that is, in amounts that do not depend on the amount of tax each person actually paid. Under Alfred Kahn's leadership, the New York State Public Service Commission did just that when it approved a charge for each call made to telephone directory assistance. Our net monthly charge for directory assistance is now 10 cents per call, less 30 cents. People who make no directory assistance calls thus actually receive a 30-cent credit on their monthly phone bill. The use of directory assistance has gone down sharply since the introduction of this charge, and subscribers who are willing to look up numbers now have lower telephone bills than before.

A lump-sum tax rebate would, for most taxed activities, actually result in a net transfer of resources from rich to poor. At the same time, the taxed activity would become less attractive to rich and poor alike. The fact that people with low incomes might curtail the taxed activity to a greater degree than do the rich is hardly a criticism of the tax approach. On the contrary, low-income persons would almost surely benefit from the opportunity of making such an exchange.

The possibility of restricting offensive behavior through the use of taxes makes it especially awkward for libertarians to insist that the state should never intervene except to prevent what Mill understood as causing harm to others. Suppose, for example, that one group finds the practice of nudism offensive and thus refuses to associate with nudists unless they consent to a stiff tax for appearing in public without clothing. The scale surplus of the larger society may be great enough that each nudist could pay this tax and continue to wear no clothing, yet still have more income left over than in the smaller, "unrestricted" society.

Even if each nudist regards himself as a libertarian in the classical natural rights tradition, what coherent argument could he then present for not joining the larger society? After all, he can continue to go without clothing there and still have all the other options he had before, *plus* some additional options as well. If these attractions cause the nudists to swallow their objections to the tax and join the larger society, what harm is there in that? Would it make sense to complain that they have somehow behaved in an unprincipled way? And, having joined the larger society, if most of the nudists decided to escape the tax by wearing clothing most of the time, would we then say, pejoratively, that they have "sold out"? Is there any sensible definition of freedom that would allow us to impugn the behavior of nudists who agree to live by the rules of the larger group rather than confront uniformly diminished options in an unrestricted smaller society?

Now, one might complain that the difficulty posed by these questions arises from the hypothetical nature of the entire exercise. Perhaps this is a fair complaint, for people are surely not able to reconstitute societies costlessly whenever circumstances might dictate. National governments are different from private clubs. Costly commitments are widespread in every society, and a workable scheme for conducting any society will have to take these commitments into account. Let us try to explore, therefore, what practical lessons the preceding discussion may have for societies in which there are already widespread commitments.

Application to Existing Societies

Our social contracting exercise has examined people with no previous commitments as they sought to form new societies. This is obviously a fanciful way of characterizing the process by which most current societies were formed. Yet, in certain important respects, this exercise resembles the circumstances under which the government of the United States emerged. Granted, the people who formed our government had to abandon many important commitments in order to constitute any government at all. But once they gained independence from England, they were in a position not unlike the original position of our exercise. They had the option of forming one society or several; and they were free to adopt whatever rules and procedures they chose. The framers of the Constitution were obviously unschooled in the language of cost-benefit analysis and risk aversion. But they were nonetheless experienced and practical-minded men who had before them a good record of the issues that had caused problems in societies past. And they had an obvious and profound regard for the rights of individuals. The fact that they reserved many important decisions for state and local governments indicates their respect for the diversity in human nature and custom. At the same time, by creating a central government, and endowing it with numerous strong powers, they showed their appreciation of the advantages implicit in larger societies. Indeed, the entire protracted debate between the Federalists and their opponents is replete with examples of the inherent tension between scale advantage, on the one hand, and the desire for custom-tailored rules on the other.[27]

Let us suppose, for the sake of discussion, that the Constitution represents the response to a problem something like the one in our social contracting exercise. What does this imply about the extent to which the state can legitimately constrain the behavior of its citizens? It hardly needs saying that the state may not do anything that is expressly proscribed by the Constitution or the Bill of Rights. Nor may those proscriptions be altered in any way except as permitted by the provisions clearly outlined in the Constitution. But what of issues that are not clearly dealt with in those documents? Or of such issues that were left purposefully vague, for legislatures to sort out as circumstances dictated? Suppose, for example, that Group 1 proposes that Congress restrict the behavior of Group 2 in some way that is not explicitly proscribed by the Constitution and ensuing legislation. What guidance does our contracting exercise offer a legislator confronted with such a proposal?

The first test to which the proposed rule may be put is to see if what Group 1 is willing to pay for the rule exceeds what Group 2 would be willing to pay to avoid it. This test will obviously be difficult or impossible to carry out in many cases. But in some instances, at least, proposals will either clearly pass or clearly fail this test. Those that clearly fail generally need be considered no further. (Some proposed rules that clearly fail this test have nonetheless been implemented because of their purportedly favorable distributional consequences. But, as noted earlier, a superior outcome is possible by avoiding such rules in favor of redistribution through the tax system.)

If the proposed rule passes this preliminary test, we may then ask whether it imposes any major costs on anyone. If so, can the victims be identified, and are there any practical means of compensating them? If they cannot be compensated, is there a tax alternative that would permit them to curtail their losses? If there are major consequences, and no practical way to compensate for them or to avoid them, there may then be reasonable grounds for abandoning the rule at this point. Suppose, for example, that Group 1 would have agreed to pass such a rule in our hypothetical original position (when people were first segregating themselves into separate societies), and that as a result Group 2 would not have joined the current society. It would then be a breach of the implicit right of freedom of association to impose such costs on Group 2 once they are irrevocably committed to membership in the current society. *Only if* not *having the proposed rule would impose comparable individual costs on members of Group 1 would respect for freedom of association then allow further consideration of the proposal.*

But suppose the issue of major losses does not arise or, if it does, that it can be dealt with adequately in some fashion. We may then seek further guidance about the proposed rule by asking the following question: If the hypothetical contract could be renegotiated today, would all the people who currently make up this society have agreed to join? That is, would they still have agreed to join knowing that the *class* of rules, of which the current proposal is one member, would be considered for passage under the positive net value criterion? If so, then the fact that Group 2 objects to this *particular* rule loses much of its force. Group 2 may even dislike each and every rule in the class that includes the currently proposed rule. But suppose that other groups would not have joined Group 2 in the absence of this class of rules. If Group 2's share of the scale surplus made possible by the presence of the other groups outweighs the costs of its having to live with this class of rules, it will then be better for Group 2 to join the others and put up with those rules. In this sense, we may say that Group 2 "approves" of the class of rules at issue. Its approval here means that it would have voluntarily joined a society that permitted this class of rules, rather than form a smaller, less productive society on its own. Group 2's approval, thus defined, together with positive net value and no major losses, creates a rebuttable presumption in favor of the rule.

It is worth noting that if the proposed restriction is passed, even the members of Group 1 may not feel pleased when it limits their own behavior. Most people recognize, for example, that mandatory tax payments are a prerequisite for even the most rudimentary form of government, yet few feel cheerful when the time comes to pay their own taxes. Buchanan refers to this phenomenon as the "paradox of being governed," and compares it to Crusoe being awakened by his alarm clock:

As the alarm bell arouses him from his nap . . . Crusoe finds himself frustrated by an external constraint on his choice set, and he feels "less free" at that moment than he might have felt in the wholly voluntary act of rising from his bed. This sense of frustration may be repeated each and every morning,

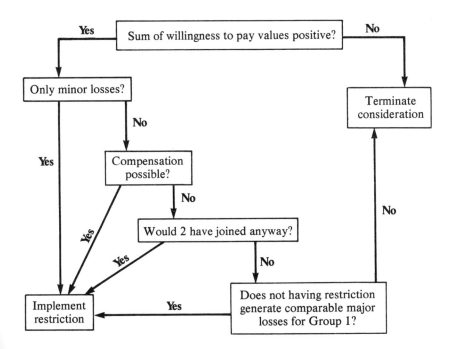

Figure 11.2 Evaluation Procedures When Group 1 Proposes to Restrict Group 2 in a Way Consistent with the Bill of Rights

but Crusoe may continue to set the governing clock each evening. The rational rule maker makes the tradeoff between liberty and planned efficiency and includes an enforcement instrument in the contract.[28]

Let me stress at this point that none of the foregoing discussion suggests that actual decisions about rules can be reduced to a series of simple formulas. Other problems aside, the difficulties associated with assessing willingness to pay would be more than enough to assure that these decisions can almost never be reached in any such mechanical fashion. Thus, there will always be room, even in policy discussions of the sort contemplated here, for the kinds of moral arguments that critics of cost-benefit analysis often emphasize.

Restrictions Motivated by Concerns about Relative Standing

The collective restrictions discussed in Chapters 7 to 10 were motivated by people's desires to escape self-defeating competitions with one another. One objection to the use of state power for these purposes is that concerns about relative standing are not legitimate concerns. By this view, it is simply not proper for state policy to cater to people who are preoccupied with where they stand in the income hierarchy. The preferences of such people are "objectionable," we are told, and deserve no weight in public policy decisions.

If everyone's preferences were carved in stone, as the economist often views them, the immediate response to this objection would be that no purpose is served by making value judgments about other people's tastes. Nor, many would argue, do we have any legitimate basis for making such judgments. If the sadist wishes to form a state that permits him to spank the masochist, it is his right to do so. From this perspective, there is no room for calling anyone's preferences objectionable.[29]

But the view that preferences are fixed and to be honored equally, regardless of their nature, is hardly a widely held view, and probably not a very sensible one either. People's values are inevitably shaped by the values of those around them. And, proper or not, many people do hold very well-defined rankings of different values and preferences. Sen refers to such rankings as people's "metapreferences."[30] Given that people have these metapreferences, and given their right of freedom of association, we can expect them to use the states they form to help instill those values they most respect.

Applying this line of thinking to people's concerns about relative standing, we may then grant the existence of all of the troublesome consequences of the various prisoner's dilemmas discussed earlier, yet still argue that the state should never take collective action in the name of concerns about position. By admitting such concerns as a valid basis for government intervention, this argument would say, the state inevitably lends society's approval to these concerns. People will thereby be encouraged to think of them as legitimate and perhaps be more inclined to dwell on them and be troubled by them. In contrast, others who have been taught at every juncture that such concerns are improper may be relatively better able to ignore or suppress them.

"You'll find there's no right or wrong here. Just what works for you."

This argument has obvious force. It evokes a similar argument often used on behalf of free speech. Although free speech occasionally permits the heretic to inflict damages on the devout that exceed the gains to the heretic, we nonetheless protect free speech. In part, surely, we do so because we believe that encouraging free speech as a value will make it easier for people to endure the negative consequences of words imprudently spoken.

Similarly, society tries to shape people's preferences to minimize the inevitable adverse consequences of invidious personal comparisons. The aim here is to encourage people to make their own accommodations to the negative feelings such comparisons provoke. Just as people can be urged to ignore unkind words that are written or spoken about them, they can also be urged to diminish the importance they attach to their positions in various income hierarchies.

As forceful as this argument appears, it nonetheless has clear limitations, at least in the case of speech. When the damage caused by a remark reaches a certain threshold, the state intervenes, despite the adverse side effects. Are the reasons that lead us to curtail free speech fundamentally different from those that might justify state action to mitigate the positional treadmill? Suppose, for example, that not regulating safety will cause almost all people to purchase much less safety than they really want, because buying the "right" amount would make them unable to provide the same advantages others do for their children. Does it then follow that we would be better off not regulating safety in any way? Suppose that not having forced savings programs will cause most people to save less than they really want to for their old age, because saving the right amount would prevent them from keeping pace with community consumption standards, with the very real costs that would entail. Does it then follow that society would be better off if it instead protected Barry Goldwater's right to choose for himself the amount he saves?

Having explored fully the possible avenues for individual adaptation, we may still find that a collective action to limit the consequences of competition for position produces an outcome that most people strongly favor. Under these circumstances, we should then ask whether the proposed collective action, including its possible unintended effects on attitudes, belongs to a *class* of actions that would have been acceptable in our hypothetical original position. Perhaps it does not. But if it does, then respect for the rights of those who oppose this *particular* action does not appear to be a valid reason for denying its legitimacy. To insist otherwise would be to show little respect for the rights of those persons who favor the action.

One might argue, of course, that the state has already enacted safety regulations and the like without placing its imprimatur on concerns about relative standing. If concern about the state's effect on people's attitudes and values is the difficulty, why not simply have the state articulate other reasons for its actions? Granted, it may in some instances be attractive to do so. Particularly in the case of income redistribution, much is gained, and very little lost, by offering altruistic concern for the poor as our reason for progressive taxation. After all, this is surely *one* of the reasons we redistribute, and the social climate stands to improve if we encourage people to adopt such a concern.

But in other cases there may be unintended negative consequences of offering misleading reasons for state policies. There are such costs, for example, when we are told that the state regulates safety because workers would otherwise be exploited by their employers. By encouraging people to believe that firms have far greater power than they do in fact have, such statements help create a climate of public hostility and distrust toward the business community. And such a climate, in turn, encourages an expansion of the economic role of the state in various ways that are harmful to the public interest. (More on these points in the next chapter.)

Additional Examples of Paternalistic Intervention

The examples discussed in Chapters 7 to 10 deal with collective action designed to modify individual behavior in circumstances where collective self-interest and individual self-interest are in clear conflict. Such circumstances account for many, but by no means all, of the paternalistic restrictions that are currently under dispute. Philip Cook, for example, discusses a class of restrictions that are motivated by concerns of a literally much more paternal nature than those discussed above.[31] Parents frustrated by their inability to monitor and control the behavior of their children may support laws that enjoin the state to act as their agent in helping carry out the parental role.

In a similar vein, Vaupel discusses our tendency to discount the future excessively as a rationale for collective action to limit individual freedom of choice.[32] Thomas Geer, who gladly accepts employment cleaning up a radiation spill at age 32, for example, might, at age 55, strongly support legislation that would have prevented his earlier behavior (see Chapter 7). Gerald Dworkin suggests that people restricted by such laws will often subsequently recognize the wisdom of the restrictions:

There is an emphasis on what could be called future-oriented consent—on what the child will come to welcome rather than on what it does welcome. Extensions of [literal] paternalism are argued for by claiming that in various respects, chronologically mature individuals share the same deficiencies in . . . capacity to think rationally and the ability to carry out decisions that children possess. Hence in interfering with such people we are in effect doing what they would do if they were fully rational.[33]

Dworkin is quick to emphasize the obvious dangers implicit in this view. But there is nonetheless clear merit in the notion that one's better-informed future self should have at least some voice regarding those actions his less-informed current self takes that may later harm him. Such considerations might be incorporated into the framework of our social contracting exercise by using not what individuals would currently be willing to pay to have or to avoid a rule, but rather something like an undiscounted sum of annual willingness-to-pay values over the course of each individual's lifetime. In a population of individuals distributed uniformly with respect to age, this sum will not differ much from the sum across individuals of current willingness-to-pay values. In any event, the contracting exercise discussed here makes clear that the middle-aged person's right to protect himself from harm is, in principle at least, no less worthy of respect than the young person's right to inflict harm on himself.

The high costs of obtaining the information relevant for certain decisions is also cited as a rationale for collective action to constrain individual behavior. People may regard the decision of whether it is safe to use a certain cleaning compound, for example, as too technically complex to make on their own. Requiring warning labels on risky substances may suffice in most instances. But where the risks are especially high, many people may place great value on avoiding the possibility of carelessly overlooking or misunderstanding such labels. They may prefer an outright ban on especially dangerous substances. Such a ban obviously limits the range of choices in a way that some careful consumers will oppose. Similarly, many people will favor laws banning drugs, prostitution, and other vices out of a desire to protect themselves from becoming personally involved in activities they believe run counter to their interests. In these cases, too, sensible policy analysis requires us to take into account the intensity and malleability of preferences on each side.

Paternalistic laws are often attacked on the grounds that they unjustly abridge individual freedom. We have seen circumstances, however, in which people with powerful rights will form governments that prohibit activities many of them value. As heavy handed as the prohibition of an activity is, it is even more heavy handed never to allow such prohibitions at all.

True individual sovereignty implies that people have not only the right not to be restricted by others—as the libertarian position stresses—but also the right not to be subjected to behavior they consider harmful. If the concept of individual sovereignty is to have any intelligible meaning at all, there can be no distinction *in principle* between the legitimacy of these two subsidiary rights: The right not to be offended is just as worthy of our respect as the right not to be restricted. Yet these rights cannot be exercised simultaneously. People must negotiate with one another and reach agreement on which rights will be respected under which circumstances. I have argued that practical considerations—in particular, aversion to risk and difficulties in measuring intensity of preference—may dictate that social contracts give priority, *under certain circumstances*, to the right not to be restricted. But not always. Hockey players, as a group, would not freely choose to live in a society that prevented them from imposing helmet rules. The libertarian who insists that the right not to be restricted cannot, as a matter of principle, ever be negotiated away, shows contempt for the rights of people to resolve such issues for themselves.

Once the issue of collective restriction of individual behavior is recognized as no more a moral than a practical one, policymakers are led to focus on the task of assessing their constituents' preferences concerning the available choices. I have argued that decision rules for collective action should be sought that mimic as closely as possible the decisions that citizens would reach themselves if they could negotiate costlessly with one another in a hypothetical unrestricted environment. In many circumstances, the best decision criteria will be linked closely to citizens' willingness to pay to have or to avoid a proposed collective action.

I also argued that, while freedom of action is not a thing to be preserved at all costs, there are nonetheless good reasons not to restrict people any more than is necessary to attain whatever objectives are sought. Where taxation of offensive behavior proves practical, it will often be a much more attractive approach than outright prohibition. Indeed, we saw circumstances where a society that restricted offensive behavior through taxation might even afford its citizens *greater* freedom of action than would be possible in alternative societies that did not restrict behavior in any way.

The existence of economies of scale at the society level plays a key role in the criticisms aimed here at the classical libertarian position. If small societies were just as efficient as large ones, and mobility between societies were costless, then an inability to restrict offensive behavior would not be very troublesome. Such behavior could simply be avoided by forming groups that do not include the offenders. But atomistic societies are not productively efficient, and mobility between such societies would not be costless even if they were. The libertarian's denial of the right to restrict offensive behavior under these circumstances will thus impose substantial unnecessary costs on people.

John Stuart Mill insisted that the only proper grounds for the state to interfere with the individual is to prevent "harm to others," an assertion with which we may continue wholeheartedly to agree, provided we are clear about what we mean by the terms "harm" and "others." In the framework discussed here, the meaning of harm was left for individuals to decide for themselves. After all, unless an individual's behavior were harmful to someone else in some way, why—barring malice—would that someone bother to restrict it? I argued that "harm" understood in this way is much more consistent with our general usage of the term than was Mill's, which rested on a shaky distinction between inner and outer spheres of being.

The interpretation of the term "others" proposed here is one that permits the 25-year-old who accepts employment cleaning up a radiation spill to be considered a different person from the 50-year-old who will later get cancer as a result. This usage coincides less with general usage than did Mill's, which would have considered these two as the same person. Still, it is a distinction that can be grounded in commonly understood behavioral terms. Indeed, it is one that is in some ways even sharper than the distinction between the 25-year-old and some completely unrelated individual. Would the 25-year-old, for example, clean up the radiation spill if, as a result, some other person would *immediately* get cancer?

The procedures set out above for social decision making do not differ very dramatically from those actually used in many contemporary societies. What does differ is the compatibility I have stressed between these procedures and the existence of powerful individual rights.

Twelve

The Libertarian Welfare State

The Pitfalls of Direct Regulation

Critics of the market system often seek to remedy its shortcomings by transferring economic decisions away from the private firms they so distrust and
into the hands of the benevolent state. But the mere observation that markets
fail to produce the best imaginable outcome is no reason to suppose that
government regulation will make matters any better. The practical choice is
never one between an imperfect market solution and a perfect government
remedy. Both alternatives will always be flawed.[1]

We have already seen circumstances, for example, where even perfectly
competitive labor markets will not offer people the safety levels they want in
the workplace. But that does not mean that government safety regulation will
improve matters. Readers who have never before seen an imperfect government regulation will learn much from a careful reading of the following
passage on ladders, excerpted from the Occupational Safety and Health
Administration's 1976 manual of workplace safety standards:

*The general slope of grain in flat steps of minimum dimension shall not be
steeper than 1 in 12, except that for ladders under 10 feet in length the slope of
grain shall not be steeper than 1 in 10. The slope of grain in areas of local
deviation shall not be steeper than 1 in 12 or 1 in 10 as specified above. For all
ladders, cross grain not steeper than 1 in 10 are permitted in lieu of 1 in 12,*

244

provided the size is increased to afford at least 15 percent greater calculated strength than for ladders built to minimum dimensions. Local deviations of grain associated with otherwise permissible irregularities are permitted.[2]

We would not be surprised if after having attempted to digest the 30 double-columned pages of standards for ladders from which this passage was taken, some discouraged firms decided simply to abandon any activities requiring the use of a ladder.

The benevolent state, it appears, has problems of its own. The bureaucrats who regulate us will almost invariably attempt to expand their sphere of control, and prescribe in great detail what we can and cannot do. Yet for such problems as workplace safety, bureaucrats will usually have insufficient knowledge to prescribe detailed solutions. Even if we suppose that careful study would reveal how best to achieve an objective at a particular moment in time, there is no reason to suppose that the same procedures would be right one year, or even one month, later. When the procedures that people and firms have to follow are prescribed by regulation, though, we can hardly update them any more frequently than that. After all, before the government requires firms to adhere to a regulation, it must hold hearings in which interested parties are given full opportunity to air their views. Various procedural requirements make this an inherently lengthy process. And in situations where technology and other important factors are changing rapidly, the likely outcome is that the procedures prescribed by regulation, even if reasonable to begin with, will quickly become obsolete.

The institutions of government control are not only often sluggish, but also subject to manipulation by special interests. In the heyday of the Interstate Commerce Commission's regulation of the trucking industry, trucking firms were generally required to obtain a "certificate of public convenience and necessity" for each specific commodity they transported across state borders. The administrative costs and delays involved in obtaining these certificates were often substantial, and there is no question that the operating flexibility of the trucking industry was greatly reduced on that account.[3] For certain commodities, however, the ICC made exceptions to this requirement. "Guano, bat," for example, which ICC regulations defined as "bat excrement, dried, but not further processed," could be transported across state borders without a certificate. On the question of why this exception did not extend to bat excrement that was dried *and* further processed, the ICC regulations were silent. But a skeptical investigator would be well advised to start by finding out who benefited most from the exception.

The general problem is that, having created a government with the ability to make and enforce rules, it is often difficult to assure that its power is used on behalf of those it governs. The democratic process provides crude checks against the most serious abuses, to be sure. Yet history is replete with reminders of the grim consequences of well-intentioned governments getting out of control. Our regulatory cures are very often more objectionable than the free-market excesses we seek to curb.

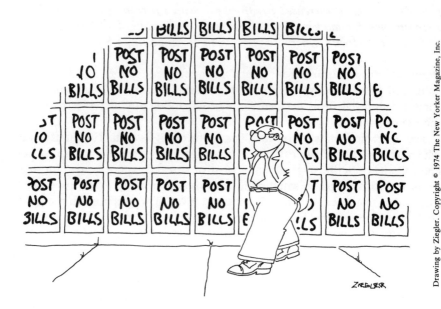

In this purely practical sense, then, it may often be prudent to avoid prescriptive government regulation, even where private markets lead to outcomes that are far from perfect. Nichols and Zeckhauser, for example, have argued that OSHA regulations may well have actually *reduced* safety levels in the workplace, in addition to causing substantial increases in production costs.[4] But whether or not that is really so, opposition to safety regulation on these grounds is very different from opposition on the grounds that such regulations abridge the right of workers to trade safety for wage income. As discussed in the preceding chapter, this right need not, in principle, take precedence over the rights of other workers to have some collective say in safety decisions.

Antidistortionary Taxation

Direct, prescriptive regulation is fortunately not the only way for society to alter a market outcome it doesn't like. As I noted in the last chapter, when an activity is accompanied by harmful side effects, it will often be more effective to tax that activity than to ban it or require it to be altered in a particular way. It is a practical impossibility, for example, to build an office building in a populated area without causing at least *some* increase in traffic congestion on the surrounding roads. Yet surely there are *some* circumstances under which most would agree that the office building should be built. (Perhaps the office building will provide a convenient place of employment for many people but increase congestion only slightly.) In such situations, the question is not whether there should be any congestion at all, but how much congestion there should be. A tax on congestion (as, for example, by requiring builders to pay a congestion-related fee) has the desirable effect of limiting construction to those projects in which the benefits outweigh the negative side effects.

Taxing harmful side effects has several other advantages over the alternative of dealing with them through prescriptive regulations. Unlike such regulations, a tax focuses on the objectionable *outcome*, rather than on the *process* that produces it. With complex, rapidly changing technologies, there is much to be said for penalizing the undesired outcome, and then allowing offenders to decide for themselves how to escape the penalty. If cleaner air is what we want, for example, does it matter whether firms install scrubbers on smokestacks or shift to low-sulfur coal? The firm itself is in the best position to know its real alternatives. When faced with a tax penalty for producing harmful effects, firms will seek out and employ the least costly way of avoiding that penalty. A tax will also provide incentives for developing new and better ways of curtailing harmful effects. And, as noted in Chapter 11, a tax on harmful effects concentrates the task of curtailing them in the hands of those who can accomplish it most cheaply.

Problems such as congestion or pollution raise a virtually identical set of issues as do problems arising out of people's concerns about position. An unfettered private market results in too much pollution because in deciding how much to pollute, firms consider only the benefits to themselves (namely, lower production costs), not the costs to others of the pollution they produce.[5] The same holds true for the decisions people make to advance their relative standing in various hierarchies. In making such decisions, people consider only the direct benefits to themselves of their actions, not the indirect costs, in terms of reduced relative standing, that those actions impose on others.[6] The same arguments that suggest that taxes are an effective way of dealing with pollution thus suggest that taxes may also be an effective way of dealing with people's concerns about relative standing.

In preceding chapters, I noted that people may do numerous things to raise their actual or apparent standing in society's income hierarchy. They may work longer hours, accept greater risks, buy more readily observed goods and fewer less readily observed goods, accept greater fragmentation of workplace tasks, and so on. To the extent that absolute consumption levels have value in and of themselves, one component of the gain from these activities is genuine. But the other component of the gain from these activities—namely, their effect on relative standing—is illusory from a collective perspective, as repeatedly discussed. It is this second component that society might therefore wish to neutralize through taxation. By taxing these activities, we can bring their private returns into balance with social returns.

Reforming and Reinterpreting the Current Tax Structure

These observations recommend a tax structure that is in many ways similar to the one we now have, but nonetheless sharply different in some important respects. They also suggest an interpretation of the welfare consequences of our current tax system that is fundamentally different from the one offered by economists generally, and by so-called supply-siders in particular.

Consider, for example, the question of how the tax system affects people's decisions about how much to work. The standard economic analysis of this question ignores people's concerns about relative standing. It says that when choosing between an extra hour of work and an extra hour of leisure, a worker should work the extra hour if the goods produced in that hour would provide more satisfaction than would be offered by the extra hour of leisure.[7] But when we tax income, this analysis continues, the worker then compares the extra hour of leisure against only the after-tax portion of an extra hour's wages. Since the latter is less than his gross earnings for that hour, he will thus be led to work fewer hours than he really should have. Supply-siders in particular have complained that our tax structure has kept workers from working as much as their own preferences would dictate.[8]

But if people are as concerned about relative standing as the evidence we have seen suggests, it then becomes clear that the supply-siders are barking up the wrong tree. The real problem is not at all that the current tax system induces people to work too little, take too few risks, and so on. On the contrary, it is a *lack* of taxation that would cause individually rational citizens to work too many hours, take too many risks, and spend too little time with family and friends.

But taxing income is itself a needlessly inefficient way of bringing private incentives more closely into line with social returns. For it is much less the

"If those soak-the-rich birds get their way, I can tell you here's one coolie who'll stop putting his shoulder to the goddam wheel."

incomes that people earn that create undesirable side effects than what they *do* with those incomes. When A saves an extra dollar, buys an extra dollar of insurance, or spends an extra dollar on medical care or on some other nonpositional good, he imposes a smaller burden on B than when he buys a private education for his child, a high-priced car, or an elegant new wardrobe. After all, since the *relative* qualities and quantities of positional goods determine much of their value, A's extra expenditures on such goods will reduce the value of the corresponding goods owned by B, whether A intends that or not. By sending his child to an expensive private school, A surely does not intend to lessen the chances for B's publicly educated child to succeed in the labor market. Yet his action nonetheless has that effect. And the loss it causes for B is not mitigated in any way by A's benign intent.

Rather than tax income, then, it would make better sense to tax only those consumption categories that impose external effects on others. Taxing positional consumption goods instead of income would create greater private incentives to save, which would help eliminate the insufficiency in savings that arises out of people's concerns about relative standing.[9] Moreover, such things as clothing, condominiums, and automobiles would become more costly, and such things as insurance and medical care would become less costly than they are now. A shift from income to consumption taxation would thus create incentives for people to spend less of their incomes on positional goods and more of their incomes on nonpositional goods. If concerns about position are as important to people as they appear to be, such a shift would improve the current allocation of resources.

Traditional economics texts never fail to warn students about the distortionary effects of taxing the goods people buy.[10] The conventional analysis, which ignores people's concerns about relative standing, follows the same approach taken by the supply-sider's analysis of income taxation. By causing consumption goods to appear misleadingly costly, it argues, sales and excise taxes induce people to buy too few of them, and to buy too many untaxed goods, such as leisure time. If people are strongly concerned about relative standing, however, then the textbook analysis has matters turned completely around. When relative standing is important, taxing the goods people buy serves to *remove* a distortion from economic life, not create one.

If we look at the history of taxation theory, these observations are not without a certain measure of irony. Economists have always recommended taxing things that will least interfere with efficient resource allocation. Henry George, for example, once proposed that all government revenues be raised by taxing land.[11] He believed that people would continue to use all of the available land no matter what its price, which means that a land tax would produce no distortions at all. In the same vein, a large literature has stressed that taxes should be concentrated on those commodities whose demands are least sensitive to price.[12] Once the importance of people's concerns about relative standing is clearly recognized, however, the tax problem we confront is fundamentally transformed. Instead of being one in which we try to minimize the distortions we *create* through tax policy, it becomes one in which we employ tax policy to *remove* existing distortions.

Now, it is easy to envision the difficulties that would arise out of any attempt to specify the practical details of a consumption tax. Special interests would undoubtedly crowd around the Congressional trough, armed with insistent arguments about why *their* particular goods should be exempt from taxation. But these difficulties would confront any serious effort at tax reform. And if anything has become clear in recent years, it is that we have no administratively simple, distortion-free alternative tax mechanism readily at hand.

The details of a personal consumption tax need not be highly complex. On the contrary, such a tax could be made much simpler than our current tax system. By adjusting the personal exemption level, and by exempting the initial blocks of various basic expenditure categories, such as housing, transportation, clothing, and food, the progressivity of a consumption tax could easily be tailored to society's wishes. Countries in Europe have relied heavily on consumption taxation for many years.[13] There is no compelling reason to believe that the details of implementing such taxes here would be any more difficult to work out than they were in those countries.

Taxing specific categories of consumption expenditures would diminish the tendencies people have to save too little money or take too many safety risks. But it would not necessarily eliminate them. No matter how the consumption tax might be designed, there would always be *some* wage premium available for accepting risky tasks, and always room, therefore, for concerns about relative standing to motivate people to accept such tasks. Whatever tax structure it may ultimately adopt, then, society may still wish to constrain the terms of private labor contracts. Even a $5 per day wage premium, for example, would probably entice a large number of willing youths to clean up a utility's serious radiation spill. Yet society may nonetheless see fit to impose legal limits on radiation exposure in the workplace.

But even where society decides to employ such regulations, it will generally be possible to aim them at final outcomes rather than at intermediate processes. The market economist's insight that people respond strongly to economic incentives is a powerful one. We generally get better results when we provide people with an economic incentive to achieve a desired outcome than when we require them to follow specific procedures.[14]

Antitrust Policy

In the particularly controversial area of antitrust policy, there is now a strong consensus that the single, overriding purpose of the nation's antitrust laws should be to "promote consumer welfare." In earlier times, it was also widely held that a proper objective of antitrust law was to prevent large firms from encroaching on the territory of smaller ones. In the words of Justice Peckham, for example, the antitrust laws were supposed to protect "small dealers and worthy men."[15]

The proconsumer-welfare goal has now all but completely supplanted this earlier view, and there is nearly universal agreement that the promotion of consumer welfare means allowing consumers to choose for themselves which firms they wish to patronize. The disagreement that remains centers on the question of which specific policies actually facilitate consumer choice. One camp, which, for want of a better label, may be called the "left," sees monopoly exploitation as the primary threat to consumer welfare. Accordingly, the left advocates expanded coverage and vigorous enforcement of laws designed to prevent the growth of market concentration.[16] The opposing camp, which may be called the "right," views firms with high market concentration in an altogether different light.[17] The firm that manages to achieve high market concentration, as the right sees things, is one that has managed to serve its customers better than its rivals have. Because people have shown a strong preference for this firm, the right argues, interfering with its growth would diminish, not enhance, consumer welfare. No strong consensus has emerged concerning the merits of these conflicting views. But it is nonetheless fair to say that the pendulum of thought has begun to swing sharply toward the right.

Both camps in the antitrust debate overlook something important here. Contrary to their implicit assumption, consumer welfare is not necessarily best served by paving the way for consumers to speak *only* in individual voices about the kinds of firms they wish to patronize. As discussed in Chapter 9, large firms often have lower prices because they are more efficient than smaller firms, which means that people who shop at small firms will lose position relative to others who shop at larger ones. Concerns about relative standing thus create strong reasons for patronizing large firms, even if, collectively, people would prefer to see the marketplace populated with the smaller establishments of years past.

I obviously have no way of knowing whether most consumers prefer to deal with small firms. But let us suppose for argument's sake that they do. If our infrequent patronage of small firms is, in part, an unintended consequence of competition for position (see Chapter 9), we may then wish to consider taking collective measures in support of smaller firms. We already do, in fact, take many such measures, as, for example, through the support services provided by the Small Business Administration.

But it does not appear sensible to recommend, as proposed anticonglomerate legislation repeatedly has done,[18] that firms be kept from growing beyond a certain size no matter how efficient they might be. The electorate may well collectively prefer small firms to large ones, other things the same. But surely there exist some cost savings sufficiently large to induce people to make at least some of their purchases from large enterprises. With small firms already receiving preferential tax treatment and other advantages, why should our antitrust laws rule out the possibility of such cost savings?

Public Policy toward Trade Unions

As noted in Chapter 8, the historical view of the trade union movement sees workers as having banded together to protect themselves against exploitation. Again, I do not claim that market power *never* permits employers to exploit workers in the way contemplated by this view. Rather, I suggested that many of the problems addressed by the trade union movement would have existed even in perfectly competitive labor markets.

But the power of the trade union to neutralize the undesirable consequences of workers competing against themselves is not without bounds. In particular, it is limited by the fact that people care about local hierarchies consisting of others besides their co-workers. As I argued in Chapter 8, the less one's personal reference group consists of one's co-workers, the less effective collective bargaining will be in eliminating the adverse consequences of interpersonal competitions. Union and nonunion workers alike care not only about how their incomes compare with those of their co-workers, but also about how large their incomes are vis-à-vis incomes in the community at large. Collective compensation agreements are therefore destined to be undermined by people who join firms that do not implement similar agreements. As discussed in Chapter 7, if A enters a collective agreement to work in a safe mine at $200 per week, and his neighbor B then works in an unsafe mine at $250 per week, A is then unable to provide the same material advantages for his family as B can for his.

Given the union workers' frustration, it is natural to suppose that they will try to force all workers in a given industry or community to submit to the same pattern of collective compensation agreements. If this cannot be accomplished by simple persuasion—which normally it cannot, because of the strong payoffs to outsiders who trade undesirable conditions for higher wages —there are then several alternatives. Workers may ask the state to require various elements in the compensation packages of all firms, union and nonunion alike (as the state already does to a certain extent). Unions may also seek the state's sanction for applying various pressures—picket lines, boycotts, and the like—against those who do not submit to their collective agreements. And they may also act without the state's sanction to apply numerous other pressures.

I have argued at length that at least *some* of the objectives that motivate the trade union movement to expand the scope of its collective bargaining power in these ways are completely legitimate. This view contrasts sharply with the traditional conservative's view that the trade union's sole objective is to separate owners from earnings that are rightfully theirs. Yet a fundamental dilemma arises when the trade union becomes so strong that it acquires effective monopoly power over the terms of the labor contract. Once the trade union has such power, what forces it to use that power in the public interest? If a trade union can exclude competition, what then prevents it from setting such a high wage as to choke off employment possibilities for those whom it excludes? What keeps it from lobbying for import controls that result in higher prices for all consumers?

There is thus a troubling tradeoff implicit in the question of what constitutes sound public policy toward the trade union movement. On one hand, the trade union movement will fall short of accomplishing many of its legitimate objectives unless it has the power to constrain nonunion firms. On the other

"Now, I'm a reasonable fellow, but it seems to me that in
case after case and time after time in these labor disputes
the fairer, more enlightened position has always been held
by management."

hand, once granted that power, there is no reason to believe that it will employ
it on behalf of all workers. There are obviously no simple solutions to this
problem. But several public policy instruments serve many of the same
objectives that the trade union movement seeks. Minimum wage laws, overtime laws, minimum safety standards, consumption taxes, and numerous
other policies all help produce the kind of compensation agreements that
union and nonunion workers alike may generally favor. There are obvious
difficulties in relying on such regulations to shape conditions in the workplace.
The alternative of granting unchecked power to the trade union movement,
however, presents difficulties of its own.

Income Distribution Policy

As discussed in Chapter 6, the practical choice society faces is not one between redistributing income and not redistributing income. There, I attempted to show that virtually everyone gains from redistribution. The major political parties obviously differ in their degree of commitment to the goal of greater income equality. But no credible political force seriously proposes that assistance for the poor be abandoned altogether. Instead, various factions advocate different *methods* of income redistribution. Let us consider the principal alternatives.

NEGATIVE INCOME TAX

A learned economist once remarked that the main problem confronting the poor is that they have too little money. And whenever some inefficient policy is recommended on the basis of its benefits for the poor, economists will almost always say, as I did in the preceding chapter, that we should instead adopt the more efficient alternative and simply give the poor some money.

Indeed, none other than the conservative Milton Friedman proposed more than two decades ago that the most sensible solution to the problem of poverty would be to adopt what he called a negative income tax,[19] which simply transfers income to people who would otherwise have too little of it. The typical negative income tax scheme starts by guaranteeing each person a minimum level of income each year, regardless of what he or she earns that year. The scheme then taxes every dollar of earned income at some rate. The result is that, beyond a certain level of income, people's tax liabilities will exceed the guaranteed income level, and they begin making net tax payments to the government. If the guarantee were set at $4000 per person per year, and the tax rate set at 50 percent, the relationship between a person's before- and after-tax income would then be as depicted in Figure 12.1. At the grant rate and tax rate assumed in Figure 12.1, the break-even income level would be $8000 per year. Persons earning more than $8000 per year would pay taxes, those earning less would receive transfers.

The appeal of the negative income tax scheme lies in its simplicity. With such a scheme in place, the state could simply eliminate its bewildering array of existing welfare programs, and dismantle the costly administrative apparatus it takes to run them. There would be no need for the poor to apply for food stamps, no need to be certified as eligible for Aid to Families with Dependent Children (AFDC), no need for energy supplements or day care allowances, no need for social workers skilled in the detection of fraud. One system of payments would replace all. And the negative income tax could be administered in much the same simple way as we run the Social Security system. The savings made possible by eliminating all of these alternative income redistribution programs would enable every man, woman, and child classified as poor in the United States today to be given an income supplement of more than $3500 per year.[20]

An additional advantage of the negative income tax scheme is that it would not have the perverse effects on family structure that current welfare pro-

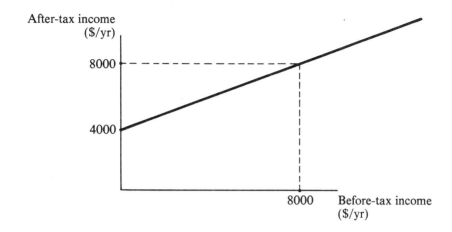

Figure 12.1 Before-Tax Versus After-Tax Income under a Negative Income Tax Program

grams appear to have had. In most states, eligibility under the current AFDC program, for example, requires recipient households to have dependent minor children and no able-bodied spouses present. A large literature documents the effect the second requirement has had in disrupting existing two-parent families. And we also know that the first requirement has created a strong incentive to start new single-parent families as a means of becoming eligible for assistance.[21]

The problem of family disintegration has been especially serious for blacks. In 1983, roughly half of all black families were headed by single women, up from 25 percent in 1965. And 55 percent of black babies born in 1983 were born to unmarried women.[22] Eleanor Holmes Norton, former chairperson of the Equal Employment Opportunity Commission in the Carter Administration, called the fragmentation of black families "a threat to the future of black people without equal."[23] The problem of providing aid for those poor families —black or white—who have small children, without simultaneously creating incentives to fragment family life, is one of the most vexing ones that confront the current welfare system. The negative income tax, by having no eligibility criteria whatever, simply sidesteps this problem.

George McGovern advocated what amounted to a negative income tax when he proposed his "demo grant" program during the 1972 presidential campaign. The guaranteed income he proposed was $1000 per person. McGovern's political opponents ridiculed his plan on the grounds that people like Nelson Rockefeller would receive such a payment. This criticism was either hopelessly naive or deeply cynical, for payouts under such a plan are obviously financed by the taxes collected from those people, such as Rockefeller, whose incomes exceed the plan's break-even level.

Attacks on the McGovern proposal were nonetheless highly effective, and it is thus ironic that Richard Nixon, shortly after his re-election, proposed his

Family Assistance Plan, which was itself a simple version of the negative income tax. During the debate on Nixon's proposal, one of the main concerns was that a guaranteed income might cause many people to drop out of the labor force. The federal government sponsored several large experimental negative income tax programs in order to assess this concern. These experiments, which were carried out in the early 1970s, produced preliminary evidence that a guaranteed income does not reduce people's attachments to the labor force.[24] But subsequent research has suggested that the effects of negative income tax programs are somewhat greater than the early studies showed.[25] One study estimated that such programs are likely to cause small reductions in the number of hours worked by husbands (an average of 103 fewer hours per year out of a total of nearly 2000 hours), with noticeably larger reductions for wives (an average of 262 fewer hours out of a total of nearly 1200).[26]

But conventional welfare programs themselves have serious adverse effects on work incentives. An important shortcoming of such programs arises from the fact that eligibility for many program benefits is linked by formula to the recipient's income level.[27] When a person who receives a rent subsidy earns an extra dollar of income, his rent subsidy will be reduced by some fraction of that amount, say 50 cents. Suppose the same person also participates in four other income-tested benefit programs, and that each also has a "marginal benefit reduction rate" of 50 percent. For this person, the consequence of earning an additional dollar of income each week would be to lose $2.50 per week in benefits. His net position would thus be $1.50 worse than if he hadn't earned the extra dollar at all. It is not necessary to have a Ph.D. in economics to recognize that such a payoff structure materially weakens people's incentives to work. Under the negative income tax, by contrast, an extra dollar of earned income must necessarily improve the recipient's net position.

Serious scholars who study the income maintenance issue seem to agree that aid could be much more effectively delivered to the poor through something like a negative income tax than through the system we currently have.[28] Yet despite this emerging consensus, welfare programs exist in much the same form today as they have for the past several decades.

Why, then, have we not adopted Friedman's negative income tax, which, on the surface at least, seems to dominate our current welfare programs? To pursue this question, it is helpful to begin by noting that the annual income necessary to sustain an urban family of four at a "lower budget" standard in 1981 was estimated by the Bureau of Labor Statistics (BLS) to be $15,323.[29] Presumably, if the negative income tax is to replace the existing array of welfare programs, the level of support it provides cannot fall too much below that figure. But suppose, for the sake of discussion, that the public is less generous than the BLS, and finds, say, $10,000 per year an acceptable level of support for an urban family of four. And suppose that level of support were established in the form of an income guarantee in a negative income tax program.

That would then mean that members of a 15-family commune in rural Mendocino County, California, would, collectively, be eligible for a total tax-free annual support level of $150,000. Now, $150,000 per year can go a long way under communal living conditions, especially when supplemented with the untaxable fruits of gardening and animal husbandry. For those who like communal living, it is possible to imagine living a very attractive life with that kind of money. Mornings could be held open for drinking coffee and having extended discussions of politics and the arts. Freed from the burdens of conventional employment, people could hone their musical skills. And there would be plenty of time for reading, writing, and exercise.

I do not mean to sell short the psychological pleasure that often accompanies productive employment. Still, it is safe to presume that a negative income tax with that high a benefit level would cause at least *some* people to quit their jobs and form communes. And given that such groups did form, there would then be an eager public audience for reports in the news media about their doings. The inevitable appearance of these groups on the evenings news would not sit well with large segments of the American public, and would soon lead to proposals to reduce the negative income tax benefit. For both legal and practical reasons, it is difficult to discriminate against unrelated individuals who elect to enjoy the economies of scale possible through group living. Lacking this ability, the public would then be faced with a choice between (1) making benefit levels so low that a small urban family could not survive on them; (2) keeping benefits high enough to support a small urban family, and continuing to watch news reports of commune members enjoying the good life at the taxpayer's expense; and (3) abandoning the negative income tax in favor of alternative welfare programs that do not guarantee long-term support to able-bodied individuals who do not work (i.e., our current system).

Given these three choices, I will assume it would not be possible to assemble a working political majority in favor of the second alternative. After all, the Terre Haute dentist—who rises at 6:00 A.M. to drive through a snowy traffic jam to reach his office by 8:00, where he spends the duration of his day on sore feet treating patients with bad breath who will accuse him of being unfair if he attempts to charge them for breaking an appointment without giving advance notice—will be understandably reluctant to see his tax dollars spent on extended holidays for commune members. The first alternative, however, is a distinct possibility. And we already know it is possible to muddle along with our current array of welfare programs. But it simply does not appear realistic to suppose that the American public would ever support Milton Friedman's recommendation that anyone who has too little money simply be given enough to live on. For all of its elegant simplicity, the negative income tax is a program that cannot be counted on as the sole means of lifting the poor from poverty.[30]

This conclusion raises troubling questions about my arguments in Chapter 11 concerning the use of cost-benefit analysis in social decision making. There I argued that, instead of adopting inefficient public projects because they happen to reduce inequality, we should adopt the most efficient alternative projects and simply transfer resources to the poor. This argument obviously has little force if it is politically impossible to carry out such transfers. And we may indeed suspect that this is an important reason that inefficient projects

Drawing by Gini Curl.

Figure 12.2 A negative income tax large enough to enable an urban family of four to subsist would support a comfortable lifestyle for large groups.

are so often adopted in the name of their beneficial distributional effects. Yet the mere fact that we cannot simply *give* money to the poor does not necessarily mean that we cannot find other, more palatable, ways of making the desired transfers.

GOVERNMENTALLY SPONSORED EMPLOYMENT

There are at least three persuasive reasons, for example, that voters might be willing to support cash transfers made in exchange for the performance of productive tasks. First, if the payment is conditional on the performance of work, there is then less risk that it will cause people to withdraw from jobs in the private sector. The more people there are who remain in private jobs, the smaller will be the overall burden on each taxpayer. Second, financing a cash transfer to others is more attractive when people get something of value in return. If, for example, the recipients of transfer payments planted trees on government land, that would be a better outcome from the taxpayer's point of view than if nothing of value had been accomplished. Finally, the very fact that recipients are required to undertake some burden will make the payments more attractive to many taxpayers. This particular attraction will exist independently of both the value of what recipients produce and the effect on their incentives to seek private employment. Even if the transfer recipient's task were to dig a hole and then fill it back up, many taxpayers would surely feel less resentful than if their tax payments had simply been given away.

Many will be troubled that the government's hiring the poor will expand what they see as an already bloated government bureaucracy. To be sure, it is hardly comforting to imagine the people who wrote the safety standards for ladders being placed in charge of how millions of citizens spend their working hours each day. Yet the government may sponsor employment for low-income persons without having to employ people directly. As discussed in Chapter 10, for example, it is possible for the government to finance education without becoming involved as a direct producer of educational services. In the same way, it would be possible for the government to provide resources to finance jobs for the poor without itself acting as the actual employer. Private companies can be invited to bid for the right to hire low-income persons to perform specified tasks, in precisely the same way that many municipal governments now invite private companies to bid for the right to perform sanitation and fire protection services. The tasks to be performed could be specified by the government, with the question of how to perform them left to the contractor. The contractor need only make sure that the employees were hired at specified wage rates and were required to put forth a specified level of effort.

Many useful tasks can be performed by persons with relatively low levels of experience and training. There is probably no city in the United States whose residents would not be pleased by the addition of new flower gardens in its municipal parks or of fresh landscaping along its highways. Given proper supervision, unskilled persons can carry out such tasks. And they can also paint government buildings; recycle newspapers, glass containers, and aluminum cans; fill potholes in city streets; replace burned-out street lamps; drive vans for the elderly and the handicapped; assist in reforestation and erosion control projects; clear away litter; remove graffiti from public places; and so on.

The success of a public-sponsored jobs approach to the income transfer problem would depend critically on making sure that such jobs were not viewed as more attractive than private-sector jobs. To guard against public-sponsored jobs appealing to those already employed by the private sector, thus making the program prohibitively costly, wages in public-sponsored jobs would have to be kept close to the minimum wage. If such jobs are not more attractive than private-sector jobs, those who apply for them will then automatically be those who need the money but cannot find suitable private-sector jobs.

One can, of course, imagine a variety of humanitarian reasons for wanting all jobs, both public and private, to be more attractive than the least attractive private-sector jobs we see today.[31] But that is not a feasible option. To make public-sponsored jobs significantly more attractive than private-sector jobs would be to eliminate any practical possibility of using public-sponsored jobs as a major income transfer tool.

TRANSFERS IN KIND

In addition to providing cash transfers in return for productive services, it may often prove attractive to redistribute through transfers in kind. Many such transfers already exist, for example, in the form of low-income housing projects and subsidized transit and medical services.

As repeatedly noted, one of the most powerful elements in people's concerns about relative standing appears to focus on the position of their children. People are often willing to suffer great inconvenience in order to prevent their children from being unduly disadvantaged because of their own financial limitations. For this reason, in part, taxpayers appear much more willing to finance programs aimed at equalizing opportunities for children than to pay for unrestricted transfers. Such programs can and do soften the most destructive social consequences that arise out of people's concerns about relative standing.

As discussed in Chapter 10, for example, people who advocate greater reliance on private markets for education often fail to appreciate the importance of a strong public school system in maintaining the social fabric. Similarly, we may question the wisdom of proposals to curtail the provision of subsidized school lunches. Unless one expects substantial numbers of children to forego eating lunch altogether, such proposals would produce no real "savings" in any event, and promise only to exacerbate social tensions. A similar case can be made for retaining public subsidies for a variety of other children's services. Although it would obviously be possible for parents to pay for after-school athletic and cultural programs privately, there are genuine advantages of providing at least some public support for such programs.

REDISTRIBUTION BY HOLDING PRICES BELOW COSTS

In large part, our conventional welfare programs have fallen short because they cannot provide adequate benefits to those we want to help without simultaneously attracting unwanted applicants. Our determination not to provide handouts to those who could fend for themselves has spawned a variety of egregiously inefficient policies for avoiding hardships to people who genuinely need assistance.

Consider, for example, the regulation of gasoline prices mentioned in Chapter 11. When the price of foreign oil increased dramatically during the 1970s, any first-year student in economics could have explained why the only efficient policy was to allow the domestic price of oil to rise to the new, higher, world price level. But rising oil prices create special difficulties for people with low incomes. And in recognition of those difficulties, a complex array of controls was employed to hold the price of domestic oil in check.

Whatever these price controls may have accomplished for the poor, they were extremely costly for the nation as a whole. The decision to use car pools, to buy a V-8, or to take a weekend trip depends largely on the difference in costs, *to individuals*, of the gasoline required by the competing alternatives. During the period in question, that difference was based primarily on the regulated price of domestic oil. Yet the cost to *society* of a gallon of gasoline is the cost of one that is refined from high-priced imported oil. The latter cost measures exactly the amount society would save if someone used one less gallon of gasoline. But by keeping prices artificially below that amount, people were led to make decisions on the basis of completely misleading incentives. They took trips they would not have taken, and they shunned car pools they would have formed had the price of domestic oil been allowed to rise to the world price level. Similarly, fuel-efficient cars were not developed as rapidly as they would have been. As events since the subsequent decontrol of domestic oil prices have demonstrated, the losses caused by these misleading price incentives amounted to billions of dollars.

Similar distributional concerns continue to dictate important pricing decisions throughout the economy. Millions of New York City residents, for example, live in artificially cheap apartments because of the fear that, without rent controls, the poor could not afford a place to live. Yet in the meantime, the least costly apartments are allowed to decay or are converted into cooperatives, because, under rent controls, their owners cannot earn a competitive rate of return.

Every electric utility regulatory commission finds itself under constant pressure to keep rates below the true economic cost of providing electric service, especially during peak demand periods, because of concerns that rates based on costs would impose unacceptable hardships on the poor. The price of natural gas, similarly, has been held by price controls at a level well below its free market price, which would put it on par with other energy sources. Conservation efforts have thus been hampered by such price restraints, since insulation and other energy use decisions depend very strongly on the prices of gas and electricity. Yet we continue to use price controls in the name of our concerns about the poor.

To the economist's standard recommendation, "let prices rise to their free-market levels and then transfer cash to the poor," society has responded that it doesn't *want* simply to hand cash to the poor. And as we have seen, there are understandable reasons for people to hold such a view. But we have also seen that *giving* money to the poor is not the only way of dealing with society's distributional concerns. A prudently designed mix of cash and in-kind transfers, together with an offer of publicly sponsored employment at low wages, would eliminate many of the perverse incentives inherent in our traditional array of welfare programs. Granted, the public might never be willing to support a negative income tax whose benefit level was high enough for a small family to live on. It may nonetheless be willing to support one with a much more modest level of support, one that would transfer at least *some* additional resources to the working poor.

Society might also be willing to broaden its network of in-kind transfers. And voters might easily support public-sponsored, low-wage employment for the poor. Single parents with preschool children could be offered jobs in public-sponsored day care centers in which their own children could also be cared for. These jobs would help solve the ever-troublesome problem of how to support single-parent families without providing incentives, as the AFDC program apparently has for some, to choose state-supported single parenthood as a way of life.

By relying on such a mix of programs to respond to society's distributional concerns, we would be much better able to target support to the groups that most need it. We might thus eliminate, or at least reduce, the gross waste caused by price controls on essential goods and services. Suppose, as in Figure 12.3, there were a negative income tax with a *modest* benefit payment, one too small to serve as a family's sole means of support. It might then be possible during times of escalating world resource prices to let domestic prices rise, and assist the poor by increasing the negative income tax benefit slightly. The same mix of transfer programs might similarly rid legislatures of pressures to adopt inefficient programs whose only selling point is their favorable distributional consequences.

MIGRATION AND THE IMPORTANCE OF UNIFORM BENEFIT LEVELS

Programs to redistribute income are surely often motivated in part by humanitarian considerations, but they are also motivated by self-interest. High-income people generally value their favored positions, yet they could not maintain these positions without redistributive action on the part of the state. Even mean-spirited, solitary persons who profess not to care about relative standing have a selfish interest in seeing that poor children are well fed and schooled. After all, children who lack these minimal advantages often grow up to be criminals or wards of the state. These considerations and more suggest that most citizens would find themselves worse off if they allowed support for the needy to fall below some level.

But when benefit levels are decided locally, each jurisdiction faces a fundamental difficulty in setting its benefit schedule at an optimal level. This difficulty arises out of migration decisions based on *relative* benefit levels across jurisdictions. For example, if community B sets its level lower than that set by community A, some of B's indigent population would move to A, thereby lowering B's tax burden. As a result, those with relatively heavier tax

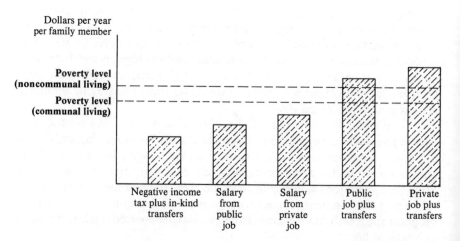

Figure 12.3 Redistribution through Public Jobs and Cash and In-kind Transfers

burdens in A will then find B an attractive community in which to relocate. But rather than lose its tax base, we may expect A (unless it is New York City) to respond by bringing its own welfare benefits levels into line with B's.

Thus, the cost of having a relatively high benefit level among jurisdictions is not limited to the direct effect of larger payments to each recipient. It includes also the indirect effects of migration. These indirect effects are not large during any one year, but over the space of several years are very substantial.[32] In precisely the same sense, then, that workers who care about relative standing may end up with too little safety, communities may end up with welfare benefits that are too low. That is, each community's natural desire not to attract the welfare beneficiaries of other communities leads it to adopt a lower benefit level than it would have chosen if communities had acted collectively. Each can attempt to outrun the bear, but all cannot succeed.

Recent proposals to shift the locus of welfare benefit decisions from the federal to the state and local levels have been received favorably by many. Yet such a shift might easily produce an outcome that most communities do not favor. Even those communities that are completely devoid of humanitarian concerns about the poor will presumably wish to set benefit levels high enough to keep peace in their streets. But, as Gramlich has noted, when benefit

"You see—the need for undertaking costly publick programs grows more desperate; the dunnage on the taxpaying element becomes more burdensome, many of that element leave the city, further lowering the tax base and thereby throwing an ever-larger share of costs on an ever-smaller per cent of Manhattan's solvent citizenry, until, before long. . . ."

decisions are shifted to the local level, each community's ability to achieve even that limited objective is compromised.[33]

Barriers to Creating a Utopia in One Country

The problem implicit in deciding welfare benefits at the community level exists on a much grander scale in the economic and social policy decisions facing the modern nation-state. Barring catastrophe, the planet earth will likely continue for many years to be partitioned into scores of sovereign nations. And when we see the world as it is, rather than as we might like it to be, it is also clear that the relative economic standing of these nations is not a matter of indifference to their citizens. Granted, some small, neutral states, such as Switzerland, occasionally manage to prosper and remain aloof from world conflict. But far more numerous are the economically weak nations whose fate is dictated by their more powerful neighbors. People who place high value on political freedom thus have no difficulty appreciating the importance of maintaining high national levels of production. Economic strength and military strength go hand in hand, and history has taught even peace-loving people to be wary of falling into a position in which they cannot adequately defend themselves.

The nation-state thus finds itself in a position similar to that of the trade union. The union is unable to control, but is nonetheless affected by, the actions of others who don't come under its collective agreements. The concern of trade union members about how their incomes compare with those of nonunion members limits what can be accomplished through collective compensation agreements. In precisely the same way, the nation-state is limited by its concern about its status vis-à-vis other nations.

The obvious and natural solution to these limitations is to negotiate verifiable, binding, arms control agreements. But as we have repeatedly seen, there are often practical difficulties to solving prisoner's dilemmas far simpler than military contests between nations. Almost needless to say, further efforts at negotiating arms reduction agreements should continue apace. Until such agreements are firmly in hand, though, the objective of maintaining material production parity with other nations will understandably receive high priority.

In industries where important economies of scale exist, one cost of a national policy that favors small firms is that firms in other countries will capture important markets that would have otherwise been served by large American firms. A clear tension thus exists between the desire to maintain parity with other nations, on the one hand, and the wish to give preferential tax treatment to smaller establishments, on the other. Similarly, the amount of leisure time it is prudent to consume will depend on the competitive balance between nations that exists at any moment. Suppose, for example, that in an isolated setting most people would choose a three-day work week. The same choice would not necessarily be best in a context where the relative material well-being of independent states is important.

The desire to maintain parity with other nations may thus limit the degree to which the citizens of any nation can act collectively to neutralize the destructive consequences of interpersonal competition. But there are also risks confronting a country that fails to take at least some such forms of collective action. I argued in Chapter 6, for example, that redistributive taxation is necessary before any heterogeneous group will voluntarily coalesce into a single society. When a country's tax system fails to maintain a sense of voluntary participation in society, increased social fragmentation will ensue, which will likely impede, rather than enhance, efforts to maintain parity with other nations.

Failure to redistribute income can thus have serious consequences for a nation. But so can redistribution policies that are not carried out in a sensible way. Because voters seem unwilling to approve cash handouts that are large enough to live on, many Western societies have adopted elaborate systems of price controls and regulations in the name of distributive justice. Such controls, as noted, often have monumental efficiency costs. Many of these costs might be avoided if instead people were given cash in return for performing useful tasks.

Similar pitfalls face the state that fails to constrain the terms of private labor contracts. As I argued in earlier chapters, concerns about position create a gap between individual and collective incentives to invest in such things as leisure, safety, diversity, and pensions. Where the state plays no role in closing this gap, workers will take matters into their own hands. We have seen, however, that the trade union movement will be frustrated in this task unless it achieves more control than most people would be willing to permit. Because completely unregulated labor markets create conditions that move workers to seek such control, it is thus not at all clear that a *laissez-faire* posture would help maintain production parity with other nations.

The Incidence of Collective Action

In Chapter 8, I argued that concerns about relative standing weigh more heavily on people near the bottom of the economic totem pole than on those nearer the top; and that the pressures to shift resources from nonpositional goods to positional goods will accordingly be stronger for the former group than for the latter. The patterns of collective action we actually take appear consistent with these observations. Workplace safety regulations, for example, most strongly affect those people who are employed at relatively low wages. The constraints they impose are generally nonbinding on workers with high incomes, who would choose in any event to work under considerably safer conditions than are required by law.

A similar observation applies in the case of forced savings programs, such as Social Security. Most persons with relatively high incomes save considerable amounts on their own. Their total savings, including the required Social Security component, are thus far greater than the amount required by law, and hence logically unconstrained by it. Anyone who feels his Social Security contribution is too high can simply reduce some other component of his savings. (Those who object most strongly to Social Security feel not that they should save less, but that they should be permitted to save in different ways.)

Chapters 7 to 10 suggested that people of all income levels face undesired pressures to invest in positional goods. Yet our regulations alter those pressures only for people with the lowest incomes. To impose constraints that were large enough to affect the behavior of people with higher incomes, we would have to impose an unacceptably difficult burden on the poor.

Under our current system of collective action, then, all but those with the lowest incomes are left, in effect, to deal for themselves with their concerns about relative standing. Overtime laws do not apply to salaried executives, who must decide individually whether it is worth staying at the office until nine each evening in order to move forward in the company. Executives who confront such a decision face the same sort of prisoner's dilemma that workers face when deciding whether to accept a risky job. The state can alter the incentives somewhat by taxing positional consumption goods. But there is no practical way for the state to resolve such dilemmas completely.

If it is impractical for the nonpoor to deal legislatively with such prisoner's dilemmas, there are nonetheless a host of useful private alternatives. To a considerable degree, people are free to choose their friends, neighbors, and co-workers. And particularly in the case of co-workers, we have seen repeated instances in which voluntary private collective actions alter the way people allocate their incomes. If an executive works for a company where she feels people work too hard or save too little, she can go to work for a different company.

Even beyond the confines of the firm, local hierarchies develop and adopt powerful norms that help shape the composition of spending. My sons and their friends, for example, are extremely disdainful of people who wear designer jeans, which has saved me a lot of money over the years. (I have been unsuccessful, however, at persuading them that jeans with plain pockets are just as good as Levi's. Perhaps they are not.)

As noted at the outset, most parents teach their children to adopt hostile attitudes toward concerns about relative standing. These teachings facilitate the formation of peer groups that resist consumption standards established by outsiders. If a person feels his friends devote too little time to humane activities, and too much to the pursuit of additional goods, he is free to seek new friends. Choosing the right pond is obviously never an easy task, and the results of our private attempts to restrain interpersonal competition will usually be far from perfect. Perhaps useful legislative steps could be taken beyond those we currently take. Many European countries take considerably stronger legislative steps than we take in the United States. Yet such steps would inevitably involve further restrictions on behavior, something that American political sentiment has never much favored.

"Fiction's nice, but it doesn't get you anywhere."

The Libertarian Welfare State

The capitalist's economics textbook says that both product and labor markets are workably competitive. In such markets, we tell our students, workers will be paid the value of what they produce, while consumers will pay prices just sufficient to cover production costs. Not everything works perfectly, the economist will naturally concede. But where occasional problems arise, they can generally be dealt with through a tax, subsidy, or some other simple change in the reward structure. With the requisite pollution taxes and transfers to the poor in place, our texts say that individuals in pursuit of their own selfish interests will bring about, as if by an invisible hand, the greatest good for all.

Although not all economists believe these claims, it is probably fair to say that most of us do. And there are others who share our views. Such claims would be received favorably, for example, by the National Association of Manufacturers, and probably by the Young Americans for Freedom. An Ayn Rand literary fan club would also greet claims of this sort enthusiastically, as would some other groups. But the total list of such groups will be small by almost anyone's reckoning. In most forums, a speaker who uttered these claims would be driven from the podium by derisive laughter.

The reason the economist's claims are greeted by such widespread disbelief is that people believe that markets are not, in fact, workably competitive. Firms with market power are said to coerce workers into producing useless products by means of fragmented tasks under unsafe, undemocratic working conditions, in exchange for unconscionably low wages. As repeatedly discussed, however, the various power imbalances contemplated by this view are largely illusory. Firms *do* in fact compete vigorously with one another, both in product and in labor markets. As a result, both the products we buy and the terms under which we work are at least in rough harmony with the demands we express as individuals.

The United Technologies Corporation recently ran an ad saying that "when forty million people believe in a dumb idea, it's still a dumb idea." The idea that markets are not workably competitive is just such an idea. Despite its massive constituency, it has neither logical nor factual content. Its incredible staying power derives from the fact that many of the conclusions it supports happen to be correct. The wage structure we see within private firms is not one in which workers are paid the values of their marginal products. Nor are the goods and services we buy in open markets the ones that best serve the needs of our communities. Nor, finally, are the terms of the unregulated competitive labor contract socially optimal in any meaningful sense. The reason they are not, however, has little, if anything, to do with the power imbalances and other imperfections stressed by critics. Instead, market outcomes fall short in the ways they do because individual goals and collective goals are in fundamental tension from the outset. Evolutionary forces saw to it that people come into the world with a drive mechanism that makes them seek to outrank others with whom they compete for important resources. But this drive mechanism, so useful in the individual's struggle to survive, could hardly have been designed to yield greater disruption for society as a whole. The specific behavioral consequences of this drive mechanism, not the consequences of excessive market power, are what we regulate in the modern welfare state.

Our failure to recognize the true purpose behind our regulations has led us to adopt a variety of policies that are ill-designed for the tasks at hand. Contrary to what their opponents say, redistributive transfer programs are in clear harmony with the interests of the well-do-do; and, with proper attention to design, we can eliminate the disruptive effects our current welfare programs have had. By taxing positional consumption instead of income, moreover, we need not rely on intrusive rules and regulations to achieve the spending patterns we seek as a community. Having penalized positional consumption through the tax system, we can achieve these patterns instead largely through voluntary actions. Ours for the taking is a society that is not only more efficient, but also more equitable and less restrictive than the one we have today. The great tradeoffs between liberty, efficiency, and equality will again confront us in the future, but for now we can have more of *all* of these things.

Although our current institutions are flawed in a variety of ways, the real message of these essays has been that, in a broad sense, they are highly adaptive. This book is in essence, then, both a reinterpretation and a reaffirmation of the status quo in the modern welfare state. There are genuine advantages as well as unavoidable tensions whenever large, heterogeneous groups gather together to form a single society. Redistributive taxation and regulation of the labor contract need not, in principle, be viewed as the assaults on freedom classical libertarians make them out to be. Rather, they are features that would inevitably be part even of perfectly voluntary societies that could form and dissolve costlessly at will. To emphasize this consistency between the institutions of modern Western societies and a philosophical orientation that assigns great value to individual liberty, I find it useful to think of these societies as "libertarian welfare states." The collectivist societies of the East, by contrast, may be usefully thought of as the result of attempting to deal with people's concerns about relative standing within a political framework that accords markedly less respect to personal liberty.

That the libertarian welfare state is a state riddled with tensions and tradeoffs is simply something that comes with the territory. The haves will naturally argue for lower taxes, while the have nots will struggle for greater benefits. Some will press for even greater standardization of the labor contract, while others will push for greater latitude to negotiate on an individual basis. Under these circumstances, it is perhaps only natural that a left should emerge to insist that the state has a moral duty to make the workplace as safe as possible; and only natural that a conservative opposition would respond that people have rights to decide such matters individually. But where individually rational and collectively rational choices point in opposite directions for many people, such disputes, we have seen, are often more practical than moral in flavor. Having provided safeguards for fundamental constitutional liberties, a system that attempts to sift through the preferences of the opposing camps in such disputes will generally outperform one that chooses aimlessly between conflicting moral platitudes.

Notes

Chapter 1

1. The late Fred Hirsch coined the term "positional goods" in his provocative 1976 book (see Bibliography).
2. Layard (1980), p. 741.
3. The following discussion is drawn from a 1983 account of the episode by Ken Wells.

Chapter 2

1. Restak (1979), p. 103.
2. Funt (1970).
3. See, for example, Hulse, Deese, and Egeth (1975).
4. See Schelling (1963), Chapter 2.
5. See Roth and Malouf (1979) and Thaler (1983).
6. See Thaler (1983).
7. See Hebb (1955) and Fiske and Maddi (1961); see also Routtenberg (1980) and Olds (1976). For an excellent nontechnical discussion of the arousal mechanism, see Scitovsky (1976), Chapter 2.
8. See, for example, McGuinness and Pribram (1980), who discuss numerous limitations of the simple arousal model presented by Hebb (1955).
9. See Mayer (1955). For an excellent nontechnical presentation, see the splendid book by Konner (1982), Chapter 15.
10. See Deutsch and Deutsch (1973) and Valenstein (1973).
11. See, for example, Reiser, Reeves, and Armington (1955); and Long, Lynch, Machiran, Thomas, and Malinow (1982).

12. Long, Lynch, Machiran, Thomas, and Malinow (1982).
13. See Raleigh, McGuire, Brammer, and Yuweiler (1983).
14. See McGuire, Raleigh, and Brammer (1982).
15. See McGuire, Raleigh, and Brammer (1982).
16. See the summary discussion by Lipton in Barchas and Usdin (1973).
17. See Coppen (1973).
18. See Mazur (1983), Mazur and Lamb (1980), and Elias (1981).
19. See Rose, Bernstein, and Gordon (1975).
20. See Duncan (1975–76). Similar findings have been reported by Gallup (1972, 1978).
21. See Bradburn and Noll (1969).
22. See Bachman, Kahn, Davidson, and Johnston (1967).
23. See Bradburn and Caplovitz (1965).
24. See Wilson (1960), quoted in Robinson and Shaver (1969).
25. See Bradburn and Caplovitz (1965).
26. See Easterlin (1973).
27. See Helson (1964).
28. See Tversky and Kahneman (1973, 1974).
29. Nisbett and Ross (1980), p. 45.
30. Nisbett and Ross (1980), pp. 53–54.
31. See, for example, Blau (1964), Davis (1959), Festinger (1954), Homans (1961), Merton and Kitt (1950), Runciman (1966), and Williams (1975).
32. See Lewinsohn, Mischel, Chaplin, and Barton (1980).
33. Lewinsohn et al. (1980), p. 210.
34. See Alloy and Abramson (1979).
35. Townsend (1979), pp. 17–18.
36. For a very thoughtful discussion of the role of absolute and relative income in the phenomenon of poverty, see Sen (1983).
37. See Duesenberry (1949).
38. See Leibenstein (1950).
39. See Scitovsky (1976), Chapter 7, and Rainwater (1974).
40. See Thurow (1973, 1975, 1980).
41. Indeed, the research of B.M.S. van Praag, Arie Kapteyn, and their colleagues at the University of Leyden in The Netherlands represents a clear exception to my claim that the importance of local status has gone unnoticed by economists. Applying very careful statistical methods to the analysis of survey data, they have made considerable progress toward quantifying the notion that people's feelings about the adequacy of their incomes depend very strongly on the incomes of those with whom they associate most closely. See, in particular, van Praag and Kapteyn (1973); van Praag, Kapteyn, and Herwaarden (1979); and van Praag and Spit (1982).
42. See Layard (1980). For a related discussion, see Boskin and Sheshinsky (1978).
43. The following list contains many of the most important papers, but is by no means exhaustive: Akerlof (1969), Archibald and Donaldson (1976), Becker (1974), Bergstrom (1970), Hamermesh (1975), McFadden (1969), Pigou (1903), Pollak (1976), Rader (1980), and Winter (1969).

Chapter 3

1. Lipsey (1960), Archibald (1969), and others, for example, have constructed models in which various barriers prevent workers from migrating between regions.
2. See Marston (1985).

3. For an extensive survey of research on cartel instability, see Brozen (1982), Chapter 5.
4. Stigler (1963), for example, found that rates of return on investment even in highly concentrated industries averaged only 8.0 percent per year for the period he studied, very little different from the 7.2 percent average return he found for unconcentrated industries. See also Peltzman (1967), Demsetz (1973), and Mann (1966). In one prominent early study, Bain (1951) found significantly higher than average profit rates for concentrated industries, but in the same data he found that profitability was highest of all (although still not high in absolute terms) in the least concentrated industries. Brozen (1973) found that the industries that are most concentrated at one date in time tended to have relatively high profit rates prior to that date, but had only average rates after that date. Weston (1980, Chapter 9) surveys numerous other studies of concentration and profitability and finds no support for the view that significant monopoly profits exist in the industrial sector of the American economy.
5. See Stigler (1946). See also Seidman (1979), and the numerous references cited therein.
6. For the details of this argument, and a more formal description of the market for local status, see Frank (1984b).
7. See Nisbett and Ross (1980), pp. 198–99. See also Lewinsohn, Mischel, Chaplin, and Barton (1980).
8. For a thoughtful discussion of the role of external group rankings, see Hansmann (1983).
9. See Smith (1910), Book I, pp. 4–11.
10. See Pencavel (1977); and Thurow (1975), Chapter 5.
11. See Thurow (1975), pp. 106–7.
12. See Thurow (1975), pp. 110–13.

Chapter 4

1. See Groves (1973).
2. See Alchian and Demsetz (1972), Lazear and Rosen (1981), and Harris and Raviv (1978).
3. The discussion that follows is based largely on Frank (1984a).
4. See, for example, Stiglitz (1975).
5. See Harris (1980).
6. See Stiglitz (1975).
7. See Mincer (1962), Becker (1964), Oi (1962), and Thurow (1975).
8. See Doeringer and Piore (1971).
9. These salary figures are a matter of public record, as required by Michigan state law. They are published once each year in the *Michigan Daily*, the university's campus newspaper.
10. See Hirschman (1970).
11. See Mincer (1983).
12. See, for example, Freeman (1980) and Mincer (1981b).
13. The military worker's pay depends only on his or her rank and length of service. Productivity can obviously affect how fast a person moves up through the military ranks, just as it affects the rate of promotion in private firms. But two workers with the same experience and rank often earn different amounts in private firms, whereas that cannot happen in the military, no matter how different their productivity levels might be.

Chapter 5

1. See, for example, Gupta (1983), pp. 103, 104.
2. See National Industrial Conference Board (1970).
3. See, for example, Belcher (1971), Brown (1962), Lupton (1963), Mahoney (1979), Marriott (1957), Purcell (1960), Whyte (1955), and Wolf (1957).
4. See McKersie (1967), p. 222.
5. See McKersie (1967), p. 222.
6. See, for example, Davison, Florence, Gray, and Ross (1958), p. 115; Lytle (1942), p. 153; Rothlisberger and Dickson (1972), pp. 30–31; Mangum (1964), p. 18; and Shwinger (1975), p. 114.
7. Roy, quoted in Whyte (1955), p. 15.
8. Whyte (1955), p. 36.
9. Whyte (1955), p. 201.
10. Mangum (1964), p. 46.
11. Roy (1972), p. 48.
12. Mangum (1964), p. 48.
13. Mangum (1964), p. 48.
14. See Shimmin (1959), p. 83.
15. See, for example, Slichter (1941), pp. 170–72.
16. As Kennedy (1945) put it: "By tradition born of bitter experience, nearly all trade unions have opposed incentive methods of wage payment at some point in their development" (p. 51). See also Slichter, Healy, and Livernash (1960).
17. See Slichter (1941), pp. 166, 167.
18. Davison, Florence, Gray, and Ross (1958), p. 50.
19. See, again, Mincer (1983).
20. See Shimmin (1959).
21. Whyte (1955), p. 212.
22. Hicks (1955), p. 390.
23. Pencavel (1977), p. 234.
24. Doeringer and Piore (1971), Chapter 4; and Thurow (1975), Chapter 3.
25. Hirsch (1976), pp. 4–5.
26. See McKersie (1967).
27. See Brill (1983).
28. Much of the following discussion is based on Anderson (1982).
29. For an extended discussion of systematically underpriced goods, see Thaler (1983).
30. *Ithaca Journal*, January 16, 1984.
31. See Thaler (1983).
32. Thaler (1983), pp. 9–13.
33. Thaler (1983), p. 26.

Chapter 6

1. *Literary Digest*, February 15, 1913, p. 326.
2. Rawls (1971).
3. See, for example, Barry (1971), pp. 109–11; and Thurow (1975), pp. 29–31.
4. Nozick (1974).
5. Nozick (1974), pp. 160, 161.
6. Friedman (1962), pp. 161, 162.
7. Nozick (1974), p. 160.

8. Nozick (1974), p. 160.
9. Rawls (1971, pp. 328, 329) does hold, however, that people should have the right to choose their own associates once they become members of society.
10. Quoted in E. F. Murphy (1978), p. 250.
11. For a general discussion of the economic theory of clubs, see the seminal paper by Buchanan (1965); see also Demsetz (1970).
12. See Buchanan (1975), Chapter 3.
13. Buchanan (1975), p. 43.
14. Manhattan Institute for Policy Research (1982), p. 12.
15. Nozick (1974), Chapter 8.
16. Nozick (1974), p. 243.
17. Nozick (1974), pp. 245, 246.
18. See Maslow (1954), p. 69.
19. Nozick (1974), p. 245.
20. Rawls (1971), p. 530.
21. Rawls (1971), p. 532.
22. Rawls (1971), p. 534.
23. Rawls (1971), p. 534.
24. See, for example, Dawkins (1976).
25. Quoted in Ratner (1942), p. 188.
26. See, for example, Campbell (1979), Chapter 2; and Williamson (1960).
27. Wolfe (1970).
28. Wolfe (1970), pp. 137, 138.
29. See Olson (1965); see also Kahn (1966).

Chapter 7

1. See, for example, Hamilton (1964). Excellent nontechnical presentations may be found in Dawkins (1976) and Wilson (1978).
2. Schelling (1978), Chapter 7.
3. See, for example, Friedman and Friedman (1979), Chapter 7; see also Siegan (1980), Chapter 4.
4. See, for example, Goldberg et al. (1976), pp. 107–11.
5. See, for example, U.S. Supreme Court (1941).
6. Quoted by Peter (1977), p. 345.
7. For a discussion of this view, see White (1981), Chapter 4.
8. Rawls (1971), p. 530.
9. This view is most commonly identified with Mill (1947).
10. See Pigou (1962), pp. 24–30.
11. See Friedman (1963).
12. Williams (1983).
13. Quoted by Peter (1977), p. 386.
14. For a more formal version of this argument, see Frank (1983).
15. For a survey of these studies, see Welch (1978).
16. Even the most steadfastly Keynesian economists do not deny the long-run validity of Say's Law, which holds that supply creates its own demand.
17. Veblen (1899).
18. Quoted by Peter (1977), p. 3.
19. See, for example, Vernon (1961).
20. See, for example, Lurie (1982).

21. For a more formal discussion of the role of consumption as ability signal, see Frank (1985).
22. Again, see Frank (1985) for a formal treatment of this point.
23. Hirsch (1976), p. 27.

Chapter 8

1. For a more formal presentation of the preceding arguments, see Frank (1985).
2. See, for example, Branson (1979), Chapter 10.
3. Duesenberry (1949), Chapter 3.
4. Modigliani and Brumberg (1955).
5. Friedman (1957).
6. Branson's treatment of Duesenberry's work (1979, pp. 202, 203) is more representative of what is found in texts generally; there it receives two pages of discussion, as opposed to more than fourteen pages for the permanent income and life-cycle theories.
7. Mayer (1966).
8. Watts (1958).
9. Diamond and Hausman (1982).
10. Diamond and Hausman (1982), pp. 36, 37.
11. For a thoughtful survey of these studies, see Mayer (1972).
12. Mayer (1972), p. 348.
13. See, for example, Menchik (1979).
14. Freeman (1981).
15. Mincer (1984).
16. Thaler and Rosen (1976).
17. For a thoughtful survey of the literature on compensating wage differentials for exposure to risk, see Smith (1979).
18. Viscusi (1980).
19. Mitchell (1903), pp. 2, 3.
20. Hirschman (1970).
21. See, for example, Clark (1980).
22. See, for example, Galbraith (1952).
23. Sinclair (1906), p. 106.
24. See the President's Commission on Military Compensation (1978).
25. See, for example, Goldberg (1982).
26. Abegglen (1973), p. 62.
27. Abegglen (1973), p. 103.
28. Abegglen (1973), pp. 102, 103.
29. Kahn (1970), p. 101.
30. See, for example, Taira (1970), pp. 183–87; Dore (1973), Chapter 3; and Abegglen (1973), pp. 100, 101.
31. Quoted by Nisbett and Ross (1980), p. 167.

Chapter 9

1. Smith (1910), Book 1.
2. Smith (1910), Book 1, p. 5.
3. Marx (1936), pp. 708, 709.

4. Bowles, Gordon, and Weisskopf (1983), pp. 167, 168.
5. Gintis (1976).
6. Gintis (1976), p. 44.
7. The classic paper on the role of authority within the firm is that of Coase (1937).
8. Galbraith (1967), Chapter 19.
9. Galbraith (1967), p. 212.
10. Galbraith (1958).
11. U.S. Bureau of the Census (1983).
12. For a discussion of the role of education in the income determination process, see Atkinson (1975), Chapter 5; see also Mincer (1974).
13. When George McGovern proposed confiscatory inheritance taxes during his 1972 presidential campaign, for example, some of the most vociferous objections came from blue-collar workers.
14. See Friedman (1953).
15. Rawls (1971).
16. The following discussion is based largely on Frank (1978).
17. Rosen (1981), p. 845.

Chapter 10

1. Dahl (1978).
2. Dahl (1978), pp. 37–39.
3. For a detailed discussion of this view, see Moore (1903), Chapter 1; and Toulmin (1950), Chapter 2.
4. See, for example, Baier (1958), Chapter 7; Gauthier (1970); and Harsanyi (1955). See also Hare (1963), Chapters 6 and 7.
5. Quoted by Goodman (1983).
6. For an economic analysis of the purported welfare gains from free markets in babies, see Landes and Posner (1978).
7. Gannett News Service (1983).
8. Gannett News Service (1983).
9. Goodman (1983).
10. Goodman (1983).
11. Quoted by Goodman (1983).
12. Goodman (1983).
13. Gannett News Service (1983).
14. See, for example, Kelman (1981a) and Culyer (1977).
15. See, for example, Little (1957).
16. See, for example, Gramlich (1981), Chapter 7; McGuire and Garn (1969); and Harberger (1978).
17. See, for example, Mishan (1976), pp. 412, 413.
18. Such is the interpretation the Environmental Protection Agency has applied to the Clean Air Act and its legislative history; see White (1981), pp. 55–56.
19. Schelling (1968).
20. Thaler (1982), p. 173.
21. For a description of this method, see Smith (1976), Chapter 3.
22. Walzer (1983), p. 219.
23. Friedman (1962).
24. Friedman (1962), p. 89.

25. For empirical estimates of the cost savings associated with private schooling, see Sonstelie (1982).
26. For references to numerous relevant studies, see Savas (1981), Chapter 6.
27. Walzer (1983), p. 219.
28. Friedman (1962), p. 92.
29. See Spence (1974), Chapters 2 and 3; see also Riley (1979).

Chapter 11

1. Rousseau (1950), p. 36.
2. Mill (1947), pp. 9, 10. For a more recent defense of the same view, see Hart (1955), p. 175.
3. Nozick (1974).
4. Hobbes (1962), Locke (1821), Rousseau (1950), and Kant (1949).
5. Nozick (1974), Chapter 10.
6. Nozick (1974), p. 310.
7. On economies of scale in defense, see Hamilton, Madison, and Jay (1961), No. 3, pp. 41–45; and Madison (1984), p. 62. On economies of scale in international commerce, see Madison (1984), p. 60.
8. Hobbes (1962), p. 100.
9. See, for example, Nozick (1974), Chapter 5.
10. See, again, Buchanan (1965).
11. These examples follow the spirit of the discussion in Coase (1960).
12. See references cited in notes 15 and 16, Chapter 10.
13. The idea that efficiency and distribution issues are separable goes back at least as far as Mill (1909). For a more recent treatment, see Hylland and Zeckhauser (1979).
14. For a discussion of this issue, see McCloskey (1982), Chapter 3.
15. In particular, the cost-benefit test, applied within this limited domain, satisfies the Pareto criterion.
16. For a discussion of these issues, see Arrow (1963) and Sen (1970b).
17. Buchanan and Tullock (1962), p. 95.
18. See, for example, the discussion of this point in McCloskey (1982), pp. 63, 64.
19. Wolff (1968), p. 24.
20. Wolff (1968), p. 24.
21. Mill (1947), p. 12.
22. Hayek (1960), Chapter 9.
23. Gramsci (1971).
24. Sen (1970a).
25. Sen (1979), p. 218.
26. For a very readable, nontechnical account, see Ruff (1970).
27. See, for example, Storing (1981), Schambra (1982), and Hamilton, Madison, and Jay (1961).
28. Buchanan (1975), p. 94. For an early discussion of the same point, see Rousseau (1950), p. 106.
29. For a thoughtful discussion of this view, see Hare (1981), pp. 144–46.
30. Sen (1974).
31. Cook (1982).
32. Vaupel (1982).
33. Dworkin (1971), p. 119.

Chapter 12

1. See Demsetz (1969) for a very lucid discussion of this point.
2. Quoted by Smith (1976), pp. 11, 12.
3. For a discussion of the effects of trucking regulation, see Alexis (1983).
4. Nichols and Zeckhauser (1977).
5. See Coase (1960) for a discussion of a class of exceptions to this proposition.
6. Exceptions may occur when, as discussed in Chapters 3 and 7, people enter into group contracts that take implicit account of the interdependencies.
7. See, for example, Musgrave and Musgrave (1976), pp. 467-68.
8. See, for example, Gilder (1982).
9. This point was first made explicit by Duesenberry (1949), Chapter 6. For more recent discussions, see Boskin and Sheshinsky (1978) and Layard (1980).
10. See, again, Musgrave and Musgrave, p. 485.
11. George (1900).
12. The original contribution to this literature is the classic paper by Ramsey (1927).
13. See, for example, Aaron (1981); see also Fullerton, Shoven, and Whalley (1983).
14. See, for example, United States Regulatory Council (1980a, 1980b).
15. Quoted by Bork (1978), p. 25.
16. For an extreme version of the left's view, see Green, Moore, and Wasserstein (1972).
17. See, for example, Bork (1978).
18. For a discussion of this legislation, see White (1981), Chapter 15.
19. Friedman (1962), Chapter 12.
20. Friedman and Friedman (1979), p. 108.
21. See, for example, Bernstein and Meezan (1975), Freeman (1974), and Boorstein (1981).
22. See Cummings (1983).
23. Quoted by Cummings (1983).
24. See, for example, Rees and Watts (1975).
25. See, for example, Hall (1975); Burtless and Hausman (1978); and Keeley et al. (1978).
26. Keeley, Robbins, Spiegelman, and West (1978).
27. See Lampman (1971), p. 160.
28. See the papers in Garfinkle (1982), and the summary discussion therein, pp. 519-23; see also Danziger et al. (1981).
29. See U.S. Bureau of Labor Statistics (1982).
30. For a discussion of public attitudes toward Nixon's Family Assistance Plan, see Moynihan (1973), pp. 245-46.
31. Bowles, Gordon, and Weisskopf (1983) have, in fact, proposed that public jobs at more than twice the minimum wage be offered to all who would take them.
32. See Gramlich and Laren (1984).
33. Gramlich (1982).

Bibliography

Aaron, H. J., ed. *The Value-Added Tax: Lessons from Europe.* Washington, D.C.: The Brookings Institution, 1981.

Abegglen, James. *Management and Worker.* Tokyo: Sophia University, 1973.

Acton, J. P. "Evaluating Public Programs to Save Lives: The Case of Heart Attacks." Research Report R-73-02. Rand Corporation. Santa Monica, Calif., 1973.

Akerlof, George A. "Relative Wages and the Rate of Inflation." *Quarterly Journal of Economics* 83 (1969):353–74.

Alchian, Armen, and Harold Demsetz. "Production, Information Costs, and Economic Organization." *American Economic Review* 62 (1972):777–95.

Alexis, Marcus. "The Political Economy of Federal Regulation of Surface Transportation." In *The Political Economy of Deregulation*, Roger Noll and Bruce Owen, eds. Washington, D.C.: American Enterprise Institute, 1983.

Alloy, L. B., and L. Y. Abramson. "Judgment of Contingency in Depressed and Nondepressed Students: Sadder but Wiser?" *Journal of Experimental Psychology: General* 108 (1979):441–85.

Anderson, Jack. "A Surefire Index to Office Status." *Ithaca Journal*, December 11, 1982.

Archibald, G. C. "Wage-Price Dynamics, Inflation, and Unemployment: The Phillips Curve and the Distribution of Unemployment." *American Economic Review* 59 (1969):124–34.

————, and David Donaldson. "Non-Paternalism and the Basic Theorems of Welfare Economics." *The Canadian Journal of Economics* 9 (1976):492–507.

Arrow, Kenneth. *Social Choice and Individual Values*, 2nd ed. New Haven, Conn: Yale University Press, 1963.

Atkinson, Anthony. *The Economics of Inequality*. London: Oxford University Press, 1975.

Auerbach, Alan. "The Theory of Excess Burden and Optimal Taxation." Working Paper 1025. National Bureau of Economic Research, November 1982.

Bachman, J., R. Kahn, T. Davidson, and L. Johnston. *Youth in Transition*, Vol. 1. Ann Arbor, Mich.: Institute for Social Research, 1967.

Baier, Kurt. *The Moral Point of View*. Ithaca, N.Y.: Cornell University Press, 1958.

Bain, Joe. "Relation of Profit Rate to Industry Concentration: American Manufacturing 1936-40." *Quarterly Journal of Economics* 65 (1951):293-324.

Barchas, Jack, and Earl Usdin. *Serotonin and Behavior*. New York: Academic Press, 1973.

Barry, Brian. "Reflections on 'Justice as Fairness'." In *Justice and Equality*, Hugo A. Bedau, ed. Englewood Cliffs, N.J.: Prentice-Hall, 1971.

Becker, Gary. *Human Capital*. New York: Columbia University Press, 1964.

———. "A Theory of Social Interactions." *Journal of Political Economy* 82 (1974): 1063-93.

Belcher, David. *Compensation Administration*. Englewood Cliffs, N.J.: Prentice-Hall, 1971.

Bergstrom, Theodore C. "A 'Scandinavian Consensus' Solution for Efficient Income Distribution among Nonmalevolent Consumers." *Journal of Economic Theory* 2 (1970):383-98.

Bernstein, Blanche, and William Meezan. *The Impact of Welfare on Family Stability*. New York: Center for New York City Affairs, New School of Research, 1975.

Blau, Peter M. *Exchange and Power in Social Life*. New York: Wiley, 1964.

Blumberg, Paul. *Industrial Democracy*. New York: Shocken Books, 1969.

Boorstein, Jane K. "A Design Promoting U.S. Population Growth and Poverty: Aid to Families with Dependent Children (AFDC)." Unpublished dissertation. Columbia University, 1981.

Bork, Robert H. *The Antitrust Paradox: A Policy at War with Itself*. New York: Basic Books, 1978.

Boskin, Michael, and E. Sheshinski. "Optimal Redistributive Taxation When Individual Welfare Depends on Relative Income," *Quarterly Journal of Economics* 92 (1978):589-600.

Bowles, Samuel, David Gordon, and Tom Weisskopf. *Beyond the Wasteland*. Garden City, N.Y.: Anchor Doubleday, 1983.

Bradburn, N., and D. Caplovitz. *Reports on Happiness*. Chicago: Aldine, 1965.

———, and C. E. Noll. *The Structure of Psychological Well-Being*. Chicago: Aldine, 1969.

Branson, William. *Macroeconomic Theory and Policy*, 2nd ed. New York: Harper & Row, 1979.

Brill, Steven. "What Recession? Why Cravath's Balance Sheet Looks as Good as Ever," *The American Lawyer*, March 1983.

Brown, C. V. *Taxation and the Incentive to Work*. Oxford: Oxford University Press, 1980.

Brown, Wilfred. *Piecework Abandoned*. London: Educational Books Ltd., 1962.

Brozen, Yale. "Concentration and Profits: Does Concentration Matter?" In *The Impact of Large Firms on the U.S. Economy*, J. Fred Weston and Stanley Ornstein, eds. Lexington, Mass: D. C. Heath, 1973.

———. *Concentration, Mergers, and Public Policy*. New York: Macmillan, 1982.

Buchanan, James. "An Economic Theory of Clubs." *Economica* 32 (1965):1-14.

———. *The Limits of Liberty: Between Anarchy and Leviathan.* Chicago: University of Chicago Press, 1975.

———, and Gordon Tullock. *The Calculus of Consent.* Ann Arbor: University of Michigan Press, 1962.

Burtless, G., and J. Hausman. "The Effect of Taxation on Labor Supply: Evaluating the Gary Negative Income Tax Experiment." *Journal of Political Economy* 86 (1978):1103–30.

Burton, John, and John Addison. "The Institutionalist Analysis of Wage Inflation: A Critical Appraisal." In *Research in Labor Economics: An Annual Compilation of Research,* Ronald Ehrenberg, ed. Greenwich, Conn.: JAI Press, 1977.

Calvo, Guillermo, and Stanislaw Wellisz. "Hierarchy, Ability, and Income Distribution." *Journal of Political Economy* 87 (1979):991–1010.

Campbell, Bruce. *The American Electorate.* New York: Holt, Rinehart and Winston, 1979.

Clark, Kim B. "The Impact of Unionization on Productivity: A Case Study." *Industrial and Labor Relations Review* 33(4), (1980):451–69.

Coase, Ronald. "The Nature of the Firm." *Economica* 4 (1937):386–405.

———. "The Problem of Social Cost." *Journal of Law and Economics* 3 (1960):144–71.

Cook, Alice H. *Union Democracy: Practice and Ideal.* Ithaca, N.Y.: Cornell University Press, 1963.

Cook, Philip J. "Evaluating Regulations of Addictive, Harmful Commodities." Mimeo. Duke University, 1982.

———, and James Vaupel. "Life, Liberty and the Pursuit of Self-Hazardous Behavior." Institute of Policy Studies and Public Affairs Working Paper. Duke University, August 1978.

Coppen, Alec. "Role of Serotonin in Affective Disorders. In *Serotonin and Behavior,* J. Barchas and E. Usdin, eds. New York: Academic Press, 1973.

Culyer, A. J. "The Quality of Life and the Limits of Cost-Benefit Analysis." In *Public Economics and the Quality of Life,* Lowdon Wingo and Alan Evans, eds. Baltimore: Johns Hopkins University Press, 1977.

Cummings, Judith. "Breakup of Black Family Imperils Gains of Decades." *New York Times,* November 20, 1983.

Dahl, Roald. "Man from the South." In *The Best of Roald Dahl: Stories from Over to You, Someone Like You, Kiss Kiss, and Switch Bitch.* New York: Vintage, 1978.

Danziger, Sheldon, Robert Haveman, and Robert Plotnick. "How Income Transfers Affect Work, Savings and the Income Distribution." *Journal of Economic Literature* 19(3), (1981):975–1028.

Davis, James. "A Formal Interpretation of the Theory of Relative Deprivation." *Sociometry* 22 (1959):280–96.

Davison, J. P., P. Sargent Florence, Barbara Gray, and N. S. Ross. *Productivity and Economic Incentives.* London: Allen & Unwin, 1958.

Dawkins, Richard. *The Selfish Gene.* New York: Oxford University Press, 1976.

Demsetz, Harold. "Information and Efficiency: Another Viewpoint." *Journal of Law and Economics* 12(1), (1969):1–22.

———. *The Market Concentration Doctrine.* Washington, D.C.: American Enterprise Institute for Public Policy Research, 1973.

———. "The Private Production of Public Goods." *Journal of Law and Economics* 13 (1970):293–306.

Deutsch, J. A., and D. Deutsch. *Physiological Psychology.* Homewood, Ill.: Dorsey Press, 1973.

Diamond, P. A., and J. A. Hausman. "Individual Retirement and Savings Behavior." Presented at SSRC-NBER Conference on Public Economics in Oxford, England, June 1982.

Doeringer, Peter, and Michael Piore. *Internal Labor Markets and Manpower Analysis.* Lexington, Mass.: D. C. Heath, 1971.

Dore, Ronald. *British Factory, Japanese Factory.* Berkeley: University of California Press, 1973.

Duesenberry, James. *Income, Saving, and the Theory of Consumer Behavior.* Cambridge, Mass.: Harvard University Press, 1949.

Duncan, Otis. "Does Money Buy Satisfaction?" *Social Indicators Research* 2 (1975–76):267–74.

Dunlop, John T. "The Task of Contemporary Wage Theory." In *New Concepts in Wage Determination*, George W. Taylor and Frank C. Pierson, eds. New York: McGraw-Hill, 1957.

Dworkin, Gerald. "Paternalism." In *Morality and the Law*, Richard Wasserstrom, ed. Belmont, Calif.: Wadsworth, 1971.

Easterlin, Richard. "Does Economics Growth Improve the Human Lot? Some Empirical Evidence." In *Nations and Households in Economic Growth: Essays in Honor of Moses Abramovitz*, Paul David and Melvin Reder, eds. Palo Alto, Calif.: Stanford University Press, 1973.

Elias, M. "Serum Cortisol, Testosterone and Testosterone Binding Globulin Responses to Competitive Fighting in Human Males." *Aggressive Behavior* 7 (1981):215–24.

Festinger, Leon. "A Theory of Social Comparison Processes." *Human Relations* 7 (1954):117–40.

———, S. Schachter, and K. W. Back. *Social Pressure in Informal Groups.* New York: Harper & Row, 1950.

Fiske, D., and S. Maddi. "A Conceptual Framework." In *Functions of Varied Experience*, D. Fiske and S. Maddi, eds. Homewood, Ill.: Dorsey Press, 1961.

Frank, Robert H. "The Economics of Buying the Best." Cornell University, Dept. of Economics Working Paper, 1978.

———. "Envy and the Optimal Purchase of Unobservable Commodities: The Case of Safety." In *The Value of Life and Safety*, M. W. Jones-Lee, ed. Amsterdam: North Holland, 1982.

———. "How Interdependent Preferences Affect Demands for Unobservable and Contingent Goods." Cornell University, Dept. of Economics Working Paper, 1983.

———. "Are Workers Paid Their Marginal Products?" *American Economic Review* 74 (1984a):549–71.

———. "Interdependent Preferences and the Competitive Wage Structure." *Rand Journal of Economics* (Winter 1984b, in press).

———. "The Demand for Unobservable and Other Nonpositional Goods," *American Economic Review* 75 (March 1985, in press).

Freeman, R. B. "The Effect of Unionism on Fringe Benefits." *Industrial and Labor Relations Review* 34 (1981):489–509.

———. "Unionism and the Dispersion of Wages." *Industrial and Labor Relations Review* 34 (1980):3–23.

Freeman, Roger A. "Welfare Reform and the Family Assistance Plan." In *Perspectives on Social Welfare: An Introductory Anthology*, Paul E. Weinberger, ed. New York: Macmillan, 1974.

Friedman, Milton. "Choice, Chance, and the Personal Distribution of Income." *Journal of Political Economy* 61 (1953):277–90.

――――. *A Theory of the Consumption Function*. Princeton, N.J.: Princeton University Press, 1957.

――――. *Capitalism and Freedom*. Chicago, Ill.: University of Chicago Press, 1962.

――――. "Windfalls, the 'Horizon,' and Related Concepts in the Permanent-Income Hypothesis." In *Measurement in Economics: Studies in Mathematical Economics and Econometrics in Memory of Yehuda Grunfeld*, Carl F. Christ et al., eds. Stanford, Calif.: Stanford University Press, 1963.

――――, and Rose Friedman. *Free to Choose*. New York: Harcourt Brace Jovanovich, 1979.

Fullerton, Don, John Shoven, and John Whalley. "Replacing the U.S. Income Tax with a Progressive Consumption Tax: A Sequenced General Equilibrium Approach." *Journal of Public Economics* 20(1), (1983):3–23.

Funt, Allen. "What Do You Say to a Naked Lady?" United Artists, 1970.

Galbraith, John Kenneth. *American Capitalism: The Concept of Countervailing Power*. Boston: Houghton Mifflin, 1952.

――――. *The Affluent Society*. Boston: Houghton Mifflin, 1958.

――――. *The New Industrial State*. Boston: Houghton Mifflin, 1967.

Gallup, George H. *The Gallup Poll: Public Opinion 1935–1971*, Vol. 3. New York: Random House, 1972.

――――. *The Gallup Poll: Public Opinion 1972–1977*, Vols. 1, 2. Wilmington, Del.: Scholarly Resources, Inc., 1978.

Gannett News Service. "Motherhood for Profit or a Great Gift," *Ithaca Journal*, June 11, 1983.

Garfinkel, Irwin, ed. *Income-Tested Transfer Programs*. New York: Academic Press, 1982.

Gauthier, David P. "Morality and Advantage." *The Philosophical Review* 76 (1967): 460–75.

George, Henry. *Progress and Poverty*. New York: Doubleday & McClure, 1900.

Gilder, George F. *Wealth and Poverty*. New York: Bantam, 1982.

Gintis, Herbert. "The Nature of the Labor Exchange and the Theory of Capitalist Production," *Review of Radical Political Economics* 8 (1976):36–54.

Goldberg, Joseph, et al. *Federal Policies and Worker Status Since the Thirties*. Madison, Wis.: Industrial Relations Research Association, 1976.

Goldberg, L. "The Effect on Enlistment Supply of Education Assistance Test Programs in Fiscal Year 1981." Center for Naval Analyses Memorandum 82, 1982.

Goodman, Ellen. "When Money Can Mean Life or Death." *Boston Globe*, September 29, 1983.

Gordon, Robert J. *Macroeconomics*. Boston: Little Brown, 1978.

Gramlich, Edward M. *Benefit-Cost Analysis of Governmental Programs*. Englewood Cliffs, N.J.: Prentice-Hall, 1981.

――――. "An Economic Examination of the New Federalism." *Brookings Papers on Economic Activity* 2 (1982):327–60.

――――, and Deborah Laren. "Migration and Income Redistribution Responsibilties." *Journal of Human Resources* (1984, in press).

Gramsci, A. *Selections from the Prison Notebooks*. London: Lawrence and Wishart, 1971.

Green, Mark, R. Moore, and B. Wasserstein. *The Closed Enterprise System*. New York: Grossman, 1972.

Grinker, R. R., J. Miller, M. Sabshin, R. T. Nunn, and J. C. Nunally. *The Phenomena of Depressions.* New York: Harper & Row, 1961.

Gross, John. *The Oxford Book of Aphorisms.* New York: Oxford University Press, 1983.

Groves, Theodore. "Incentives in Teams." *Econometrica* 41 (1973):617–31.

Gupta, Udayan. "Who's Who in Buyout Financing?" *Venture,* August 1983.

Hall, Robert E. "Effects of the Experimental Negative Income Tax on Labor Supply." In *Work Incentives and Income Guarantees: The New Jersey Income Tax Experiment,* Joseph Pechman and P. M. Timpane, eds. Washington, D.C.: The Brookings Institution, 1975.

Hamermesh, Daniel S. "Interdependence in the Labour Market," *Economica* 42 (1975):420–29.

Hamilton, Alexander, James Madison, and John Jay. In *The Federalist Papers,* Clinton Rossiter, ed. New York: The New England Library Limited, 1961.

Hamilton, W. D. "The Genetical Theory of Social Behavior." *Journal of Theoretical Biology* 7 (1964):1–32.

Hansmann, Henry. "Exclusive Organizations." Yale University Law School Working Paper, December 1983.

Harberger, Arnold. "On the Use of Distributional Weights in Social Cost-Benefit Analysis." *Journal of Political Economy* 86(2), (1978):S87–S120.

Hare, Richard. *Freedom and Reason.* London: Oxford University Press, 1963.

——. *Moral Thinking.* Oxford: Oxford University Press, 1981.

Harris, Milton. "A Model of Tenure Contracts." Carnegie-Mellon University Working Paper, 1980.

——, and A. Raviv. "Some Results on Incentives Contracts with Application to Education and Employment, Health Insurance, and Law Enforcement." *American Economic Review* 68 (1978):20–30.

Harrison, Russell. *Equality in Public School Finance.* Toronto: D.C. Heath, 1976.

Harsanyi, John. "Cardinal Welfare, Individualistic Ethics, and Interpersonal Comparisons of Utility." *Journal of Political Economy* 63 (1955):309–321.

Hart, H. L. A. "Are There Any Natural Rights?" *The Philosophical Review* LXIV (1955):175–91.

Hayek, F. A. *The Constitution of Liberty.* Chicago, Ill.: Chicago University Press, 1960.

Hebb, D. "Drives and the C.N.S." *The Psychological Review* 62 (1955):243–54.

Helson, Harry. *Adaptation-Level Theory.* New York: Harper & Row, 1964.

Hicks, John R. "Economic Foundations of Wage Policy." *Economic Journal* 65 (1955):389–404.

Hirsch, Fred. *The Social Limits to Growth.* Cambridge, Mass.: Harvard University Press, 1976.

Hirschman, Albert. *Exit, Voice and Loyalty.* Cambridge, Mass.: Harvard University Press, 1970.

Hobbes, Thomas, *Leviathan.* New York: Macmillan, 1962.

Homans, George C. *Social Behavior: Its Elementary Forms.* New York: Harcourt Brace and World, 1961.

Hulse, S. H., J. Deese, and H. Egeth. *The Psychology of Learning,* 4th ed. New York: McGraw-Hill, 1975.

Hylland, Aanund, and Richard Zeckhauser. "Distributional Objectives Should Affect Taxes but Not Program Choice or Design." *Scandinavian Journal of Economics* 81(2), (1979):264–84.

Kahn, Alfred. "The Tyranny of Small Decisions." *Kyklos* 19 (1966):23–47.

Kahn, Herman. *The Emerging Japanese Superstate.* Englewood Cliffs, N.J.: Prentice-Hall, 1970.

Kant, Immanuel. *Critique of Practical Reason and Other Writings in Moral Philosophy.* Chicago: University of Chicago Press, 1949.

Kapteyn, Arie, and B. M. S. van Praag. "A New Approach to the Construction of Family Equivalence Scales." *European Economic Review* 7 (1976):313–35.

Keeley, M. C., P. K. Robbins, P. K. Spiegelman, and R. W. West. "The Estimation of Labour Supply Models Using Experimental Data." *American Economic Review* 68 (1978):873–87.

Kelman, Steven. "An Ethical Critique of Cost-Benefit Analysis. *Regulation* 5(1), (1981a):33–40.

———. *What Price Incentives: Economists and the Environment.* Boston, Mass.: Auburn House, 1981b.

Kennedy, Van Dusen. *Union Policy and Incentive Wage Methods.* New York: Columbia University Press, 1945.

Klein, Benjamin, and Keith Leffler. "The Role of Market Forces in Assuring Contractual Performance." *Journal of Political Economy* 89(4), (1981):615–41.

Konner, Melvin. *The Tangled Wing.* New York: Holt, Rinehart and Winston, 1982.

Lampman, Robert J. *Ends and Means of Reducing Income Poverty.* Chicago, Ill.: Markham, 1971.

Landes, Elisabeth M., and Richard A. Posner. "The Economics of the Baby Shortage." *Journal of Legal Studies* 7(2), (1978):323–48.

Lave, Lester. "An Empirical Approach to the Prisoner's Dilemma Game." *Quarterly Journal of Economics* 76 (1972):424–36.

Layard, Richard. "Human Satisfactions and Public Policy." *The Economic Journal* 90 (1980):737–50.

Lazear, Edward. "Why Is There Mandatory Retirement?" *Journal of Political Economy* 87 (1979):1261–84.

———, and Sherwin Rosen. "Rank Order Tournaments as Optimal Labor Contracts." *Journal of Political Economy* 89 (1981):841–64.

Leibenstein, Harvey. "Bandwagon, Snob and Veblen Effects in the Theory of Consumers' Demand." *Quarterly Journal of Economics* 64 (1950):183–207.

Lewinsohn, P., W. Mischel, W. Chaplin, and R. Barton. "Social Competence and Depression: The Role of Illusory Self-Perceptions." *Journal of Abnormal Psychology* 89 (1980):203–12.

Linder, S. B. *The Harried Leisure Class.* New York: Columbia University Press, 1970.

Lipsey, Richard G. "The Relation between Unemployment and the Rate of Change of Money Wage Rates in the United Kingdom, 1862–1957: A Further Analysis." *Economica*, new series, 127 (1960):1–31.

Literary Digest, February 15, 1913.

Little, I. M. D. *A Critique of Welfare Economics*, 2nd ed. Oxford: Oxford University Press, 1957.

Locke, John. *Two Treatises on Government.* London: John Bumpus, 1821.

Long, Jack M., James J. Lynch, N. M. Machiran, Sue A. Thomas, and Kenneth Malinow. "The Effect of Status on Blood Pressure during Verbal Communication." *Journal of Behavioral Medicine* 5(2), (1982):165–71.

Lupton, T. *On the Shop Floor.* New York: Macmillan, 1963.

Lurie, Alison. *The Language of Clothes.* New York: Random House, 1981.

Lytle, Charles Walter. *Wage Incentive Methods.* New York: Ronald Press, 1942.

Madison, James. *Journal of the Constitution Convention.* E. H. Scott, ed. Volumes 1 and 2. Chicago: Albert, Scott Co., 1984.

Mahoney, Thomas. *Compensation and Reward Perspectives*. Homewood, Ill.: Irwin, 1979.

Mangum, Garth L. *Wage Incentive Systems*. Berkeley: Institute of Industrial Relations, University of California, 1964.

Manhattan Institute for Policy Research. *Manhattan Report on Economic Policy*, Vol. 2, No. 6, 1982.

Mann, H. "Seller Concentration, Barriers to Entry, and Rates of Return in Thirty Industries, 1950–1960." *Review of Economics and Statistics* 48 (1966):296–307.

Marriott, R. *Incentive Payment Systems: A Review of Research and Opinion*. London: Staples Press, 1957.

Marston, Stephen. "Two Views of the Geographic Distribution of Unemployment." *Quarterly Journal of Economics* (1985, in press).

Marx, Karl. *Capital*. New York: Modern Library, 1936.

Maslow, A. H. *Motivation and Personality*. New York: Harper, 1954.

Mathewson, Stanley B. *Restriction of Output among Unorganized Workers*. New York: Viking, 1931.

Mayer, Jean. "Regulation of Energy Intake and the Body Weight: The Glucostatic Theory and the Lipostatic Hypothesis." *Annals of the New York Academy of Sciences* 63 (1955):15–43.

Mayer, Thomas. *Permanent Income, Wealth and Consumption*. Berkeley: University of California Press, 1972.

———. "The Propensity to Consume Permanent Income." *American Economic Review* 56 (1966):1158–77.

Mazur, Allan. "Physiology, Dominance, and Aggression in Humans." In *Prevention and Control of Aggression*, A. Goldstein, ed. New York: Pergamon, 1983.

———, and T. Lamb. "Testosterone, Status, and Mood in Human Males." *Hormones and Behavior* 14 (1980):236–46.

McCloskey, Donald. *The Applied Theory of Price*. New York: Macmillan, 1982.

McFadden, Daniel. "A Simple Remark on the Second Best Pareto Optimality of Market Equilibria. *Journal of Economic Theory* 1 (1967):26–38.

McGuinness, Diane, and Karl Pribram. "The Neuropsychology of Attention: Emotional and Motivational Controls." In *The Brain and Psychology*, M. C. Wittrock, ed. New York: Academic Press, 1980.

McGuire, Martin, and Harvey Garn. "The Integration of Equity and Efficiency Criteria in Public Project Selection." *Economic Journal* 79 (1969):882–93.

McGuire, Michael, M. Raleigh, and G. Brammer. "Sociopharmacology." *Annual Review of Pharmacological Toxicology* 22 (1982):643–61.

McKersie, Robert B. "Payment by Results Systems in the United States." In *International Management Seminar on Forms of Wage and Salary Payments for High Productivity*. Versailles (1967), supplement to final report.

Menchik, P. L. "Intergenerational Transmission of Inequality: An Empirical Study of Wealth Mobility." *Economica* 46 (1979):349–62.

Mendeloff, John. *Regulating Safety: An Economic and Political Analysis of Occupational Safety and Health Policy*. Cambridge, Mass.: MIT Press, 1979.

Merton, Robert, and Alice Kitt. "Contributions to the Theory of Reference Group Behavior." In *Continuities in Social Research: Studies in the Scope and Method of Reference Group Behavior*, Robert Merton and Paul Lazarsfeld, eds. Glencoe, Ill.: The Free Press, 1950.

Mill, John Stuart. *On Liberty*. Arlington Heights, Ill.: AHM Publishing, 1947.

———. *Principles of Political Economy*. New York: Longman Greens and Co., 1909.

Mincer, Jacob. "On-the-Job Training: Costs, Returns, and Some Implications." *Journal of Political Economy* (Supplement 1962):50–79.

——. *Schooling, Experience, and Earnings.* New York: National Bureau of Economic Research, 1974.

——. "Unemployment Effects of Minimum Wages." *Journal of Political Economy* 84, Part 2 (1976):S87–S104.

——. "The Economics of Wage Floors." In *Research in Labor Economics*, Ronald G. Ehrenberg, ed. Greenwich, Conn.: JAI Press, 1984.

——. "Union Effects: Wages, Turnover, and Job Training," In *Research in Labor Economics* (Supplement 2), Ronald G. Ehrenberg, ed. Greenwich, Conn.: JAI Press, 1983.

Mishan, E. J. *Cost-Benefit Analysis.* New York: Praeger, 1976.

Mitchell, John. *Organized Labor.* Philadelphia: American Book and Bible House, 1903.

Modigliani, Franco, and R. Brumberg. "Utility Analysis and the Consumption Function: An Interpretation of Cross-Section Data." In *Post-Keynesian Economics*, K. Kurihara, ed. London: Allen & Unwin, 1955.

Moore, G. E. *Principia Ethica.* Cambridge: Cambridge University Press, 1903.

Moynihan, Daniel Patrick. *The Politics of a Guaranteed Income.* New York: Vintage, 1973.

Murphy, E. F. *The Crown Treasury of Relevant Quotations.* New York: Crown, 1978.

Musgrave, R. A., and Peggy Musgrave. *Public Finance in Theory and Practice.* New York: McGraw-Hill, 1976.

National Industrial Conference Board. "Incentive Plans for Salesmen." *Studies in Personnel Policy* 217 (1970):75–86.

Nelson, Phillip. "Advertising as Information." *Journal of Political Economy* 82 (1974): 729–54.

Nichols, Albert, and Richard Zeckhauser. "Government Comes to the Workplace: An Assessment of OSHA." *The Public Interest* 49 (1977):39–69.

Nisbett, Richard, and Lee Ross. *Human Inference: Strategies and Shortcomings of Social Judgment.* Englewood Cliffs, N.J.: Prentice-Hall, 1980.

Noll, Roger, and Bruce Owen. *The Political Economy of Deregulation.* Washington, D.C.: American Enterprise Institute, 1983.

Nozick, Robert. *Anarchy, State, and Utopia.* New York: Basic Books, 1974.

Oi, Walter. "Labor as a Quasi-Fixed Factor." *Journal of Political Economy* 70 (1962):538–55.

Olds, James. "Behavioral Studies of Hypothalamic Functions: Drives and Reinforcements." In *Biological Foundations of Psychiatry*, Vol. 1, R. G. Grenell and S. Gabay, eds. New York: Raven, 1976.

Olson, Mancur. *The Logic of Collective Action.* Cambridge, Mass.: Harvard University Press, 1965.

Palmer, John, ed. *Creating Jobs: Public Employment Programs and Wage Subsidies.* Washington, D.C.: The Brookings Institution, 1978.

Paul, Randolph E. *Taxation in the United States.* Boston: Little Brown, 1954.

Peltzman, Sam. "Profits, Data and Public Policy." In *Public Policies toward Mergers*, J. Fred Weston and Sam Peltzman, eds. Pacific Palisades, Calif.: Goodyear, 1967.

Pencavel, John. "Work Effort, On-the-Job Screening, and Alternative Methods of Remuneration." In *Research in Labor Economics: An Annual Compilation of Research*, Ronald Ehrenberg, ed. Greenwich, Conn.: JAI Press, 1977.

Peter, Laurence. *Peter's Quotations: Ideas for Our Time.* New York: William Morrow, 1977.

Pigou, A. C. *The Economics of Welfare,* 4th ed. London: Macmillan, 1962.

———. "Some Remarks on Utility." *Economic Journal* 13 (1903):58–68.

Pollak, Robert A. "Interdependent Preferences." *American Economic Review* 66 (1976):309–20.

The President's Commission on Military Compensation. Washington, D.C.: U.S. Government Printing Office, April 1978.

Purcell, Theodore V. *Blue Collar Man.* Cambridge, Mass.: Harvard University Press, 1960.

Rader, Trout. "The Second Theorem of Welfare Economics When Utilities Are Interdependent." *Journal of Economic Theory* 23 (1980):420–24.

Rainwater, Lee. *What Money Buys.* New York: Basic Books, 1974.

Raleigh, Michael, M. McGuire, G. G. Brammer, and A. Yuwiler. "Social and Environmental Influences on Blood Serotonin Concentrations in Monkeys." *Archives of General Psychiatry* (in press, 1984).

Ramsey, Frank. "A Contribution to the Theory of Taxation." *Economic Journal* 37 (1927):47–61.

Ratner, Sidney. *American Taxation.* New York: W. W. Norton, 1942.

Rawls, John. *A Theory of Justice.* Cambridge, Mass.: Harvard University Press, 1971.

Rees, Albert, and Harold Watts. "An Overview of the Labor Supply Results." In *Work Incentives and Income Guarantees: The New Jersey Income Tax Experiment.* Washington, D.C.: The Brookings Institution, 1975.

Reiser, M. F., R. B. Reeves, and J. Armington. "Effect of Variations in Laboratory Procedures and Experimenter upon the Ballistocardiogram, Blood Pressure, and Heart Rate in Healthy Young Men." *Psychosomatic Medicine* 17 (1955):185–99.

Restak, Richard. *The Brain: The Last Frontier.* New York: Warner, 1979.

Riley, David P. "Taming GM . . . and Ford, Union Carbide, U.S. Steel, Dow Chemical . . ." In *With Justice for Some,* Bruce Wasserstein and Mark Green, eds. Boston, Mass.: Beacon Press, 1970.

Riley, John G. "Testing the Educational Screening Hypothesis." *Journal of Political Economy* 87 (1979):S227–S251.

Robinson, J., and P. Shaver. *Measures of Social Psychological Attitudes.* Ann Arbor, Mich.: Institute for Social Research, 1969.

Roethlisberger, F. J., and W. J. Dickson. "Management and the Worker." In *Payment Systems,* Tom Lupton, ed. Middlesex, England: Penguin Books, 1972.

Rose, R., I. Bernstein, and T. Gordon. "Consequences of Social Conflict on Plasma Testosterone Levels in Rhesus Monkeys." *Psychosomatic Medicine* 37 (1975):50–61.

Rosen, Sherwin. "The Economics of Superstars." *American Economic Review* 70 (1981):845–58.

———. "Authority, Control, and the Distribution of Earnings." *Bell Journal of Economics* 13 (1982):311–23.

Roth, A., and M. Malouf. "Game Theoretic Models and the Role of Information in Bargaining." *Psychological Review* 86 (1979):574–94.

Rousseau, Jean-Jacques. *The Social Contract.* New York: Dutton, 1950.

Routtenberg, Aryeh. *Biology of Reinforcement: Facets of Brain Stimulation Reward.* New York: Academic Press, 1980.

Roy, Donald. "Quota Restriction and Goldbricking in a Machine Shop." In *Payment Systems,* Tom Lupton, ed. Middlesex, England: Penguin Books, 1972.

Ruff, Larry. "The Economic Common Sense of Pollution." *The Public Interest* 19 (1970):69–85.

Runciman, W. G. *Relative Deprivation and Social Justice.* New York: Penguin, 1966.

Samuelson, Paul. *Economics.* New York: McGraw Hill, 1980.

Sargent, Thomas J. *Macroeconomic Theory.* New York: Academic Press, 1979.

Savas, E. S. *Privatizing the Public Sector.* Chatham, N.J.: Chatham House Publishers, 1982.

Schambra, William. "The Roots of the American Public Philosophy." *The Public Interest* 67 (1982):36–48.

Schelling, Thomas. *The Strategy of Conflict.* New York: Oxford University Press, 1963.

———. "The Life You Save May Be Your Own." In *Problems in Public Expenditure Analysis*, Samuel B. Chase, ed. Washington, D.C.: The Brookings Institution, 1968.

———. *Micromotives and Macrobehavior.* New York: W. W. Norton, 1978.

Schoeck, Helmut. *Envy.* New York: Harcourt Brace and World, 1966.

Scitovsky, Tibor. *The Joyless Economy.* New York: Oxford University Press, 1976.

Seidman, Laurence. *The Design of Federal Employment Programs.* Lexington, Mass.: D.C. Heath, 1975.

———. "The Return of the Profit Rate to the Wage Equation." *Review of Economics and Statistics* 61 (1979):139–42.

Seligman, Edwin B. *Progressive Taxation in Theory and Practice.* Princeton, N.J.: Princeton University Press, 1909.

Sen, Amartya. "The Impossibility of a Paretian Liberal." *Journal of Political Economy* 78 (1970a):152–57.

———. *Collective Choice and Social Welfare.* San Francisco: Holden Day, 1970b.

———. "Choice, Orderings, and Morality." In *Practical Reason*, S. Korner, ed. Oxford, England: Blackwell, 1974.

———. "Liberty, Unanimity, and Rights." *Economica* 43 (1976):217–45.

———. "Poor Relatively Speaking." *Oxford Economic Papers* 35 (1983):153–67.

Shaul, Ben-David, Allen Kneese, and William D. Schultze. "A Study of the Ethical Foundations of Benefit-Cost Analysis Techniques." Mimeo. New Mexico University, 1979.

Shavell, Steven. "Risk Sharing and Incentives in the Principal and Agent Relationship." *Bell Journal of Economics* 10 (1979):35–53.

Shimmin, Sylvia. *Payment by Results: A Psychological Investigation.* London: Staples Press, 1959.

Shwinger, Pinhes. *Wage Incentive Systems.* New York: Wiley, 1975.

Siegan, Bernard. *Economic Liberties and the Constitution.* Chicago, Ill.: University of Chicago Press, 1980.

Sinclair, Upton. *The Jungle.* New York: Sinclair, 1906.

Slichter, Sumner H. *Union Policies and Industrial Management.* Washington, D.C.: The Brookings Institution, 1941.

———, James J. Healy, and E. Robert Livernash. *The Impact of Collective Bargaining on Management.* Washington, D.C.: The Brookings Institution, 1960.

Smith, Adam. *The Wealth of Nations.* New York: Everyman's Library, 1910.

Smith, Robert S. "Compensating Wage Differentials and Public Policy: A Review." *Industrial and Labor Relations Review* 32 (1977):339–52.

———. *The Occupational Safety and Health Act: Its Goals and Achievements.* Washington, D.C.: The American Enterprise Institute, 1976.

Sonstelie, Jon. "The Welfare Cost of Free Public Schools." *Journal of Political Economy* 90 (1982):794–808.

Spence, A. Michael. *Market Signaling: Informational Transfer in Hiring and Related Screening Processes.* Cambridge, Mass.: Harvard University Press, 1974.

Streeten, P. "Wages, Prices and Productivity." *Kyklos* 15 (1962):723-33.

Stigler, George. "The Economics of Minimum Wage Legislation." *American Economic Review* 36 (1946):358-65.

———. *Capital and Rates of Return in Manufacturing Industries.* Princeton, N.J.: Princeton University Press, 1963.

Stiglitz, Joseph. "Incentives, Risk, and Information." *Bell Journal of Economics* 6 (1975):552-79.

Storing, Herbert J. *What the Anti-Federalists Were For.* Chicago: University of Chicago Press, 1981.

Taira, Koji. *Economic Development and the Labor Market in Japan.* New York: Columbia University Press, 1970.

Thaler, Richard. "Precommitment and the Value of a Life." In *The Value of Life and Safety*, M. W. Jones-Lee, ed. Amsterdam: North Holland, 1982.

———. "Using Mental Accounting in a Theory of Consumer Behavior." Ithaca, N.Y.: Cornell University Graduate School of Management, 1983 (processed).

———, and Sherwin Rosen. "The Value of Saving a Life: Evidence from the Labor Market." In *Household Production and Consumption*, Nestor Terleckyj, ed. New York: National Bureau of Economic Research, 1976.

Thurow, Lester. "The Income Distribution as a Pure Public Good." *Quarterly Journal of Economics* 85 (1971):327-36.

———. "Toward a Definition of Economic Justice." *The Public Interest* 31 (1973): 56-80.

———. *Generating Inequality.* New York: Basic Books, 1975.

———. *The Zero Sum Society.* New York: Basic Books, 1980.

Tomes, Nigel. "The Family Inheritance and the Intergenerational Transmission of Inequality." *Journal of Political Economy* 89 (1981):928-58.

Toulmin, Stephen. *Reason and Ethics.* Cambridge, Mass.: Cambridge University Press, 1970.

Townsend, Peter. "The Development of Research on Poverty." In *Social Security Research: The Definition and Measurement of Poverty.* Dept. of Health and Social Research. London: HMSO, 1979.

Tversky, A., and D. Kahneman. "Availability: A Heuristic for Judging Frequency and Probability." *Cognitive Psychology* 5 (1973):207-32.

———. "Judgment under Uncertainty: Heuristics and Biases." *Science* 185 (1974): 1124-31.

U.S. Bureau of Labor Statistics. *Urban Family Budgets and Comparative Indexes for Selected Urban Areas.* April 16, 1982.

U.S. Bureau of the Census. *Current Population Reports Series* 134 (1982).

———. *Current Population Reports Series P-60* 140 (1983).

U.S. Senate. Committee on the Judiciary. *Federal Restraints on Competition in the Trucking Industry: Antitrust Immunity and Economic Regulation.* Washington, D.C.: U.S. Government Pringing Office, 1980.

United States Regulatory Council. *Innovative Techniques in Theory and Practice: Proceedings of a Regulatory Council Conference.* Washington, D.C.: U.S. Regulatory Council, July 1980.

———. *Regulating with Common Sense: A Progress Report on Innovative Regulatory Techniques.* Washington, D.C.: United States Regulatory Council, October 1980.

U.S. Supreme Court, Darby Decision (1941).

Valenstein, Elliot. *Brain Stimulation and Motivation.* Chicago, Ill.: Scott-Foresman, 1973.

van Praag, B. M. S., and Arie Kapteyn. "Further Evidence on the Individual Welfare Function of Income: An Empirical Investigation in the Netherlands." *European Economic Review* 4 (1973):33–62.

———, Arie Kapteyn, and F. G. van Herwaarden. "The Definition and Measurement of Social Reference Spaces." *The Netherlands Journal of Sociology* 15 (1979):13–25.

———, and Jan Spit. "The Social Filter Process and Income Evaluation." Report 82.08, Center for Research in Public Economics, Leyden University, 1982.

Vaupel, James. "Sharing the Gains of Restricting Self-Hazardous Behavior." Mimeo. Duke University, 1982.

Veblen, Thorstein. *The Theory of the Leisure Class.* New York: Macmillan, 1899.

Vernon, Philip E. *The Structure of Human Abilities*, 2nd ed. New York: Wiley, 1961.

Viscusi, W. Kip. "Unions, Labor Market Structure, and the Welfare Implications of the Quality of Work." *Journal of Labor Research* 1 (1980):175–92.

Walzer, Michael. *Spheres of Justice.* New York: Basic Books, 1983.

Watts, H. W. "Long-Run Income, Expectations, and Consumer Savings." In *Studies in Household Economic Behavior*, Yale Studies in Economics, Vol. 9. New Haven, Conn.: Yale University Press, 1958.

Welch, Finis. *Minimum Wages: Issues and Evidence.* Washington, D.C.: American Enterprise Institute, 1978.

Wells, Ken. "Tongan Chic in Utah Is Horsemeat Luau and Kava and Rugby." *Wall Street Journal*, May 13, 1983.

Weston, J. Fred. *Domestic Concentration and International Competition.* Unpublished monograph. UCLA Graduate School of Management, 1980.

White, Lawrence. *Reforming Regulation: Processes and Problems.* Englewood Cliffs, N.J.: Prentice-Hall, 1981.

Whyte, William F. *Money and Motivation.* New York: Harper and Brothers, 1955.

Williams, Robin. "Relative Deprivation." In *The Ideal of Social Structure: Papers in Honor of Robert K. Merton*, Lewis A. Coser, ed. New York: Harcourt Brace Jovanovich, 1975.

Williamson, Chilton. *American Suffrage: From Property to Democracy, 1770–1860.* Princeton, N.J.: Princeton University Press, 1960.

Wilson, Edward O. *On Human Nature.* Cambridge, Mass.: Harvard University Press, 1978.

Wilson, W. *An Attempt to Determine Some Correlates and Dimensions of Hedonic Tone.* Unpublished Ph.D. dissertation. Northwestern University, 1960.

Winter, Sidney G., Jr. "A Simple Remark on the Second Optimality Theorem of Welfare Economics." *Journal of Economic Theory* 1 (1969):99–103.

Wolf, William B. *Wage Incentives as a Management Tool.* New York: Columbia University Press, 1957.

Wolfe, Tom. *Radical Chic and Mau-Mauing the Flak Catchers.* New York: Farrar, Straus & Giroux, 1970.

Wolff, Robert Paul. *The Poverty of Liberalism.* Boston: Beacon Press, 1968.

Index

Aaron, Henry, 250n.13
Abegglen, James, 171, 172nn.27,30
Ability
  and compensation, 149
  and return to education, 211
Ability signaling, 148–52
  and education, 211
  and job seeking, 149
  and lawyers, 150
  and marriage, 149–50
  and research professors, 150
  and small-town consumption patterns,
    151
Abramson, L. Y., 34n.34
Absolute income
  and consumption, 156–60
  and welfare, 35–36
Accidents, 169. *See also* Safety
Advertising, 184–87
Age and consumption patterns, 151–52
Aid to Families with Dependent Children,
  254–55, 261
Air conditioning and wages, 137. *See also*
  Compensating wage differentials
Airbags, 214
Air pollution. *See* Externalities
Akerlof, George A., 37n.43
Alchian, Armen, 64n.2

Alexis, Marcus, 245n.3
Alienation, 177–81
Allen, Woody, 29–30
Alloy, L. B., 34n.34
Altruism
  and the competitive wage structure, 61–
    62
  and redistributive taxation, 108, 127, 240
  and workplace safety, 167
Anderson, Jack, 101n.28
Antitrust policy, 250–51
Arab oil embargo, 179, 222, 260
Archibald, G. C., 37n.43, 42n.1
Armington, J., 23n.11
Arms control, 136, 264
Arousal, 22
  and consumption, 152–53
Arrow, Kenneth, 225n.16
Atkinson, Anthony, 188n.12
Auction model of competition, 74
Auctions
  as an allocation method, 48
  of seats on overbooked airline flights,
    200, 221
  for top-ranked positions, 50–51
Automobiles and auto industry
  advertising of, 184–86
  sales dealerships, 65, 68–71, 74, 75

Automobiles and auto industry (*continued*)
  as signals of ability, 150
  and worker control, 179
Availability, 33

Babies, markets for, 195–99
Bachman, J., 30n.22
Bacon, Francis, 173
Baez, Joan, 197
Baier, Kurt, 195n.4
Bain, Joe, 43n.4
Barbers, 71
  and fair prices for haircuts, 105
Bargaining, 21
Barry, Brian, 110n.3
Barton, R., 34n.32, 56n.7
Baseball, 3, 10
Becker, Gary, 37n.43, 41, 73n.7
Belcher, David, 90n.3
Bergstrom, Theodore C., 37n.43
Bernstein, Blanche, 255n.21
Bernstein, I., 27n.19
Berra, Yogi, 97, 217
Bill of Rights, 236. *See also* First
  Amendment; Sixteenth Amendment
Black lung disease, 137
Black market. *See* Ticket scalping
Blasphemy, 230–31. *See also* Freedom of
  speech; Freedom of religion
Blau, Peter M., 33n.31
Body parts, markets for, 194–201
Boorstein, Jane, 255n.21
Bork, Robert, 250n.15, 251n.17
Boskin, Michael, 37n.42, 249n.9
Bowles, Samuel, 177, 259n.31
Boxing, 13–14
Bradburn, N., 30nn.21,23,25
Brammer, G. G., 25n.13, 26n.14, 27n.15
Branson, William, 157nn..2,6
Brickmaking, 40–41, 45–55
Brill, Steven, 99n.27
Brown, Wilfred, 90n.3
Brozen, Yale, 43nn.3,4
Brumberg, R., 157
Buchanan, James, 118nn.11,12, 119,
  218n.10, 225, 237
Bureaucracy
  and inefficiency, 208, 244–45, 259
  and special interests, 245
Burtless, G., 256n.25

Callahan, Daniel, 195
Campbell, Bruce, 128n.26
Camus, Albert, 143
Capital income, 43–44, 169

Capital markets, imperfections in, 180
Caplovitz, D., 30nn.23,25
Cartels, 43, 177
Censorship, 232–33
Chaired professorships, 100–101
Chamberlain, Wilt, 110–11, 130–31
Chaplin, Charles, 176
Chaplin, W., 34n.22, 56n.7
Civil Aeronautics Board, 200
Clark, Kim, 167n.21
Class-reunion effect, 56
Clothing, 12, 153. *See also* Wardrobe
Clubs, 118, 235
Coal mining, 44, 140–41
Coase, Ronald, 178n.7, 219n.11, 247n.5
Co-brokered sale, 72
Cohesiveness, social. *See* Social
  fragmentation
Collective bargaining. *See* Trade unions
Collective preferences, 13, 131, 135, 141,
  169, 268
Compensating wage differentials
  for amenities, 137
  for control, 177–79
  for risk, 250
  for status, 51–55
  for variety, 176–77
Compensation
  for injury caused by rules, 220–23, 226
  nonpecuniary, 99–102. *See also* Fringe
  benefits
Competition, 42–45, 138, 267–68
  and wages, 41–42, 66–67, 189
  and working conditions, 176–77
Compromise, 218
Computers, 141–42, 144
Concerns about relative standing
  moral arguments against, 120, 122–25
  rationality of, 123–24
  as a basis for redistributive taxation,
    114–15
  as a basis for regulation, 140–43, 238–40
Condominiums
  as positional goods, 248
  and rent controls, 261
Conglomerate firms
  and antitrust policy, 251
  internal wage structure of, 88–90
Conservation, 261
Conspicuous consumption, 146–53
Consumer choice
  and antitrust policy, 250–51
  and advertising, 184–87
Constitution, U.S., 217, 235–37
  and economies of scale, 217, 235

First Amendment to, 231
Sixteenth Amendment to, 126
Consultants, 877
Consumer sovereignty, 184–87
Consumption
  and relative income, 155–56
  as a signal of ability, 148–52
Consumption taxes
  effects on the poor, 234
  on positional goods, 249
  and supply-side economics, 248–50
Contests
  for position, 7–11
  properties of, 4
Contingent commodities, 143–44
Contracts. *See also* Social contract
  the Constitution as a, 216–17
  as precommitment devices, 21
  for public services, 259
Cook, Philip, 240
Coppen, Alec, 27n.17
Cornell University, 78–81, 99
Corporate spin-offs, 88–90
Cost-benefit analysis
  and constitutional rights, 216–17, 221
  and distributional effects, 201, 221–23, 234
  and environmental cleanliness, 202
  ethical objections to, 201–5
  and human lives, 203
  measurement problems, 202, 204, 205, 229–33
  reciprocal nature of, 220, 228
  and religious freedom, 230–31
  and rules, 218–21, 257
  and safety, 14, 138, 139, 203
  as a social welfare function, 225
  and the unanimity criterion, 220–21, 223–24, 226
Cravath, Swaine, and Moore, 99
Credentials in hiring, 211–12
Cross-subsidies, 210
Cultural relativism, 15–16
Culyer, A., 201n.14
Cummings, Judith, 255nn.22,23

Dahl, Roald, 193
Danziger, Sheldon, 256n.28
Davidson, T., 30n.22
Davis, James, 33n.31
Davison, J., 91n.6, 94n.18
Dawkins, Richard, 124n.24, 132n.1
Deese, J., 20n.3
Defense, 217–18, 264
Democracy in the workplace, 167, 177–81

Demonstration effects, 37, 146–53
Demsetz, Harold, 64n.2, 43n.4, 118n.11, 244n.1
Depression
  and self-perception, 34–35
  and serotonin, 27
Deutsch, D., 23n.10
Deutsch, J. A., 23n.10
Diamond, Peter, 158
Diamonds, 7–8
Dickson, W. J., 91n.6
Differentials, wage. *See* Compensating wage differentials
Diminishing marginal utility, 155
Directory assistance, 234
Discounting the future, 142–43, 241
Distribution of income. *See* income distribution
Division of labor. *See* Specialization of labor
Doeringer, Peter, 41, 73, 95
Dominance
  and serotonin, 23–25
  and testosterone, 27–28
Domino effect, 59–60, 116
Donaldson, David, 37n.43
Dore, Ronald, 172n.30
Drugs
  laws against, 241
  prescription requirements, 148
Dueling, laws against, 12
Duesenberry, James, 37, 38, 157, 160, 249n.9
Duncan, Otis, 28, 29n.20
Dworkin, Gerald, 241

Earnings
  of auto salespersons, 68, 69
  of concert soloists, 190
  distribution of, 187, *See also* Income redistribution
  of real estate salespersons, 65ff., 71–73
  of research professors, 76–82
  of tax accountants, 189
  versus marginal productivity, 40–41
Easterlin, Richard, 31
Ecological niche, 32, 124
Economies of scale
  in conglomerate enterprises, 88–89
  and national retail chains, 183
  and preferential tax treatment for small firms, 264
  as a reason for firms, 60–61
  and redistributive taxation, 125–26
  role in social choice, 218–21, 227, 242

Edinburgh, University of, 17
Educational requirements of jobs, 211
Educational vouchers, 207–12
Efficiency, 265, 268
Effluent charges. *See* Taxes on externalities
Effort
  monitoring of, 20–21
  and reward, 97, 109
  and wages, 96
Egeth, H., 20n.3
Einstein, Albert, 20
Electricity, price regulation, 261
Elias, M., 27n.18
Emotion, 23
Energy conservation, 261
Enforcement mechanisms, 135
Envy, 14, 117, 123
Equal Employment Opportunity
    Commission, 255
Equity 10, 61–63, 126–27. *See also* Fairness
Estate taxes, 188
Ethical norms
  adaptive significance of, 195
  against cost-benefit analysis, 201–5
  costs to violators of, 199
  against markets for babies, 196–201
  against markets for transplantable
    organs, 196–97
  against private markets for education,
    205–12
  against prostitution, 198
Evolution
  of behavior 19, 31–32, 32–33
  and the ecological niche, 124
  and motivation, 268
  and time preference, 141
Exploitation, 43–44, 136, 167, 174
Externalities
  congestion, 246–47
  in education, 206–7
  and envy, 122–23
  interracial handholding, 122–23
  negotiated solutions to, 218–21
  noise, 204–5, 219–20
  pollution, 123
  positional consumption, 249
  taxation of, 233–35, 246–50, 268

Fair Labor Standards Act, 145
Fair prices, 102–6
  for concert tickets, 105
  for haircuts, 105
  and relative standing, 104
  for restaurant meals, 105
Fairness, 10, 11

  and competitive wages, 61–63
  and cost-benefit analysis, 221–23
  and immigration laws, 108
  and redistributive taxation, 10, 11, 108,
    126–30
Falkson, Micky, 71
Family Assistance Plan, 256
Family formation incentives, 254–55, 261
Faulty telescopic faculty, 142–43
Festinger, Leon, 33n.31
Firm-specific training, 73–74, 76
First amendment, 231
Fiske, D., 22n.7
Fixed costs, 68, 81, 165, 217
Fixed labor costs, 165
Florence, J., 91n.6, 96n.18
Food stamps, 254
Football, 12, 13
Ford, Henry, 137
Fragmentation. *See* Social fragmentation;
    Stratification
Frank, Robert H., 51n.6, 65n.3, 144n.15,
    151nn.21,22, 156n.1, 189n.16
Frazier, Walt, 149
Freedom
  and less-than-unanimous collective
    action, 119, 225–26, 237–38
  of religion, 228–31
  and restrictive rules, 225
  of speech, 231–33, 239
Freedom of Association
  and competitive wage rates, 10, 48–51
  and externalities, 218–21
  and redistributive taxation, 113–14
  and restrictive laws, 216, 232, 236
Freeman, Richard B., 83n.12, 162–65
Freeman, Roger, 255n.21
Free-rider problem, 118, 125
Friedman, Milton, 111, 115, 136n.3, 142,
    157, 188n.14, 206–8, 210n.28, 254, 257
Friedman, Rose, 136n.3, 254n.20
Fringe benefits, 100
  of government workers, 101–2
  in Japan, 171–72
  in union firms, 162–65
Frogs, as choosers of ponds, 9, 39, 88
Fullerton, Donald 250n.13
Funt, Allen, 18

Galbraith, John Kenneth, 167n.22, 184, 186
Gallup Surveys, 35, 36
Garfinkle, Irwin, 256n.28
Garn, Harvey, 201n.16
Gasoline price regulation. *See* Price
    controls

Gasoline rationing, 222
Gauthier, David, 195n.4
George, Henry, 249
Germany, 31
Gilder, George, 248n.8
Gintis, Herbert, 177–79
Global status, 47
Goldberg, Joseph, 136n.4
Goldberg, L., 171n.25
Goldwater, Barry, 14, 240
Goodman, Ellen, 195n.5, 197nn.9,11
Gordon, David, 177, 259n.31
Gordon, Robert, 157
Gordon, T., 27n.19
Gore, Albert, 197
Government, local control of, 227, 262
Government regulation. *See* Regulation
Gramlich, Edward M., 201n.16, 263n.32
Gramsci, A., 232
Grantsmanship, 78–82
Gray, Barbara, 91n.6, 94n.18
Groves, Theodore, 41, 64n.1
Guaranteed jobs, 258–60
Gupta, Udayan, 89n.1

Hackle-raising, 132–34, 151
Half, Robert, 148
Hall, Robert E., 256n.25
Halo effect, 57–58, 85
Hamermesh, Daniel S., 37n.43
Hamilton, Alexander, 217n.7, 235n.27
Hamilton, W. D., 132n.1
Hansmann, Henry, 58n.8
Happiness surveys, 28–30
Harberger, Arnold, 201n.16
Hare, Richard, 195n.4, 238n.29
Harm to others, 215, 229, 230–232, 243
Harris, Milton, 69n.5
Harsanyi, John, 195n.4
Hart, H. L. A., 215n.2
Harvard University, 7
Hastings Center, 195
Hausman, Jerry, 215n.2
Hayek, Friedrich, 232
Health care
  for the poor, 197
  preventive, 148
Healy, James, 93n.16
Hebb, D., 22n.7
Helson, Harry, 31n.27
Hicks, Sir John, 95
Hierarchies
  of co-workers, 47, 48. *See also* Reference
    group
  of needs, 122

Hirsch, Fred, 7, 36, 96, 153
Hirschman, Albert, 83, 167
Hobbes, Thomas, 216–18
Hockey helmet rules, 133, 242
Homans, George C., 33n.31
Housing. *See* Rent control
Hull, Cordell, 108, 126–27
Hulse, S. H., 20n.3
Hunger, 22, 23, 152
Hylland, Aanund, 223n.13

Identified lives, 203
Imitative behavior, 7. *See also* Peer pressure
Immigration, 117
Imperfect information
  and paternalistic rules, 241
  and safety regulation, 137–38
  and wage compression, 64–65
Imperfect mobility
  and constitutional rules, 227, 235–38
  and redistributive taxation, 118–25, 127–
    28
  and wage compression, 42–43
Implicit market for status
  and income variations, 96–98
  and price variations, 58, 82–86
Import controls, 252
Incentives
  and effort, 109
  and family formation, 255
  and pay schemes, 88, 96
  and regulations, 250
  and welfare programs, 256–57
Income
  and the demand for leisure, 96
  and the demand for status, 48, 96–99
  and the incidence of regulations, 265–66
  and savings rates, 157–61
Income comparisons
  reference groups for, 33–34
  and welfare, 55
Income inequality
  and cost-benefit analysis, 221–23
  resulting from class privilege, 188
  resulting from rank order effects, 189–90
  and social fragmentation, 114–15, 118–19
Income redistribution
  policies for achieving, 254–65
  as a public good, 118
  and self-interest, 10, 115, 254
Income taxes
  and fringe benefits, 165
  and work incentives, 249
India, 5
Indirect costs, 78–82

Inherited wealth, 188
In-kind benefits, 259–60
Insurance
  as a contingent commodity, 143
  as a fringe benefit, 162–63
  and risk aversion, 226
Internal labor market, 73–75
Internal wage structure
  as affected by demand for status, 51ff.
  for auto sales agencies, 68–71
  military versus civilian, 84
  for real estate agencies, 71–73
  for research professors, 75–82
  union versus nonunion, 83
  U.S. versus Japan, 172
Interstate Commerce Commission, 245
Invisible hand, 4, 210, 267
Ivy League, 12

Jackson, Michael, 102
Japanese labor contract, 171–72
Jay, John, 217n.7, 235n.27
Job tenure
  in Japanese firms, 171
  in union firms, 83, 94
  in universities, 83
Job titles, 99–101
Johnston, L., 30n.22
Justice, entitlement theory of, 110–111

Kahn, Alfred, 131n.29, 234
Kahn, Herman, 172n.29
Kahn, R., 30n.22
Kahneman, Daniel, 33
Kant, Immanuel, 216
Kapteyn, Arie, 37
Keeley, M., 256nn.25,26
Kelman, Steven, 201n.14
Kennedy, Van Dusen, 93n.16
Kidneys, market for 195, 197
Kitt, Alice, 33n.31
Klein, Benjamin, 184
Konner, Melvin, 23n.9

Labor relations, 167
Labor unions. *See* Trade unions
Ladders, regulation of, 244–45
Laissez-faire, 265
Lamb, T., 27n.18
Lampman, Robert, 256n.27
Landes, Elizabeth, 196n.6
Laren, D., 263n.32
Layard, Richard, 9, 37, 249n.9
Lazear, Edward, 41, 64n.2
League rules, 11

Leagues, 9
Learning effect, 58, 85
Leffler, Keith, 184
Leibenstein, Harvey, 37
Leisure
  and the demand for status, 145–46
  and tax policy, 248
  versus income, 248
Leveraged buyouts, 88–90
Leviathan, 214
Levin, Michael, 120, 126
Levi's, 266
Lewinsohn, P., 34n.32, 34n.33, 56n.7
Libel, 123, 231
Libertarian welfare state, 267–69
Libertarians
  and paternalistic regulation, 4, 215, 242–
    43
  and redistributive taxation, 113–15, 120,
    126, 127, 130, 190
  and safety regulation, 14–15, 142
  and tax penalties, 234–35
  and unanimously supported rules, 219,
    221
Life, value of, 197–98, 203–4
Life-cycle hypothesis, 157–60
Limbic system, 23, 152
Lipsey, Richard G., 42n.1
Little, I. M. D., 201n.15
Livernash, E. Robert, 93n.16
Local autonomy, 227
Local governments and welfare benefits,
    262–63
Local hierarchies, 30–35, 47–48, 55
Local status. *See also* Relative standing, 9,
    17, 32, 34–35, 47–48
Locally owned businesses, 183–84
Locke, John, 216
Long, Jack M., 23nn.11,12
Los Angeles and air pollution, 131
Lupton, T., 90n.3
Lurie, Allison, 149n.20
Luxury goods, 156
Lynch, James J., 23nn.11,12
Lytle, Charles, 91n.6

Machiran, N. M., 23nn.11,12
Maddi, S., 22n.7
Madison, John, 217n.7, 235n.27
Mahoney, Thomas, 90n.3
Mailer, Norman, 12
Major losses
  compensation for, 226
  and constitutional rights, 227
  defined, 223

as an exception to the cost-benefit test, 226-27
and risk aversion, 226-27
Malinow, Kenneth, 23nn.11,12
Malouf, M., 22n.5
Mangum, Garth, 91n.6, 92n.10, 93nn.12,13
Mann, H., 43n.4
Marginal productivity theory, 40-41
criticisms of, 42-45
and the internal labor market, 73-75
and measurement problems, 64-65, 75-77
and risk aversion, 69-71
Market concentration, 251
Market power, 191
Markets
for babies, 195-99
for education, 206-12
for quietude, 204-5
for seats on overbooked flights, 200-201
for sex, 194-98
for slaves, 198
for status, 48-51
for transplantable organs, 195-97
Marriage laws, 228-29
Marriott, R., 90n.3
Marston, Stephen, 42
Martin, Billy, 12
Marx, Karl, 176
Maslow, A. H., 122n.18
Mayer, Jean, 23n.9
Mayer, Thomas, 158-60
Mazur, Allan, 27n.18
McCloskey, Donald, 225n.14, 226n.18
McFadden, Daniel, 37n.43
McGovern, George, 188n.13, 255
McGuinness, Diane, 22n.8
McGuire Martin, 201n.16
McGuire, Michael, 23-27
McKersie, Robert, 90nn.4,5, 97n.26
Means-tested benefits, 256
Medicaid, 197
Meezan, William, 255n.21
Menchik, P. L., 160n.13
Mencken, H. L., 5
Merton, Robert, 33n.31
Metapreferences, 238
Migration. *See also* Mobility
between cities, 42, 138
of corporations, 42
between firms, 43
between planets, 116-17
in response to welfare benefit differentials, 262-63
Military compensation, 169-71
and fringe benefits, 170-71

variability in, 84
Mill, John Stuart, 139n.9, 215, 229-31, 233n.3, 243
Mincer, Jacob, 41, 73, 83, 94n.19, 165, 188n.12
Minimum wage laws, 13, 138, 144-46, 253
Minority rights, 227. *See also* Rights
Mischel, W., 34n.32, 56n.7
Mishan, Ezra, 201n.17
MIT, 57
Mitchell, John, 167
Mobility. *See also* Freedom of association; Imperfect mobility; Migration
of firms, 42
and individual rights, 119-20, 237
of labor, 42, 45-46, 138
and redistributive taxation, 119-20
and social choice, 218-21
Modern Times, 176
Modigliani, Franco, 157
Monogamy, 228-29
Moore, G. E., 195n.3
Moral arguments
and cost-benefit analysis, 201-3
and policy analysis, 136, 238, 269
against redistributive transfers, 120, 122-25
and safety legislation, 138-39, 214
Motivation, 19, 22-23, 268
Motor Vehicles, Department of, 208
Moynihan, Daniel P., 257n.30
Multiple listing service, 71-72
Murcer, Bobby, 3, 4
Murphy, E. F., 116n.10
Musgrave, Peggy, 248n.7, 249n.10
Musgrave, Richard, 248n.7, 249n.10

National Association of Manufacturers, 267
National Football League, 12
Natural gas regulation, 261
Natural rights, 216, 232. *See also* Rights; Bill of Rights
Natural selection, 19, 141. *See also* Evolution
Navratilova, Martina, 20
NCAA, 136
Necessity, 156
Needs, 9, 121
Negative income tax, 254-58
Nelson, Philip, 184n.
Net value criterion
defined, 223
examples, 224
Neurotransmitters, 23-25
New York City, 32, 263

New York Yankees, 3
Nichols, Albert, 246
Nigeria, 31
Nisbett, Richard, 33, 56n.7, 171n.31
Nixon, Richard, 74, 255
Noll, C. E., 30n.21
Nonpositional goods, 153, 248
Norms, 32, 33. *See also* Reference standard
Norton, Eleanor Holmes, 255
Nozick, Robert, 109–13, 121–23, 130, 215,
      217, 218n.9
Nudism, 234–35

Occupational Safety and Health Act, 136.
      See also Safety, regulation of
Occupational Safety and Health
      Administration
   and effects on workplace safety, 246
   safety standards for ladders, 244–45
Oi, Walter, 41, 73
Olds, James, 22n.7
Olson, Mancur, 130
Opportunity costs, examples of, 43, 201
Orange juice experiment, 6
Organized crime, 135
Original position, 109, 190
Overtime laws, 13, 144–46, 163, 253

Pareto optimality, 225n.15
Paternalism, 14–16, 240–42
   and imperfect information, 241
   and the military, 171
   and rationality, 241
   and risk aversion, 241
   and safety regulation, 136, 139, 167
Peckham, Justice, 250
Pedestrian overpasses, 139
Peer pressure, 17–18, 151–52. *See also*
      Imitative behavior
Peffer, William, 125
Peltzman, Sam, 43n.4
Pencavel, John, 61n.10, 95
Pension plans, 13, 148, 162–63, 170
Permanent income hypothesis, 157–60, 173.
      See also Consumption; Savings
Peter, Lawrence, 137n.6, 143n.13, 148n.18
Petroleum geologists, 87
Pets, 15, 121, 229
Piece-rate earnings
   guarantees on, 93
   and income, 98
   limitations on, 90–96
   and team production, 98, 99
Pigou, A. C., 37n.43, 142
Piore, Michael, 41, 73, 95

Poker, 11
Police, 15, 118
Pollak, Robert A., 37n.43
Polygamy, 228–29
Pond, choosing the right, 9, 10, 39, 88, 266
Pony roasting, 15
Positional goods
   clothing as, 13, 150–51
   defined, 7, 153
   diamonds as, 7–8
   education as, 7, 211, 248
   jobs as, 8–9
   taxing, 248
Positive reinforcement, 20
Posner, Richard, 196n.6
Poverty, and absolute income, 35-36, 126
Precommitment, 21
Prescription drugs, 148
Pribram, Karl, 22n.8
Price controls, 222, 260–62
Prices, of top-ranked positions, 50–51, 84–
      86
Prisoner's dilemma
   and alienation in the workplace, 181
   and arms races, 136
   and baby-selling, 194–201
   defined, 133–35
   and democracy in the workplace, 181
   and hackle-raising in animals, 132–35
   and hockey helmet rules, 132–35
   limits to resolving, 266
   and locally owned businesses, 183
   and markets for transplantable organs,
      194–201
   and minimum wage laws, 144–46
   and noise pollution, 204–6
   and overinvestment in education, 211–12
   and overtime laws, 144–46
   and prostitution, 194–201
   and risk taking, 143–44
   and safety regulation, 136–42
   and savings, 147
   and Social Security, 147–48
Private schools, 206–12
Production complementarities, 60–61
Production quotas, 90–96
Productivity
   of faculty, 75–82
   and morale, 61
   of salespersons, 65–73
   and specialization, 60–61, 175–76
   and wages. *See* Marginal productivity
      theory
Productivity decline, and the implicit
      market for status, 97

Professors' salaries, 75–82
Profits, 43–44, 105–6, 138, 176, 210
Public employment, 258–59
Public goods, 118–19
Public schools, 206–12, 260
Purcell, Theodore, 90n.3

Quality control, 94
Quotas, and piece-rate pay schemes, 90–96

Racism, 122–23
Rader, Trout, 37n.43
Radiation exposure, 142–43, 243, 250
Rainwater, Lee, 37
Raleigh, Michael, 25n.13, 26n.14, 27n.15
Ramsey, Frank, 249n.12
Rand, Ayn, 267
Rat race. *See also* Prisoner's dilemma
    in education, 211–12
    and pay variability, 96
Rate of return
    to education, 211
    on invested capital, 43–44
Rationality
    collective versus individual, 130–33, 143–
        44, 269. *See also* Prisoner's dilemma
    and feelings of envy, 123–24
    and paternalism, 241
    and safety regulation, 141
    and savings, 160
    and self-serving behavior, 139
    and vivid information, 152–53
Rationing by auction, 48, 50–51
Ratner, 126n.25
Raviv, Artur, 64n.2
Rawls, John, 109–10, 112–13, 123–24, 126–27,
    188, 190
Reagan, Ronald, 74
Real estate sales, 65, 71–73
Reame, Nancy, 196, 197
Redistributive taxation. *See* Income
    redistribution
Rees, Albert, 256n.24
Reeves, R. B., 23n.11
Reference groups. *See also* local hierarchy,
    30–35, 83, 89–90, 169, 172, 252
Reference standard, 32–33
Regulation
    of bat guano, 245
    in Europe, 266
    of the labor contract, 136ff.
    of ladders, 244–45
    of the marriage contract, 228–29
    pitfalls of, 244–46
    of prices, 260–61

of safety. *See* Safety regulation
    and special interests, 245
Reiser, M. F., 23n.11
Relative deprivation, 120
Relative income hypothesis, 157
Relative standing. *See also* Local status;
        Reference group
    and affective disorders, 30
    and alienation, 181–83
    and excessive specialization, 181–83
    and fair prices, 22, 102–6
    and feelings of well-being, 23–30
    and fringe benefits, 100–102
    and health, 30
    and heart rate and blood pressure, 23–24
    between nations, 264–65
    and poverty, 5, 35–36, 127
    and serotonin, 23–27
    and testosterone, 27–28
    thought experiments involving, 6–7, 116–
        17
    and worker control, 181–31
Religious freedom, 228–31
Rent control, 261
Rescue efforts, and cost-benefit analysis,
    203
Research universities, 75–82
Reservation price, 103
Restak, Richard, 17n.1
Retail chain stores, 183–84
Retirement plans. *See* Pensions; Savings
Revealed preference, 125, 205
Rights. *See also* Constitution; Bill of Rights
    and costs of adjustment, 125
    to the fruits of one's labor, 120, 126
    and imperfect mobility, 118–19, 217
    and major losses, 226–29
    and measurement problems, 229–31
    minority, 227
    reciprocal nature of, 14, 119–20, 242
    and risk aversion, 226
    and self-interest, 227
Riley, John, 211n.29
Ripple effects on wages, 39, 78, 88, 94
Risk
    and relative standing, 143–44
    and reward, 109–10
Risk aversion
    and competitive wage rates, 69–71
    and constitutional rights, 226
    and income redistribution, 110
    and insurance, 143–44, 226
    and major losses, 226–27
    and paternalism, 241
Rizzuto, Phil, 3, 4

Robbins, P. K., 256n.26
Robinson, J., 30n.24
Rockefeller, Nelson, 255
Rockefellers, 9
Roethlisberger, F. J., 91n.6
Role models, 19
Rolling Stones, 103
Rose, R., 27n.19
Rosen, Sherwin, 64n.2, 166, 190
Ross, Lee, 173n.31
Ross, N. S., 91n.6, 94n.18
Roth, A., 22n.5
Rousseau, Jean-Jacques, 214, 216, 238n.28
Routtenberg, Aryeh, 22n.7
Roy, Donald, 91, 92n.11
Ruff, Larry, 233n.26
Rules, 11–14. *See also* Regulation
Runciman, W. G., 33n.31

Safety
  automobile, 13, 186
  commercial airline, 13
  pedestrian, 138–39
  regulation of, 13–14, 136–42, 239–40, 253
Sales commissions, theory of, 65–67
Sales tax, 248–49
San Francisco Giants, 10
Sargent, Thomas, 157
Savas, E. S., 208n.26
Savings, *See also* Pensions
  in Japan, 172
  life-cycle theory of, 157–61
  in the military, 170, 171
  permanent income theory of, 151–61
  relative income theory of, 147, 151–61
  as a share of income, 156–60
  and Social Security. *See* Social Security
  in union firms, 162–63
Say's Law, 145n.16
Scale surplus, 219, 221–22, 230
Schambra, W., 235n.27
Schelling, Thomas, 21, 133, 203
Schlichter, Sumner, 93nn.14,16
School lunch programs, 260
Schools. *See* Educational vouchers
Scitovsky, Tibor, 22, 37n.39
Seidman, Laurence, 44n.5
Self-discipline, 4
Self-esteem, 120
  and differentiating characteristics, 121
  and local status, 34–35
  and relative income, 120, 123–24
Self-perception, 34–35

Sen, Amartya, 36n.36, 225n.16, 232, 238
Seniority, and fringe benefits, 163–65
Serotonin
  and affective disorders, 27
  and behavior, 27
  and local status, 23–25, 59
Shavell, Steven, 41
Shaver, P., 30n.24
Sheshinsky, E., 37n.42, 249n.9
Shimmin, Sylvia, 93n.14, 95
Shoven, John, 250n.13
Shwinger, Pinhes, 91n.6
Siegan, Bernard, 136n.3
Signature loans, 180
Sinclair, Upton, 169
Sixteenth Amendment, 125–26
Small Business Administration, 251
Smith, Adam, 4, 60, 175, 210
Smith, Robert S., 166n.17, 204n.21, 254n.2
Smog, 130. *See also* Pollution; Externalities
Social choice, 119, 219–33
Social contract
  and income redistribution, 112–15, 130
  and paternalistic rules, 216ff.
Social fragmentation, 114–15, 118–19, 216, 265. *See also* Stratification
Social Security, 13–14, 148, 170, 240, 265–66. *See also* Pensions; Savings
Social welfare function, 225
Sonstelie, Jon, 208n.25
Specialization of labor, 60, 175–76
Specific training, 73–75
Spence, A. Michael, 211n.29
Spiegelman, P., 256n.26
Spin-offs, 88–89
Spit, Jan, 37n.41
Stability, social. *See* Social fragmentation
Statistical lives, 203
Status. *See also* Local status; Relative standing
  markets for, 9–10, 48–51
  reciprocal nature of, 9, 45, 99, 127
Stevenson, Robert Louis, 20
Stigler, George, 43n.4, 44n.5
Stiglitz, Joseph, 41, 69n.4, 70n.6
Storing, Herbert, 235n.27
Stratification
  in the labor market, 10, 51–55
  among sales firms, 75
  of school populations, 210
  of society. *See* Social fragmentation
Super Bowl, 103
Supply and demand, for top-ranked positions, 48–51

Supply-side economics, 248
Surrogate motherhood, 196–99
Sweden, 218
Switzerland, 264

Taira, Koji, 172n.30
Tax accountants, 189
Taxes
  on estates, 188
  on externalities, 233–35, 245–46
  on income. *See* Income redistribution
  on land, 249
  on positional consumption, 247–50
  redistributive. *See* Income redistribution
  simplification of, 189
Team production, 64
Testosterone, 27–28
Thaler, Richard, 22, 102, 104, 203
Thomas, Sue A., 23nn.11,12
Thought experiment
  on interplanetary travel, 116–17
  on marginal productivity, 76–77
Thurow, Lester, 37, 41, 61, 73, 95, 110n.3
Ticket scalping, 102–5
Tolerance, 120–21
Top-ranked positions
  markets for, 10, 48–51
  prices of 10, 51–55, 84–86
Toulmin, Stephen, 195n.3
Townsend, Peter, 35
Trade unions
  and collective consumption agreements,
    161–69
  and democracy in the workplace, 167
  and exploitation, 167–69
  and fringe benefits, 162–69
  goals of, 167–69, 252
  public policy toward, 251–53
  and wage variability, 83, 94
  and worker grievance procedures, 167
Training, firm-specific. *See* Firm-specific
    training
Transactions costs, 223–26. *See also*
    Imperfect information; Imperfect
    mobility
Transfer programs, voluntary, 117–18. *See
    also* Income redistribution, policies for
    achieving
Trucking industry, 245
Tullock, Gordon, 225
Tversky, Amos, 33

UCLA, 23
Ulysses, 21

Unanimity
  and collective action, 119, 220–21, 225
  and cost-benefit analysis, 220–24
  and liberty, 232–34
Unemployment, 174
UNICEF, 62
Unions. *See* Trade unions
United Technologies Corporation, 268
University of Michigan, 76–77, 79
University of Texas, 81
Unsystematic preferences, 224
Utilitarian, 216, 232
Utility maximization, 155

Vacations, paid, 146
Valenstein, Elliot, 23n.10
Values. *See* Metapreferences
van Herwaarden, F. G., 37n.41
van Pragg, B. M. S., 37n.41
Vaupel, James, 241
Veblen, Thorstein, 146
Veil of ignorance, 109
Vernon, Philip, 149n.19
Vervet monkeys, 23–27
Vice presidents, 99–100
Viscusi, W. Kip, 166–67
Vividness
  and consumption, 152–53
  defined, 33
  and identified lives, 203
  and the reference group, 33, 57
Voluntary associations. *See* Freedom of
    association
Voucher plan for schools. *See* Educational
    vouchers

Walzer, Michael, 206, 210
Wardrobe, as positional good, 12, 151
Watts, Harold, 158, 160, 256n.24
Wealth, distribution of, 187–90
Weinberg, Steven, 81
Weisskopf, Thomas, 177, 259n.31
Welfare reform. *See* Income redistribution,
    policies for achieving
Wells, Ken, 15n.3
West, R. W., 256n.26
Weston, J. Fred, 43n.4
Whalley, John, 250n.13
White, Lawrence, 138n.8, 202n.18, 251n.18
Whyte, William F., 90n.3, 91n.7, 92, 95
Williams, Mary, 142
Williams, Robin, 33n.31
Williamson, Chilton, 128n.26
Wilson, Edward O., 132n.1

Wilson, W., 30n.24
Wimbledon, 103
Winter, Sidney, 37n.43
Wolf, William, 90n.3
Wolfe, Tom, 130
Wolff, Robert Paul, 229, 230
Worker control, 178–83

Working conditions and wages. *See* Compensating wage differentials

Young Americans for Freedom, 267
Yuweiler, A., 25n.13

Zeckhauser, Richard, 223n.13, 246